PERFORMING LAW

The words "all rise" announce the appearance of the judge in the thespian space of the courtroom and trigger the beginning of that play we call a trial. The symbolically staged enactment of conflict in the form of litigation is exemplary of legal action, its liturgical and real effects. It establishes the roles and discourses, hierarchy and deference, atmospheres and affects that are to be taken up in the more general social stage of public life. Leading international scholars drawn from performance studies, theatre history, aesthetics, dance, film, and law provide critical analyses of the sites, dramas, and stage directions to be found in the orchestration of the tragedies and comedies acted out in multiple forums of contemporary legality. This title is also available as open access on Cambridge Core.

Peter Goodrich is a professor of law at Cardozo School of Law (Yeshiva University), and a visiting professor in the Division of Social Science, New York University Abu Dhabi. His most recent excursus was *Vision in Decision* (2023).

Anna Jayne Kimmel is an assistant professor of dance and affiliate faculty at the Nashman Center for Civic Engagement and Public Service at George Washington University. She is an associate editor at *Performance Research* and a board member of Performance Studies international. Her scholarship appears in *Dance Research Journal, Performance Research, Lateral, The Drama Review,* and *The Brooklyn Rail,* as well as various edited volumes.

Bernadette Meyler is the Carl and Sheila Spaeth Professor of Law at Stanford University. She is the author of *Theaters of Pardoning* and a coeditor of *The Oxford Handbook of Law and Humanities.*

LAW IN CONTEXT

Since 1970, the Law in Context series has been at the forefront of a movement to broaden the study of law. The series is a vehicle for the publication of innovative monographs and texts that treat law and legal phenomena critically in their cultural, social, political, technological, environmental and economic contexts. A contextual approach involves treating legal subjects broadly, using materials from other humanities and social sciences, and from any other discipline that helps to explain the operation in practice of the particular legal field or legal phenomena under investigation. It is intended that this orientation is at once more stimulating and more revealing than the bare exposition of legal rules. The series includes original research monographs, coursebooks and textbooks that foreground contextual approaches and methods. The series includes and welcomes books on the study of law in all its contexts, including domestic legal systems, European and international law, transnational and global legal processes, and comparative law.

Books in the Series

Acosta: *The National versus the Foreigner in South America: 200 Years of Migration and Citizenship Law*
Alaattinoğlu: *Grievance Formation, Rights and Remedies*
Ali: *Modern Challenges to Islamic Law*
Alyagon Darr: *Plausible Crime Stories: The Legal History of Sexual Offences in Mandate Palestine*

Anderson, Schum & Twining: *Analysis of Evidence, 2nd Edition*
Ashworth: *Sentencing and Criminal Justice, 6th Edition*
Barton & Douglas: *Law and Parenthood*
Baxi, McCrudden & Paliwala: *Law's Ethical, Global and Theoretical Contexts: Essays in Honour of William Twining*
Beecher-Monas: *Evaluating Scientific Evidence: An Interdisciplinary Framework for Intellectual Due Process*
Bell: *French Legal Cultures*
Bercusson: *European Labour Law, 2nd Edition*
Birkinshaw: *European Public Law*
Birkinshaw: *Freedom of Information: The Law, the Practice and the Ideal, 4th Edition*
Blick: *Electrified Democracy: The Internet and the United Kingdom Parliament in History*
Broderick & Ferri: *International and European Disability Law and Policy: Text, Cases and Materials*
Brownsword & Goodwin: *Law and the Technologies of the Twenty-First Century: Text and Materials*
Cakal: *Law and Torture: Widening the Apertures, from the Doctrinal to the Critical*
Cane & Goudkamp: *Atiyah's Accidents, Compensation and the Law, 9th Edition*
Clarke: *Principles of Property Law*
Clarke & Kohler: *Property Law: Commentary and Materials*
Collins: *The Law of Contract, 4th Edition*
Collins, Ewing & McColgan: *Labour Law, 3rd Edition*
Corrias: *Law and Inhumanity: Dehumanization, Silent Claims and Atrocity Crimes*
Cowan: *Housing Law and Policy*
Cranston: *Making Commercial Law Through Practice 1830–1970*
Cranston: *Legal Foundations of the Welfare State*
Darian-Smith: *Laws and Societies in Global Contexts: Contemporary Approaches*
Dauvergne: *Making People Illegal: What Globalisation Means for Immigration and Law*
David: *Kinship, Law and Politics: An Anatomy of Belonging*
Davies: *Perspectives on Labour Law, 2nd Edition*
Dembour: *Who Believes in Human Rights?: Reflections on the European Convention*
de Sousa Santos: *Toward a New Legal Common Sense: Law, Globalization, and Emancipation*
Diduck: *Law's Families*
Douglas-Scott: *Brexit, Union, and Disunion: The Evolution of British Constitutional Unsettlement*
Dowdle: *Transnational Law: A Framework for Analysis*
Dupret: *Positive Law from the Muslim World: Jurisprudence, History, Practices*
Dutta: *A Jurisprudence of Conversations: Law, Life and Feminism in Post-colonial India*

Emon: *Jurisdictional Exceptionalisms: Islamic Law, International Law, and Parental Child Abduction*
Estella: *Legal Foundations of EU Economic Governance*
Fortin: *Children's Rights and the Developing Law, 3rd Edition*
Garnsey: *The Justice of Visual Art: Creative State-Building in Times of Political Transition*
Garton, Probert & Bean: *Moffat's Trusts Law: Text and Materials, 7th Edition*
Ghai & Woodman: *Practising Self-Government: A Comparative Study of Autonomous Regions*
Glover-Thomas: *Reconstructing Mental Health Law and Policy*
Gobert & Punch: *Rethinking Corporate Crime*
Goldman: *Globalisation and the Western Legal Tradition: Recurring Patterns of Law and Authority*
Graber: *The Technosystem of Free Speech: Enriching Fundamental Rights in a Digital Society*
Haack: *Evidence Matters: Science, Proof, and Truth in the Law*
Harlow & Rawlings: *Law and Administration, 4th Edition*
Harris: *An Introduction to Law, 8th Edition*
Harris, Campbell & Halson: *Remedies in Contract and Tort, 2nd Edition*
Harvey: *Seeking Asylum in the UK: Problems and Prospects*
Herring: *Law and the Relational Self*
Hervey & McHale: *European Union Health Law: Themes and Implications*
Hervey & McHale: *Health Law and the European Union*
Holder & Lee: *Environmental Protection, Law and Policy: Text and Materials, 2nd Edition*
Hommes: *The Convention and the Kingdom: How the Netherlands Received the European Convention on Human Rights*
Jackson & Summers: *The Internationalisation of Criminal Evidence: Beyond the Common Law and Civil Law Traditions*
Jeutner: *The Reasonable Person: A Legal Biography*
Kennedy: *Inducing Intimacy: Deception, Consent and the Law*
Kostakopoulou: *The Future Governance of Citizenship*
Kreiczer-Levy: *Destabilized Property: Property Law in the Sharing Economy*
Kubal: *Immigration and Refugee Law in Russia: Socio-Legal Perspectives*
Lewis: *Choice and the Legal Order: Rising above Politics*
Likosky: *Law, Infrastructure and Human Rights*
Likosky: *Transnational Legal Processes: Globalisation and Power Disparities*
Lixinski: *Legalized Identities: Cultural Heritage Law and the Shaping of Transitional Justice*
Loughnan: *Self, Others and the State: Relations of Criminal Responsibility*
Lunney: *A History of Australian Tort Law 1901–1945: England's Obedient Servant?*

Maughan & Webb: *Lawyering Skills and the Legal Process, 2nd Edition*
McGaughey: *Principles of Enterprise Law*
McGlynn: *Families and the European Union: Law, Politics and Pluralism*
Mertens: *A Philosophical Introduction to Human Rights*
Miller: *An Introduction to German Law and Legal Culture: Text and Materials*
Moffat: *Trusts Law: Text and Materials*
Monti: *EC Competition Law*
Morgan: *Contract Law Minimalism: A Formalist Restatement of Commercial Contract Law*
Morgan & Yeung: *An Introduction to Law and Regulation: Text and Materials*
Nash: *British Islam and English Law: A Classical Pluralist Perspective*
Ng: *Political Censorship in British Hong Kong: Freedom of Expression and the Law (1842–1997)*
Nicola & Davies: *EU Law Stories: Contextual and Critical Histories of European Jurisprudence*
Norrie: *Crime, Reason and History: A Critical Introduction to Criminal Law, 3rd Edition*
Norrie: *Rethinking Criminal Justice: Punishment, Abolition And Moral Psychology*
O'Dair: *Legal Ethics: Text and Materials*
Oliver: *Common Values and the Public–Private Divide*
Oliver & Drewry: *The Law and Parliament*
Palmer & Roberts: *Dispute Processes: ADR and the Primary Forms of Decision-Making, 1st Edition*
Palmer & Roberts: *Dispute Processes: ADR and the Primary Forms of Decision-Making, 3rd Edition*
Petersen: *Practices of Restitution: Law and Aesthetics in Modern Germ*any
Picciotto: *International Business Taxation*
Pieraccini: *Regulating the Sea: A Socio-Legal Analysis of English Marine Protected Areas*
Probert: *The Changing Legal Regulation of Cohabitation, 1600–2010: From Fornicators to Family, 1600–2010*
Qiao: *The Authoritarian Commons: Neighborhood Democratization in Urban China*
Radi: *Rules and Practices of International Investment Law and Arbitration*
Reed: *Internet Law: Text and Materials*
Richardson: *Law, Process and Custody*
Roberts & Palmer: *Dispute Processes: ADR and the Primary Forms of Decision-Making, 2nd Edition*
Rowbottom: *Democracy Distorted: Wealth, Influence and Democratic Politics*
Sauter: *Public Services in EU Law*
Scott & Black: *Cranston's Consumers and the Law*
Seneviratne: *Ombudsmen: Public Services and Administrative Justice*

Seppänen: *Ideological Conflict and the Rule of Law in Contemporary China: Useful Paradoxes*
Siems: *Comparative Law, 3rd Edition*
Stapleton: *Product Liability*
Stewart: *Gender, Law and Justice in a Global Market*
Tamanaha: *Law as a Means to an End: Threat to the Rule of Law*
Taylor: *Fortin's Children's Rights and the Developing Law, 4th Edition*
Tuori: *Properties of Law: Modern Law and After*
Turpin & Tomkins: *British Government and the Constitution: Text and Materials, 7th Edition*
Twining: *General Jurisprudence: Understanding Law from a Global Perspective*
Twining: *Globalisation and Legal Theory*
Twining: *Human Rights, Southern Voices: Francis Deng, Abdullahi An-Na'im, Yash Ghai and Upendra Baxi*
Twining: *Jurist in Context: A Memoir*
Twining: *Karl Llewellyn and the Realist Movement, 2nd Edition*
Twining: *Rethinking Evidence: Exploratory Essays, 2nd Edition*
Twining & Miers: *How to Do Things with Rules, 5th Edition*
Varney: *Disability, Human Rights and Contract Law*
Wan: *Film and Constitutional Controversy: Visualizing Hong Kong Identity in the Age of 'One Country, Two Systems'*
Ward: *A Critical Introduction to European Law, 3rd Edition*
Ward: *Law, Text, Terror*
Ward: *Shakespeare and Legal Imagination*
Watt: *The Making Sense of Politics, Media, and Law: Rhetorical Performance as Invention, Creation, Production*
Wells & Quick: *Lacey, Wells and Quick: Reconstructing Criminal Law: Text and Materials, 4th Edition*
Woodhead: *Caring for Cultural Heritage: An Integrated Approach to Legal and Ethical Initiatives in the United Kingdom*
Yeung and Ranchordás: *An Introduction to Law and Regulation: Text and Materials, 2nd Edition*
Young: *Turpin and Tomkins' British Government and the Constitution: Text and Materials, 8th Edition*
Zander: *Cases and Materials on the English Legal System, 10th Edition*
Zander: *The Law-Making Process, 6th Edition*

International Journal of Law in Context: A Global Forum for Interdisciplinary Legal Studies

The *International Journal of Law in Context* is the companion journal to the Law in Context book series and provides a forum for interdisciplinary legal studies and offers intellectual space for ground-breaking critical research.

It publishes contextual work about law and its relationship with other disciplines including but not limited to science, literature, humanities, philosophy, sociology, psychology, ethics, history and geography. More information about the journal and how to submit an article can be found at http://journals.cambridge.org/ijc

CHAPTER 1

Introduction

Peter Goodrich and Anna Jayne Kimmel

A SMALL, SOLITARY FIGURE OF AN ADVOCATE IN ROBES, surrounded by monumental columns, climbs the lengthy flight of stairs that leads into the Belgium *Palais de Justice* (see Figure 1.1). The actor, an old Latin term for lawyer, is a diminutive, costumed figure engulfed by the imperial surroundings and majestic spectacle in which they will play their evanescent part. The shadow of a shadow, a fleeting image, the jurist thespian enters an exemplary theatre of legality, the colossus of the courthouse, to take up a costumed role and scripted part in the spectacle that awaits beyond the hardwood doors of the various courtrooms. This still from a video artwork by artist Carey Young arrests the viewer in its symmetry and scale. Emptiness defines the scene: To the right a vacant chair symbolises the absence of any populace. Authority reveals itself as structure, the vicarious delegation of majesty and power as places occupied, as offices and duties rather than individual attributes. The space exudes a sense of the past as other: The architectural imposition, the scale of *forensis* with its Doric sentinels, and the sheer magnitude of the building all indicate the environment and atmosphere as entry into a social sanctum, a space that is itself spectacular and simultaneously a threshold to the structural stages and stagings of law as performance.

This is the site of open justice where, in the old language of the ecclesiastics, law is published and 'sped' to populace and public. The performing of law, its enactment as a spectacle, carries on and indeed augments massively with the presence of cameras, monitors, lenses within what was previously the intimate public sphere of legality. The spectres of

1.1 Carey Young, *Palais de Justice* (still), 2017. Single-channel HD video (from 4K); 16:9 format, colour, quadraphonic sound. 17 minutes, 58 seconds.

trial and figures of litigation now increasingly circulate on social media, on viral and streamed sites, while both publicising and diffracting the doctrines and other scenes relayed. Law, in sum and trajectory, now inexorably joins the more general politics of the imaginal that marks the contemporary epoch and impinges increasingly upon the disciplines. Just as the robed advocate is swallowed up by the sheer scale of the building, so law anxiously awaits the arrival of precisely the technologies and modes of circulation that Carey Young's secretive video of the *Palais* both portends and relays in images that transgress the antique divide between licit and illicit. Like it or not, lawyers in their lairs now have to come alive to the fact that they exist in a mediated environment through which they nevertheless have to perform.

It has become commonplace to assert that *everything is a performance.* From presidential debates streamed with zealous pomp and circumstance to social media accounts carefully curated toward superficial connection to corporate mimicry of interpersonal rhetoric intended to virtue signal, it is all too easy to point to the ambivalent use of the performative in today's society. The theatrics of our times are undeniable, as media, politics, and the wider attention economy inundate our daily lives. For others yet, *performance is everything.* The stage has moved beyond established concert venues to pop-up theatres, museum and gallery installations, viral videos, one-on-one performances in the home, and puppet parades involving entire cities and crossing continents. In a post-pandemic society, the ability to attend live art has been received with renewed welcome. Attendance, attention, audition, and audience rule the day online as also in real time and space, one bolstering the other, doubling and redoubling in feedback loops and viral enumerations.

Law has never been entirely immune to the rigmarole of image and spectacle as atmospheric locators and transmitters of legal structures. Early in the Western tradition the drama of legal duels, enacted as symbolic stagings of conflict, replaced the melody of nomos or Pythagorean harmony as a musical model of settling disputes. The legal form was and is a belligerent tradition, historically often a mode of literal combat. The *duillum* or duel was a legal procedure that survived until the late sixteenth century, but over time the rules of legal procedure and the ceremonies of the process sought to mask the element of antagonism and to secrete and separate the duelling parties, the crown and the accused, or the litigants, in a discrete and secluded theatre of legal actions *in curia* but not *in camera*, as one early text formulates it.[1] The rituals of trial were specifically gauged to give the appearance of a liturgical function and the theatrical dimensions of lawsuits were hidden, as Carey Young so vividly portrays, in vast sepulchres, in arcane argot, windowless courtrooms, ecclesiastical architecture, aesthetics, and costumes. The historical atmosphere of law and the symbolism of its ceremonies were very much *in camera* in the sense and materiality of separate and somnolent mausoleums, chambers, libraries, but until recently not on camera.[2] Digitisation,

[1] Edward Waterhous, Fortescutus Illustratus *or, A commentary on that nervous treatise* De Laudibus legum Angliæ (London: Roycroft, 1663), at 100, meaning that the sovereign should be seen to decide cases in court by his judges and not in private by his will.

[2] For the most recent UK report on cameras in court, urging yet again that, for purposes of civic legal education and to save the law from obscurity and desuetude, trials should be transmitted and archives accessible digitally, see the Ministry of Justice report, 'Call for Evidence: Open Justice, the Way Forward – Summary of Responses', Gov.uk, 24 February 2025, www.gov.uk/government/consultations/open-justice-the-way-forward/outcome/summary-of-responses. For discussion of the background, see Peter Goodrich, 'Unveiling Law: The History of a Ban and of Its Lifting', in Ozan Kamiloglu and Kanika Sharma (eds.), *The Courtroom on Camera: Visions of Justice* (Abingdon: Routledge, 2026).

however, broke down the walls of the legal archive, and omnipresent recording, online blogging, streaming, and screen capture have all entered the courtroom and other sites of lawmaking and law enforcement. Law's performances, its bodies, rites, and stages, as also its agon, polarisations, and the politics of decision, are increasingly visible and evanescent events, spectacles in the public sphere.

And yet despite the overwhelming ubiquity of the theatrical, the performative, spectre and spectacle, performance studies has frequently been siloed in marginal academic spaces, held at arm's length from the more traditional disciplines of the academy and specifically the lucubrations of jurists and philosophers of law. Theatre and training in the rhetorical arts of gesture and delivery were intrinsic to the Renaissance and early modern fabrication of common law, as well as to its internal pedagogy and mooting. The Inns of Court were next to the playhouses of London, and barristers would learn to perform 'to the pit', the audience, both by attending plays and through their own training exercises and revels.[3] The separation occurs with the broadly Protestant attack on imagery and its theatrical manifestations, and then later in the continuance of that hostile stance in the Enlightenment attack on theatre that led to an ever-increasing reliance upon the textualisation of law and particularly the systematisation of law reporting. The common opinion of the bar, the thespian sense of what was argued and heard in court as oral memory of performance, as dialogue and exchange, gets replaced by written reason and solemnity of judgment. The specialisation of the profession and the emergence of law schools in the United Kingdom and the United States in the second half of the nineteenth century moved the common lawyers to their own faculty, housed most usually in their own building and frequently on the edge of or just off campus. The marriage, or in legal terms, *altera coniux*, the other love of the lawyers, their revels and dances, plays and ludic inventions, were abandoned in favour of the text. The scission extends most distinctively and formidably

[3] On which, see Subha Mukherji, *Law and Representation in Early Modern Drama* (Cambridge: Cambridge University Press, 2006), 1–16; Paul Raffield, *Images and Cultures of Law in Early Modern England 1588–1660* (Cambridge: Cambridge University Press, 2004); Jessica Winston, *Lawyers at Play: Literature, Law, and Politics at the Early Modern Inns of Court, 1558–1581* (Oxford: Oxford University Press, 2016).

to the gulf between legal practitioners and those who practice theatre. Perhaps in US contexts the Establishment Clause designating what is now the increasingly fragile separation of church and state accounts for this anxiety, given the ease with which performance has been frequently elided with ritual, ceremony, the fictive, the occult, and the magical.[4] Or perhaps performers' refusal to be recorded resists the authoritative archival logics tethered to Western jurisprudence. Regardless of the reason, intentional or not, it remains true that two of the disciplines most rooted in public engagement of the populace remain the most distinct from one another in the modern university.

This absent disciplinary attention and dysfunctional dialogic lacuna extends in both directions. When originary figures in performance studies such as Jon McKenzie defined the field through the paradigms of cultural, organisational, and technological performance practice, space for the legal and juridical was made peripheral, if not left out altogether.[5] As performance studies pushed forward in directions of the political and methodological, traces of legal engagement fell from central view in spite of early attentions. Consider Joseph Roach's oft-cited work, *Cities of the Dead.* This monograph advances generative themes of surrogation, counter-memory, and circum-Atlantic performance, as taught in many introductory courses to performance studies and cherished by pedagogues and scholars alike. Yet less frequently highlighted is 'Bodies of Law', a section in the second chapter that sutures Richard Schechner's definition of performance's 'restored behavior' to law. Here, Roach writes: 'Law functions as a repository of social performances, past and present. … Indispensably, performance infuses the artifacts of written law with bodily action, a meaning that obtains when it is said that a party

4 See most emblematically Jean-Jacques Rousseau, 'Letter to d'Alembert on the Theatre', in Allan Bloom (ed.), *Politics and the Arts* (Ithaca: Cornell University Press, 1991); and for an extensive study, see Jonas Barish, *The Anti-theatrical Prejudice* (Berkeley: California University Press, 1985). In English history, see, for example, Jeremy Collier, *A Short View of the Immorality and Profaneness of the English Stage* (London: Keble, 1698), and in continental literature, Jacques Bénigne Bossuet, 'Maximes et rélexions sur la comédie', in Jacques Bénigne Bossuet, *Oraisons funèbres et sermons* (Paris: Mignot, [1694]).

5 Jon McKenzie, *Perform or Else: From Discipline to Performance* (London: Routledge, 2001).

to a contract "performs."'[6] In a broader historical sense, a legal action – *legis actio* – is expressly a mode of political manifestation and public appearance of law in the social sphere. For lawyers, in the old formula, *scribere est agere*, to write is to act, and the juridical writ or edict are illocutionary modes of what Emanuele Coccia terms 'efficacious language', pronouncements that give effectiveness to formulae and rules.[7] What is actually figured, what materialises, appears in public space or assembly as present and real is precisely the display, the liturgical efficacy of the legal act, and in the traditional language of both laws, *actus legitimi* materialising on the social stage as performance. The lawyer, as noted, was in classical terms an actor, a player upon the political scene, but one who shrouded that performance in a religious cloak of gravity and truth that had the ironic effect of hiding the essentially thespian character of these stagings behind technical argot and theological robes. The gilded separation of law from other disciplines, the specialism necessary to legal action, the distinct and secreted spaces of juristic apparition, as well as the jurisprudential call to pure reason, all tended to segregate the legal from performance studies and the everyday of social play. Antiquity, meaning the legal tradition, hates novelty, or *novum omne cave* as the maxim goes, meaning beware of the new, and the mobile and rapidly changing ephemera of performance were ignored by a law determined to stay for the *longue durée*, symbolically reflected in religious garb and ceremonies, architecture, archives, and the use of dead languages.

Similarly, when legal theory widened its scope toward the humanities, embracing or borrowing from other disciplines, the ambit of these couplings or fetters were constrained by the textualism of legal analysis and equally restrained by the esoteric and at times occult character of its tradition, language, and rules. From the law and literature movement to

[6] Joseph R. Roach, *Cities of the Dead: Circum-Atlantic Performance* (New York: Columbia University Press, 1996), 55.

[7] Emanuele Coccia, *Goods: Advertising, Urban Space, and the Moral Law of the Image* (New York: Fordham University Press, 2018), vii. On the *oikonomia* of liturgical effects, see also Giorgio Agamben, Opus Dei: *An Archaeology of Duty* (Palo Alto: Stanford University Press, 2013). For the legal meanings of *effectus*, see Pierre Legendre, *God in the Mirror: A Study of the Institution of Images* (London: Routledge, 2019), *Id efficit quod figurat*, 139–155.

critical legal studies to critical race studies, the less conventional (which is to say, the less textual) shunned the field of performance studies, which was not invited to the party until most recently and even still quite tentatively. Occasional essays in early critical legal studies took the form of dialogues, and in one case a fictive correspondence on writing and copyright law was performed live at an annual conference, but the presentations were pitched as literary and cogitative, readings gauged to subsequent publication, rather than rooted in the gestural or ephemeral realms of performance and play.[8] While rhetoric was also highlighted as a central device in the maintenance of the legitimacy of the legal order, it was the figures of speech that were marshalled to provide critical analyses of statutory and precedential texts rather than addressing directly their playbook, the social enactment of law, or the visual semiotics of its transmission.[9] The discipline of print, so fundamental to the concept of 'black letter law', and the Gothic typeface of permanent rule, confined critique of law to the page, to an inveterate textualism that ramiculated into the variants of radical lawyering that superseded critical legal studies, particularly in the United States.

Although central figures in critical race studies, such as Kimberlé Crenshaw, featured the work of performers in their analyses, not least the 2 Live Crew in her famed essay, 'Mapping the Margins', such an action never became a trend in spite of the centrality of representation and agency implicit to both fields.[10] As Subha Mukherji noted some time back of the relation of law to theatre, rhetoric and specifically its third component, delivery, suffered 'a reduction of the role of the legal rhetorician and the displacement of rhetoric from law to literature'.[11] In

8 For dialogue, see Duncan Kennedy and Peter Gabel, 'Roll over Beethoven' (1984) 36 *Stanford Law Review* 1–55; and for theatre, see Costas Douzinas and Ronnie Warrington, with Shaun McVeigh, *Postmodern Jurisprudence: The Text of Law in the Law of Texts* (London: Routledge, 1991), ch. 12, 'Suspended Sentences'.

9 James Boyd White, *Heracles' Bow: Essays on the Rhetoric and Poetics of Law* (Madison: Wisconsin, 1985); Peter Goodrich, *Reading the Law: A Critical Introduction to Legal Methods and Techniques* (Oxford: Blackwell, 1986).

10 Kimberlé Crenshaw, 'Mapping the Margins: Intersectionality, Identity Politics, and Violence against Women of Color' (1991) 43:6 *Stanford Law Review* 1241–1299.

11 Mukherji, *Law and Representation*, 5. This follows, of course, on a lengthy tradition of viewing rhetoric as ornament, as flowery deceit. Within the Anglican tradition of

making a return to law, the literary is deemed safely narrative and operates in multimodal forms that have more recently provided lawyers, conservative and critical alike, with a textual outlet that hides the elements of dialogue and performance in the discursive regimentations and monochromacity of the page. The radicals remain lawyers, their critique circumscribed by modernist frames of legal rationality as a disembodied discursive enterprise of rule application. Thus metaphor, and more recently the neo-materialist matterphor, reference transference and materialisation in discourse rather than directly addressing the performative character and corporeal enactment of both text and utterance.[12] Narrative figures, stories, and calls for rights displace rhetorical attention on delivery or *hypokrisis* as essentially and extrinsically thespian endeavours.

The historical confinement of legal studies to the linearity of the page and the scripture of reason – *ratio scripta* – is a complex historical phenomenon of the *longue durée* of juridical theology. In the common law tradition, the modern roots of what Sir Edward Coke termed the sedentary, and in consequence short, life of lawyers lie in the Protestant reforms that swept England during the early modern period. The reformers' very creditable juristic maxim *sola scriptura* fed into the epistemological break of the Enlightenment and captured the heart of early modern lawyers.[13] It led to an ever more formal separation of legality and theatricality, erasing both the history and the histrionics of the legal

common law such a dismissal of the rhetorical can be found most expressly in the reformist work of Bishop John Jewel, notably in his *Oratio contra rhetoricam* (*Oration against Rhetoric*), translated in Wayne Rebhorn, *Renaissance Debates on Rhetoric* (Ithaca: Cornell University Press, 2000), ch. 15. Note should also be taken of Roland Barthes, 'L'Ancienne rhétorique: Aide-memoire' (1970) 16 *Communications* 172; and Gérard Genette, 'Rhetoric Restrained', in Gérard Genette, *Figures of Literary Discourse* (Oxford: Blackwell, 1982).

12 See the special issue, edited by Daniela Gandorfer and Zulaika Ayub, 'Matterphorical' (2021) 24 *Theory and Event*, and Daniela Gandorfer, *Matterphor: Laws of Theory* (Durham: Duke University Press, 2026).

13 Sir Edward Coke, *A Book of Entries containing perfect and approved presidents of Courts, Declarations … and all other matters and proceedings (in effect) concerning the pratick part of the laws of England* (London: Streeter, 1610, 1671 ed.) at fol. A 5 a: noting that the student of law 'having *sedentariam vitam*, is not commonly long lived; the study [is] abstruse and difficult, the occasion sudden, the practice dangerous'.

tradition as an art of actors and acting. To paraphrase a Renaissance critic of common lawyers, the jurists sought jealously to guard the distinctiveness of their profession: 'You would love the law, but *sine rivali*, you would reign, but alone, *hinc illae lachrymae*.'[14] The desire for isolation and autonomy, guild pride in law as a distinct discipline and practice serve to veil the dramaturgic dimension of court and trial. Hubris and denial are triggered by the need to make claims to legitimacy and to enforce the interests of governance. These lead to disguising theatricality as religious ritual and treating an at times absurd gravitas as a form of anti-theatricality. It is this point of scission, the fissure between theatre and law, thespian performance and legal practice, that the present collection picks up, examines, and aspires to move beyond.

Julie Stone Peters' book *Law as Performance: Theatricality, Spectatorship, and the Making of Law in Ancient, Medieval and Early Modern Europe* first appeared, meticulous, mellifluous, and monumental, in print in 2022. It was clear immediately that its provocations and taunting historical and theatrical detail would challenge scholars in their scholist siloes and secluded specialisms. Her painstaking reignition of the theatrical narratives, trainings, and performances of lawyers across time and jurisdictions has been an efflorescent sign of the times and a moment seized to maximum effect. It has rippled forth toward a fuller deluge of new avenues in law and humanities and specifically has generated a bridging of the chasm separating law and performance.[15] Arguing in intense historical detail that the force of law lies in its aesthetics, in the style of its performances, Peters signals a seismic shift of focus and attention. The downcast eyes of judges and jurisprudes are raised again to the corporeal and scenic avenues of law's enactment, the blindfold is removed from the eyes of justice, and in the manner of poor theatre, the audience's role in the judgment of law is seen and acknowledged.[16] *Law as Performance*

[14] Abraham Fraunce, *The Lawiers logike; exemplifying the praecepts of logike by the practice of the common law* (London: How, 1588), vi.

[15] Julie Stone Peters, *Law as Performance: Theatricality, Spectatorship, and the Making of Law in Ancient, Medieval and Early Modern Europe* (Oxford: Oxford University Press, 2022).

[16] Peters, *Law as Performance*, at 5, 'Law's aesthetic power is essential to its force.' On poor theatre and theatrical jurisprudence, see also Marett Leiboff, *Towards a Theatrical Jurisprudence* (London: Routledge, 2020), 91–106.

emerges as the culmination of prior inclinations, and as a mode of building toward a subdiscipline that understands the embodiment of legal action. It is a trajectory expressed in a number of Peters' shorter, more polemical pieces. Most famously, in a much mooted article that opens with a theatrical scene of a failed conference dialogue between professors of literature and legal academics, she argues that law and literature is 'an interdisciplinary illusion': The lawyers seek to work through their fantasies of escape by exiting into literature, while the literary critics seek meaningful substance for their work in law.[17] Neither group experiences fulfilment. The putative interdisciplinarity was in fact, Peters argues, an anti-interdisciplinarity, and its positive outcome is the realisation that the illusion lies in the attempt to separate the two enterprises, namely that there is no firm boundary between what are essentially two intertwined normative literary programs or, in Bradin Cormack's version of the argument, conjoint and so competing jurisdictions.[18]

In 'Theatrocracy Unwired', Peters examines the impact of the modern mediasphere on the visibility of the legal and the consequent trial by media that now suffuses the polity as both entertainment and political trending. The remediation of law also forms the topos of an historical analysis that traces the shift in law's performance from the thaumaturgic character of classical legal judgment to the accelerated crowdsourced quality of contemporary relays going viral, 'the *coup de force* is here turned into a *coup de théâtre*'.[19] Certain other scholars, including Alan Read in his *Theatre and Law*, and the anthology *Law and Performance*, give scope to an emergent subdiscipline and line of active critical inquiry.[20] The key point is not that Peters has a few fellow travellers, but rather that *Law as Performance* immediately and uniquely

[17] Julie Stone Peters, 'Law, Literature, and the Vanishing Real: On the Future of an Interdisciplinary Illusion' (2005) 120 *PMLA* 442.

[18] This is the principal theme of the excellent Bradin Cormack, *A Power to Do Justice: Jurisdiction, English Literature, and the Rise of the Common Law* (Chicago: University of Chicago Press, 2009).

[19] Respectively, Julie Stone Peters, 'Theatrocracy Unwired: Legal Performance in the Modern Media Sphere' (2014) 26:1 *Law and Literature* 31; Julie Stone Peters, 'Legal Performance Good and Bad' (2008) 4 *Law, Culture and the Humanities* 179.

[20] Alan Reed, *Theatre and Law* (London: Macmillan, 2015); Austin Sarat, Lawrence Douglas, and Martha Umphrey (eds.), *Law and Performance* (Amherst: University of

spawned future research inquiries and responses. Colloquia in Toronto and New York, London and Los Angeles, Oxford and online, as well as a series of three panels extending themes of law and performance at the 2022 Association for the Study of Law, Culture, and the Humanities conference at Emory University School of Law in Atlanta, Georgia, exemplify this energetic reception and aesthetic force of the author and work, and it is from those varied and dynamic sessions that the present volume originates.

Performing Law responds to the generative scholarship advanced following the publication of Peters' magnum opus. It seeks both to capture a sampling of the theoretical and conceptual questions opened by her text, while also itself advancing new lines of interdisciplinary research. Intimate frictions between the disciplines of law and the humanities animate its pages, further blurred by a new embrace of the live arts, not least the amorphous category of performance and contested neologism of performativity. These concepts and their theatrical practices, of course, have a lengthy history that law has at times attempted to quash, as with the Roman edict that banned citizens from performing on stage under penalty of *infamia*, meaning civil death. The prohibition on citizens acting was an attempt to exclude the competitor to legal theatre, Greek tragedy, fearing that its foreign and exotic histrions would displace, seize, or otherwise distract attention from the forensic stage on which the legitimate drama of public life was to be played out.[21] Lawyers' uses of theatrical techniques and oratorical arts of delivery, of codes of gesture and instructions on bodily postures, elocution and enunciation borrowed from drama, has tended more often, however, to generate a covert relationship between the performative and the legal, hidden

Massachusetts Press, 2018). There is also, as noted, the incisive thespian intervention of Leiboff, *Towards a Theatrical Jurisprudence*.

21 *Digest* 3.2.1 records that any citizen who 'appeared on the stage to act or recite' was subject to the penalty of *infamia*, meaning loss of citizenship. The two-century-long prohibition is discussed in Florence Dupont, 'La scène juridique' (1977) 26 *Communications* 62–77, and interpreted in Peter Goodrich, 'Law', in Thomas Sloane (ed.), *Encyclopedia of Rhetoric* (Oxford: Oxford University Press, 2001). See further, Florence Dupont, *L'Orateur sans visage: Essai sur l'acteur romain et son masque* (Paris: Presses Universitaires de France, 2000) 67–73.

borrowings, *sotto voce* incorporations, divagating uses. Yet lawyers themselves are not the only bodies whose performances manifest the law. In the classical formula, the function of the juridical is to exemplify the recognisable structure of the social, to identify and circumscribe persons, relations, and actions – the tripartite bases of the public sphere and playbook. Law provides the parameters within which subjects, persons as players, appear on the social stage. The jurist desires enactment, the embodiment of rules as the encoding of a daily life which in its conversational and performative forms in turn provides the animus that mobilises and in time responds and contributes to the customs and uses that signal changes in both mores and laws.

Divided into three parts, *Performing Law* proposes to move through law to performance and so to shift attention from the constrained analogy of law to theatre, to an expanded focus on an unconstrained, mobile, and transitive sense of enacting law in the everyday embodiments of persons and polities. Part I thus addresses the history of law's performance, namely the classical staging of the legal, *forensis* as that which pertains to the forum and to the formality and formulae of lawyers. The theatricality of law, both in text and context, is addressed in genealogical style as a series of dramatic occasions and choreographed events, including its venue. Part II directly addresses the affective play of legality, *homo juridicus* as *homo ludens,* and specifically focuses on the theatres of affect and resistance, the agon and agonistics of legal action here being understood as the push and pull of play that emerges in juridical conflict, casuistry, and decision, and effectively attaches subject to norm. As a structural feature of the social, of language and symbolic, law gets under the skin. Part III engages with performance studies to look toward transgressive encounters, good and bad, between legal actors and the comedians, as also the variable inhabitation of these roles by either or both genres. *Performing Law* opens, finally, to the contemporary, social-media-generated, viral, and unwired performativity manifest both in virtual websites and in real life. The two are inextricably interlaced and appearances online are as likely to generate recognition and resistance, accession or opposition to legal regulation as an extraneous or alien form and formalism of staging the social.

PART I: FORENSIS

The space and stage of law's performance, the architecture and atmosphere, provide the manifest visual entrance to any account of law as performance. To aid in that conjunction each section of the work is entered and introduced through an image taken from the work of visual artist Carey Young. Her expansive oeuvre has increasingly challenged perception of law's more performative life through covert and cunning use of images shot through the windows of closed doors, through partings of curtains, cracks, and distances that allow the observer to be unobserved. Many photographs simulate camera apertures, peeping scopic views, purloined images – Young did not have permission to film – inviting visual and sensorial counterpoint to the historical and methodological rubric of law's downcast eyes and the abstractions of academicism.[22] For Part I: Forensis, a colour still, 'Installation View', from the series *Palais de Justice* evinces law becoming strangely real. It captures the silhouette of a museumgoer at Modern Art Oxford, reclined on a bench to look back at the outcast glance of a female judge from her bench. The immediate visual impact is of a camera obscura, a portal of light entering an enclosed space – a blank page – and inverting its content. The judge and robed lawyer are in dialogue, pensive, and for the viewer, the portal into the enclosure. The courtroom produces an image that escapes into the darkened auditorium. There is a doubling effect – the spectator viewing an audience member returns the gaze of the judge looking out – and in doing so, in this further refraction, inculcates and displays an expanded sense of law's public, at once constituted for and by this optical intrusion upon the *in camera* of the courtroom spectacle.

Forensis, derived from forum, is the Latin term for the publicity of law, designating the juristic space in which trials were conducted, as well as being used to reference the advocate – *forensis* – who would play the part of representing the litigants. *Forensis* thus references the space where trials were publicly conducted and the meaning develops in medieval Latin to include the lay participants and other foreigners to the law. The etymology is taken up and extended in performance studies into a variety of action-related verbs: to witness, to spectate, to appreciate, to respond,

[22] See Jeanne Gaakeer, Ruth Herz, Joan Kee, et al., 'Carey Young's *Palais de Justice*' (2018) 12 *Law and Humanities* 278.

active modalities that reverberate through the contributions of these chapters and disrupt an imaginary of law rooted in the discursive. 'The windows and the camera's lens are suggested as an interwoven series of oculi', submits Young, 'in which we watch justice as performance and are ourselves implicated as witnesses and voyeurs'.[23] Dim lighting and digital projection otherwise haunt the photograph, shuttling the viewer into temporal tension, a scene of sci-fi effect in the afterglow shattered by the iconographic sartorial folds of black robing in the nineteenth-century halls of justice in Brussels. Here a phenomenon of the camera obscura, elsewhere the cloaked contours of law illuminated through the suggestion of law as performance in which the script is flipped. From law's enunciation to its mise-en-scène, these opening chapters amplify the fundamental ways in which law has always been framed through performance, ceremonially promulgated in both its historical pageantry and its itinerancy as well as being distinctively enacted for public relay and consumption in its various forums.

Regardless of the historical, political, and epistemological differences that both led to and sustained the artificial separation of law and live performance, this volume expands upon the long-standing entanglements of the two but also the importance of taking that entanglement seriously. Law without theatre is a broken reed, a dead letter, a public vacuum, an irrelevance, in the specific sense that to manifest, to appear and become real require staging, delivery, and visibility. To ignore such facets of the legal process as ornamental and trivial in comparison to substantive textual elaborations misunderstands both a key modality of legal transmission and ignores the theatrical content of legal enunciations, be they legislative, administrative, case reports, trial transcripts or enforcement practices. For actors – and we can recall again that the classical term for lawyers was precisely *actores*, and later *narratores*, a structural sign of commonality embedded in the language – to be in the public sphere is to be on stage, to manifest and appear, to be a spectacle engaged in the *aisthesis* of representation and performance.[24]

[23] 'Palais de Justice'. Carey Young. 2017. www.careyyoung.com/palais-de-justice.

[24] We borrow here from Barbara Carnevali, *Social Appearances: A Philosophy of Display and Prestige* (New York: Columbia University Press, 2020), ch. 2.

As Peters formulates it at the outset of her study, aesthetics is essential to the force of law, to which she adds circumspectly that 'law and its aesthetic representation are not always radically distinct kinds of things, their differences often more a matter of degree than of kind'.[25] The commonality lies in costume, staging, and the unities of action, time, and place – a shift from representation to presentation, from the textually bound to the embodied.

Reflecting on the obviousness of law's theatrical character and the sheer scope of examples of histrionics in the emergence of the modern tradition, tracked most recently and expansively in *Law as Performance*, the starting point for interdisciplinary repair looks first to the performativity of legal texts. The foundational works of the early modern legal tradition, particularly noticeable in common law, were dialogues, scripted conversations, often in ambulant form, enacting both juristic principles and substantive transmission underscored through rhetorical attentions. There, we find dialogues between Chancellor and Prince, Doctor and Student, a Philosopher and Common Lawyer, or a between Cardinal and a Scholar on the possibility of transitioning from common law to continental Roman formulae.[26] The text, in dialogic form, evidences both a dialectic of conversation and difference, an awareness of sources and derivations, as well as concordances and refutations. The printed text – as an earlier work by Peters, *Theatre of the Book*, well expounds – carried elements of performance into the textual archive with which law becomes synonymous.[27] We see this as well in the peculiar style of early printed law, with emblems and illustrated letters, including the case of Sir Edward Coke's foundational *Institutes* where three

25 Peters, *Law as Performance*, 5.

26 Respectively Sir John Fortescue, De laudibus legum Angliae: *On the Laws and Governance of England* [*c.* 1460] (Cambridge: Cambridge University Press, 1997); Christopher Saint German, *The Dialoges in Englishe betweene a Doctor of Divinitie and a student of the Lawes of Englande* (London: Tothill, 1575); Thomas Hobbes, *A dialogue between a philosopher and student, of the common laws of England* (Oxford: Oxford University Press, 2005); Thomas Starkey, *A dialogue between Pole and Lupset* (London: Royal Historical Society, 1989).

27 Julie Peters, *Theatre of the Book 1480–1880* (Oxford: Oxford University Press, 2000) makes the extensive point that modern theatre and the printing press grow up together in reciprocal engagement.

columns jostle together and interact on the folio page in Latin, French, and English.[28] These were, in a dual sense, playbooks, texts that both manifested and concealed in scriptural form and linear regimentation the performances that the book had and will propel. Moving across *didascalia*, the textual directions, in dialogue, oration, and forensic play, the focus in this section extends to the ambulation of the law through the countryside, the pageant that precedes and accompanies entry into the portals of the courthouse, the movement of judges and lawyers both across and in composition of their jurisdiction. The skiagraphic observer, the shadow figure of the viewer in Young's image of the camera obscura of the courtroom is inherited from the careful pageantry of legal spectacles, the florid progress of the Assize judges, and in the extreme the scaffold on which public executions and hangings were historically performed for lay consumption.

This volume thus begins in refusal: of norms, customs, and literary dominance. Juridical *hypokrisis* becomes suddenly hypocritical because performance makes the playbook of law both visible and contestable, if not always risible or lachrymose. For Lorna Hutson, in an adroit chapter on the relation of theatre to rhetoric to performance, the anti-theatrical drive of lawyers is delineated as motivated by a desire to restrain performance and prevent it taking on a life or laughter of its own. The prejudice against acting seemingly parallels the historical restraint of rhetoric as administrative and juridical regimes seek to mute the playful character of proceedings. This, as Florence Dupont aptly argues, is because law and theatre are both in significant measure exercises in words and gestures that are distinguished primarily by the context of their enunciation.[29] Law, in being intrinsically theatrical, becomes paradoxically anti-theatrical as a mode of saving its identity and autonomy as law, rather than being only or merely theatre. Another way of formulating the competition between lawyer and thespian, judge and player, in Hutson's analysis, is to point to the capacity of the two regimes to inspire a forgetting of the world

[28] Sir Edward Coke, *The First Part of the Institutes of the Lawes of England. Or, A Commentarie on Littleton, not the name of a lawyer only but of the law itself* (London: Society of Stationers, 1628).

[29] Dupont, 'La scène juridique', 70.

in favour of the fictive scene conjured by the play or by the law play. The public stage, according to the jurisprudence of the Bar and prior formulations of forensic oratory, should be kept for legal theatrics, for serious social speech, while from Rousseau's *Letter to d'Alembert* onwards, the playwright was simply divagating, dissembling and distracting from the real themes, concerns and faiths of the polity. This is the result of the force and impact, Hutson argues, of a novel fictionality that is transmitted to English theatre from the new Italian *commedia erudita*, which underspecifies the fiction so as to allow the audience to imagine and fill in the world to which the narrative and action belong. At this point of intersection, particularly, the two genres of performance had to be kept strictly distinct and hierarchically juxtaposed for law to retain its gravity and gravitational field. The jurist had to appear to shun the playful, the wiles of the actor, and the efflorescences or exornations of the flowers of rhetoric that could only serve to distract the viewer from the liturgical solemnity, apposite ceremony and gravamen of the secular equivalent of the biblically inscribed Last Judgment.

The concept that the theatre of law is somehow real in the ontological sense of being non-fictive, stated rather than performed, also depends upon a strict separation of the legal from the social. As Subha Mukherji points out both in earlier work and in her contribution here, the law needs credibility, persuasiveness, and effective presence. It depends upon the triumphal spectacle of legality, and this in turn necessitates embodiment and the techniques of theatre and rhetoric to relay both the form and the content of the norm. She starts from the tears that failed to flow in the lawsuit between Johnny Depp and Amber Heard.[30] In contradistinction, the failed expression and tearless weeping of the actress were received as a paradoxical yet key signifier of inauthenticity, a visibly absent ontology where in theatrical *poiesis* the lachrymose is properly the figure and punctum of the face, the opening to the affects of the soul. In seeking to make inward truths visible, law codes the expressions

[30] It is not without note that during the US trial, Depp, using the handle #JusticeForJohnnyDepp, received 20 billion views. See Scott Stump, 'How Social Media Could Influence Other Cases after Depp, Heard Trial', TODAY.com, 3 June 2022. www.today.com/popculture/popculture/social-media-could-influence-other-cases-after-depp-heard-trial-rcna31804.

of tears and laughter, solemnity and levity as also the gestures and colours, intensities and movements of bodily presence and performance both to authenticate evidence and to relay a spectacle of trial, enactment, and governance. Drawing on an unparalleled archive of renaissance dramatics, Mukherji goes on to show how the schools of law at the Inns of Court not only depended upon a profound familiarity with the techniques of theatre, but also how training as a barrister was an adventure in dramatics, a playbook of laws, and also an exercise in revels, in the wild playfulness of the emotions and the persuasive expressions of the affective body performed for a public.

Reaching beyond the page, it is what appears in law, the substance of the staging, that engrosses Piyel Haldar, whose chapter traces the public appearance of law to that other staging that so impregnates both common and Gallic law, namely the concept of laws of the earth, or *leges terrae*, the alluvial source or divinely given tellurian basis of a most just earth. Starting from the last trial by combat in the common law tradition, the grand staging in Tothill Fields, recounted in detail in Peters' opening chapter, Haldar embarks upon a reconstruction of a peculiarly English open-air theatre of law comprised of mythical 'ley lines', geographical law vectors of force that transect the English countryside and produce a pattern, interpreted by many as a species of early modern earth jurisprudence or Druidic tellurian harmony that precedes and undergirds the common law as its natural infrastructure. The court is a place, an alluvial architectural space in which ley lines and other forces conjoin as the common substrate and natural norm, a nomos of the earth, upon which law's legitimacy so proximately depends. For Haldar, the theatre of law is predicated upon its staging in and out of the architectural space of the courtroom as an itinerant symbolic scheme of sovereign communication as much as it was a substantive body of rules. Law travels not only in time, for posterity, but also in space, transfixing its jurisdiction through the act of traversing it.

Derek Miller returns us to a critical review of the four corners of the document in the subtle and literal sense of how the modern legal text still incorporates in concealed or generally overlooked form the markers of performance, reading these scripts for the residual indicators of dramatic texts aligned to the theatrical directions for their enactment, past or future. It is the relay and exchange, the dialectic of record and act, that is quarried in thespian markers, and specifically dialogue, speech prefixes, stage directions, paratexts, and *didascalia* (markers that encode and direct emotion). Careful scrutiny or proper exegesis of legal texts, of trial transcripts, law reports, affidavits, and of Hansard, the official record of English parliamentary legislative debates, now warily viewed by courts attempting to interpret statutory texts, all bear the imprimatur of the live performances that produced them. That they might perform or not is the driving question that challenges a more flippant view of all law as performative and so poses the question that Young inscribes implicitly through her 'Installation View' of the effect of the image that escapes, the literal optics of the exchange between viewer and viewed, which is doubled in the gaze of the spectator opening to the photograph.

PART II: AFFECTATIONS

An opening onto another opening, a lush red theatrical curtain frames a marbled corridor leading to another door, this one ajar, half open, simultaneously beckoning and concealing. Entry to law is both physical and affective, the archway of a courthouse is not separate from the felt sensations of passing through. In a 'Theatre of Punishment', a video still by Young included in the wider Before the Law series, the curtain separates the scene, marking – or inventing – a proscenium boundary between law's public and its authorised actors. It situates the viewer downstage as recipient of a carefully curated performance meant to be viewed with respect to the fourth wall. Behind peeks a plain bench, radiator, and open door, the mechanics of law's performance revealed through parted folds. These uncomfortable way stations for the attendant public discourage congregating and exude a barren formality, a hushed bureaucratic injunction to quietude, obeisance, and awe. The photograph thus challenges the affective register of law in a dual form. The geometry of the space suggests hierarchy, waiting, and passage to an unseen *arcanum* or space before the law. It offers both the opulent and the retracted, the installed artifice of the drapery barely masking the attempt at self-importance required to maintain the authority of law's performance against the more banal bureaucracy held in the linear folds of the plush velvet curtains and more strikingly in the bare corridor and sparse furniture that discourage any lingering presence. This may be an exotic scene but it is not a welcoming one. When viewed as an exhibition-sized print, Young laments, one can see silver pins on the curtain hem, suggesting the curtain is not only 'handmade but unfinished': Law abides by theatre's own thirty-foot rule.[31] Young's work affirms the impetus of this section, that 'law operates in its affects' and emotional territories.[32] Part II of this volume shifts our attention from the rhetoric of law and its formulae of emplacement to its affective spaces of conjunction and disjunction. The curtain rises or here opens as a theatrical potential for animating dialogues, conjuring affects, constraining viewing and presence so as to absorb the potency and the unruly affective resonances which linger in between the formal stages of the legal process. Here, contributors attend to atmospherics, the auratics of the courts, the imaginal presence of law and lawyers that form the less obvious and in some senses less visible structures that stage legal performance. This attention also allows a shift from the presumed gravitas and authority of law to more fleeting emotions and humours, to the play of anger, laughter, sorrow, and anxiety that riddle the form and engender performances both public and private, manifest and suppressed.

Part II begins, historically and theatrically, with the affective spaces of dialogue, the scripted roles and staged performances that Miller earlier discusses in terms of *didascalia* or stage directions. Jesús Velasco takes this structural feature of legal discourse as dramatic enactment as the starting point for an account of the history of illegalism, the fight for the survival of affective spaces that exist in externality to juristic orthodoxy and resist its regulatory forms. These illegalisms are both inside and outside of the lawscape, the atmosphere of legality and its scripted modes. Dialogue assigns roles and places to the actors in the juridical drama and assigns the spaces that these players will occupy. It is these spaces that become the focus of Velasco's critical analysis of legal performance as a practice that

31 Personal note from artist.

32 Interview with the artist, January 2024. www.paulacoopergallery.com/exhibitions/carey-young5#tab:slideshow;tab-1:thumbnails.

necessarily occupies and expresses an affective space that challenges the authority and the containment of the dialogue that it relays. The atmosphere of law provides the context, the affective outside that contains the legal dialogue and also mingles in and with it. Affect roams freely, and like the image, it exceeds what can be said; it has to be seen, sensed, and felt. Dialogue, in the expanded sense in which Velasco elaborates its historical and legal role, escapes both literature and law as pure performance, as bodily habiliment and ontographic expression. It generates a space of feeling, an affective atmosphere and exchange whose embodied dimensions and sensory relay take dialogue and role beyond themselves and into the new media, the mobile scopic, auditory and holographic forms of contemporary performance as differing modes of conjoined promulgation of mores or the moral censures that give effect to governmentality.

In the next chapter Simon Stern examines shifting patterns of performance and its affect within the courthouse and trial procedures with a specific focus upon the emergence of the modern form of cross-examination as a key dimension of legal dialogue in courtroom action. When the world comes into the space of law, the atmosphere changes. Focusing on the trend toward a somewhat more explicit advocacy from the judicial bench, Stern is concerned to address the role of the community in the performance of law, paying particular attention to the ways in which the audience, spectators in the courtroom – in critical perspective, in the pit – and in the jury, impress communal views upon the legal advocates and the judges. Performance, in other words, is always for someone, for an audience, and that dynamic between advocates, judges, and spectators is nowhere more evident than in the recent tendency of the judiciary in the US Supreme Court to seek to use humour and to elicit laughter from those below. This is in many respects an exercise of power, an expression of Hobbesian superiority, legal one-upmanship, but it is also a rift and fissure in the solemn appearance of law, a hostage to humour that opens legal dialogue both to alternative performances and to critical revision.

Court TV and streaming services augment and accelerate that interplay of the ludic and the legal, and in consonance with Velasco's disassembling of dialogue stands Francis Bacon's dictate that law take nothing from theatre, which leads into the theme of *Performing Law*, which is that law takes, if not everything, at least *multum ex scena*, or as Bentham put it, to take much from theatre 'is to say, lose no occasion of speaking to the eye. In a well-composed committee of penal law, I know not a more essential personage than the manager of a theatre'.[33] The boundaries or rather the confusion and lack of boundaries are the disturbing focus of Jisha Menon's analysis of two controversial plays on child sex offenders, *The Hunt* and *The Woodsman*. Adopting an intersectional and open perspective upon the moral panic and carceral drive that inform and blur social responses to paedophilia, Menon analyses the possibility of a non-binary approach to both offender and victim. The accused is rapidly, and without process or trial, subject to *infamia*, to the public response of *caput lupinum* or outlawry, a vindictive herd reaction or social panic that dehumanises in seeking sudden and swift retribution for the extremity of the allegation rather than inquiring into the context and relationships, contacts, and communications that actually occurred. A restorative understanding of sex offenses greatly complicates the easy and totalising binaries of perpetrator and victim by showing how the roles can be reversed by social frenzy and misinformation. This is particularly evident in the context of the vulnerability, shame, and wounding of a wrongly accused sex offender, but is equally pertinent to recovery and rehabilitation that has to recompose relational dynamics and understand both the source of the paedophile's desire and the avenues to its redirection. In all of this, Menon's critical analysis scrutinises and unpacks the troubled relation of law to social anxieties and sexual panics, the rage and the projections that play into the legal process as well as stemming from it. Hate, exclusion, and stereotyping as well as sexual, racial, and class divisions play into the analysis and intersect any simplified distinction or singular boundary between legal process and sociopolitical action – a partiality framed back in a theatre of punishment.

PART III: TRANSGRESSIONS

The intersection of performance and law carries theatre into legal proceedings while equally extending the themes and fictions of trial,

[33] Jeremy Bentham, *Works* (1962 ed.), 5:21, col. 2, cited in Peters, *Law as Performance*, 298, and reprised in Jisha Menon's chapter.

regulation, and enforcement into the increasingly virtual spaces of the social. Courtroom drama has been the focus of performance studies' attention toward the juridical: Catherine Cole writes on the Truth and Reconciliation Commission as a performance of public ritual and national theatre as much as transitional justice; Michelle Castañeda writes on the hidden theatres of US immigration law that criminalise race; and Minou Arjomand writes on post-war show trials, including the Nuremburg trials, the Eichmann trial, and the Auschwitz trials, as staged showcases of both truth and artifice, norm, and performance.[34] Collectively these works mark a shift in the boundaries of the disciplines and the hierarchy of social stagings of governance as a diverse array of normative practices made visible in their liveness. Legal theatre – that is, theatre that addresses law and legal events, be it Sophocles' *Antigone* or Shakespeare's *The Merchant of Venice*, Reginald Rose's *Twelve Angry Men* or Wole Soyinka's *Death of a King's Horseman* – transitions toward a concept of living law, the perception of legality as necessarily and intrinsically performative, material, and embodied, and thus meriting attention in terms of gesture and movement, colour and costume, spectacle and screening. The divide between law and performance is destabilised and pluralised by the blurring of the boundaries between the two. But performance studies as method further transgresses the line between theatre and law, norm and practice by addressing the corporeal immediacy, the intimate visibility, and the shared quality of social enactments of juridical forms. The performance of law, in its intimate, corporeal and fleshy modalities, mediatised and streamed, seen on screen, in mobile fragments, clips and memes, breaks down the barriers, the walls of the courtroom and the mystique of its argot and rites, its dialogue and formulas, to show the juridical as yet another part of the gestural and symbolic diversity and diversions of transient, transitional, and transgressive modes of social action.

[34] Catherine Cole, *Performing South Africa's Truth Commission* (Bloomington: Indiana University Press, 2009); Michelle Castañeda, *Disappearing Rooms: The Hidden Theaters of Immigration Law* (Durham: Duke University Press, 2023); Minou Arjomand, *Staged: Show Trials, Political Theater and Aesthetics of Judgement* (Columbia University Press, 2018).

The final Carey Young still included in the volume features the four corners of the document recast through the four limbs of the body, the reach of the self, imprinted on the surface of law. A set of blue handprints and footprints mark where a body has been, already indicating where a yet unnamed body will inevitably be. The radial extension harkens to the induced corporeality of legal authority, 'Hands Up, Don't Shoot', the interpellation of the subject with stop and search, with arrest, and Transportation Security Administration body scans compelled in the silhouette. The silence of the white space, here staged between the cinder blocks of an intake room rather than a blank abyss of paper, reverberates in the absence of the human form, its marks alone left on the impassive, slightly sepia tone of the wall. The footprints mark a presence, a standing before the law, a station that obviously enough goes no further into the doorless barricade or windowless cube of legality. It is a sign of what is sometimes termed *la salle des pas perdus*, of the legal labyrinth, where causes are lost and litigants 'lose their feet and their time' endlessly searching for a resolution that is ever delayed.[35] The hands are blue as in the Blue Man Group, or more recently the business attire colour chosen by protesting women in the Tasmanian case of *Lau* v. *Moorilla,* where in uniform hue thirty-five women danced in and out of the court-house where their discrimination case was heard. Transgression occurs as poor theatre or incursion of the audience upon the stage.[36] For Young, the monotone plaster surface repels advances but registers marks of presence. Thus framed, it speaks to a history of obstruction, presenting a visual relationship between law and the bodies that encounter legality in the diversity of its forms, and here in an art gallery.[37] They can strive to enter, to participate, to engage, but the scene is set, the rules are laid down, and as audience and auditors they enter on law's terms and in the striking image of 'Intake Room' there are only the marks, the prints of

[35] A point well made in Linda Mulcahy, 'Before the Law', in Gaakeer et al., '*Palais de Justice*', 292.

[36] *Moorilla Estate* v. *Lau* [2024] TASSC 49 overturned the first-instance tribunal decision and makes no mention of the dancing in and out of court, nor of the silent well choreographed performance inside the tribunal chamber.

[37] Interview with the artist, January 2024. www.paulacoopergallery.com/exhibitions/carey-young5#tab:slideshow;tab-1:thumbnails.

their extremities, their presence otherwise a blank. No face, no torso, no front or back; it feels as if the identity is absorbed in the indifference, the adiaphorism of the law. This photograph completes a larger photographic series, 'Surfaces of Law', which captures spaces of discipline in which the body is implicated, if absent. In Part III of this book, like Young, scholars turn toward the ways in which law is performed and transgressed, through absence, interruption, non-performance, hilarity, laughter, and the various eruptions that follow.

In the spirit of revision, borrowing a term from early modern lawyer Thomas Blount's *Glossographia*, Peter Goodrich centres the transgressive history of comedy more directly through a study of legal texts as comediographic records. His chapter starts from an image preceding a dialogue between Emperor Hadrian and Epictetus, published in the years of the plague in Renaissance France by Italian jurist Andrea Alciato and translated and commented by constitutional theorist Jean de Coras. The comediographer is defined as one who takes an altercation, a conflict, and develops a narrative that elaborates and expands upon the discontent and then ends it in happy, which is to say comic, popular resolution. Law may seem more tragic, more prone to disillusion than contentment, but it follows a similar trajectory to comedy, one drawn inexorably to resolution and to social harmonisation of antithetic views. Casuistry has its own comic relay, its instances of the absurd as well as its everyday occasions of the unforeseen, unexpected, and untoward. Tracking these glimpses of the playbook, of epistolary exchange and dialogue between theatre and law, casuist and comedian, persona and performance, allows for an appreciation of the manner in which law appears, a reasoning that adds to the inductive protocol of law proceeding *ad similia*, that of proceeding *ad apparentiam* and in the mode of play. The popular appeal of legal drama lies not only in its agon, the thrill of contestation, but also in the affective projection of the viewing self into the phantasmatic spaces of the tradition, costume, and comedy of conflict resolution.

Extending this historical reflection on comedy, laughter is the driving theme of Başak Ertür's contribution to the minor jurisprudence of affect and its transgressive interruptions to the solemn space of law. Where Simon Stern, at the end of his chapter, addresses the propensity of judges to elicit laughter as a form of advocacy, seeking to persuade the audience of the veracity of the judicial position or opinion, Ertür examines a uniquely rambunctious courtroom drama in Marleen Gorris' film *A Question of Silence.* Here a different, explosive, and more equalising laughter takes hold of a murder trial of three women and spreads to their female psychiatrist and then to the audience. The world erupts in the court in rebellion against the absurdity of the formal procedures, and the laughter becomes contagious. The women on trial have remained silent throughout the process, they 'can communicate but see no point in it', the sonic absence, or abstinence, echoed in Young's trace remainder of the body. The women refuse, and laughter is the modality of their breaking away from the agelastic sexism of the proceedings. Laughter shatters both their silence and the discourse of the lawyers in a gelascopic fashion. Ertür argues that a complex hybrid of emotions, what could be termed *risus iratus,* mixing anger and absurdity, the ribald and the resistant, the cachinnation opens an alternative space within the dialogue of court proceedings, interrupting and taking over the trial through the intervention of an untameable flow and wild contagion of mirth. The drama performs an exquisite reversal in which what the dictionary defines as psychiatrically inappropriate hilarity takes hold also of the psychiatrist expert witness. The spectacle of laughter, which recent studies indicate that the US Supreme Court uses to validate their decisional proceedings,[38] here gets upended in a feminist filmic fiction that hints at the critical role of the comic and the transgressive force of laughter. The restrained comedy of the Justices of the Supreme Court is here potentially pitched against an affective hilarity that inverts and undoes the solemn gravitas and occasional, generally mocking humour of the high judiciary whose bids for laughter are always accompanied by the *meiosis* or mockery of dogmatic superiority. For Ertür the focus is on the women defendants and a laughter that laughs back, that takes over the court and silences the judges. But it is a fiction, an aspiration that in the argot of the legal philosopher is defined as *non-entia imaginaria,* an imaginal intervention

[38] For a recent conspectus of theories of laughter in the US Supreme Court, see Tonja Jacobi and Matthew Sag, 'Taking Laughter Seriously at the Supreme Court' (2019) 72 *Vanderbilt Law Review* 1423–1496.

rather than a real trial. As the image 'Intake Room' shows, blue prints on a bare and seemingly unreceptive and nonresponsive wall are the only vestiges, the austere marks of sensory presence and performance, laughter and tears, that passed before but not through the law.

The dual potential for legal texts to script action, but also in many instances to fail to do so, undergirds the more contemporary theorisation of the non-performative. Pointing to the shadow side of the Austin–Butler conception of the performative as a constituting utterance or act, Sara Ahmed draws our attention to the non-performative: 'the failure of the speech act to do what it says is not a failure of intent or even circumstance, *but is actually what the speech act is doing* . . . naming can be a way of not bringing something into effect'.[39] The critical role of the non-performative, the conflict of theatres, and more precisely of genres of the theatrical, take centre stage in Marco Wan's account of increasingly tense political struggles in Hong Kong that came to a head in the peculiar rite of swearing the oath of office upon being returned to the legislature, after election victories. The performative ceremony of oath taking was seized upon by prodemocracy, oppositional politicians to literally stage a protest, capture the camera, and turn law's performance of induction against itself. Six elected representatives chose different facets of the oath-taking ceremony to enact the oath differently, by changes in tone and speed of diction, in deportment, in accessories such as a flag with an anti-China message on it, or an enormous yellow umbrella, by sudden interruptions of the recitation, or in one case by pausing six seconds between each word. In the last mentioned instance, the court held the oath invalid for being theatrical, rendering this performative event oddly non-performative. The expanded pauses between words make the performance, the medium of oral delivery, the subject of the swearing, and so deflect successfully both from the seriousness of the legal rite, resisting the imposition of the role of subject who swears an

[39] Sara Ahmed, 'The Nonperformative of Antiracism' (2006) 7.1 *Meridians* 104–126. Judith Butler, *Notes towards a Performative Theory of Assembly* (Cambridge, MA: Harvard University Press, 2015) 34–37, develops a similar point in relation to recognition and recognisability of subjects in the fields of social appearance. Non-recognition is a mode of exclusion.

oath by subverting the illocutionary act and turning the form of affirmation against its substance. The decision against the recalcitrant actor, in a reprise of earlier legislation against acting, and in common with the anti-theatrical tradition, makes visible the covert element of play in juristic and governmental culture. Such exposure or stripping bare of the law by its makers threatens the *status quo ante comœdium* or the state of affairs prior to the histrionics of their performance.[40] The theatre of law can neither admit poor theatre nor let popular performance into the sanctified interior of the legal assembly. As Wan argues it, the illocutionary force, the power of the juristic performance, its liturgical effect, was undone by the explicit theatricalisation of the legal process. The irony of this profanation of communist legality has a peculiar force or redoubling effect, opening the viewer's eyes in this context not so much to the emperor's lack of clothes as to the empire's lack of closure.

The oath takers' revelry in alternate modes of acting out the oath of office sought not only sympathy from the auditors but also engagement in politicising the ritual of investiture into a constrained yet contested official role. Indeed, in deed, the secret of successful performance, according to Charles Lamb, was a subtle and tacit understanding whereby the audience is drawn without knowing it into the scene.[41] They participate unconsciously, and it is precisely that convention, the legal atmosphere, the exegetical literalism of the avowal, which portends an otherworldly judgment, an exodus from quotidian secular time and space that is challenged by the loudly explicit performance of laughter or, in the Hong Kong case, the self-consciously thespian style of swearing the oath.

Gender, race, and performance in contemporary contexts of conflict emerge dramatically upon the social stage of law enforcement in the figure of 'Naked Athena', the subject, both literal and matterphoric, of Kimmel's chapter on the wayward aesthetics of exposed bodies. The figure in question was that of a woman who, wearing only a face mask

[40] One can note here Simon Critchley, *On Humour* (Abingdon: Routledge, 2002) 29: 'If humour is human, then it also curiously marks the limit of the human. Or, better, humour explores what it means to be human by moving back and forth across the frontier that separates humanity from animality, thereby making it unstable.'

[41] Charles Lamb, *The Essays of Elia* [1823] (New York: Wiley and Putnam, 1845), 2:21.

and stocking cap, confronted police lines during demonstrations in Portland, Oregon. She stood alone and adopted what came to be captioned balletic poses in front of the heavily overdressed and armed police lines: 'Through her balletic performance of resistance, themes of discipline, elegance, and decorum swirl against the indecent, vulgar, and obscene labels afforded other protesters in the same scene.' The choreographic apparition of Naked Athena, the performance as a bare and unnamed actress, staged a semiotic alternative or other scene of protest. The exposure of the body was deemed neither pornographic nor a threat to public order, and the mask, which in other protests has been deemed of itself to threaten violence, was seen as the *prosopon* of a stage player.[42]

Resistance, demonstration, and political manifestation on the streets of the polity often results in conflict with the law in which disorder confronts the militarised forces of the state. The protesters occupy the streets in opposition to the routine and the extant status quo. In the example of Naked Athena, however, a singular naked performance, dance postures, and a silent semiotic resistance were capable of stepping outside and above legal rules of public order and social decorum that most probably were conceived without contemplating such a bare manifestation of public and public expression. The most effective art is sometimes the simplest, and the naked adoption of poses not only confronted the latent violence of the police riot lines but also managed to break the law in the alternative sense of breaking out of law and entering an untamed space of *an-archos* not dissimilar to, but more real than the laughter in court that ends the trial scene in *A Question of Silence*. Where laughter interrupts and collapses the binary distinction between speech and silence, the stripping bare and performing stage poses in front of police lines makes the medium of protest, the body, both inordinately visible and vulnerable, collapsing in turn the sumptuary binary between the clothed and the uniform, protest and the forces of order, and in a complex historical sense between gender and norm, love and law.

[42] There are numerous U.S. anti-mask statutes, and for a case of a demonstrator wearing a mask being arrested and charged, see *Gates* v. *Khokhar* 884 F.3d 1290 (2018).

Returning to our starting point, the antagonism between law and theatre, two different and competing stages for the unravelling of public life, is both challenged and reshaped by the shift of focus to performance. As Peters has argued at length in *Law as Performance*, the binary opposition or duelling dyad misrepresents the history of law's intrinsic theatricality while also failing to appreciate the law internal to theatre. The opposition, as the performances of Naked Athena so well illustrate, is really a case of frustrated desire for social place and legal recognition. Law is intrinsic to the social forms and patterns of performance, to social dressage, the codes of gesture (*lex gestus*), to the rhythms of dance, to the circulations and ambulations that organise the protests and processions, the occasions and the events, the persons and plays that appear and so are recognised in the public, and intimate public spheres. Law carries over the order of religious and social rites, and the judge takes the place of the priest to be the one who dances first – *praelatus* – in the secular social sphere. On the other side of the collapsed equation, the emergence of performance studies gives new weight to the theatricality, the plurality of actors and acting, that is at the heart of legality. To perform is to manifest, to institute, to produce and transform. In an age of omnivoyance, in the viral videosphere, it is increasingly the ephemera of performance, the unmarked signs of law, that now govern.

PART I

FORENSIS AND FORENSIC ACTORS

I.0 Carey Young, *Palais de Justice* (still), 2017. Single-channel HD video (from 4K); 16:9 format, quadraphonic sound. Installation view from *Carey Young: Appearance*, Modern Art Oxford, 2023.

CHAPTER 2

Law, Rhetoric and Fictionality in 'the Age of Theatre'

A Literary Response to Law as Performance

Lorna Hutson

2.1 LAW AS THEATRE

The trope of law-as-theatre, writes Julie Stone Peters, is older than the figure of Justice as blind, but just as devastatingly ambivalent. Instead of insisting that Justice, to be impartial, *should not see*, it insists that Justice, to be effective, should *be seen*. But the trope of law as theatre is not just an analogy; it is also an antithesis. Justice defines itself against the theatre. Theatre is compromised by its desire to please, its repertoire of tricks and sleights, its masks, wigs and bags of blood. The 'dispassionate reason, objectivity, discipline, and the sovereignty of the truth' that is law, argues Peters, should have no truck with such arts, for obvious reasons.[1] But this pristine, dispassionate, abstract Law cannot avoid meddling with showmanship. It must condescend to embody itself, to make itself visible, 'to showcase justice, visibly represent its own force and dignity . . . deploy the passions of the crowd, produce a theatre for vengeance' (8–9). So the analogy and the antithesis coexist simultaneously, registering two opposing attitudes. On the one hand, there is 'legal theatricality (law needs theatre); and legal antitheatricality (law must avoid theatre at all costs)'. The trope, Peters writes, 'marked these out as antinomies, but also revealed them as, often, perilously proximate. Recognising law as a performance practice, it identified theatre as both a source of law's

[1] Julie Stone Peters, *Law as Performance: Theatricality, Spectatorship, and the Making of Law in Ancient, Medieval, and Early Modern Europe* (Oxford: Oxford University Press, 2022) 8. Hereafter references are given by page number in the text.

power and an embarrassment' (9). Peters' latest book, *Law as Performance*, argues that these antinomies are not just anecdote material, but lie at the definitional heart of legal theory in the West. '"What is law?"' Peters asks, ventriloquising legal philosophers since law began. '"Not theatre!"' she choruses back, still in their voices. But then she adds, mischievously, in her own: 'Except *when it is*' (9, my italics).

In this strikingly original and erudite study, Peters uses the terms 'theatre' and 'performance' more or less interchangeably, which is not to say that she is not conscious of and discriminating about these words' different etymologies and semantic range. Early cultures, as she notes, did not have a single word for what we call 'performance'. Indeed, as Luke Wilson has pointed out, the terms 'perform' and 'performance' in sixteenth-century legal English are primarily set in conceptual opposition to the 'promise' of which they signify the fulfilment.[2] Peters scrutinises a range of other words: '*hypokrisis*', '*actio*', '*pronunciatio*' and 'delivery', along with a range of words for audiences and spectators (17). We could say, broadly, then, that Peters is interested in theatre in its *performative aspect.* As soon as we come on to the history of law as 'theatre', however, another term becomes important: *rhetoric.* Chapter 1, vividly describing the theatricality of the Athenian law courts, identifies *hypokrisis* as the art of acting, but also as that of legal oratory. So we have two terms, 'theatre' and 'rhetoric', both of which are associated with, indeed largely defined by, a third term: live 'performance' before an audience. And yet neither 'theatre' nor 'rhetoric' coincides completely with 'performance'. If performance is an aspect of theatre, so is dramatic composition. And if, as *pronunciatio*, performance is an aspect of rhetoric, then so is the discovery of persuasive arguments, known as *inventio.* It is to these compositional or inventive aspects of early modern theatre and rhetoric – which are also in various ways held to compromise the rational and dispassionate workings of the law – that this chapter will in due course turn.

[2] Luke Wilson, *Theaters of Intention: Drama and the Law in Early Modern England* (Stanford, CA: Stanford University Press, 2000) 165–166. See also Jonathan Powell, 'Scarce Expressible in English': Theatre and the Common Law, *c.* 1597–1624, PhD thesis, King's College, University of London.

My aim, in this response to Peters' timely, powerful work, is both to acknowledge its transformative force for legal studies and at the same time to introduce some distinctions that may be of some value in distinguishing discussions of the 'theatricality' of law (in the sense of reconstructing law as live performance) from the emergence of a modern understanding of 'theatre' as the production of coherent and powerful fictions enacted by characters. The early modern period (1500–1650) is described, in chapter 5 of Peters' study, as 'the age of theatre'. If Peters shows how judicial proceedings draw on the performative aspects of rhetoric and theatre, I hope, conversely, to show how, in the 'age of theatre', theatre's distinctive *fictionality* – every bit as important as the fictionality of 'the rise of the novel' – drew on the fiction-generating power of probable argument and inferential reasoning, as taught in legal rhetoric.[3] First, however, to attend to the argument of *Law as Performance.*

2.2 LAW AS PERFORMANCE

Julie Stone Peters is well known as an academic crosser of literary and legal disciplinary boundaries, combining the writing of prize-winning books on early modern book history with being at the cutting edge of contemporary debates on women's rights and law as a media spectacle.[4] Yet her work is characterised not so much by boundary crossing as by the investigation of boundaries as generators of antitheses which in turn give rise to definitional desire and disavowal. Peters' work bracingly confronts all that is disavowed in the definitional boundaries that sustain and produce institutional knowledge. When I used to teach early modern literature and law, I would start my students off with Peters' 2005 *PMLA* article, 'Law, Literature and the Vanishing Real: The Future of an

[3] For an argument that identifies 'fictionality' with the rise of the novel, see Catherine Gallagher, 'The Rise of Fictionality', in *The Novel,* vol. 1 ed. Franco Moretti (Princeton, NJ: Princeton University Press, 2006) 336–363 and for a counter-argument for the 'fictionality' of early modern poetry and drama, see Benedict S. Robinson, 'The True Story of Fictionality', *Critical Inquiry,* 50.3 (2024) 547–568.

[4] Julie Stone Peters, *The Theatre of the Book, 1480–1880: Print, Text and Performance in Europe* (New York: Oxford University Press, 2000); Julie Stone Peters and Andrea Woper, eds., *Women's Rights, Human Rights: International Feminist Perspectives* (New York: Routledge, 1995).

Interdisciplinary Illusion'. This article opened with a bold satire on professional critical desire, an imagined scenario in which literature professors demanded of their legal counterparts real-world effectiveness against injustice, while law professors craved from their literary peers some amalgamation of a razor-sharp deconstruction of truth as metaphor with a warmly empathetic response to human 'story telling' and 'narrative'. The implication was that the illusions of interdisciplinarity that went by the name of 'law and literature' were fantasies shaped by what professionals in each discipline felt their own discipline lacked, each distorting the other into the desired antithesis and complement.[5]

Law as Performance is similarly bracing in that it confronts and dismantles what is argued to be a defining distinction between law and theatre from the legal point of view. Law has a theatrical dimension, but theatre must know its ancillary place. Law cannot, must not, be *reduced to mere theatre.* So the official story goes – but Peters shows that, in the end, in the publicity of the court, in those moments in which two advocates argue and present evidence (using every technique of rhythmic speech, appropriate gestures, timely revelations, emotively human props or mocking rituals) *mere theatre* is exactly what law is. Quintilian, contrasting the listener's experience with that of the reader, writes that, for the former, 'everything is alive and stirring, we welcome every fresh thought as it is born with joy and anxiety, and are moved not only by the fortunes of the trial, but the risks of the speakers ... In reading, on the other hand, judgement is surer, because a listener's reactions are frequently distorted by personal inclination or by the noisy cries of the applauding audience'.[6] Peters foregrounds the extent to which law has depended, across the centuries and across different jurisdictions, on these live, collective audience responses rather than on solitary readerly judgement. Auditory and sensory reactions and distractions (whether anticipated by forensic technique or unexpectedly emerging in the trial) shape legal decisions that, once codified or assimilated to the body of

[5] Julie Stone Peters, 'Law, Literature, and the Vanishing Real: On the Future of an Interdisciplinary Illusion', *PMLA*, 120.2 (2005) 442–453.

[6] Quintilian, *The Orator's Education*, tr. Donald A. Russell (Cambridge, MA: Harvard University Press, 2001), 5 vols., vol. IV, pp. 260–261, 10.1.16.

knowledge called law, are promptly abstracted and insulated from the crowd-pleasing compromises of their origins.

This analogy-as-antithesis (law as performance, but also everything but) energises Peters' wide and erudite sweep across Western legal history, 2,000 years of trials, ranging, geographically, from Athens to Rome through Bologna, Toulouse, Innsbruck, Lisieux and Bamberg as well as Paris and London. She begins with ancient confrontations and codependencies, some quite familiar (Plato versus Aristotle; Quintilian's textbook Cicero), and, moving through legal treatises and trial records of the high and late Middle Ages, reaches sixteenth-century France and the Netherlands and, finally, London with its much-investigated Inns of Court. What distinguishes Peters' treatment from earlier studies of these confrontations between law and theatre is her methodology. She highlights those aspects of forensic theory and practice that most explicitly acknowledge theatrical uses of bodily movement, signs of emotion, physical props. She is sceptical of legal-historical narratives that accept at face value reforming accounts of a law which has wrested control of trial procedure from the contingency of the publicly accessible live event. She looks, in the official record, for what it does not want to tell us: indications of what the space felt like; the sensory sway of the crowd; the jostling, the cacophony, the emotionally heightened, embodied experience of witnessing the trial's unfolding in a public space. Legal historians, she notes, have looked to literary texts for this kind of colour, but complex poetic artefacts do not tell us much about real people in real situations. She reads between the lines of ancient, medieval and early modern theoretical texts as well as medieval texts of legal reform and archival records of trials.

Theoretical treatises of forensic oratory, from the Greeks to the Romans, provide explicit instructions in *hypokrisis*, *actio* and *pronunciatio* – how to speak, how to move the body, how to deploy clients and props to most pathetic effect. The early modern period sees the fullest pedagogical revival and development of these techniques, but Peters persuasively insists that medieval legal-rhetorical theory from the eighth to the fourteenth centuries was far from underestimating the importance of *actio* and *pronunciatio*, far from uninterested in the body, the visceral, the embarrassing, the emotive. As she comes on to the high and late Middle

Ages, Peters confronts and challenges the methodological assumptions of histories that have treated official legal ideology as empirical and experiential. Scholars have identified two moments in early European legal history in which power shifts away from the contingency of communal and public arenas of justice and towards a more authoritatively controlled, scripted and regulated process. The first of these ostensibly occurred when the church and jurists took over in the twelfth century and law 'became a privileged tool in the hands of experts' (146). The second, taking place in the late fifteenth and early sixteenth centuries, was influentially characterised by John H. Langbein as the transition, across several European jurisdictions, from public, accusatory criminal procedures to one based on the law of the Roman canon inquisition, an '*Inquisitionsprozess*'.[7] In both cases, Peters argues, the success of attempts to script judicial procedures and to control public access to them has been assumed from the aspirational texts of the reformers, the motivations and aims of which tell a very different story. In 1455, Thomas Basin, Bishop of Lisieux, proposed a scheme for a perfectly functioning trial procedure involving the silent exchange of written documents to replace the noisy, disorderly and temporally distended public trials of the Norman customary courts. Yet his proposals themselves alert us to the inescapable presence of the crowd in places of trial, before and after he wrote. This, Peters shows, is true across Europe in this period, whether those places of trial be outdoor or indoor. And with the presence of this public audience comes the contingency and reversibility of live theatre.

One of the three propositions with which Peters opens her book is that performance, though essential to law, cannot be completely controlled by a script. It 'has a tendency to take on a life of its own' (5). In challenging these narratives of procedural shifts from public accusation to private *Inquisitionsprozess*, Peters reads between the lines of trial records for those moments of the autonomous life of performance, moments in which the official theatrical script fails to deliver its desired effects. The trial and defrocking of Jan Hus in 1415, for example, degenerates into a *Noises Off*-like farce of revealed backstage business as the ecclesiastical

[7] See John H. Langbein, *Prosecuting Crime in the Renaissance: England, Germany, France* (Cambridge, MA: Harvard University Press, 1974).

judges engage in a decidedly unslick, not to say cumbersome, series of costume changes. In order to perform the judicial ritual of defrocking Hus, the bishops had first to get him into his frocks, which meant several senior clergy wrestling the heretic into the elaborate vestments of ecclesiastical high office – alb, amice, stole, cincture, maniple and chasuble – only in order to wrestle them all back off again. And while they were about it, Hus took the opportunity to subvert the iconography of the event by elevating his arms and addressing the crowd in full sacerdotal regalia, possibly appearing to be performing the Mass in the person of Christ himself.

This is a powerful reading, brilliantly illustrative of the book's central thesis. Peters' wide-ranging exploration of the antinomies of law-as-theatre (the analogy that sparks antitheses) seems to pay off again and again. Peters' book will undoubtedly be generative for legal, social and cultural historians as well as literary scholars of early modern England. To take two recent examples of work on English law and literature by younger scholars: Clare Egan's study of provincial libels emphasises how carefully the court of Star Chamber framed libellous words in order to make 'sure the material contained was not laughed at in the court itself', testifying to the unruly power of performance to disrupt legal proceedings.[8] Lucy Clarke's work on the role of performance in constituting magisterial authority at a local level is similarly supported and enriched by Peters' central trope of law as performance.[9]

Yet this ingenious central rhetorical trope, illuminating as it is, may nevertheless be a little too neat for its own good. In equating theatre first with performance and second with rhetoric, Peters' book may be eliding complex and incommensurable differences that matter. I do not think these elisions detract in any serious way from the book's central argument about the theatricality of law in ancient, medieval and early modern Europe. But I do think that noticing them helps explain why what Peters has to say about law 'in the age of theatre' (the early modern period)

[8] Clare Egan, 'Jacobean Star Chamber Records and the Performance of Provincial Libel', in *Star Chamber Matters: An Early Modern Court and Its Records*, ed. Krista J. Kesselring and Natalie Mears (London: University of London, 2021) 135–153, 137.

[9] Lucy J. S. Clarke, 'Public Men on Public Stages: The Performance of State Authority by Magistrates in Popular Drama, 1590–1610', DPhil, Oxford University, 2021).

seems largely unilluminating about what was distinctive and new in that period's achievements in *theatre* itself, as opposed to in the theatricality of law. And the period's achievements in theatre – that is, in dramatic writing – would have, in the long run, a more significant legacy for poetic and legal meaning-making in the West.

2.3 NOT JUST PERFORMANCE: RHETORICAL INVENTION AND THEATRICAL FICTIONALITY

It is, then, worth unpacking the differences between early modern theatre, rhetoric and performance, not because these are ever entirely separable practices but because, on the contrary, their necessary interaction and interdependence cannot be properly appreciated unless we consider their separate qualities and see how they work together. I will sketch out how we might supplement Peters' account of law's theatricality in terms of rhetorical *pronunciatio* and courtroom performance with another account of how theatre, borrowing and adapting legal rhetoric's techniques of *inventio*, became imbued with powerful qualities of fictionality and credibility, acquiring a new capacity to elicit an audience's imaginative participation in the bringing alive of invented stories and fictional characters.[10]

The Renaissance of theatre in early modern Europe was the effect of a revival of forensic rhetoric as well as topics-logic or dialectic. We could, to borrow Katrin Ettenhuber's term, say it was the effect of a revival of 'the rhetorico-logical art of language' adapted to the practice of composing and enacting powerfully enduring theatrical fictions.[11] On the rhetoric side, then, we're not talking solely about those aspects of rhetoric that Peters identifies most closely with theatre and performance (*hypokrisis, actio, pronunciatio*). Rather more significant for the composition of dramatic plots was rhetoric as *inventio* and *dispositio*, the invention and emplotment of arguments. The dramatic masterpieces composed in

[10] Robinson, 'True Story'; Lorna Hutson, *Circumstantial Shakespeare* (Oxford: Oxford University Press, 2015).

[11] Katrin Ettenhuber, *The Logical Renaissance* (Oxford: Oxford University Press, 2023) 43.

the sixteenth century are less vehicles for improvisatory performance than invitations to an audience to infer a whole fictional world, incorporating back story and offstage. These plays aim, through ingenious plot composition, to elicit a profound and complex emotional response to a whole enacted, invented narrative. This was a truly new achievement in the European vernaculars: nothing like it had existed since the drama of the ancient world. I have already mentioned Peters' third opening proposition – that 'performance can take on a life of its own'. This proposition pinpoints precisely how 'law-as-performance' is *unlike* the theatre of the European Renaissance. For in the 'age of theatre' dramatists desired performance less to take of an improvised life of its own (as it had traditionally done) than to bring into being the more complex poetic life of the play in the audience's imaginations.[12] When Hamlet tells the players to 'let those that play the clowns speak no more than is set down for them' because talented improvisers can obscure 'some necessary question of the play then to be considered', he expresses theatre's new concern that the precise poetic under-specification that invites audience to conjecture and imagine ('some necessary *question* of the play') should not be drowned out by unscripted performance practice.[13]

2.4 RENAISSANCE THEATRE'S NEW FICTIONALITY: FROM ITALY TO ENGLAND, 1500–1650

So what, precisely, was new about theatre in sixteenth-century Europe? Most of what we take for granted about much theatre today – the fact of theatre's fictionality, the fact that plays and TV and movie dramas enact stories about invented characters whose motives and feelings interest us, the fact that we imagine a 'world of the play' beyond the stage or fictional

[12] The classic study of the interactive, audience-oriented theatrical culture of the fifteenth century is Robert Weimann's magisterial *Shakespeare and the Popular Tradition in Theater: Studies in the Social Dimension of Dramatic Form and Function* (Baltimore, MD: Johns Hopkins University Press, 1978).

[13] William Shakespeare, *Hamlet*, ed. Ann Thompson and Neil Taylor (London: Bloomsbury Arden Shakespeare, 2016) 3.2.36–7. For 'under-specification', see Terence Cave, *Thinking with Literature: Towards a Cognitive Criticism* (Oxford: Oxford University Press, 2016) 27.

spaces beyond what the camera shows us and that we infer or project a coherent order of events on to the mix of representational effects that we see – all these ordinary assumptions of theatrical, cinematic and televisual drama, are the legacies of sixteenth-century innovations in theatre. And it all started in Italy. 'Italy', as Louise Clubb has written, 'was unique in producing the technology of modern theatre'. And she goes on:

> From the Cinquecento (the 1500s) into the Seicento (the 1600s) it developed a new system of play-making, comprising generic structures, methods of acting, and innovations in scene design, as well as theoretical principles and vocabulary ... that would appear in theatrical structures throughout Europe and would be carried from *commedia erudita* and *commedia dell'arte* to Molière and Shakespeare and beyond.[14]

Adapting the plot structures of Latin comedy, Ludovico Ariosto and his imitators and followers produced comedies that were modern, recognisable fictions of contemporary Italian urban life, 'presenting fiction onstage so as to capture and embody in the vernacular the causality and illusion of quotidian reality'.[15]

Prior to the Italian avant-garde experimentalism of the early sixteenth century, European vernacular theatre – the *sacre rappresentazioni* of fifteenth century Italy, say, or Corpus Christi or penitential drama of fifteenth-century England – was of course already doing profound and significant things with performance. The Corpus Christi plays, as Sarah Beckwith has persuasively demonstrated, performatively enacted the body of Christ as a divine jurisdiction exercised through community reconciliation.[16] Yet these culturally powerful forms of theatrical performance lacked *fictionality* – they lacked any capacity to invite the audience to infer or imagine an implied world offstage, or action happening between scenes. Late fifteenth-century English drama displays few

[14] Louise George Clubb, *Renaissance Theatergrams: From Italy to England.* SKENÈ Texts and Studies (Pisa: Edizione ETS, 2024) 25.

[15] Clubb, *Theatergrams*, 31.

[16] Sarah Beckwith, *Signifying God: Social Relation and Symbolic Act in York Corpus Christi Plays* (Chicago, IL: University of Chicago Press, 2001).

techniques for 'conveying offstage action and extramimetic locations'.[17] When actors go offstage, they do not enter an imagined elsewhere that is part of the play; they simply cease to be until their next performative appearance. Peter Womack, referring to the late fifteenth-century play *Mankind*, puts it thus:

> The performers come on, do their performance and leave, and nobody pretends that they are going anywhere except to their dressing rooms. The performance may generate a 'character' (a singer adopts the voice of a lover, a wrestler cultivates an artificially aggressive stage personality); but if so, the character does not acquire enough imaginative solidity for us to attribute continuing life to it. Rather, it is a trope, or a colour, within *the always dominant discourse of the performance itself.*[18] (my italics)

This is not a criticism of fifteenth-century sacred drama, but a recognition of its distinctive kind of theatricality. As sacramental drama, there is no imaginative dimension to the offstage, writes Womack, because 'the on-stage space is *complete*' as an allegory of human salvation in which the audience is already implicated.[19] Womack's analysis enables us to distinguish a late medieval theatrical culture, with its 'always dominant discourse of the performance itself', from the radically innovative fictionality of the early modern theatre that succeeded it. Early modern or Renaissance theatre offers us fictions and characters (Hamlet, Falstaff) to whom later generations have attributed a 'continuing life'. Early modern theatre also produces fictional worlds, imagined theatrical space. One of the assumptions of modern theatregoers, as Womack says, is that of the metonymic relation of onstage and off. We assume that 'if the stage is a drawing-room, the characters are entering it from the dining-room; if it is a street, the upstage door leads into somebody's house' and so forth.[20] But this assumption – which Womack names 'fictional adjacency' – is predicated precisely on the further assumption

17 Charles Whitworth, 'Reporting Offstage Events in Early Tudor Drama', in *Tudor Theatre: 'Let There Be Covenants . . .'*, ed. Andre Lascombes (Bern: Peter Lang, 1998) 45–66, 58.

18 Peter Womack, 'Off-Stage', in *Oxford Handbook of Early Modern Theatricality*, ed. Henry Turner (Oxford: Oxford University Press, 2013) 74–75.

19 Womack, 'Off-Stage', 75.

20 Womack, 'Off-Stage', 73.

that what a play presents is *a coherent fictional world*. And that, in turn, is an assumption inherited from the achievement of European theatre in the sixteenth century.

Peters shows compellingly how public pleading in legal trials inevitably has qualities of live theatre which open it to the contingencies of performance. Conversely, however, I want to show how sixteenth-century theatre became more powerful as *fiction*. The story I will tell is partial; it is focussed on what Italian comedy conveyed to England by way of a mastery of vivid techniques for engaging the audience's imagination in the plot. Although this is just one strand of how European theatre developed in the sixteenth century, it is significant and pertinent partly because it drew on forms of argumentative proof originally formulated for the law courts, codified in Roman forensic rhetoric and adapted in the 'forensic disposition' of Roman New Comedy. Ludovico Ariosto, the great innovator of early modern theatre, made dazzling use of the 'forensic disposition' of Terence and Plautus's comedies: that is, in actions that seem always to anticipate litigious consequences, in 'argumentation that borrows the strategies of forensic discourse: above all, in a readiness to formulate attacks and defenses ... to rehearse evidence and to supply proofs'.[21] Ariosto's plots involved young men's attempts to get access to courtesans or citizens' daughters by various forms of entrapment, impersonation and credit fraud, deploying the kinds of proofs that Quintilian, after Aristotle, called 'artificial' or 'technic' – that is, the rhetorico-logical strategies subsumed under the general term of 'arguments'.[22] We need to see these strategies not just as 'let's pretend' versions of real legal strategies of proof, but as the resources of a new theatrical fictionality predicated on the audience's readiness to infer, from characters' uses of probable arguments, all the backstories, motives and hidden truths of the play's story.

[21] Adele Scafuro, *The Forensic Stage: Settling Disputes in Graeco-Roman New Comedy* (Cambridge: Cambridge University Press, 1997) 28.

[22] Quintilian, *Orator's Education*, 5.8, 5.10. For examples of how these rhetorico-logical proofs were deployed in the plays of Terence and Plautus, and how sixteenth-century schoolboys were taught to recognise them, see Lorna Hutson, *The Invention of Suspicion: Law and Mimesis in Shakespeare and Renaissance Drama* (Oxford: Oxford University Press, 2007) 46–47, 164–170, 286–288.

For example, Ariosto's first comedy, *La Cassaria* (1508) involves a plot of legal entrapment adapted from Plautus's *Poenulus.*[23] To help a young man extract the courtesan he loves from the hands of her pimp, the young man's servant, Volpino, plots to plant a coffer full of valuable merchandise in the pimp's house so they can accuse him of stealing it. But by Act 4, the scheme has gone wrong: the young man's father and owner of the coffer has come home early, so Volpino starts to improvise, accusing the pimp of stealing the old man's coffer. The old man is deeply sceptical, reluctant to go to the authorities without more proof, but Volpino confidently lies. 'If I come along with you, I'll present the governor with so many indications and conjectures, so much proof (*tali indizii e coniettureet prove*) that even if he didn't want, he couldn't help but believe you'.[24] Volpino's conjectures and *indicia* (a term Sir Thomas Smith was later to gloss in the English legal context as 'tokens' or 'evidence') turn out to be ingeniously detailed and vividly visualised narratives designed to elicit the false inferences which drive the engine of the comic plot.[25] Important to grasp, however, is the homology between these comic uses of artificial proof to devise plausible but false narratives and the newly illusionistic power of theatre to make audiences think they have seen things they have not seen, and to infer and imagine the fictional world of the play. The poet does not lie, but the lies of his characters produce the knot of confusion and false surmise to which the audience must attend and in making sense of which it becomes imaginatively involved.

Audience attention, inferring causes and motives, thus begins, with Ariosto and his imitators, to contribute to a new imaginative participation in making theatrical fictions feel realistic or *verisimile.* Writing to an actor friend, the dramatist Giovanni Battista Giraldi Cinthio proposed,

[23] See Lorna Hutson, '"Che indizio, che prova . . . ?" Ariosto's Legal Conjectures and the English Renaissance Stage', *Renaissance Drama*, 36/7 (2010) 179–205.

[24] Ariosto, La Cassaria, in *Tutte le Opere di Ludovico Ariosto* ed. Cesare Segre, vol. 4, ed. Angela Casella, Gabriella Ronchi and Elena Varsi (Mondadori: 1974) 4.2.159–160; for a translation, see *The Coffer* in *The Comedies of Ariosto*, tr. and ed. Edmond M. Beame and Leonard G. Sbrocchi (Chicago, IL: University of Chicago Press, 1975) 4.2, p. 28.

[25] Sir Thomas Smith, *De Republica Anglorum*, ed. Mary Dewar (Cambridge: Cambridge University Press, 1982) 114.

controversially, that a newly invented or fictive (*finta*) tragedy might even be more moving than one based on history, since the spectator of a fictive tragedy will be aware that the only way he can know the story is through this theatrical representation, and so will pay very close attention: 'Aware that the action about to be represented can be known only through the representation', Cinthio speculates, 'the spectator no sooner tastes the plot and thinks that it might be ingeniously constructed (*ingegnosamente composta*) than he concentrates his attention and tries not to lose one word'.[26] It is thus auditors' own imaginative participation in following the intricate situations enacted before them – inferring connections, imagining motives, causes and emotions – that gives the fiction credibility and life. That a fiction should seem *verisimile*, like truth or like life, is not an effect of its 'copying' some concept of everyday 'reality', but rather of what Terence Cave calls 'bold and highly precise forms of underspecification' which afford 'limited but suggestive indications about a character and his or her behaviour that would allow us, in the case of a real person, to infer their cognitive profile and anticipate their likely utterances or actions'.[27] Or, as Benedict Robinson puts it, fictionality demands probability, because 'every inference from actions to passions or from passions to actions depends on a socially constituted sense of what is probable'.[28] In early Italian *commedia erudita* the complication of the intrigue invites auditors to be proactive in inferring and anticipating, so that although this theatre can seem to us to be mere plot and no psychology, its particular precise forms of under-specification were paving the way for the greater characterological interiority we associate with Shakespearean theatre. Cinthio accordingly derives effects of verisimilitude from the poet's care in tying the 'knot' of the play, by which he says he means 'the weaving together or composition of the story' (*la testura, ò la compositione della fauola*) and then untying or resolving it so that, the story being brought to its end, the mind of the auditor or reader (*l'animo di chi*

[26] Giovanni Battista Giraldi Cinthio, *Discorsi di M. Giovambattista Giraldi Cinthio . . . intorno al comporre de I Romanzi, delle Comedie, e delle Tragedie, e di alter manière di Poesie* (Venice: Gabriel Giolito, 1554) 209–210; see also Giovanni Battista Giraldi Cinthio, 'Discourse or Letter on the Composition of Comedies and Tragedies', tr. Danial Javitch, *Renaissance Drama*, 39, new series (2011) 207–255, 212.

[27] Cave, *Thinking with Literature*, 27. [28] Robinson, 'True Story', 562.

ascolta, ò di chi legge) is fully satisfied; false inferences will be naturally explicated and resolved without any *deus ex machina* other than the artifice of its unfolding. This does not always happen in ancient drama, says Cinthio, but Ariosto's *Cassaria,* in that 'it almost naturally unties itself, surpasses in artifice all his other comedies'.[29] Note too that the kind of attentiveness Cinthio describes is that of audience and reader indiscriminately (*chi ascolta, ò . . . chi legge*), overriding Quintilian's previously cited distinction between the groupthink of listening and the independent judgement of reading.

Moreover, this newly discovered theatrical power of inferential plotting and artificial proof intersected with a new way of producing imaginative or fictional space. In the Italians' avant-garde comedy of the sixteenth century, when an actor goes offstage, he is not (as in *Mankind*) simply absenting himself *as actor*; for, as an *invented character* he is engaged in vividly producing the 'elsewhere' within the fiction – perhaps an interior space such as a young virgin's bedroom or a convent full of excitable nuns, or another part of town, where there are pubs and market stalls, pigeon sellers and officers of the law. Of Ariosto in this respect, Louise Clubb writes, 'what really electrified audiences in 1508 and 1509 were his settings, namely contemporary Italian cities: his second comedy, *I Suppositi,* brought onstage the bourgeois Ferrara of merchants, customs officers, and travelers, with the offstage court invoked as a guarantor of order'.[30] The brilliant, illusionistic realism of Ariosto's theatrical depiction of Ferrara had been remarked by the poet's contemporaries too. In 1519 Tomà Lippomano wrote of Ariosto's *I Suppositi,* 'The comedy was such, that it feigned a Ferrara' (*che'l fu fento un Ferrara*).[31] Critics have discussed the innovative sets, involving houses and doors, that contributed to the '*citta ferrarese*'.[32] But the city was also feigned or fictionalised *in language,* in speeches made by characters about their actions and whereabouts in between their appearances onstage.

[29] Cinthio, *Discorsi,* 214; Cinthio, 'Discourse', 214. [30] Clubb, *Theatergrams,* 78.

[31] Cited by Sergio Costola, 'Ludovico Ariosto's Theatrical Machine: Tactics of Subversion in the 1509 Performance of *I Suppositi,* unpublished PhD thesis, University of California, Los Angeles, 2002 (UMI microform 3078154), 56.

[32] Nino Pirrotta and Elena Povoledo, *Music and Theatre from Poliziano to Monteverdi* (Cambridge: Cambridge University Press, 1982), 302, 316–317.

The mistaken impression often given by anglophone criticism of Italian Renaissance comedy is that its adherence to neo-Aristotelian 'unities' of time and place was a mechanical, rule-bound restriction of imaginative vitality. 'Fixed-locale staging restricts the action in certain ways,' writes Alan Nelson. 'All conversations, including the most private must occur outdoors.'[33] But if we reverse Nelson's thinking we can see how the fixed locale staging makes the audience's imagination work overtime. It contributes to the electrifying effect of seeing on stage 'a Ferrara as precise as the real one', producing a vivid sense of the city's streets and shops and of the unseen the interiors of houses.

In Ariosto's *La Lena* (1528) we have such an effect in Act 2, scene 3, when a servant, Corbolo, who has been dispatched by his young master to buy some nice fat quails or pigeons for a feast at Lena's, describes his travails seeking vainly among the delicatessen shops (*pizzicagnoli*) in front of the Palazzo Ducale. The pigeons were all so scrawny, he says, they looked as though they had had the quartan fever, but then, at the *porta del Cortile*, the archway now known as the *Volta del Cavallo*, some of the Duke's gamekeepers (*uccellatori*) were waiting to go into the Gorgadello – the local pub. One of these sold Corbolo a pair of decently plump pheasants on the condition that he would keep the transaction secret. 'The statue of Duke Borso will not be quieter than me,' promises Corbolo ('*Non è la statua / Del duca Borso là di me più tacita*'), referring to the statue of the Este Duke towering above the very *Volta del Cavallo* beneath which we imagine this conversation to take place.[34] This is an audacious joke: for it is the silence of the ruling Este family – in the form of the complicity of the ducal decrees which prohibit the sale and consumption of game – that creates the dearth of edible fowl in the shops by the Palazzo and fuels the lucrative black market exploited by the Duke's gamekeepers. Corbolo's narration of his voyage in search of the ingredients for the feast therefore presents to the Este family seated before the stage in the Sale Grande of

[33] Alan H. Nelson, 'The Universities: Early Staging in Cambridge', in *A New History of Early English Drama*, ed. John D. Cox and David Scott Kastan (New York: Columbia University Press, 1997) 59–67, 64.

[34] Ariosto, *La Lena* in Ariosto, *Opere*, vol. IV, 543–626, 2.3.448–97.

the Palazzo Ducale not 'an opulent, well-regulated Ferrara', but a city 'inferior to all others', corrupt and full of secrets.[35]

Even more electrifying, however, were the implications of this inferential plotting for the imagining of what characters might be getting up to when not even present or embodied by actors onstage. *La Lena* offers a wonderful example of the libidinal possibilities of the inferential plot on the fixed locale stage in the little episode of a dispute over a barrel. In Act 4 of the comedy, all sorts of people – creditors, law officers, surveyors, tenants, relatives and friends – seem to have converged just inside and outside of the stage exit signifying the house of the eponymous Lena and her slothful, penurious husband, Pacifico. It seems that the house's owner, their neighbour, Fazio, has decided to put it on the market (hence the surveyor) and the rumour of this has made Pacifico's many creditors rush to the house to reclaim what is owed to them before sale. Among the disputed objects is a barrel which a relative of Pacifico's claims he lent Pacifico last wine harvest to get rid of a bad smell, but now he's worried it will be seized by debt collectors and wants it back. An altercation ensues, temporarily settled by Fazio, who says he'll adjudicate the case later and orders the barrel to be rolled into his house. But the barrel is not – at least in the audience's imagination – *empty*. For the audience must (if they have been paying any attention) infer that it contains the nearly naked body of a lustful young merchant's son called Flavio who has, since the play's opening, been trying to gain access to Fazio's closely guarded daughter, Licina. Following the usual contours of Roman comedy, *La Lena* opens with Flavio on the doorstep of Lena's house, promising Lena money if she could get him access to Licina. Annoyed that he does not have the cash, Lena makes Flavio undress so his clothes can be sent to the pawnbrokers. At this point, Flavio undresses and goes *offstage* – that is, into the imagined interior of Lena's house. But when news comes in Act 3 of Fazio arriving with a surveyor to check out Lena's house, a panicked discussion ensues about where to stow the naked Flavio so Fazio will not see him. It concludes with a plan to *stuff*

[35] Paul Larivaille, 'Spazio Scenico e Spazio Cittadino ne La Lena', in *La Corte e lo Spazio: Ferrara Estense, ed. Giuseppe Pagano and Amedeo Quondam*, ed. Gusieppe Papagano and Amadeo Quondam (Rome: Bulzoni Editore, 1982), 257–278, 262.

him into an empty wine barrel that someone left in the house. The audience never sees this action; however, when they later see Fazio loftily ordering this same wine barrel to be trundled into his house, what the audience 'knows', or imagines they know, is that Flavio will soon be making love to Licina – though of course the actor playing Flavio has been unseen since Act 1 and will never reappear until the final applause at the end of the play. The whole momentous sexual encounter announced by servants in the last scene is created by the audience's imagination, activated by their attentive following of the plot.

This unprecedented new potential for activating audiences' imaginations – including their libidinal imaginations – was certainly not lost on English poets and playwrights later in the sixteenth century. Nor could they have failed to notice the logico-rhetorical basis of Italian theatrical fictionality and its affinity with forensic strategies of proof. Writing to lawyer William Fleetwood, to whom he dedicated his translation of Cinthio's *Epitia*, George Whetstone condemned English playwrights for neglecting plot probability. The English playwright 'groundes his worke, on impossibilities ... not waying, so the people laugh, though they laugh them (for theyr follyes) to scorne'.[36] Yet while Whetstone implicitly lauded the probability of Italian plots, he lamented their lewdness: 'at this daye, the *Italian* is so lasciuious in his cōmedies, that honest hearers are greeued'. Whetstone wrote these words a decade or so after Fleetwood had likely been in the audience of one such comedy, George Gascoigne's translation of Ariosto's *I Suppositi* (1509) performed at Gray's Inn in 1566.

Gascoigne's choice of *I Suppositi* was a daring one: even now, his play seems surprisingly sexually permissive for the period, far less concerned with female chastity than any of Shakespeare's plays. *I Suppositi* involves an amorous intrigue, announced in the opening words, when a Ferrarese citizen's daughter comes onstage and confides to her nurse 'in the street' (because, the nurse says, indoor walls have ears!) that a household servant, Dulippo, who has been her lover for the past two years, is really a merchant's son called Erostrato who wants to marry her. This shocking

[36] George Whetstone, *The Right Excellent and famous Historye of Promos and Cassandra* (London: Richard Jones, 1578) sig. A2v.

revelation is at once a joke about this avant-garde theatre's not being able to show an interior scene and an announcement to the listening audience that in this new style of theatre their presence is going to be *ignored*. The nurse's first words, as the two step out onstage before the listening audience, are 'Here is no body, come foorth, Polynesta, let us looke about lest any man heare our talke.'[37]

The lawyers in the audience would surely have burst out laughing at this risqué opening. Nor, as they attended to the plot, could they have failed to notice the way that the play's ingenious 'untying of the knot' of supposes, or false inferences, was itself dependent on proofs that were equally suppositious, conjectural and possibly false, even in their supposed legal denouement. The young Sicilian student Erostrato has, on arriving in Ferrara, changed identities with his servant Dulippo so that he can enjoy Polynesta while Dulippo keeps house in his place and courts her officially, fending off a rival suitor, a rich lawyer, Cleander. But when Cleander ups his offer of a dower, the boys need to fake a counter-offer, so they con a passing Sienese merchant into assuming the identity of Erostrato's father, Philogano, and signing a bond. Naturally it all goes horribly wrong in Act 4, when the real Philogano arrives in Ferrara only to be denied admittance and confronted with a his Sienese doppelganger and his old servant claiming his son's identity. He assumes the worst: his son must have been murdered by this gang of imposters.

The question then turns on problems of proof: how, when witnesses in Ferrara support the claims of the imposters, is Philogano to prove his own identity? Philogano's servant Litio spends a lot of Act 4 slandering Ferrara for its falsehood and lack of judicial safeguards: 'have you not often heard tell of the falsehood of *Ferrara*', he asks, berating a native of the city: 'in deed your officers are most to blame, that suffer such faultes to escape unpunished'. The Ferrarese citizen defends the judicial system: 'we have potestates, we have Judges, and above all, we have a most juste prince, doubt you not, but you shall have justice if your cause be just'; but Litio is again sceptical, for how will the matter be proved? 'If there be

37 George Gascoigne, *The Supposes*, in *An Hundreth Sundrie Flowres*, ed. George W. Pigman III (Oxford: Oxford University Press, 2002) 1.1.1–4.

many such witnesses in this country, men may go aboute to prove what they will in controversies here.'[38]

Litio's scepticism has the last word, for the lawyer summoned to help Philogano is none other than the rival for Polynesta's hand, Cleander. Cleander is as perplexed by the problems of proof as everyone else: 'Yea, but how will ye prove that he is not *Erostrato*, having suche presumptions to the contrarie?', he asks, 'or how shal it be thought that you are *Philogano*, when an other taketh upon him this same name, and for proofe bringeth him for a witnesse, which hath bene ever reputed here for *Erostrato*?'[39] The question seems irresolvable, certainly within the scope of the play, when it conveniently dawns on Cleander that Philogano's servant Dulippo must be none other than the son, Carino, whom he lost at the battle of Otranto. Recognitions of this kind, as Terence Cave has shown, always have a strong whiff of scandal in their facile reliance on easily falsified signs and tokens.[40] So it is no surprise that when Cleander exclaims, 'What nedeth me more evident tokens? this is my sonne out of doubt whom I lost eighteen yeares since, and a thousand thousand times have I lamented for him: he shuld have also a mould on his left shoulder,' Litio sceptically and obscenely replies, 'He hath a moulde there in deede: and an hole in an other place too, I woulde your nose were in it.'[41] Ariosto's prologue explicitly links the 'evident tokens' of this resolution to the deceptions made possible by *suppozioni,* or merely probable and possibly false inferences. The play, his prologue announces, is called *Suppositi* because it is full of '*suppozioni*'. The nuances of the Italian word *suppositi* range from supposition to substitution and further to 'placed under, after or behind'. As the prologue slyly announces that children have been '*per l'adrieto . . . suppositi*' ('substituted in the past', or 'exposed from behind') so sodomitical innuendos accumulate alongside disparaging references to logical sophistry. Supposes are evidently deeply scandalous, not to be trusted and neither is the brilliantly vivid fiction of the play.[42]

38 Gascoigne, *Supposes*, 4.6.2–3,7–9; 4.8.14–15, 35–37. 39 Gascoigne, *Supposes*, 5.5.1–5.

40 Terence Cave, *Recognitions* (Oxford: Oxford University Press, 1988).

41 Gascoigne, *Supposes*, 5.5.132–3.

42 Ariosto, *I Suppositi* in *Opere*, vol. IV, 197–198, 'Prologo', 1–16; see Ariosto, *Comedies*, 95–96; Costola, 'Theatrical Machine', 175–178; Clubb, *Theatergrams*, 31.

Gascoigne's *Supposes* thus marked the arrival in English of a new kind of theatrical fictionality. When Shakespeare adapts the *Supposes* plot as the subplot of his *The Taming of the Shrew,* he acknowledges its illusionistic realism by having its powerful fictionality dispel the embryonic fiction of the induction, which dramatises the common anti-theatrical complaint that boys playing women's parts incited men to lust. As Christopher Sly beckons the cross-dressed page Bartholomew to come to bed with him, the players intervene with a comedy – *The Taming of the Shrew* – which forever defers Sly's lust for the boy player; Sly and the boy player simply disappear and with them the anti-theatrical prejudice. But in splicing the *Supposes* plot of clandestine courtship with a plot of successful wife-taming, Shakespeare defeats the anti-theatricalists by containing, disciplining and even 'beshrewing' the sexually permissive implications of the Ariosto–Gascoigne plot of erotic subterfuges.

The dazzling intelligence of Shakespeare's solution to the scandal of *Supposes* should not prevent us from seeing its connection with the bumpy ride Gascoigne's play had on first publication in 1573, when it was called in by the High Commission (who included William Fleetwood).[43] Gascoigne published a 'reformed' version of the text in 1575 and in the same year reformed the plot of *Supposes* itself by rewriting it as a play called *The Glasse of Government* in which the amorous adventures and impostures of students in the city of Antwerp are detected and severely punished by a diligent magistrate. A whole scene is devoted to the magistrate's forensic examination of the parasite Eccho, whom he suspects but cannot prove to have ensnared the students and made them customers of the prostitute – 'I haue examined them', he later worries, 'but truly I can not finde hitherto any proofe against them, whereby they ought to be punished'. It is only by going over events in the first two acts with the boys' tutor that the magistrate uncovers the lies – or 'supposes' – that give him 'good cause to punish Master Eccho' while the boys themselves meet ignominious ends, one hanged and the other whipped and left for dead in a village outside Geneva. The audience is finally invited not to applaud, but to wring its hands. Gascoigne dedicated this

[43] See Hutson, *Invention,* 202–213.

extremely grim play to William Fleetwood's friend and fellow High Commissioner Sir Owen Hopton.[44]

The story I have been tracing is, as I have said, only one strand in the history of how the balance between the performative and the fictional in European theatre changed in the sixteenth century and how the rhetorico-logical strategies of argument, drawn from Cicero and Quintilian and from Roman New Comedy, informed new inferential plot structures which made audiences proactive in anticipating and imagining (or supposing) likely outcomes. The strand I have emphasised is that of *commedia erudita,* but there are, of course, many others. There is not scope here for more than a sketch of how Shakespeare's playwriting built on the foundations I have described. Briefly, Shakespeare worked out an ingenious way of dissociating the inferential techniques of the Italian intrigue structure – so effective for engaging the audience's imagination in producing the fiction – from unavoidably libidinal conclusions. Where in Italian comedy the emplotment can lead the audience to imagine sexual activity just offstage, Shakespeare's circumstantial dramaturgy allows for such possibilities, but in place of sexual explicitness offers figurative proofs that require construal or that are irresolvably ambiguous along a fault-line between speculation and fact. Things may or may not have happened; there are doubts, suspicions, hallucinations – but it may all be just in someone's head. A good example is Shakespeare's *Comedy of Errors*, probably performed at Gray's Inn in 1594, which features a husband locked out of his house, but ensures that while he nearly goes mad thinking his wife is playing him false, an interior scene shows the audience that she is chaste and innocent.

Shakespeare thus also dissociated the inferential technique of the Italian comic plot from its dependence on Italian innovation in scene design, on the fixed-locale stage and temporal unity. This is not to say that Shakespeare simply abandoned, because he did not need, the 'rules' of the neoclassical unities. As I have argued elsewhere, constraints of time and space on the Italian stage were not so much rules as prompts to new forms of inferential and imaginative activity recognisable as a new

44 George Gascoigne, *Glasse of Gouernement* (London: 1575) 5.7, sig. L8v; sig. M1r. See dedication, sig. A2r.

dramaturgical resource. Shakespeare and other dramatists of the 1590s and 1600s did not ignore or reject these. What Shakespeare did was to adapt the inferential value of temporal and spatial specificity by developing a drama in which time and place are 'circumstances', that is, *topic questions structuring our experience of the play.* Circumstantial questions of time, place, motive and manner are also constantly deployed by characters in ways which deliberately invite audiences to imagine their inner lives, and which give specificity and reality to the world of the play.[45] This is rhetoric as *inventio* contributing to theatre's *fictionality.*

2.5 RHETORIC AS INVENTION: THE WORK OF SIMILITUDE IN *LAW AS PERFORMANCE*

In her interpretation of the Dutch engraver Crispijn de Passe's image of *Rhetorica* (*c.* 1599) Peters perhaps comes closest to an elision of the contribution of rhetoric as *inventio* with its contribution as performative technique. De Passe's engraving shows a female figure holding a scroll, her head turned towards the viewer while her body is turned the other way, to the left of the image. The background is an urban scene, divided in two. On the right, two men earnestly argue a legal case, while on the left, a scene is being played at the theatre. Rhetorica's striding out to the theatre on the left, stepping across what Peters identifies as Rome's Cloaca Maxima, illustrates the image's caption, which reads, 'If I say what is to be said well, coloring the words, any cause is to be made good through my eloquence' (223). In the scene's division between law and theatrical performance, the latter – identified with Rome's sewer – has won. In Peters' interpretation, de Passe is identifying theatrical *performance* with law's power to make the worse seem the better cause. But if the moral is that law-as-truth is being subverted by law-as-rhetoric, then surely subversion takes place as much at the level of rhetorical *invention* and theatrical *fictionality* as it does at the level of performance. It is by the skilful invention of arguments, by the rhetorico-logical art of language, that the worse may be made to seem the better cause. This art of rhetorico-logical argument is, as I have shown, also fundamental to the

[45] Hutson, *Circumstantial.*

rise of a theatrical fictionality – a theatre of supposes and surmises. This is a theatre which, though it exploits the uses of deception and false inference to engage the audience's imagination, is capable of dramatising and exposing law's venality and is true in its depiction of human passions.

Julie Stone Peters' colleague at Columbia Kathy Eden published a book in the same year as Peters' *Law as Performance*, called *Rhetorical Renaissance*, and the cover of this book is adorned by another female figure of 'Rhetorica'. This Lady Rhetorica, an image by Mantegna (1431–1506), is not stepping over a sewer to head to the theatre. She is a warrior queen brandishing an unsheathed sword. Among Renaissance humanists Lady Rhetorica could also, as Eden acknowledges, be portrayed less flatteringly as a courtesan, a meretrix. But even in that guise she was a mistress of debate, overthrowing powerful statesmen with her arguments, her skilful deployment of such forensic techniques of proof as *status* theory, refutation and similitude.[46] Julie Stone Peters' book is overpoweringly persuasive partly because of the way its central figure of similitude – 'law as theatre' – generates its own antithesis. She uses it to challenge older legal histories by a technique not unlike that used to such great effect in 'Law, Literature and the Vanishing Real'. In the claims of philosophers of law, the texts of legal reformers, the efforts of officials to control the trial script and excluded the disorderly crowd, 'performance' emerges as something like the repressed in psychoanalysis. Law disavows its inevitable dependence on performance practice. This is a brilliant, powerful argument. We could, without discrediting it, however, also appreciate it as the effect of Peters' *rhetorical* artistry, her exploitation of the affinity that similitude has, as a mode of proof, with techniques of refutation, sharpening, as it does, our perceptions of difference and dissimilitude. It is in Kathy Eden's book that we learn of the development of similitude in Roman forensic rhetoric and in humanist preaching, law and poetry, from Socratic techniques of refutation.[47] '"What is law? … Not theatre!" Except when it is.' Julie Peters' brilliant central antithesis,

[46] Kathy Eden, *Rhetorical Renaissance: The Mistress Art and Her Masterworks* (Chicago, IL: University of Chicago Press, 2022) 5–6.

[47] Eden, *Rhetorical Renaissance*, 93–94.

derived from the similitude of law *as* theatre shows that the power of rhetoric – and therefore its threat to law as pure, abstract truth – lies not just in theatrical *performance*, but in the invention of figures and tropes that shape arguments, form thoughts and produce imaginatively compelling fictions. I am entirely persuaded by what Peters says about law's relation to theatrical performance from ancient, through medieval to early modern times. My act of desynonymy – insisting that rhetoric, theatre and performance are not substitutable for one another – while subtracting nothing from Peters' dazzling argument, makes a bit of room for thinking about its implications for the history of literature, including theatre, and for the longer-term implications for trial by social media in the present day.

CHAPTER 3

The Poetics of *Hypokrisis* in Early Modern Judicial Theatre

Subha Mukherji

IN A DRAMATIC MOMENT IN HER CLOSING REMARKS IN THE *Depp* v. *Heard* defamation trial on 27 May 2022, Johnny Depp's advocate Camille Vasquez offered an arresting evocation: 'She [Amber Heard] came into this courtroom prepared to give the performance of her life. And she gave it. Miss Heard's acting coach … testified that Miss Heard has difficulty crying when she is acting. You saw it. Miss Heard sobbing without tears.'[1] This took me right back to the economy of bodily self-evidence and affect in the early modern English courtroom – the context I have engaged with most closely – and its mediation through drama, to the rhetoric of distinction between authenticity and performance that Renaissance plays both stage and trouble. It was a moment that reached back almost seamlessly to a context that opens into the prehistory of the legal focus on tears as an ultimate proof of essence against show, manifestation against mask. It also signalled the abiding embeddedness of ideas from classical forensic rhetoric in the popular evidential imaginary, not just in early modern England where rhetorical texts had been freshly revived and widely read, but all the way down to our own times. It vivified the way in which, as the editors write in Chapter 1, the digitisation of law in our times has brought the agon and the bodily performance of law back into view, in the public sphere, against what

[1] Accessed through live relay of trial on 27 May 2022: *Johnny Depp* v. *Amber Heard*, Fairfax County Circuit Courthouse, Fairfax, Virginia. Cf. www.youtube.com/watch?v=px7CWV02FYs, 26.33 mins–26.58 mins. Also reported by several news outlets: e.g. www.independent.co.uk/arts-entertainment/films/news/johnny-depp-amber-heard-fake-crying-camille-vasquez-b2089031.html or www.newsweek.com/camille-vasquez-accuses-amber-heard-sobbing-without-tears-1710914.

they see as the accretive masking of law's theatre in the Western tradition. But that masking itself turns out to be less of a stable or continuous history if we know where to look for the dramaturgy of law, at what historical moments, and the epistemic and ontological stakes shared by judicial drama and the theatre of legal process. The emplotment of the affective body and its semiotics in the contemporary courtroom functioned as a window on how historically determined traditions reshape themselves at different junctures to animate something essential about the way we want the law to make our inward, inaccessible truths visible, whether '*in camera*' or on camera, whether in a formal court of law or in human 'scenes' of adjudication or ascertainment.

But the moment sincerity is coded, it becomes performable. The freighting of signs with meaning comes with a risk. The authentication procedure undercuts authenticity. Lear, in Shakespeare's *The Tragedy of King Lear*, asks incredulously at the moment of reunion with his daughter Cordelia: 'Be your tears wet?' He has seen too much hypocrisy – or indeed *hypokrisis* in the original classical forensic sense of judicial delivery – to believe that he has not only regained his long-lost child but also her forgiveness when he has only deserved judgement at her hands. 'No cause, no cause', Cordelia remonstrates – meaning that there is no cause for her to judge him for his wrongs or to deny him love[2] – while the audience hear a pun on legal cause or *causa* – and an echo of Othello's 'It is the cause, it is the cause my soul: [...] It is the cause', repeated with fervour three times (5.2.1–3) in Shakespeare's *Othello*; or indeed Brabantio's insistence in the same play that his allegation against Othello is 'not an idle cause' (1.2.95).[3] Lear's question, however, does not just come out of a longing to ascertain that Cordelia is weeping, but, more specifically, to know that her tears are moist, and thus, genuine – intimating an awareness that even tears can be faked and performed as a

[2] William Shakespeare, *The Tragedy of King Lear*, 4.6.65 and 69, in René Weis, ed., *King Lear: A Parallel Text Edition* (London: Longman, 1993). All references to *King Lear* are to this edition.

[3] William Shakespeare, *The Tragedy of Othello, Moor of Venice*, in *The Riverside Shakespeare*, ed. G. Blakemore Evans (Boston: Houghton Mifflin, 1974). All references to Shakespeare's plays and poems are to this edition unless otherwise specified (as in the case of *King Lear*).

persuasive device. Or perhaps that one can sob without tears. This induces a more radical sense of being adrift in a sea of semiotic incertitude.

Tears are, of course, a part and punctum of face and body, opening into the legal fixation with natural self-evidence – which focuses on a human need to bank on the irrepressible manifestation of the inward in the physical form. The textual hunger as well as frustration inscribed in legal performance is translated into literature's depictions of the judicial imagination in moments of epistemic crisis. The narrator in Shakespeare's *Lucrece* comments on Lucrece's inability to read and thus judge the treacherous book that her rapist Tarquin's face is – with 'subtle shining secrets' written in its 'glassy margents' (*Lucrece*, 99–102). Cicero's Crassus says, 'All delivery is an expression of the soul, and the face is the image of the soul, and the eyes are the pointers to it [*Nam ut imago est animi voltus sic indices oculi*].'[4] Quintilian, so familiar to the English Renaissance through the humanist curriculum, turns to tears as the most unmediated sign of feelings, when the face looks too much like a mask. Through early modern literature, not least drama, tears are the touchstone of authenticity, and their faking is cited as the worst kind of desecration: witness the distraught Imogen's lament, in Shakespeare's *Cymbeline*, at discovering Posthumus' intemperate, murderous misjudgement which she compares to the false Sinon's performance of grief: a blemish on the truest of men and on the sanctity of tears:

> True honest men being heard, like false Aeneas,
> Were in his time thought false, and Sinon's weeping
> Did scandal many a holy tear.
>
> (*Cymbeline*, 3.4.59–61)

But 'weeping', as Cornelius informs him, was one of the 'shows' of the wicked queen to convince King Cymbeline of her love while plotting to poison him; a 'craft' to secure her unworthy son's royal adoption (5.5.52–6). Not even tears, any more than face and body, are free from inference. In *Lucrece*, 'those round, clear pearls of [Sinon's] move [Priam's] pity': how could they not (1553)? And 'So Priam's trust false Sinon's tears doth

4 Cicero, *De Oratore (The Orator's Education)*, 18.60.

flatter/That he finds means to burn his Troy with water' (1560–1). It is the perjured Sinon's face – graced with 'outward honesty, but yet defiled/With inward vice' (1545–6) – that Lucrece rips apart in the tapestry of the siege of Troy, having identified so much with Hecuba's sorrow as to fail to distinguish between its immediate instrument, Sinon, and the agent of her own destruction, Tarquin.

In a comic key, the performability of tears is foreshadowed in Shakespeare by the Lord's instruction on acting to his page Bartholomew in *The Taming of the Shrew*, to keep an onion in a napkin to 'enforce a watery eye', 'if the boy have not a woman's gift/To rain a shower of commanded tears' (1.1.120–4). But the theatre is acutely alive to the generic scope and range of this recognition of radical performability. It can provide inventive delight at what Ben Jonson calls 'quick comedy' in *Volpone* (Prologue, 30), such as the feigned decrepitude of his own ceaselessly performative Volpone, for feigning is inseparable here from protean acting.[5] Volpone plays so long and so unstoppably that he sabotages his own legal victory over his virtuous and woefully wronged accusers across two trial scenes in Act IV. But as the 'fox' (*vulpes*) is caught in his own snare and led in shackles to prison, Volpone the dramatic character – mimetic creature and master of ingenious plot reversals – breaks free of his confinement, steps out of the reductive tool of the beast-fable and re-emerges to speak the Epilogue. And in doing so, he destabilises the judgment of the law court at the end of a final act that need not even have existed, if only he had been content to stop playing after the favourable legal outcome of the previous act.[6] Effecting the final *peripeteia*, he at once constructs and appeals to an alternative jurisdiction, enlisting the verdict of the jury of the audience as delight exceeds and floods the judicial 'cause' internal to the dramatic plot in the wider

[5] Ben Jonson, *Volpone, or The Fox*, ed. David Cook (London: Methuen, 1984, first pub. 1962). All references are to this edition.

[6] Dryden spotted the gratuitousness and irrationality of the final act long ago: see John Dryden, *Of Dramatic Poesy*, *Works*, Vol. XVII, ed. Samuel H. Monk and A. E. Wallace Maurer (Berkeley: University of California Press, 1971), 49. For a review of critical responses to the 'false ending', see also Stephen Greenblatt, 'The False Ending in *Volpone*', *Journal of English and Germanic Philology*, 75.1/2 (January–April 1976), 90–104.

courtroom of the theatre, driving a provocative wedge between legal and aesthetic judgment:

> The seasoning of a play is the applause.
> Now, though the Fox is punished by the laws,
> He yet doth hope there is no suffering due
> For any fact which he hath done 'gainst you.
> If there be, censure him: here he doubtful stands;
> If not, fare jovially, and clap your hands.
>
> (5.7.152–7)

Julie Stone Peters admires the orator in the equally admirable early fourth-century invective *Against Alcibiades* (attributed unreliably to Andocides) for demanding the judicial expulsion of the Athenian statesman Alcibiades who, bolstered by sycophantic judges and aspirant Athenian youths, has abused the law in mistreating and throwing offstage the non-Athenian Taureas in the midst of a theatrical competition. The orator sides instead with the theatre audiences who cheer the wronged Taureas and condemn the tyrannical act of Alcibiades (*LP*, 51–2). The radical provocation of *Volpone* is to blur the distinction between legally culpable 'deed' and courtroom *actio*, and to challenge the 'democratic power of applause' that Peters identifies as a motor of righteous judgement from the example of pre-Platonic speech (52). The role of performance is less feel-good than we would like: the collaborative participation it elicits does not safeguard accountability but complicates it. The innocuousness of the 'salt' that the Prologue promises to rub the audience's cheeks with, leaving them 'red, with laughter' (Prologue, 33–6), proves deceptive; unlike the 'entertainment' that Peters sees as 'spectacular diversion' inseparable from the law (*LP*, 21, 25, 4, 6), it proves unassimilably subversive. This is a play where comedy is the medium of the anarchic potential of the performative that nestles at the heart of legal training and procedure. Volpone wins the first trial through consummate role-playing – the charismatic impersonations and dissimulations that Peters shows to be the substance of 'Legal Performance Education in Early Modern England' (*LP*, chapter 6); but because that is what turns him on – he '[glories]/More in the cunning purchase of [his] wealth/Than in the glad possession' (I.i.30–2) – it overflows the institutional ends of legal performance, shaping an unsettling chiasmus between conscience and craft, punishment and pleasure, justice and jouissance.

But the opposite affective markers of laughter and tears are equally productive – though distinct in their probative purchase – for a medium that finds in law not so much a model for judgment as a ground-plot for the relation between reality and representation, subjectivity and semiotics. For the theatre also knows how not only *hypokrisis* itself, but an awareness of it, can tragically undo us as it does Shakespeare's over-integrated Othello when it faces us with the essential unknowability of the other as well as the impossibility of representing oneself to the world. For, as early modern drama, not least Shakespeare, repeatedly shows us, law shapes the imagination at moments of crisis because we feel that it meets a human need for justice and knowledge, vindication and certainty. But does it? And if not, what work does it do? And what do its failures speak to? This chapter shows how dramatists, at once inheritors of the rhetorical tradition – at the very least through the humanist curriculum of grammar schools, and familiar with the law – whether through Inns-of-Court education, or their own brushes with the legal system, mine law as an imaginative resource, both in its discernment and its obscurities, its hermeneutic success and its cognitive limits, its evocations and its obfuscations, its rigours and its risks. Un-anxious to find resolution or arrive at verdict, plays can, instead, probe the uses of the ludic content *in* law as well as use the ludic as their own method to question and complicate the veridical assumptions of judicial process. My use of a contemporary legal moment as an entry point into early modern drama's mining of the complexities of *hypokrisis* at once draws on Peters' excavation of theatrocracy and offers a provocation against her assumption of a fundamental difference between the fiction of the theatre and the truth and reality of the law court. When Lear, faced with the flagrant lack of justice in his world and its institutions, stages his own mock trial on the bare heath in the 1608 Quarto of Shakespeare's *King Lear*, is the play merely presenting a fib, or is it tuning in to the fiction, construction and the affective realties underpinning 'real' trials?

> I'll see their trial first. Bring in their evidence.
> [To Edgar] Thou robed man of justice, take thy place;
> [To Fool] And thou, his yokefellow of equity,

Bench by his side. [To Kent] You are of the commission,
Sit you, too.

Q 3.6.31–6

As Lear choreographs his meagre company into a law court to try Goneril and Regan, the daughters who have kicked him out of doors and blinded his loyal retainer, Gloucester, the fantastic nature of the trial lays bare the performative insides of the legal machine, its fictive ontology: the ways in which any place could be shaped into a trial by the structure of the action, the ecology of relations, the blocking of characters in space and the psychic impulses and epistemic fantasy that call for 'trial' in human affairs, or for a mock trial in a Godless world where one must anatomise hearts on a heath because no court, human or divine, will do it. The theatre can mine this dimension of the ontology of law the more freely because it does not share institutional law's investment in factual truth or its veridical telos. Remember Adorno: 'Art is magic delivered from the lie of having to be truth.'[7] What might be the yield of replacing a hierarchy between 'what real people did in real legal arenas' and the 'fiction' of 'literary texts' that needs to be sifted from 'fact' (*LP*, 22) with a horizontal placement of legal and theatrical engagements in counterpoint with the role of the performative imagination in expressing, accessing and shaping truth?[8] Their dynamic tells us more about legal performance than either discipline can in isolation: it reveals it to be both an extractive agent of moral understanding and a tool of persuasive artifice, with all the representational and moral implications of that duality.

If Vasquez and her historical predecessors in Elizabethan or Jacobean London or the Athenian or Roman law court are unerring at unmasking the supposed performance of defendants and accusers, the plays that stage the composite drama of the legal scene are canny at piercing the performativity of advocacy itself. Peters uncovers the legal

[7] Theodor Adorno, *Minima Moralia: Reflections from Damaged Life*, trans. Edmund F. N. Jephcott (London: Verso, 2020) (first published in German, 1951), section 143, p. 236.

[8] Julie Stone Peters, *Law as Performance: Theatricality, Spectatorship, and the Making of Law in Ancient, Medieval and Early Modern Europe* (Oxford: Oxford University Press, 2022), p. 22.

terrain in granular detail through the sixteenth-century French lawyer Etienne Pasquier's masterly translation of the rhetorical precepts of advocacy (*LP*, 244–50). Pasquier is shown to recast the tears of Bobie – his client Jean d'Arconville's opponent – as a manipulative mask, and Arconville's own dry eyes as a sign of masculine, stoic integrity, while also, at the same time, emplotting Arconville's wife's tears as an unmediated sign of distress and a trigger for judicial pathos. It is as if the self-reflexive impersonations written into legal practice (not to speak of the *mise-en-abyme* of legal training so brilliantly reconstructed by Peters) unmoor the very touchstones of sincerity. Is Cicero weeping the tears that his client Milo cannot – a suggestive moment for Peters (*LP*, 19) – an example of a lawyer manipulating emotion by performing its coded proof? After all, Cicero emplots Milo's tearlessness as manly stoicism, much as Pasquier emplots Arconville's. Or is this rather an instance of what Quintilian presents as suasorial empathy, becoming one with the subject he speaks for, embracing mimesis as an act that stirs the self itself:

> ... let us assimilate ourselves to the emotions of those who really suffer [...] [...] Will [the hearer] weep when the speaker's eyes are dry? [...] Will we be moved before we try to move others. *The Orator's Education*, 6.2.27–8

> ... let us not plead the case as though it were someone else's, but take the pain of it on ourselves for the moment. *The Orator's Education*, 6.2.34–5

Curiously, the idea of temporary identification is similar to the passionate plain style of affective preaching that seventeenth-century Protestant preachers such as William Perkins advocated – the paradox of the preacher being a mere vehicle for the Holy Spirit but needing to be transformed by it in order to be an effective medium and move his congregation.[9] Quintilian's reassuring distinction between an orator and an actor is as unsustainable in the courtroom practice of arousing emotion as the paradoxical precepts of English Reformed preaching style, whose demand of dispassionate passion is complicated by its own

[9] *The Orator's Education*, 6.2. William Perkins, *The Art of Prophesying* (1607), passim.

tripartite interpersonal economy between '1. God, 2. the *Preacher*, and the *Hearer*'.[10] One remembers Herbert too, a priest and poet who feels a wrench every time he renounces artifice in his poetry, but who makes a firm distinction between holiness and eloquence in characterising sermons.[11] The inter-discursive location of the fractured facts of legal performance is nowhere so clear as in the syncretic fictions of imaginative literature. But that is another chapter of the story.

Early modern plays reflect on both sides of the equation. They are sharply aware of how lawyers can play to – and indeed play – the affective needs of the audience. But they also understand what performance and being, artifice and nature, can do for each other, and how sometimes one slides into the other in a juridical context. In the mock trial of Q *Lear* – the theatre staging the theatricality of law – legal roles shift and coalesce like aspects of the judicial impulse. As Lear slides from judge to accuser to plaintiff, Edgar says in an aside: 'My tears begin to take his part so much/ They mar my counterfeiting' (Q55/F18–19). In an extraordinary semantic glide, Edgar's tears are at once the irrepressible sign of authenticity piercing his theatrical 'part' as 'poor Tom', *and* Lear's advocate, defending him through affective representation, in a trial where Lear has none to take his 'part'. After all, Quintilian argued that the parts of a forensic speech – or *partitio* – was a vital part of an individual question and an aspect of proof.[12] The transference of emotion that Peters locates in Quintilian's idea of effective legal representation haunts the moment: the sense that legal role-play is an extractive form of art, not just histrionics is almost inextricable from genuine empathy as a disruptor of performance. Tears in this play are nothing if not fluid.

The stakes of self-representation in court are of course different from those of advocacy – or people speaking *for* others, staging others' bodies for ethos and pathos. In a necessarily indicative rather than exhaustive discussion, I will glance at a selection of early modern texts, either

[10] Lancelot Andrewes, *XCVI Sermons*, London, 1629 (RSTC 606), 130.

[11] George Herbert, *A Priest to the Temple* (1652), chap. VII: accessed via Early English Books Text Creation Partnership at https://quod.lib.umich.edu/e/eebo/A43381.0001.001/1:12?rgn=div1;submit=Go;subview=detail;type=simple;view=fulltext;q1=he+is+not+witty.

[12] *The Orator's Education*, 4.5.22. See also 4.5.1.

dramatic or folding drama into the narrative, to show how literature gets into the ethical and affective crevices of the forms of representation that law demands as well as makes available. I also intuit and suggest that literature uses the structure of interpersonal encounter to address these implications. Lucrece laments her rape copiously for some 2,000 lines, but when it comes to writing to her husband, Collatinus, about it, she ends up tearing all her drafts and writing a one-liner, choosing instead to 'hoard' 'the life and feeling of her passion' (1317)

> [...] to spend when he is by to hear her;
> When sighs and groans and tears may grace the fashion
> Of her disgrace, the better so to clear her.
>
> (1319–20)

She has mentally constructed the scene of disclosure as a trial where she has to clear herself from the world's 'suspicion' by choosing the theatrical over the textual, relying on embodied presence. Her resolve taps into the intersection of a physiognomic idea with a legal one. A fragment from *De Pace Regis et Regni* (1609) by Ferdinand Pulton of Lincoln's Inn throws light on the thinking behind this: in a criminal trial, 'the defendant must answer [the indictment] in proper person, and not by Atturney' – because then 'his countenance, or gesture will shew some tokens therof, or by his simple speeches somewhat may be drawne from him to bolt out the veritie of the cause'.[13] Raleigh famously was denied benefit of counsel in his treason trial. Yet when he demanded to meet the witness against him 'face to face', the crown prosecutors denied his request – a landmark in the historical development of the right of confrontation in criminal cases which became the norm in English common law courts by the later seventeenth century. The model of encounter as a sifter of truth was a gift of the law, yet its place in the ecology of law itself was uneasy to start with.

[13] Ferdinand Pulton, *De Pace Regis et Regni* (1610), fol. 184v–185. On the importance of 'the Manner of a Witness's delivering his testimony', see also Sir Matthew Hale, *The History of the Common Law of England* (1971; first pub. 1713), p. 163; *Historia Placetorium Coronae*, 2:276–7; William Best, *Principles of the Law of Evidence*, sixth ed. (1875), pp. 18, 22 and 24.

In *Arden of Faversham* (1592), an obviously judicial play, two men travel together with 'a pretty tale' told by Franklin to Arden to '[beguile] the weary way'.[14] It is an account of the trial of a woman taken in adultery, now repentant, being interrogated by her husband – whether in a formal or domestic court. 'I wonder how she looked,' Arden interjects. Franklin replies:

> First did she cast her eyes down to the earth,
> Watching the drops that fell amain from thence;
> Then softly draws she forth her handkercher,
> And modestly she wipes her tear-stained face;
> Then hemmed she out, to clear her voice would seem,
> And with a majesty addressed herself
> To encounter all their accusations.
>
> (ix, 81–7)

The gendered fantasy of the expressive body becomes here a prettifying aesthetic code for authentic demonstration. The *mise-en-abyme* of this moment encases encounter within response. The woman is speaking for herself, but Franklin is offering a commentary. That interface marks a space where access is lost even as it is scripted in reception. By contrast, the trial of the guilty but compelling Vittoria Corombona in Webster's *The White Devil* stages an attempt at scripting so that the audience witness both the defendant's self-representation and the prosecutor Monticelso's attempt at reading and reducing her. Peters dwells on how the classical tradition placed attention to 'character' at the heart of oratorical *prosopopoeia* (78). In their courtroom collision, M vents his frustration with her wayward body which, in its very fairness, fashions a false semiotic, and calls her a whore. She retorts, 'Whore? Ha – what's that?' Here's Monticelso's reply.

> Shall I expound whore to you? sure I shall;
> I'll give their perfect character. [...][15]

14 *The Tragedy of Master Arden of Faversham: The Revels Plays* (London: Methuen, 1973), scene ix, l. 92. All references are to this edition.

15 John Webster, *The White Devil*, ed. John Russell Brown (Manchester: Manchester University Press, 1996), 3.2.78–9. All references are to this edition.

And he proceeds to present a twenty-four-line exercise in the aphoristic Inns-of-Court genre of character-writing which sketched deeds to make intent quickly legible. It falls flat against Vittoria's protean performance and her shrewd counter-images. Quick to recognise Monticelso's formal strategy, Vittoria retaliates: 'This character 'scapes me' (l. 101). Webster himself had written thirty-two character sketches. But here, he flamboyantly sets apart the deep play of dramatic characterisation from the naïve fantasy of indexical demonstration. Associating the latter with both physiognomy and providentialism, he shows how law co-opts both through the factually correct but representationally naïve lawyer Monticelso whose attempt to demonstrate Vittoria's corruption falls on its face in this densely rhetorical play. 'I will but touch her and/Straight you will see she will fall too soot and ashes,' he says (ll. 66–7), almost quoting from his own 'character' of the 'Ordinary Widow' – but she does not.[16] The theatrical conditions – the boy in a frock impersonating the complex woman flaunting her femininity on the dock – only align the playhouse 'auditory' (whom she co-opts as the common man's jury) with the superior aesthetics of her action (l. 15). Ironically, while striking at legal procedure, she is a creature formed out of the ethically insouciant logic and craft of impersonation in moots: thus almost embodying the ancient and paradoxical combination of affinity and rivalry between law and drama that Peter Goodrich has unearthed.[17] The white devil of the play 'characterises' the inscrutable face, and the illegible defendant haunting the legal imagination, but she also signals that aspect of the play-texts which is defiantly pensive, like Roland Barthes's classic text, holding back 'some ultimate meaning … whose place it keeps free and signifying' (S/Z).[18] An example of how law's subjects turn subjection around into irreducible subjecthood, 'acutest at its vanishing'.[19]

16 See *The Complete Works of John Webster*, ed. Frank L. Lucas (London: Chatto & Windus, 1927), Vol. IV, 'Characters', p. 39.

17 See Peter Goodrich's foundational article 'Law', in Thomas O. Sloane, ed., *Encyclopedia of Rhetoric* (Oxford: Oxford University Press, 2001), pp. 417–26.

18 Roland Barthes, *S/Z: An Essay*, trans. Richard Miller (New York: Hill and Wang, a division of Farrar, Straus and Giroux, 1974; first pub. 1970), p. 216.

19 Phrase borrowed from Wallace Stevens, 'The Idea of Order at Key West', l. 34. See Wallace Stevens, *Collected Poems* (London: Faber & Faber, 2006; first pub. 1954), pp. 110–11 (111).

A similar inwardness is forged in a 1590s play with an almost opposite evidentiary semiotic – the anonymous *A Warning for Fair Women* which, like *Arden*, was based on a real-life adultery and murder story. The guilty wife, Mistress Sanders, comes into court with a white rose 'in token of her spotless innocence', but the rose changes colour (presumably as she turns and squeezes a sheep's heart or some such). Her attempt to fashion her own semiotic is hijacked by the theatre of God's judgement in this providentialist play, where insides are already always visible because God is the ultimate spectator as well as dramaturge. But when she is in prison and actively repentant, the generic shift to pathos, almost tragedy, is an effect of the very rhetoricity built into theatrical presence:

> ... were my breast transparent,
> That what is figured there, might be perceiv'd,
> Now should you see the very image of poore
> And tottred ruines, and a slaine conscience ...[20]

The lack of devices to make the inward visible becomes a mimetic index of the invisible theatre of the heart. Law becomes a seam at which tears, faces, bodies, selves and texts are shown to play and play out their games of knowledges, intimating a live, intractable, inexpressible core.

In a secular context, this takes a slightly different form – one that can be peculiarly poignant in cultural encounters. Once the performability of sincerity is understood, can genuineness make itself legible? Consider Othello the 'hypocrite'. Summoned to answer Brabantio's 'cause' (1.2.95) 'in [his] own part' (1.3.74), alleging Othello's use of witchcraft to seduce Desdemona, he begins by protesting his lack of eloquence – 'Rude am I in speech' – only to proceed to a vivid re-enactment of his persuasion of her through recountings of the 'moving accidents' that brought him from Africa to Venice, slavery to military decoration. 'This only is the witchcraft I have used,' he rests his case. So magnificent is his oratory that the critical reception has been cynical of his 'round unvarnished tale' – the 'credibility problem' Peters refers to when one is too good an orator. The Duke responds, 'This tale would win my daughter too'

[20] Anon., *A Warning for Fair Women*, ed. Charles Dales Cannon (The Hague: Mouton, 1975), ll. 2654–7.

(1.3.170). Is this conviction to be uttered admiringly, ruefully or cynically? 'Tale' evokes a story that might be invented and incredible. Yet perhaps Othello's 'story' is also his 'history' (words he uses interchangeably, as did the period); when Desdemona responds to its '[strangeness]', perhaps she registers the source of its force in a radically other, unified and simpler world, though liable to be swiftly reconstructed in hyper-civic Venice where performance is sharply distinct from being. Where the semblance of racial tolerance proves a dissemblance, the black but un-obscure Othello becomes judicially opaque, and over-read. The poetics of *hypokrisis* that Peters says Plato left incomplete is drawn out by playwrights in this legally obsessed culture into a poetics – and a politics – of relation. The theatre also challenges legal theory's tendency to essentialise 'performance', and Peters' implicit corroboration of it: '"performance" ... may diagnose a universal ontological condition: the fact that what appears as natural is in fact produced and reproduced through performance on the stage of life' (*LP*, 18). But the *stages* of life are plural, and the hermeneutics of performance as well as reception are culturally specific, often inflected not only by gender but also race, class or place.

But does prosopopoeia – as opposed to self-presentation – guarantee the ethics of emotion in the law court, as Peters suggests? If we take on trust Quintilian's idea that when we speak for another we take on their pain, perhaps so. But if we look at what Renaissance plays do with Plato's worry about theatrocracy's 'contamination' of justice with pleasure and pain, how they disaggregate and counterpoint the two, and locate pleasure at the heart of law's own performativity, we will see how an affective challenge of the ethics of representation is enabled by the twinning of law and performance. In Shakespeare's *Titus Andronicus*, the immediate aftermath of an offstage crime is mediated to us by Marcus, who runs into his niece, the raped and mutilated Lavinia, arrests her mid-flight, and turns her into a still image as he makes her turn to face him and describes her in a vivid forty-seven-line testimonial address (2.4.11–57). 'Shall I speak for thee? Shall I say 'tis so?' he asks (l. 33), and then we see prosopopoeia going horribly wrong as it is infected by the pleasure of rhetorical ornamentation and the temptation of poetic decorum. The rhetorical coupling of *enargeia* as poetic resource and as forensic tool is ruptured as ravishing description converts the ravished Lavinia into a series of elegant tropes as we face her onstage, bleeding. Framing the scene as a chance meeting – one that inscribes Lavinia's mute recoils – courts a deeper indecorum, to question the ethics of response and representation. The elocutionary asymmetry grants semiotic power to Lavinia and evokes the dialogue that can never happen. And finally, *ekphrasis* sharpens the judicial stakes of shaping *enargeia* into encounter. Lavinia's onstage presence in the face of Marcus' ekphrastic vividness brings the audience face to face with a perversely redundant mediation. Quintilian talks of (good) *enargeia* as a function that conjures up presence in absence. But Marcus' *enargeia*, while we look at Lavinia, collapses presence into hideous absence – after its conversions of art, language perversely bodies forth the non-existent:

> O, had the monster seen those lily hands
> Tremble like aspen-leaves upon a lute,
> And made the silken strings delight to kiss them,
> He would not then have touched them for his life.
> Or had he heard the heavenly harmony
> Which that sweet tongue hath made …
>
> (44–9)

Not all instances of *enargeia* in Shakespeare make the objects of representation, or their scenes 'present'. In Erasmus' mimetic hierarchy, the richest kind of enargeic descriptions are messenger speeches in tragedies, 'because they are presented instead of the spectacle and … report the things … impossible or inappropriate to present on the stage'.[21] Think of death by drowning – like sex and murder, impossible to stage. Gertrude, in *Hamlet*, is witness and messenger of Ophelia's suicide. But listen to her *enargeia*:

> There is a willow grows aslant a brook
> That shows his hoar leaves in the glassy stream.
> There with fantastic garlands did she come
> Of crow-flowers, nettles, daisies, and long purples

[21] Desiderius Erasmus, *On Copia of Words and Ideas*, trans. Donald B. King and H. David Rix (Milwaukee: Marquette University Press, 2012), p. 48 (Book II).

> That liberal shepherds give a grosser name,
> But our cold maids do dead men's fingers call them.
> There, on the pendent boughs her coronet weeds
> Clambering to hang, an envious sliver broke;
> When down her weedy trophies and herself
> Fell in the weeping brook. Her clothes spread wide;
> And, mermaid-like, awhile they bore her up;
> Which time she chanted snatches of old tunes,
> As one incapable of her own distress,
> Or like a creature native and endued
> Unto that element: but long it could not be
> Till that her garments, heavy with their drink,
> Pull'd the poor wretch from her melodious lay
> To muddy death.
> Laertes: Alas, then is she drowned.
>
> (*Hamlet*, 4.7.141–58)

In Aristotelian rhetoric, *enargeia* is the tool for both poet and orator to reimagine and then present absent things with 'the vividness of an eye-witness'.[22] The later, Latin rhetorical tradition, immediately proximate to the English Renaissance, translates *enargeia* as *evidentia.*[23] What kind of evidence does Gertrude's aestheticising speech provide of Ophelia's motive, agency or physical reality as she drowned? The phonetic gap between melodious and muddy is entirely elided in the poetic images – *eikon*s? – it spawned, from the pre-Raphaelite necrophilia of John Everett Millais' iconic painting *Ophelia,* to Hitchcock's cinematic adoption in the scene in *Vertigo* where Kim Novak's Madeleine drowns 'mermaid-like' with 'her clothes spread wide' in a pool of water strewn with flowers from her bouquet. But that gap is also the space of what Erasmus calls the 'exercise or display of genius' – when the whole evidentiary business 'looks to pleasure'.[24] Erasmus distinguishes between two kinds of objects

22 Aristotle, *Poetics*, 17, 1455a22–6.

23 See, e.g., Quintilian, *The Orator's Education*, 6.2.31: 'The result will be *enargeia*, what Cicero calls *illustratio* and *evidentia*, a quality which makes us seem not so much to be talking about something as exhibiting it. Emotions will ensue just as if we were present at the event itself.'

24 Erasmus, *On Copia of Words and Ideas*, p. 49.

of vivification that, together, contribute to enargeic *copia*: 'living things' and 'woven things'.[25] Gertrude's account knits the living thing (which, here, is also the dying thing) into a woven thing with a liveliness that complicates both ethical insouciance and aesthetic enjoyment.

Different in specifics but comparable in kind is the displacement of erotic frisson into narrative jouissance in Iachimo's evidential narratives in Shakespeare's *Cymbeline*. Though Iachimo is not speaking for anyone but himself, his judicial reports take me back to the layering of performativity in the contemporary trial I started with, one that early modern culture was dense with, not just in the theatre of the courtroom, as Peters brilliantly unpacks, but in the courtroom of the theatre. Vasquez's vivid conjuration and framing of a moment already watched by the court audience could have come straight out of *Cymbeline*, where the original scene of criminal action – Imogen's bedroom – is first staged; then vividly reported in another space and time by the villain Iachimo as he tries to persuade her husband Posthumus of her supposed infidelity through false proofs consisting of a heady mix of material tokens and enargeic narrative; and then reported again in the final trial scene in Iachimo's supposed confession speech which becomes a self-delighting bravura performance. The compositional aspect of rhetoric and the performance of law that Lorna Hutson distinguishes in Chapter 2 in this volume come together in Iachimo's repeated efforts at persuasion. Ontologically, they are a variation on the crafted whimsy of Vittoria's report of her 'foolish, idle dream' (*White Devil*, 1.2.232) to her lover Bracciano, insinuating her wish that he should get rid of her husband and his wife, which Bracciano rightly interprets as the first stage of a mutual composition, swearing to give her thoughts 'the invention of delight/And the fruition' (265–6). But the dramatic context of purported confession and revelation in the finale of *Cymbeline* embeds the rhetorical in the performative. As Iachimo launches into his evidential aria, 'Once upon a time, unhappy was the clock ... ' (5.5.153), the dilations and delays of his narrative, his melodramatic 'faint', his leisurely, relishing embellishments, his self-congratulatory asides – 'O cunning, how I got it!' (205) – elicit anguished impatience from this onstage audience; witness Cymbeline's outburst: 'I stand on fire./

25 Ibid., p. 50.

Come to the matter' (168–9). Rhetorical temptation overtakes legal necessity, as in *Volpone*. And like Volpone, Iachimo is not interested in the supposed legal purpose – or 'profit' – of this confession: disclosure, testimony and repentance. He is absorbed, instead, by the pleasure of his bravura performance, his Italianate aria evoking his earlier ingenuity of deception. Like his false, testimonial narrative to Posthumus, but unlike the fictional world of *Volpone*, the focus here is on affect and ethics, as narrative retardation sharpens anticipation and causes avoidable pain, in a context of interpersonal ecology. The painful and the comic, the poignant and the perverse, jostle in this tragicomic disclosure to uncover the generic components that make up the insides of the legal machine, which need the extractive work of the theatre to be realised in their fully affective dimensions.

But Gertrude's speech, or Marcus', *can* be played to draw on the affective scope of absence; their strange, dislocated pathos can be made to speak out of a longing that reaches across the gap between *res* and its representation. Interestingly, the context in which Erasmus conceives of *enargeia* as a vehicle of longing is a meditation on real presence – and indeed on mediation – in *Convivium Religiosum (The Godly Feast)* (1522). This is a dialogue structured around Eusebius' guided tour of his house for his guests. His commentary preserves the opacity and enigma of certain forms in the garden, whether natural, artificial or textual: these becomes the loci of plenitude, precisely because they generate epistemic desire. Erasmus' reflection on the deceptiveness of appearance, and on the elusiveness of the reality beyond it, is immediately followed by this comment: 'the very appearance of the place invites one to pray'.[26] The proto-Pauline figure of the transenna or lattice-window – '*veluti per transennam vidisse*' – stands in at once for seeing through a glass, dimly, and the pursuit of seeing and knowing face to face.[27] This throws light in turn on the slippage between *energeia* – the Aristotelian sense of motion, and *enargeia* – the evidential idea, in *De Copia*. Could we see the intrinsic

[26] Desiderius Erasmus, *Convivium Religiosum*, in *Omnia Opera Desiderii Erasmi* (Basel: Froben, 1540), p. 579. Also at https://archive.org/stream/erasmus-the-godly-feast-1522/ERASMUS%20-%20%27%27The%20Godly%20Feast%27%27%20%5B1522%5D_djvu.txt, fo. 134.

[27] Erasmus, *Omnia Opera*, p. 567.

elusiveness of Vittoria's 'character' as theatre's way of translating into a secular idiom the untranslatable *copia* of the self's presence in the face of exegesis?

I end, then, with these intimations of how law's disknowledge becomes the poetic condition for theatrical knowledge – an ironic variance that maps on to the chiasmus shaping the relation between Aristotle's preference of probable proof and the English law courts' privileging of direct and inartificial proofs for creating conviction.[28] The vivid invisibilities in the performance of evidentiary practice, and the knowingness of drama's deep play with the affordances and limits of *energeia,* underline the slippage between the two in legal thinking and action that allows playwrights to push as well as test the limits of empathy, and, paradoxically, forges personhood precisely as its invisibility is inscribed. Theatrical performance acknowledges and looks beyond the invisible object of representation – the truths of intention and emotion – at how their very elusiveness intensified the need for these signs, the desperation to map what is visible on to what is not, to make presence figure absence. The epistemic yearning structuring judicial encounters, the proficiency of legal representation at playing to it, the semiotic remit of subject-positions, and the pain and pleasure of the *scaenius* of law need the *scaenius* of the theatre to be fully explored: for the theatre is at home in *hypokrisis.*

[28] Aristotle, *Rhetoric* I.i.3–11; I.ii.2. Cp. *Poetics* 16 on the corresponding hierarchy of signs.

CHAPTER 4

The Outdoor Stages of Common Law

Piyel Haldar

STAGING LAW OUTDOORS

The study of law suggests that its performances, largely through the format of trials, take place behind the closed doors of its offices and courtrooms. Little of the exterior would seem to intrude upon its routines and, vice versa, little of what might constitute law's performativity occurs outside of its bounded architectural habitat. Yet this has not always been the case. Numerous examples of outdoor performances provide a rich study into the siting of legal performance. They direct our attention away from the familiar environments in which law's monumental and bureaucratic presence is most directly felt. Hitherto, no study has taken place of those institutional performances that historically took place in the outdoors. The argument presented in this chapter is that it was the outside that provided the initial stage and staging of law. Asserting the presence of law across the various and remote parts of the realm required performances of its majesty on the very surface of the earth. It required acts heralding, inscribing and publicising common law as the law of the land and so it was the land that had to become the physical platform and the scene of its delivery. The evolution of common law depended upon the rudiments of landscape, on the plotting of the countryside, and on the elemental matter of the earth. Such features formed a stage on which the emergence of common law not only took place but was very much performed.

It is as well to note that from the perspective of a pre-common law history, customs that were eventually assimilated into early common law were already, and in the main, matters of the land. The materiality of the earth established customs as regional, local, agrarian, riparian, of the forest and of the soil. Feudal relations revolved around land usage. For early common lawyers, the spirit and antiquity of customary laws initially festered in and were inherited with the territory. For Coke, it was earth that held the memory of the law. Interred in England's soil were the bones of common law sages that had survived 'the worm of oblivion'.[1] Rights and customs not only subsisted in the soil. They were also activated and reactivated through heavily symbolic performances that took place upon the land. Consider, as an initial example, the ritual practices around livery of seisin in which land was passed from one title-holder to another in 'solemn ceremony'.[2] Completion of conveyance could not be perfected until both parties met on the land and 'a carve of land be delivered to the other party'. The symbolic transfer of a carve or clod of land (sometimes substituted by a twig) is what entitled the new owner to be 'seized of the land'. It was, however, the grounds of the property itself that mattered and that became both stage and medium for the transmission and transfer of all the rights and appurtenances that inhered therein.

In shifting the legal stage from inside to out, the claim is that a new perspective on law emerges. It is a perspective that has links to an observation made by Julie Stone Peters that often, and in spite of the law's control of its own performances, a more earthly and insurgent drama manages to break through the legal artifice. This is given exemplary expression in her account of a judicial trial by battle held in 1571.[3] The duel is performed on Tothill fields, where scaffolds were erected for onlookers and a dais raised for the judges and the Chief Justice of Common Pleas, who had decamped and reconstituted their court in open air. The outdoors is, quite obviously, a highly practical venue for men of steel to take ten paces back and 'fight until the stars appear in the

[1] Sir Edward Coke, 'Preface', *in The Reports of Sir Edward Coke, Volume 1* (J. Moore: Dublin, 1793 ed.) iv.

[2] Sir Edward Coke, *The Reports of Sir Edward Coke,* Volume II (Alexander Towar: Philadelphia, 1836 ed.) 297.

[3] Julie Stone Peters, *Law as Performance: Theatricality, Spectatorship, and the Making of Law in Ancient, Medieval and Early Modern Europe* (Oxford University Press: Oxford, 2022) 1–2.

evening'. It is, nevertheless, symbolic of law's return to outdoor locations. It ought to be remembered that the Court of Common Pleas ordinarily sat in its fixed location at Westminster Hall. However, prior to the constitution of the Curia Regis by Henry II, and, certainly, prior to Conquest, the court sat al fresco. Other descriptions of Naylor's flamboyant character and the theatricality of his retinue are well attended to by Peters.

One point, however, deserves further attention. On his way to Tothill fields, Nayler (along with his retinue) pauses outside Westminster Hall. None of the accounts give any reason for the pause, and, perhaps, it was simply a matter of respect for the institution. Nevertheless, a pose was adopted, one that constituted a rhetorical caesura in theatrical form and allowed the retinue to view the court of law from the outside. There was, in other words, a symbolic reorganisation of legal resources, reducing the law to a mere phenomenon of architecture. So that what might appear as performative obeisance could also be regarded as an audacious and impudent objectifying of law, as if by adopting an external position, and marching past the building, there is an assertion (or an attempt at an assertion) of an exteriority to law. The outside – the earthy and the quotidian – may threaten and challenge legal authority. It also threatens the presumption that law is an immobile and intransitive institution that fails to move either in time or in tune with the earth. An appreciation of outdoor legal performances might be read, or unearthed, not simply as a corrective counter memory to institutional stagecraft but as a part of its repertoire that, while forgotten, subsists deeply rooted within the genealogy and ontology.

The duel at Tothill fields is not the only mention of outdoor events in Peters' book. Elsewhere she emphasises the embedded and public nature of outdoor trials held 'at hills, at columns, crosses, statues, or bridges; in tents … or in the open market square'.[4] Reference is made to 'Law Days' – days set apart from the quotidian – held outside the city of Hereford and on Cutthorne Mound outside Southampton.[5] These outdoor courts join a vast typology of other legal events, whose provenance lies in caliginous ages, and that were held outdoors. Common law, in

[4] Peters, *Law as Performance*, 159n3. [5] Peters, *Law as Performance*, 160n3.

part, owes its institutional character to customary formalities of open-air moot hills, 'thing' assemblies, *wapentakes* and *burghemots*. Even those institutions that were eventually harboured within architecturally safe environments, such as piepowder, manorial and hundred courts and halimots, were initially held as outdoor public events. In these theatrical environments, the use of the earth becomes loaded with significance in order to construct a sense of make-believe.

In more general terms, we might note that as platform and as ground, the stage is more than a merely terranean under-structure, and provides the legal drama with more than the boards upon which actors tread.[6] In any performance, it is the stage that allows for the allocation of props, bodies and action during performance and becomes as significant as dialogue, character or plot. More essentially, it provides a medium for foundation. This sense of the stage as a medium for foundation emerges in Martin Puchner's analysis of theatre's existential problem with locality and place.[7] Puchner draws links between theatre's concern for ground and the philosophical project of foundations for metaphysical norms. The rostrum, raised above the level of the floor, situated in indoor theatre venues, as Puchner notes, had the effect of uprooting theatre from its initial open-air environments (as, for example, the flat floor of amphitheatres in ancient Greece), on which performances were held. In the process of lifting performances onto an indoor raised platform, the dynamic and foundational relationship between the earth and theatre had become lost.

The legal equivalent of Puchner's analysis would be to draw a link between the stages on which legal performances were housed, and Hans Kelsen's formulation, in his *Pure Theory of Law*, of the *Grundnorm* (as the most basic and ultimate foundation of law) thereby linking performative

[6] It is interesting to note in this context that the Roman ban on theatre was a senatorial prohibition on the building of theatres, a denial of the space in which play could be become art and threaten thereby the primacy of the art of law. See Florence Dupont, 'La scène juridique' (1977) 26 *Communications*, 62–77. Thanks to Peter Goodrich for the reference.

[7] Martin Puchner, 'The Problem of the Ground: Martin Heidegger and Site-Specific Performance', in *Encounters in Performance Philosophy, ed.* Laura Cull and Alice Lagaay (Palgrave Macmillan: London, 2014) 65–86.

action to a foundational principle.[8] The *Grundnorm* is more often than not translated as basic norm. A literal translation, however, from the German might render *Grund* as ground. In its earliest forms to which this essay refers, the *Grundnorm* was taken up as the most material of grounds, namely that of the platform of earth itself. It was the earth – humus and loam – that provided the common law with the most basic foundational norm. It was its *Grund* and source, and the stage from which all other norms arose. It is less a 'pure theory of law' than a soiled theory. In both legal and non-legal senses of the word, performance relies upon a foundational platform, and it is the choice of venue and stage that becomes key. The concern here is to retrieve the ground as an alternative sense of law's foundation and stage. In doing so, there is the further claim that any analysis of legal performance loses its sense of the material ecology (the relationship between law and the natural environment) that is locked into the emergence of common law unless it takes into account the notion of the outdoor stage and the peculiarity of al fresco rituals.

THEATRE OF THE ASSIZES

The ecology of common law emerges most notably through those outside performances that marked the transition from disparate religious and sovereign practices to a sense of a common law. In particular, it is the itinerant assize courts and eyres of medieval England that provide the historical background. The assize courts were the primary mechanism for assimilating local customary rules and observances practised in the various shires of medieval England into common law. As Paul Raffield neatly summarises: 'As well as exercising the functions of a court of law (in civil and criminal matters), the eyre served as an itinerant form of central government, exercising a supervisory and regulatory role over local government and local customs.'[9] Both were comprised of a corps of

8 Hans Kelsen, *Pure Theory of Law* (University of California Press: Berkeley, 1967).

9 Paul Raffield, 'Custom and Common Law', in *The Cambridge Companion to Medieval English Law and Literature*, ed. Candace Barrington and Sebastien Sobecki (Cambridge University Press: Cambridge, 2019) 40–53 at 45.

justice-errants periodically sent out from Westminster to ride the preset routes of provincial circuits, collect taxes and hear pleas. Initially, twenty-one judges toured the country divided into the four inaugural circuits. These four circuits were later increased to eight in order to 'facilitate perambulation by Royal agents'.[10] Such judicial visitations and incursions into areas remote from London, the centre of judicial and legislative power, established what Frederic Maitland called 'the great council of the nation'.[11] The circuit courts of assizes and eyres were launched during the twelfth century as a means of replacing the seigniorial courts (the private franchise jurisdiction of manor lords determined by the collective of arcane rights of sake and soke, toll and team, and ingfangthief).[12] In replacing these baronial and private manor courts (courts that largely relied on local customary laws), circuit courts instituted a machine for colonising boroughs and shires, bringing them structurally closer to the Curia Regis, the King's Court. They took over adversarial causes between warring barons, as well as other similar private duels. The assizes, in particular, became the first resort for cases that had hitherto fallen under the jurisdiction of manor lords, or sheriffs. In more conceptual terms, the assizes provided a key institution in the state monopolisation of hitherto private feuds, and in the more general pacification of social relations.

It was by sending the judges on circuit that the assizes more deeply settled common law upon a geographical and sublunary terrain. To cite Maitland and Pollock's felicitous phrasing, 'the English circuit system struck its roots deep into the soil'.[13] Or, as William Dugdale put it: their task was to distribute justice *jura per pagos*, in each town throughout the country.[14] In its turn away from the centre of power,

10 James S. Cockburn, *A History of English Assizes 1558–1714* (Cambridge University Press: Cambridge, 1972) 15.

11 Frederic William Maitland, *The Constitutional History of England* (Cambridge University Press: Cambridge, 1963) 69.

12 Frederic William Maitland, *Domesday Book and Beyond: Three Essays in the Early History of England* (Fontana Press: London, 1960) 110–138.

13 Frederic William Maitland and Frederick Pollock, *The History of English Law before the Time of Edward I* (Cambridge University Press: Cambridge, 1815) 615.

14 William Dugdale, *Historical Memorials of the English Laws, Antient Parliaments, Courts of Justice, Forms of Trial before the Norman Conquest: Also of the Four Inns of Court, the Inns of Chancery, &c, Volume 1* (London, 1790) 58.

the institution of the assizes created a minor revolution in legal technique. It may have been untelevised, but this itinerant spectacle of the assizes reoriented law's theatrical performance towards a drama of social action defined by topography and the surface of the land rather than the grand architectonic structure of court buildings. Of course, the elementary attributes of the body politic remained. The central conceit of Crown authority remained intact, and the King acted *deus ex machina.* Circuit judges, representing regal authority, were deployed 'front of stage' to perform in character. The act, of course, depended on the suspension of disbelief that judges carried the memory of the law in their breasts. In this fashion, according to Francis Bacon in his *Speech for the Summer Circuits 1617,* they 'preserve[d] laws pure'.[15]

What is important to note, however, is that the performance of law took place on a wider stage than those provided by the assize courts themselves. In striking its roots deep into the soil, assize performances were not restricted to those that took place in courts located in towns. Indeed, assize trials and the court buildings in which they were held were no more than nodal points in an organised network of communication that extended over the entire social and geographic terrain. And, while it cannot be denied that assize trials were theatrical and even melodramatic events, while they performed the ultimate function of decision-making, it was the itinerancy of the regional circuits themselves that provided a larger, more significant stage for the presentation of law.

For Bacon, this outdoor stage of the circuits was first and foremost conditioned by cosmic forces. If the earth provided the law with a stage, then planetary and horoscopic energies ensured its integrity. Astronomy conspired to pattern the circuits in its own image according to which the Crown took on the characteristics of an all-seeing mechanism, a *primum mobile* in a Pythagorean/heliocentric system that set the whole mechanism of the circuits in motion. As Bacon puts it; 'You that are Judges of the Circuits are as it were the planets of the Kingdom . . . Do therefore as they do; move always and be carried with the motion of your first mover, which

15 Sir Francis Bacon, *Speech for Summer Circuits in James Spedding, Robert Leslie Ellis and Douglas Denon Heath* (Cambridge University Press: Cambridge, 2011) 13:211–214 at 211.

is your sovereign.'[16] Bacon's sentiments are not simply metaphorical and are to be taken as symptomatic of the Pythagorean ethos of the Elizabethan and Jacobean era.[17] In their circuits and revolutions, microcosm resembled macrocosm and revealed the greater order of the universe.

Put differently, the assize court trial was no more than a play set within a much grander play that communicated a more grandiloquent message. Each individual assize trial was no more than the equivalent of Hamlet's *Mouse Trap* mirroring the larger plot. With its own interchangeable cast of stock characters (malevolent defendants, mischievous troublemakers, inept solicitors, hapless officials), the trial merely confirmed the words of the main script that was acted out on the move and on the paths and routes between shires and assize towns.

These were paths already wired into the landscape. In one, admittedly eccentric reading these routes were ley lines that followed the flows and currents of druidic energies.[18] Ancient trackways made good through customary usage and the assertion of customary rights and which already gave rise to many various usages that would be assimilated into common law were ready-made for the transition from customary to common law and provided a geographical platform for the most visible and outward appearance of law as it moved cross-country. Since the court travelled with the judges, the journey along the circuits was the journey and performance of the law. Crime committed on the road and in the presence of a judge 'was done as in the presence of the Prince ... As that if a *justice* of assize shall happen by any of his circuit to be slain, the Law adjudgeth it to bee *Lese Crimen Majestasis*'.[19]

Accordingly, if the Lord Chancellor might be regarded as having provided directions, instructing the errant judges from the centre of

[16] Bacon, *Speech for Summer Circuits*, 211.

[17] See Eustace M. W. Tillyard, *The Elizabethan World Picture* (Chatto & Windus: London, 1943).

[18] See Piyel Haldar, 'The Imaginary Origins of the Common Law', in *The Cabinet of Imaginary Laws*, ed. Peter Goodrich and Thanos Zartoloudis (Routledge: New York, 2021) 1–10.

[19] Sir Edward Coke, 'Speech and Charge to Norwich Assizes 4th August 1606', in *Selected Writings and Speeches of Sir Edward Coke*, ed. Stephen Shepherd (Liberty Fund: Indianapolis, 2003) II:529.

legal power, and if the countryside provided the stage, then the paths might be regarded as replete with its own set of stage furniture. Positional and 'on-set markers' were provided by stone crosses, oak trees, tumps and megaliths that sat at significant junctions and presented itinerant judges with locations for ad hoc roadside hearings along the way. The itinerancy of law officiated on these once pagan sites of significance. It colonised, for the purposes of its own staging, sites of geological, lithic and arboreal weight.

The journey itself was designed as a spectacle performed and accounts of assize judges on the move are worth considering in detail. Setting off from Holborn, a retinue (or a *posse comitatus*) of valets, clerks and guards travelled with the judge, riding pack horses from assize town to assize town: 'When they moved, crimson and gold, burnished steel and floating ancient [pennants] gladdened the eye: at the same time the ear was addressed by the blare of trumpets.'[20] Barristers followed in their own coaches, or on horseback, or even on foot: 'Royal justices with attendant trains of clerks and officers ... passed from shire to shire drawing after them as they went a great crowd of recogniters, parties, essoiners and others.'[21] Even on route and in between court sessions, judges were on show. According to the 'Historical Memorials' of William Dugdale: 'When riding judges and serjeants are to wear a coat of good broad cloth with sleeves, and faced with velvet. They have used of late to lace the Sleeves of the Serjeant Coat, thick with lace. And they are to have a Sumpter, and ought to ride with six men at the least.'[22]

With the country providing its stage, the scenography to common law's performance was provided by the English landscape. Take the description of his journey by John Alderson Foote, a late nineteenth-century circuit judge: 'It was a goodly land and fair through which His Majesty's judges followed those well worn ways.'[23] His approach into

[20] John Cordy Jeaffreson, *Pleasantries of English Courts and Lawyers* (James Cockcroft: New York, 1876) 94.

[21] Charles Chadwick-Healey, 'Introduction', in *Pleas (Civil and Criminal) from the Rolls of the Itinerant Justices* (Harlison and Sons: London, 1897) xviii.

[22] William Dugdale, *Origines Juridiciales* (F and T Warren: London, 1666) 101.

[23] John Alderson Foote, *Piepowder Courts Being Dust from the Courts by a Circuit Tramp* (University of Michigan Press: Michigan, 1973) 11.

Salisbury for assizes is marked by the sudden rise of its cathedral spire over the southern uplands, by wild roses and 'everlasting hills'. Mounted on the English stage, the setting provided an idyllic geography. This landscape becomes an illusion, a matter of stagecraft and part of the designated proscenium. There is even lighting and sound design where the circuit is described as 'bathed in sunshine' and Devizes silently sleeps. What emerged, as the backdrop to this theatre, is the make-believe scenery of 'merrie' England as a rural idyll, 'time worn' and 'everlasting', against which the myth of common law appeared. Foote's account mirrors the more doctrinally nuanced observations made by Coke on his way to the Norwich Assizes:

> Mee thinkes, that oftentimes when I ryde by the way, I see the Effects of Justice rightlie resembled, when I behold a River with a silver currant, bounded in her equall course, with what just proportion shee doth disperse her streames, without bewraying any little rage of intemperate violence.[24]

Not only did the scenography represent a bucolic idyll, the English countryside – with its furniture and props of rivers and streams – gently reflecting the decorum of justice. Merrie England was justice because it was equal, proportionate and temperate. Distance and lighting hid the defects of quotidian life, mob unhappiness. Space, as it is with any element of scenography, was synthesised into an illusion of place. Where the usual elements of stagecraft employ perspectival technique, painted backcloths or Piranesian *trompe l'oeil*, these judicious descriptions of landscape served to create the sense of a place situated in time immemorial in order to stage the romance of common law.

The entry of the itinerant circuit into the assize towns deserves further attention since it is here that law's dramatic realisation on the territorial stage reached its climax and was expressed with full pageantry. Any stage requires attention to design and layout. Proscenium arches, trapdoors, fly-towers and bridges are typical and indeed essential to the delivery of performance. So too are exit and entry points in determining the positioning and movement of actors. The outdoors, as any other stage, was

[24] Coke, *Speech and Charge at the Norwich Assizes*, 532.

similarly laid out for devising performance and the directions for exiting/entering geographical territory required ritual and ceremony. Crossing county borders, arriving in a town, were essentially acts of becoming visible. It was a play of transferring from one jurisdiction to another, from one atmosphere into another, but also an act of transferring from invisibility to the point of visibility. Most accounts of the entry of processions into assize towns tend to assume that the ceremony provided a prelude to the main business of hearing assizes at court.[25] In this sense, they were no more than an insertion into an overall chain of events leading up to proper matters to be decided in court. It might be supposed that these outdoor civic performances established what Butler describes as: 'the temporal conditions for making the speech act [that] precede[s] ... the momentary occasion of its enunciation'.[26] Nevertheless, such analyses miss the point that territorial borders and the geography of entry points were configured on the outdoor set as specifically dedicated liminal points. The minor geography was in fact the major stage, the point of entry and exit, as also the source of the customs that constituted the law of the land, the *leges terrae*, and the audience for, as well as recipient of the proto-liturgical pronouncements of the assize court itself.

The pageantry of these entrances mixed and enjoined judicial and civic performances as an essential part of staging the machinery of state-sponsored justice. From the twelfth century until as recently as 1972 (when the assize circuits were abolished), the county sheriff would meet the travelling justices at the county border with elaborate ceremony. 'The sheriff with his *posse comitatus* used to receive the judges at their entrance into the city, and attend them till they were received by the sheriff and *posse comitatus* of the next county.'[27] In his description of the

[25] Ernest Turner, *May It Please Your Lordship* (Joseph: London, 1971); Frank Douglas MacKinnon, *On Circuit 1924–1937* (Cambridge University Press: Cambridge, 1940); Thomas Walmysely, *The Expenses of Judges Riding the Western and Oxford Circuits, Temp. Elizabeth, 1596–1601* (Camden Society: London, 1858).

[26] Judith Butler, *Notes toward a Performative Theory of Assembly* (Harvard University Press: Cambridge, MA, 2015) 176.

[27] 'Debate in the Commons for the Assizes to be Held at Aylesbury, Buckinghamshire AD 1748', in William Cobbett, *Parliamentary History of England* (Longman: London, 1813) XIV:226.

assizes to Charles Villiers (the courtier and favourite of Charles II), Bacon stipulated the 'attendance of the sheriffs of the counties, accompanied with the principal gentlemen, in a comely equipage, upon the judges of assize at their coming into the place of their sitting'.[28] Whether Villiers was directly concerned with the 'comely equipage' of anyone other than the king is moot, but Bacon's advice emphasises the theatrics of law's arrival into town. Descriptions of assize processions are legion, and we need only summarise the large retinue of significant gentry, trumpeters and javelin men on horseback, followed by aldermen, tradesmen, magistrates and the sheriff, travelling in ceremonial carriages (the latter of which is used to collect and transport the visiting judge). The earliest use of the accompanying retinue may well have been to act as bodyguards for the justices. Local tenants and cottagers armed with halberds/javelins were employed for the task. Sheriffs were instructed to 'have in readiness a strong and decent guard for receiving [the judges], which guard must consist of the potents, knights, esquires, and gentlemen of the county with their men arrayed in liveries, with a trumpet for their convoy'.[29] They evolved, however, from a performance of protection to one of symbolic ritual. Under shrieval and mayoral arms and with the continued use of javelin men, trumpeters rode and blew on and announced the iconic presence of law. A description taken from John Wesley's sermon before the assizes at Bedford concentrates on the minute solemnities necessary for civic values. 'For these also, by means of the eye or ear, may more deeply affect the heart: and when viewed in this light, trumpets, staves, apparel, are no longer trifling or insignificant, but subservient, in their kind and degree, to the most valuable ends of society.'[30]

In terms of the development of common law, the border marked the point at which local, rural, franchises ceded rights, authority and jurisdiction to the royal judges. As Hale noted, the assizes brought the law 'Home to the Parties in the Countries ... near where they live'.[31] These

[28] Bacon, 'Letters and Life Advice to Villiers', in *Speech for Summer Circuits*, 13:27–55.

[29] Lord Henry Cockburn, *Circuit Journeys* (David Douglas: Edinburgh, 1889) 297.

[30] John Wesley, *The Great Assize: A Sermon Preached at Bedford, 1758* (John Mason: London, 1829).

[31] Matthew Hale, *A History of the Common Law of England* (Chicago University Press: Chicago, 1973), 161.

ceremonies staged the occupation and colonising of the land, a patterning of authority in accordance with what ought to be held in general across all England. The pageants reversed the flow of law's energy from sources of local customs (rooted in local soil) to a more centrally located hierarchical organisation of authority that took over the whole terrain. Thus, even in the localised and custom-driven context of civic authority, daily life and quotidian existence in assize towns had to surrender to the extraordinary appearance and arrival of law. A long-standing statute from the thirteenth century, for example, forbade the continuation of markets during the time of visiting assizes and eyres.[32] The country had to be awoken for the show and individual locales had to make way for 'the place of law's appearance'.[33]

A BRIEF DIGRESSION ON THE COURTS OF PIEPOWDER

The business of moving across the country required from the wandering judges a particular appreciation of other courts that would eventually be assimilated into the institutional repertoire of common law. In particular, the courts of piepowder (alternatively, the courts of pied poudres, pipoudler or pye poudre) deserve brief mention. These courts were held during market fairs and matters that fell within its jurisdiction were only those that were incidental to specific markets. Essentially, in the terms of the day, they were *curia parvi ponderis summarli.* Claims invariably were small and the presence of foreign traders at market fairs, meant justice needed to be speedy and simple. The courts (much to Blackstone's appreciation) ministered justice with model efficiency and speed.[34] They were, it is important to note, located at the gateways of urban or larger rural settlements. Two points on the materiality of the stage might here be made. First, it is the geographical positioning of the piepowder courts that brought them into contact with itinerant justices as the latter rode into and sat at the gates of the city. The particularities of the

32 '*Articulii et Sacramenta Ministrorum Regis in Itinere Justiciariorum* 1232', in *Statutes of the Realm* 1810 (Dawsons: London 1965) I:232.

33 Hale, *History of the Common Law of England,* 161.

34 William Blackstone, *Commentaries on the Laws of England* (Chicago University Press: Chicago, 1979) 3:21.

aforementioned spectacles are not worth repeating except to stress that it is the liminal point of gateways and boundaries that here provide a stage for the meeting of laws as well as the meeting of jurisdictions. The second point adds a footnote as it were. What is interesting about piepowder courts is that the discourse of elevation that attaches to the assizes surrenders to its opposite and retains, in a more material sense, the importance of earthly matter as material foundation for the staging of law. Courts of piepowder were, Blackstone says, 'the lowest ... court of justice'. Indeed, it is only once he provides an account of these courts that he then continue to write about other courts of the legal system by 'ascending gradually to those of the most extensive and transcendent power'. Blackstone claims that the name (pluralised from piepowder and translated from *pye-poudre,* or *cura pedis pulverizati*) derives from the dusty feet (the pied poudre) of the suitors to the court. These travelling merchants, itinerant chapmen, shepherds, vagabonds and drovers were those who not only traversed geographical space but 'by their motion raise *pulvererm vel lutum* (dust and mud)'. An alternative explanation for the name is given by Cowell and refers to the feet of the whole court; 'it hath the name of dustie feet which we commonly get by sitting neere the ground'.

The staging of the assizes depended upon a cosmologically determined ecosystem of itinerant circuits. The earthly stage provided the landscape of 'merrie' England. Paths and natural furniture provide on-set markers. To this we ought to add that it was the very material quality of dust that determined jurisdiction. That is to say, the dust in question had a forensic value. The dusty foot, if we are to believe Blackstone's etymology, belonged to those travellers from other urban areas plying their trades at the relevant marketplaces. It was the very material of the stage, namely the dust specific to a region, that marked the stranger as coming from another region. It might, however, be speculated that what applied to the traveller also applied to the wandering justices, who might equally have brought their own dusty boots into town. If dust on the traveller's foot provided a marker of regional differences, it also provided, on the part of those judges who rode through the gateways of market towns, an erasure of those differences and a mixing of regional soils to provide a unified stage.

FEIGNING THE DEATH OF PERFORMANCE

In one restricted and administrative sense, the functional performance of common law across the geographical stage of the country continued well into the twentieth century. Its continued existence, however, was more often than not considered a matter of nostalgia and anachronism. Towards the end of the nineteenth century, and perhaps under the spirit of utilitarian reform, assize processions had become enfeebled and assumed a mantle of mere pageantry. Many of the insignia of shrievalty that marked these quarterly street performances of the assizes were priced by Parliament, and had succumbed to money-saving reforms. It might be assumed that such reforms were purely driven by economic motivation. Hansard records, however, show that such reforms were ideological. In a House of Commons debate, Mr Edwin Jones is reported as declaring that there is 'no pageantry in having twenty four decrepit old men moving before the judge, and preceded by an asthmatic trumpeter'.[35] In the same debate and vein, Sir John Shelley derided the 'idle paraphernalia of the number of men in red-coats, accompanied by trumpeters discoursing very ineloquent music'.[36] Faced with the alternative proposition that aesthetics becomes and empowers the law, Shelley continued:

> [that he] could not see what honour was given to the judges by putting in a gilt coach at the station the man with whom they travelled cheek by jowl in the railway carriage, and who perhaps made his appearance on the platform in a wide-awake [hat] and a shooting jacket.[37]

Arguments against the overt pageantry of conducting law, as Julie Stone Peters reminds us in her analysis of the Tothill duel, are not anti-performance. They merely posit a licit form of performance as being more a propos to the proper function of law. The alternative to the use of javelin men and asthmatic trumpeters would remain performative.

[35] Edwin Jones, *Hansard House of Commons Debates, 27 July 1859* (Longmans: London, 1859) 155:494.

[36] Sir John Shelley, *Hansard House of Commons Debates, 27 July 1859* (Longmans: London, 1859) 155:490.

[37] Shelley, *House of Commons Debates*, 490.

The arguments presented in Parliament, however, typify the old split between the body politic (or body judicial) and the body natural. Masks are let slip and judges are believed to be as much a maladroit body as any other. The stage, from the perspective of reformers, was no longer considered necessary and judges on the road were no longer considered to be providing a performance. Visiting brethren were mere flesh and blood, separated from us only by cheek and jowl. Once out of their judicial robes, their fashions – an un-feathered, wide-awake hat and gentleman's shooting jacket – are, or were, no different to the rest of fare-paying passengers on the railways. Even as an anachronism, the theatre of assizes continued to function in the historical imagination. The argument that pageantry is ersatz, comically out of touch and out of time, is a key part of the theatre of law. Indeed, what seems to substitute for the fetish of judicial dignity is a performance in which it is the physical body of the judge that becomes the object of obsession. Often, this reverse fetish is expressed through the comic. Anecdotes that relate incidents of mishaps during the assizes take the theatre of law into the realms of the absurd.[38] Take the instance where Justice Rokeby had to be carried out of his digs at Trinity College (Cambridge) on a chair because the entrance to the college was too narrow for the ceremonial coach and horses.[39] Or the same judge having to cope with a coach horse falling down dead during the procession: 'just as the high sheriff met us, one of the horses in my coach fell down dead'.[40] Another author derides the scene of assize judges smoking cigars while in procession and belching beer during sermons.[55] A peep backstage, or a comic interlude, allowed the mask of judicial authority to slip, but this slippage only served to enhance and reify what happened on the front stage. Laughter became the new medium of faith and kept the mystical theatre afloat. If pageantry highlights anachronism, it is because

[38] The argument that the absurd becomes a modern characteristic of the foundation of law is pursued at length in Piyel Haldar, '*Credo Quia Absurdum*', in *The Courtroom on Camera: Visions of Justice, ed.* Kanika Sharma (Routledge: London, 2025).

[39] Thomas Rokeby, *The Diary of Mr Justice Rokeby* (Privately printed: London, 1887) 39.

[40] Rokeby, *Diary of Mr Justice Rokeby*, 27.

anachronism is key to the timelessness of ceremony and to the exceptional and non-ordinary spectacle of law.

The transhistorical transposition of circuit theatre (from the twelfth to the twentieth centuries) proceeded along the lines of all legal performances, reinforcing the conditions of faith and collective behaviour. It reasserted the common law myth of time immemorial. What disappears, however, during this relatively long history is the direct confrontation between law and the natural environment. It would seem as if the play had been performed and the stage had served its purpose. Common law had long since settled its purchase on the land. There is, in other words, a denial of the proper extent of law's ecology. With the few exceptions of judicial memoirs from circuit judges in the late nineteenth and early twentieth centuries, the idea of common law's dependency on nature is increasingly excluded. Land is externalised and subject largely to the topics of private law. Earth no longer exists as a stage, or a functional and active agent in law's performance. What is lost is not simply a connection to the material ecology of law but a relationship between law and a sense of location with all the social, political and cultural memories that therein subsist.

THE PERSISTENCE OF THE OUTSIDE

The outdoor stage, read somewhat historically and with only the barest of attention to the present, determined the performance of law. The question that arises is: what is lost to legal performance once the outside moves indoors and into the relative comfort of purpose-built architecture? Since 1972 the assize circuits have been discontinued along with their attendant performances. Law seems no longer to mobilise the natural environment, nor does it need to perform directly on it. Any analysis of current legal performances would have to attend to action taking place in a dust free, airless environment sequestered from the planetary impulses, cosmic energies and matters of the earth. That the third rock from the sun once provided the ground for legal stagecraft might seem to turn a purposeless and perverse study into a moribund topic. Nevertheless, given that the stage, in itself, is an *actant*, always performing and always staging its drama, there is no reason to suppose that its effect has disappeared.

Consider the symbolic elements of the relatively new building for the UK Supreme Court that deliberately redraws the curtains to reveal an ecology embedded in the legal imaginary. The court replaced the former House of Lords, was housed in the refurbished Middlesex Guildhall and opened in 2010. The building is state-of-the-art and, in its interior design, far removed from the ecological conditions and earthly stage of the assize circuits. The props, stage layout and scenography seemingly reflect an interior designed for businesslike functionality. Yet, in both the foyer and in Court number one at the Middlesex Guildhall, carpets have been laid depicting the natural sigils of the four nations of the United Kingdom; the rose of England, the leek of Wales, the thistle of Scotland and the flax of Northern Ireland. The carpet is a matter of pride, described in the various press releases and brochures as a 'pop art carpet designed by Sir Peter Blake of Sergeant Pepper fame [that] brightens up the room with symbols representing the four nations of the United Kingdom'.[41] Nature has been brought inside as a synthetic representation of the Supreme Court's territorial and conceptual jurisdiction. The carpet provides a stage for the highest appeal cases and remains an efficient and postmodern simulacrum of the stage that provided common law with its initial platform. The material ecology of the archaic and historic stage has been emblematised and distorted. Despite being simulated, the symbolic mobilisation of law's ecological provenance remains visible. Judges, lawyers and a host of attendants continue to perform upon an extension of territory.

Other tropes that attach to the legal stage speak to the insistence of the earth in legal performance. In her analysis of the Supreme Court of India, Rahela Khorakiwala comments on its circular architecture.[42] She notes that while resembling a mamelon, the rotunda of the court

[41] https://supremecourt.uk/about-the-building/architecture.

[42] Rahela Khorakiwala, 'Justice in Circles'. www.scobserver.in/75-years-of-sc/justice-in-circles. See also Rahela Khorakiwala, *From the Colonial to the Contemporary: Images, Iconography, Memories and Performances of Law in India's High Courts* (Hart: New Delhi, 2020).

building, seen from above, has been interpreted by some as a phallic architectural image.[43] The rotunda connects architecture to the invisibility of women in the Indian judicial system. It is an expression of the unsatisfactory civic ordering of life. We can add to this. The dome – whether on the Indian Supreme Court or the Old Bailey – speaks to law's love for discourses of elevation. The hemispherical idiom locks into a persistent tradition that begins with the hill upon which early lawyers would moot or, the mountain from which laws are received. Alternatively, and from the perspective of the inside, the dome is a hemispherical vault that makes manifest the heavens. In this sense, the dome is a proscenium arch that recalls an observation made by Francis Bacon that the assize circuits were patterned and choreographed according to laws of planetary movement.[44] Lawyers that once circulated around the assizes now do so, 'in motion all day', beneath curvilinear vaults that bring the heavens inside.

More generally, Khorakiwala intimates, circularity organises the pathways of lawyers and ushers us towards an aspect of their performance that is as visible – perhaps more so – as those that occur in the courtroom. Little-analysed features of court architecture such as the corridor, function equally as much as the courtroom as places of legal theatre. As Mark Jarzombeck reminds us, the architectural history of the corridor is linked to the organisation and appearances of social interaction.[45] Rules of etiquette required country houses to be built with separate corridors for masters and servants. Charles Barry's design for the Houses of Parliament used corridors to segregate the Lords from the Commons. The Lord Chancellor had his own corridor just as judges in modern court buildings have theirs. As Jarzombeck notes of the Royal Courts of Justice on the Strand, the judges were able to access their corridor directly from their carriage via a magnificent stairway panelled with wainscot.[46]

[43] Shailesh Kumar, 'Interpreting the Scales of Justice: Architecture, Symbolism and Semiotics of the Supreme Court of India' (2017) 30.4 *International Journal for the Semiotics of Law* 637.

[44] 'You that are Judges of the Circuits are as it were the planets of the Kingdom.' Bacon, *Speech for Summer Circuits.*

[45] Mark Jarzombeck, 'Corridor Spaces', 36.N4 (Summer 2010) *Critical Inquiry*, 728–770.

[46] Jarzombeck, 'Corridor Spaces', 754.

Circulation as a medium of legal performance takes its cue from the bringing of the outside into the courthouse. Corridors are the modern pathways, or, as Le Corbusier calls them, 'internal streets' (*rue interieure*). Where assize judges once heard cases on the move, en route and on the roadside, lawyers, with their own retinue, now perform in corridors. More than utilitarian spaces, corridors are places of argument, of deals and bargains between competing parties. They have become the extension of the territorial pathways and rural circuits where the acting and the action take place.

CONCLUSION

Attending to the history of the legal stage, to its earthbound platform, its former material ecology and its fractured persistence, reveals a different performative history of law. Such a history cannot be inattentive to the deep nationalism at stake in the mythologising of the English country stage. A history of blood and soil is woven into the ecology of law. Equally, however, a sense of the stage on which law performs and has performed its drama reminds us that law is a specifically located institution and built upon local and geological fault-lines. The theatrical is often invoked as a matter of providing a scene of make-believe, a founding reference or the underside of legal rationality that masks the credo/*fides quia absurdum.*[47] As a modest contribution and addendum to studies of legal performance, it can only be proposed that this underside be examined as that platform which exists beneath the sandal. As Freud discovered, 'stones speak'.[48] The materiality of the stage, its land, soil and scenery opens up the chance to consider the stage on which law performs as matter through which a richer ecology of law might be activated, other voices heard and its current forms mocked.

47 Haldar, '*Credo Quia Absurdum*', n.38.

48 Sigmund Freud, 'The Aetiology of Hysteria', in *The Standard Edition of the Complete Works of Sigmund Freud,* trans. James Strachey (Hogarth Press: London, 2024) 2:192.

CHAPTER 5

Law – Text – Performance

Derek Miller

TWO PROPOSITIONS ABOUT THE LAW: (1) Law is an endless flow of paperwork, a relentlessly, overwhelmingly textual practice. From contracts to briefs to opinions to treatises, law lives in its texts. There is no law without text. (2) Law produces authenticity and authority through performances. Witness testimonies, pleadings, and trials all enact law through the bodies of participants. There is no law without performance.

Legal texts; legal performances: These practices exist in a kind of opposition – the fixed finality of text; the fleeting ephemerality of performance – but also produce and reproduce each other. Legal texts record or script legal performances (transcripts, oaths); legal performances inspire or enact legal texts (testimonies, opinions read from the bench).

To understand law as dependent on both text and performance, we must study how law moves between these two domains. This chapter examines law's textuality and its theatricality in tandem by probing legal performances as they move between texts and acts. By drawing on theater studies and the history of dramatic texts, I offer methods for reading legal texts as scripts that precede or follow legal performances. Examples from Anglo-American law reveal that legal documents' typographical and formatting conventions encode law's anxious reliance on performance. Paying close attention to the relationship between the law's texts and its performances would better serve the law and, most importantly, justice.

To begin locating performance in legal texts, we must first know what we are looking for: What does performance look like in a text? There are many ways to encode performances in writing, but perhaps

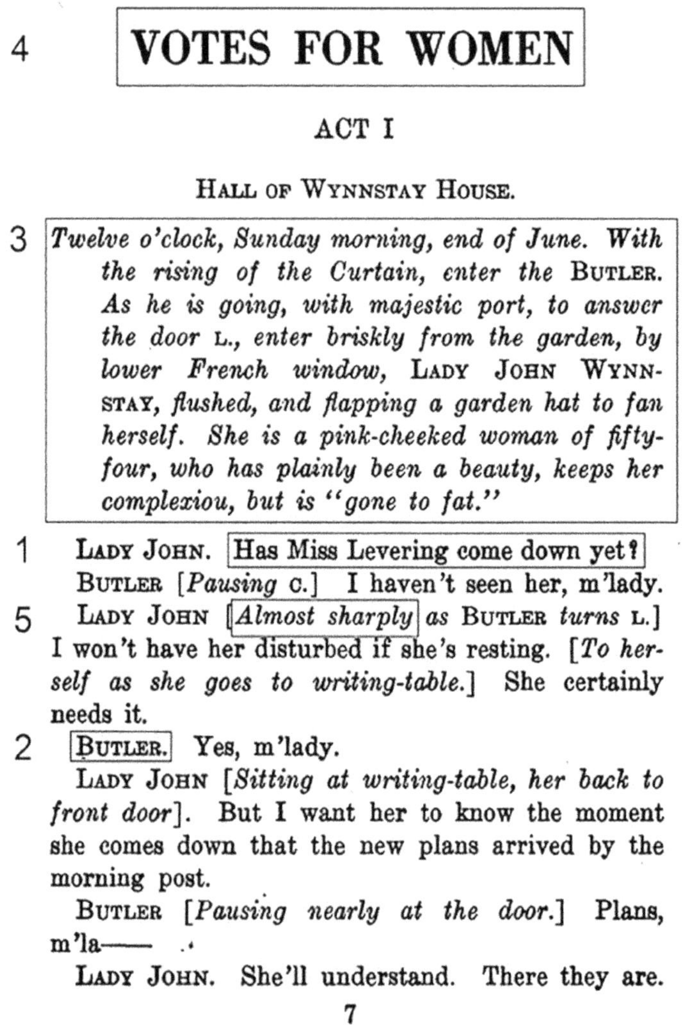

4 VOTES FOR WOMEN

ACT I

HALL OF WYNNSTAY HOUSE.

3 *Twelve o'clock, Sunday morning, end of June. With the rising of the Curtain, enter the* BUTLER. *As he is going, with majestic port, to answer the door* L., *enter briskly from the garden, by lower French window,* LADY JOHN WYNNSTAY, *flushed, and flapping a garden hat to fan herself. She is a pink-cheeked woman of fifty-four, who has plainly been a beauty, keeps her complexiou, but is "gone to fat."*

1 LADY JOHN. Has Miss Levering come down yet?

BUTLER [*Pausing* C.] I haven't seen her, m'lady.

5 LADY JOHN [*Almost sharply as* BUTLER *turns* L.] I won't have her disturbed if she's resting. [*To herself as she goes to writing-table.*] She certainly needs it.

2 BUTLER. Yes, m'lady.

LADY JOHN [*Sitting at writing-table, her back to front door*]. But I want her to know the moment she comes down that the new plans arrived by the morning post.

BUTLER [*Pausing nearly at the door.*] Plans, m'la——

LADY JOHN. She'll understand. There they are.

7

5.1 Elizabeth Robins, *Votes for Women* (The Dramatic Publishing Company, 1907).

the best known and most widely disseminated is the set of conventions surrounding dramatic texts (also called playscripts or scripts). The modern playscript consists of five main elements. Figure 5.1, from The Dramatic Publishing Company's edition of Elizabeth Robins's *Votes for Women,* shows us the five elements now common in printed drama.

Most plays distinguish these elements through typographical variation: A combination of text size, font, capitalization, indentation, and spacing indicates the different functions of each element.[1] (Numbers refer to boxed elements in the figure.)

1. *Dialogue* furnishes the words spoken by performers, printed here in a regular font, fully justified.
2. *Speech prefixes* indicate who speaks each line of dialogue (and, sometimes, who performs specific actions on stage). These appear in this text indented at the start of each line of dialogue, in small caps and followed by a period.
3. *Stage directions* both describe the scene and direct the movement of actors. This edition prints them in italic font, with a hanging indent when they occupy a full paragraph.
4. *Paratext,* such as the play title (in a large, bold type, all capitals, center-aligned) or the page number (a center-aligned regular font at the bottom of the page), control the structure of the play and the text as a material artifact.
5. *Didascalia* are stage directions that indicate not action ("*Pausing nearly at the door.*") but a character's emotion or manner, such as "*Almost sharply.*" Didascalia often look like regular stage directions, but they are less concrete than a practical stage direction and sometimes far more discursive, as in the plays of Bernard Shaw.[2]

The history of printed drama traces two developments in the playscript's form: (1) the elements' individuation, and (2) the changing print conventions that distinguish them from each other.[3] Even in any given era (including the present day), one can find huge variety among plays: the presence or absence of any given element, the use of different typographical indicators for the common elements. Each element is a convention

[1] Elizabeth Robins, *Votes for Women* (The Dramatic Publishing Company, 1907).

[2] On the evolution of discursive stage directions and modern developments, see William B. Worthen, *Print and the Poetics of Modern Drama* (Cambridge University Press, 2009) and Bess Rowen, *The Lines Between the Lines: How Stage Directions Affect Embodiment* (University of Michigan Press, 2021).

[3] For an early history of this story in England, see Claire M. L. Bourne, *Typographies of Performance in Early Modern England* (Oxford University Press, 2020).

with a history. How texts differentiate among them changes depending on shifting methods, tastes, and needs in the theater and in the printing and publishing industries.[4]

An example from this history of theater's evolution in print, discussed alongside a similar change in some legal print practices, demonstrates the potential of this analytic method. Prior to the consolidation of the conventions for printed drama just enumerated, dialogue-based genres did not reliably distinguish dramatic from narrative forms, instead intermingling them. As Julie Stone Peters explains in her history of printed European drama, "medieval verbal arts foregrounded their use of direct speech and indirect speech in combination, their conjoined use of both characters speaking in their own voices and an author's or narrator's voice describing the action."[5] The Renaissance consolidation of theater's artistic identity went hand in hand with a new style in printed drama. The emergent style for dramatic texts minimized "the voice of the poet" and maximized characters' direct speech, in part by distinguishing typographically between dialogue and other aspects of the script (stage directions, arguments, etc.). Those nondialogic elements retained traces of an authorial, narrative function, but without corrupting the dialogue, the essence of printed drama.[6] The dramatic action (primarily spoken by characters) and the narrative circumstances (inscribed by stage directions and other textual materials) thus adopted distinct typographical forms.

Compare the history of reporting speeches in Britain's Parliament. Not until 1909, when *Hansard* became an official report commissioned by each House of Parliament, were all members' speeches printed fully in the first person. (Or, at least "substantially" verbatim.)[7] Previously, printed parliamentary debates appeared as indirect speech, a form of narration that suggests, but is not true dialogue:

> MR. H. BERKELEY believed that if this Bill became law it would have the effect of turning every pothouse into a theatre, and every theatre into a pothouse.

[4] For a longitudinal study of such developments, see Julie Stone Peters, *Theatre of the Book 1480–1880: Print, Text, and Performance in Europe* (Oxford University Press, 2000).

[5] Peters, *Theatre of the Book*, 167. [6] Peters, *Theatre of the Book*, 173.

[7] Michael MacDonagh, *The Reporters' Gallery* (Hodder and Stoughton, 1913), 441–3.

MR. BRADY also thought the passing of the Bill would reduce the drama to the lowest pitch it had ever stood at in the country.

MR. LOCKE said, he was not disposed to accept mere assertions as an answer to his arguments.[8]

Here we find a combination of direct and indirect speech. We can imagine the named members speaking, but only through an act of implicit translation from this printed form. The use of "believed" and "thought," as well as "said" without quotation marks, all either interiorize or simply narrativize what was actually a set of speech acts, that is, a dialogue. One could imagine a naive reader thinking that Berkeley did not speak at all, but that the debate's author omnisciently reports Berkeley's "beliefs." Why did parliamentary reports appear this way? In part because, until the 1890s, the reports were produced by cobbling together articles from multiple newspapers. The narrative style disguised the fact that the debates were summaries of summaries.

Modern *Hansard* transcribes Parliament's debates more clearly, treating speech like speech. In other words, it looks more like a dramatic text – complete with speech prefixes in bold followed by a colon. *Hansard* today purports to represent directly what was said by MPs, and thus to increase the transparency of parliamentary actions and to improve citizens' knowledge of government by making their representatives accountable for their speech. Parliamentary reports' old narrative–dramatic style, with its indirect discourse, could only gesture at such accountability. It never adopted – as a standard or as a format – the direct connection between speech and the speaking subject upon which dramatic texts insist. Thus we see in the evolution of printed parliamentary debates the belated adoption of a process that theatrical texts underwent in the Renaissance. These changes in legislative reporting, defined in part by adopting drama's print conventions, improved democratic transparency and accountability.

Changing how parliamentary reports transcribe spoken words and actions changes the legal character of those reports themselves. Such change is only possible after we have recognized the gap between the legal form and its (often disregarded) dramatic cousin. When we see

[8] HC Deb 13 June 1865, vol. 180, cols 178–83.

what legal forms elide in their failure to be fully dramatic, we can identify the shortcomings of the former and the possibilities inherent in the latter. In this particular case, once one recognizes that parliamentary debates might be written as dramatic texts, the apparatus of a dramatic text becomes available to bring Parliament to book in a new, newly legible form. Many other legal texts may benefit from a similar analysis – but first we must locate the dramatic potential that their current form suppresses.

Let us explore legal writing by seeking in legal documents – primarily legal transcripts – the elements of printed dramatic texts. By searching for dialogue, speech prefixes, stage directions, paratext, and didascalia, we will find some of law's essential performances – sometimes concealed, sometimes hiding in plain sight. Because law really is, sometimes, a type of performance, how law does and does not engage with drama's textual elements may help us learn what legal texts prioritize and exclude from the legal performances they encode or anticipate. Seeking the elements of printed drama, we will discover the slippages between legal texts and legal performances, and identify places where more care for that dynamic may create a better form – literally and figuratively – of law.

DIALOGUE

Unlike dramatic texts, most legal texts are not scripts for performance. Ex post facto scripts of legal performances – that is, transcripts, such as parliamentary reports – are far more common. A deposition transcript, for instance, is something designed not to be performed by others but to document what was already said. And yet legal material does encode dialogue. For instance, the Constitution of the United States includes a kind of dialogue: the oath to be administered when swearing in the president. Here is how the Constitution introduces the oath:

> Before he enter on the Execution of his Office, he shall take the following Oath or Affirmation: – "I do solemnly swear (or affirm) that I will faithfully execute the Office of President of the United States, and will to the best of my Ability, preserve, protect and defend the Constitution of the United States."

This differs from stage dialogue's formatting in two important ways. First, there is no speech prefix, but simply an order that the president-elect "shall take" the oath. Second, the oath's text appears in quotation marks – not, of course, the way dramatic texts indicate speech. Should we, then, regard the oath of office as dialogue at all?

The Constitution's text suggests we should not. And yet inaugural ceremonies have adopted traditional practices that transform the Constitution's pseudo-script into a real script for legal performance. In practice, the presidential oath truly is a dialogue. The dialogic nature of the oath begins with the addition of an oath administrator (traditionally, the Chief Justice of the Supreme Court) as the second speaker in the ceremony. Until the 1930s, the oath's administrator would read the oath as a question, to which the president-elect merely replied in the affirmative. In playscript form, that might look something like this:

> ADMINISTRATOR: Do you, George Washington, solemnly swear that you will faithfully execute the Office of President of the United States, and will to the best of your Ability, preserve, protect and defend the Constitution of the United States?
>
> PRESIDENT-ELECT: I do.

This form of dialogue gives all the words of the oath to a new, supporting actor, transforming the president-elect's "line" into a question delivered by the administrator. In this version, the president-elect, surprisingly, never speaks the constitutionally assigned dialogue at all, but instead speaks an entirely different line ("I do."), inherited from the normal form of oath-taking (e.g., weddings, sworn testimony). In other words, pre-1930s inaugurations relied on the implicit script of oaths and affirmations to transform the Constitution's unclear dialogue into a recognizable performance of oath-taking.

With Franklin Delano Roosevelt, the inaugural oath transformed into a new performance script. In a letter from February 1933, Roosevelt asked the clerk of the Supreme Court "whether it would be better for me to repeat the oath after the Chief Justice."[9] Chief Justice Charles

9 Franklin Delano Roosevelt to Charles Elmore Cropley, February 25, 1933, National Archives and Records Administration [NARA], FDR-FDRPSF, Inaugurations.

Evans Hughes affirmed this suggestion as "the more dignified and appropriate course" than the "I do" of previous generations.[10] Thus, since the 1933 inauguration, the oath's administrator has read each clause of the Constitution's oath to the president-elect, who replies piecemeal, thereby cumulatively saying all of the oath's language. Oath takers have also begun appending "so help me God." The script – and the hands of inaugural participants may well hold a printed script – might look like this:

ADMINISTRATOR: Please raise your right hand and repeat after me: I, Joseph Robinette Biden, Junior, do solemnly swear –

PRESIDENT-ELECT: I, Joseph Robinette Biden, Junior, do solemnly swear –

ADMINISTRATOR: – that I will faithfully execute –

PRESIDENT-ELECT: – that I will faithfully execute –

ADMINISTRATOR: – the Office of President of the United States,

PRESIDENT-ELECT: – the Office of President of the United States [etc.]

However formatted on the page, both the old and the modern forms of the oath differ significantly, in their text, from the Constitution's script for the oath. Each version transforms the Constitution's implicit text for performance into a proper script.

This may seem a rather overwrought, quibbling history of presidential oath-taking.[11] Yet to execute the Constitution's mandate, we must answer questions that document leaves unresolved: What does it mean to "take" an oath? What is the proper script for oath-taking? What words must be said, by whom, at what time? By understanding presidential oath-taking as a scripted performance, we notice how American law has left the assumption of executive power somewhat mysterious. The plain constitutional text requires rewriting and reformatting to be performed.

Theater scholars are accustomed to plumbing this magical space between print and performance, and to demystifying how the forms of dramatic texts enable particular performances. Less common to theater studies is the

[10] Charles Evans Hughes to Franklin Delano Roosevelt, February 28, 1933, NARA.

[11] Of course American law has a long tradition of such quibbling: No stretch of imagination is necessary to envision a federal lawsuit by various radical lawyers declaring the first 160 years of American executive branch actions unconstitutional because the president never "took" the oath properly.

examination of scripts derived from performances. Law, however, inverts theater's literal priority of the written word (i.e., the dramatic text that precedes the performance), depending less on performing implicit scripts than on producing ex post facto transcripts of legal performances. The legal system has not ignored the challenges posed by translating speech to writing; many conventions have developed to control some of the messiness inherent in that act of transformation. The Federal *Guide to Judiciary Policies* for producing court transcripts, for instance, features sixteen pages of guidelines.[12] These rules range from the material (paper sizes) to the visual (margins, lines per page, indentations) to the organizational (headings) and more. Such conventions help stabilize legal performances into reliable, purportedly neutral texts. (Intriguingly, the Judicial Conference seems to have established these rules initially only to regularize transcript fees charged by court stenographers.[13]) By standardizing transcripts, the rules predetermine what can and cannot be meaningfully recorded about a legal performance.

One rule stands out as particularly relevant when considering the relationship between legal and dramatic texts, a rule that determines what counts as "verbal content" in a transcript. The rule posits that, while the proceedings "must be transcribed as spoken," nevertheless,

> In the interest of readability, false starts, stutters, uhms and ahs, and other verbal tics are not normally included in transcripts; but such verbalizations must be transcribed whenever their exclusion could change a statement's meaning.[14]

Transcripts necessarily smooth out the messiness of speech: translate run-on thoughts into neat sentences and paragraphs; remove ambiguities; make what we hear with comprehension into something we read with understanding. But speech is not writing, and some of the information that speech carries is in precisely those things that writing seeks to suppress.[15] (As any good playwright knows, making meaning from

12 *Guide to Judiciary Policy*, Vol. 6: Court Reporting, §520.20.

13 *Record of the Judicial Conference*, September 1944. 14 *Guide*, §520.40.10(b)(2).

15 Were I so minded, I would offer a Derridean version of this argument. But I am not. See Jacques Derrida, "Signature/Event/Context," in *Limited Inc.*, trans. Samuel Weber and Jeffrey Mehlman (Northwestern University Press, 1988), 1–23.

"false starts, stutters, uhms and ahs" is a task at which actors excel.) Forensic linguist Anne Graffam Walker observed this problem in a 1986 essay that surveyed appellate justices about their use of transcripts. Appellate judges, she found, use transcripts "not just to get the facts, but to get at the meaning of the original proceeding which produced the facts by forming impressions of the setting and the participants in an effort to reach intelligent and fair decisions."[16] Significantly, judges rely on "contextual features" and "disfluencies" of language to get at that meaning.[17] In other words: Judges read transcripts like theater artists read scripts, mining them for clues about character and intent. Court proceedings are just as likely to carry meaning in those easily missed, suppressible aspects of speech as any line of Chekhovian dialogue.

A recent play that dealt with the relationship between American law and women presented a magnificent example of unexpected meaning in precisely such verbal clutter from a court proceeding. Heidi Schreck's *What the Constitution Means to Me* plays some of the recorded oral argument in *Griswold* v. *Connecticut*, the case that established a right to privacy, specifically a right to access birth control. To fully appreciate the effect of this scene, one must listen to the oral argument itself, which, in this written chapter, I cannot offer readers. But Schreck's script reproduces the necessary portion of it, with her own – rather than the court's – formatting and details. Her transcript reads:

> JUSTICE POTTER STEWART: Now that I've interrupted you, you've told us that in Connecticut the sale of uh . . . these devices is uh . . . not molested because they're sold for the prevention of disease. Is this uh . . . true about all of these devices that are covered uh . . . that each of them has the potential dual function of acting in a contraceptive capacity and as a prevention of disease, or only with respect to some of them?
>
> WILLIAM I. EMERSON: It's probably only true with respect to some, but some get by under the term "feminine hygiene," and uh . . . others uh . . . (*Cough*) uh . . . (*Cough*) uh . . . I – I – I just don't know about, but uh (*Cough*) uh . . . (*Cough*) They are, they are all sold in Connecticut drug stores on one theory or another.

[16] Anne Graffam Walker, "Context, Transcripts and Appellate Readers," *Justice Quarterly* 3, no. 4 (1986), 422.

[17] Walker, "Context, Transcripts and Appellate Readers," 425.

JUSTICE EARL WARREN: Is there anything in the record to (*Cough*) to indicate uh . . . (*Cough*) the uh, stem of the birth rate in Connecticut vis-à-vis the States that don't have such laws?[18]

Schreck is wholly uninterested in the substance of this dialogue. She plays the recording so the audience can hear these men's evident discomfort when talking about birth control. The audio recording and Schreck's transcription feature persistent, loud throat-clearing first from lawyer Thomas I. Emerson (Schreck mistakenly names him William) and then Chief Justice Earl Warren.

By contrast, here is what that passage looks like in the court's official transcript:

THE COURT: Now that I've interrupted you – you've told us that in Connecticut the sale of these devices is not molested because they're sold for the prevention of disease. Is this true about all of these devices that are covered, that each of them has the potential dual function of acting in a contraceptive capacity and as a prevention of disease, or only with respect to some of them?

MR. EMERSON: It's probably only true with respect to some, but some get by under the term "feminine hygiene," and others I just don't know about. But they are all sold in Connecticut drugstores on one theory or another.

THE COURT: Is there anything in the record to indicate the extent of the birth rate in Connecticut vis-a-vis the states that don't have such laws?[19]

No coughs; no throat clearing; just words. Yet as Schreck and her audience recognized – laughter was plentiful at both performances I attended, and can be heard in the film made of the stage production – the throat-clearing recharacterizes the entire argument, permeating the meaning of the men's purportedly substantive statements with a stark awareness that their speaking on this issue at all is injust.[20] The court's

[18] Heidi Schreck, *What the Constitution Means to Me* (Theater Communications Group, 2017), 34–5.

[19] Oral Argument in *Griswold* v. *Connecticut*, Supreme Court of the United States, argued March 29, 1965, 13.

[20] *What the Constitution Means to Me*, dir. Marielle Heller (Amazon Studios, 2020).

transcript, of course, records only what legal transcribers considered essential dialogue: the words.[21]

SPEECH PREFIXES

Speech prefixes in the law appear in striking forms. Some legal documents include a paratextual relative of speech prefixes, a list of *dramatis personae*. In case names, the central players in the dramatic conflict called litigation constitute the title itself: plaintiff v. defendant.[22] The printed *US Reports* go further, opening each volume with a list of the justices, along with the officers of the court. Opinions name the attorneys arguing and supporting each case, along with the filers of *amicus curiae* briefs.

Speech prefixes proper appear in transcript of arguments or depositions. The transcript from *Griswold*, for instance, refers to the lawyers by name, but to the justices – who do not, sad to say, speak simultaneously, like a Greek chorus – simply as "The Court." At some point since 1965, that practice changed, and modern Supreme Court transcripts do indicate which justice asked which question. The *Guide to Judiciary Policy*, however, still indicates that transcripts must refer to judges as "THE COURT." Lawyers maintain their identity – though the policy, in superannuated detail, insists on identifying female lawyers by their marital status ("MRS., MS., OR MISS"). Criminal defendants, after an initial identification by name, lose theirs: a defendant becomes simply THE DEFENDANT, like a character in a medieval morality play.

Yet all of these titles fall by the wayside during witness examinations. Witness examination transcripts record dialogue in a format that almost eliminates speakers as speaking persons. The proper prefixes are simply "Q" and "A" for "question" and "answer" (Figure 5.2).

The transcript is a pure dialogue, denuded of persons speaking, recording only the linguistic pursuit of truth.[23] Most examinations, however, also include some haggling about procedure, a "colloquy." And

[21] For a related critique of extra-verbal content at the Supreme Court, see Tonja Jacobi and Matthew Sag, "Taking Laughter Seriously at the Supreme Court," *Vanderbilt Law Review* 72, no. 5 (October 2019), 1423–96.

[22] Many plays could be retitled this way: *Romeo and Juliet* v. *Montagues and Capulets*.

[23] Deposition of Lawrence Paterson, Ohio Supreme Court, Case No. 2010–2029, 33.

him to define it. I asked him if he had any.

A When you say "photocopying machine," what do you mean?

Q Let me be clear. The term "photocopying machine" is so ambiguous that you can't picture in your mind what a photocopying machine is in an office setting?

A I just want to make sure I answer your question correctly.

Q Well, we'll find out. If you can say yes or no, I can do follow-ups, but it seems -- if you really don't know in an office setting what a photocopying machine is, I'd like the Ohio Supreme Court to hear you say so.

A I just want to make sure I answer your question correctly.

MR. CAVANAGH: There's different types of photocopiers, Dave.

MR. MARBURGER: You're speaking instead of -- you're not under oath. This guy is.

MR. CAVANAGH: I understand that, but I understand what his

5.2 Deposition of Lawrence Paterson, Ohio Supreme Court, Case No. 2010-2029, 33.

colloquies, unlike the questioning proper, revert to named speakers, but with different indentation, with each new speaker identified beginning "on the tenth space from the left margin." The convention results in an effect like a play within a play.

But which is the metatheatrical frame and which the staged performance? Colloquies control the flow of the question and answer, stepping out of the performance of the Q&A to negotiate the rules of engagement. Law's procedure, rules about what may be asked, what counts as badgering a witness, etcetera, all direct the play of Q&A. And yet the transcription format suggest that the question and answer is the main event. Q and A's dialogue is left-justified without indentation, while colloquies begin inside, as it were, the Q&A. And the abstraction of "Q" and "A," a kind of Beckettian scholasticism, implies large questions of major import, compared to the piddling asides of squabbling, named lawyers. Indeed, even in the formidably absurd deposition in Figure 5.2, Mr. Cavanaugh's casual, dismissive "There's different types of photocopiers, Dave" seems petty and insignificant next to A's profound semantic query – yes, A asks a question! – "When you say 'photocopying machine,' what do you mean?"

STAGE DIRECTIONS

Legal scripts thus follow their own, somewhat strange practices for speech prefixes. The rules for stage directions are far less clearly defined. Legal texts do not deal significantly with a legal proceeding's setting. Legal documents usually provide only vague indications of place-as-jurisdiction: the Southern District of New York, for instance. Dockets, perhaps, add some sense of geographic movement, with their indication of a case's journey through different jurisdictions. In legal texts, legal scenery is sparse.

This does not mean, however, that legal scenery does not exist or is unimportant. Linda Mulcahy argues that "the environment in which the trial takes place can be seen as a physical expression of our relationship with the ideals of justice."[24] Federal courts recognize this in their *Design Guide*, which combines Levitical detail about the sizes of clerks' desks with observations such as "Courtroom ceiling heights should reflect the solemnity of court proceedings. The raised judge's bench and ceiling

[24] Linda Mulcahy, *Legal Architecture: Justice, Due Process and the Place of Law* (Taylor & Francis, 2010). See also Martha J. McNamara, *From Tavern to Courthouse: Architecture and Ritual in American Law, 1658–1860* (Johns Hopkins University Press, 2004).

height contribute to the order and decorum of the proceedings."[25] The *Design Guide* attends to both the practical and the affective registers of architecture, recognizing that courts are environments loaded with symbolic and emotional meaning.

But on the page, law loses attention to space. The *Guide to Judiciary Policy* does not require transcripts to reveal in which physical venue proceedings took place. Without such information, we cannot grasp how each trial participant's relationship to the courtroom space may affect their behavior. Many actor training paradigms urge actors to familiarize themselves with the play's set, so as to make the actor comfortable enough to act truthfully.[26] Little wonder that the strange courtroom environment creates tension for so many people, or that law enforcement officers and expert witnesses perform so well on the stand: They may be familiar not only with court procedures, but with the very rooms in which they find themselves. (Even a seasoned witness may feel uncomfortable in a new courtroom.) As the *Design Guide*'s existence demonstrates, legal spaces matter. The absence of information about legal scenery in most legal texts does not imply neutral settings, but merely inattention to the physical environment's effects on legal performances.

Although scenery is usually absent from legal texts, information about the actions of bodies is not uncommon. The *Guide to Judiciary Policy* indicates that "It is the responsibility of the attorneys, as well as the judge in some instances, to note for the record any significant nonverbal behavior (i.e., physical gestures, and lengthy pauses on the part of a witness)." A court transcript will also indicate recesses, the commencement and conclusion of a proceeding, and even the jury's entrances and exits. In tracing the movement of bodies, as well as the discrete "scenes" of legal action, transcripts can look very much like plays. Yet law remains ambivalent about the import of legal actors' bodies. On the one hand, law often insists on presence in the

25 Judicial Conference of the United States, *US Courts Design Guide* (2021), 4–5, "Ceiling Height."

26 In other words, you have to create actual comfort and familiarity by rehearsing in the proper space, with the right furniture. See, for example, Uta Hagen, *Respect for Acting* (Wiley & Sons, 1973), chapter 8.

courtroom. Debates about televising trials still bring up fierce resistance from many in the judiciary.[27] On the other hand, the appellate process, for instance, turns the human beings in the case into merely dramatis personae.

Does the law script movement, as well as record its having occurred? The blank signature line on a contract is a kind of stage direction: The line instructs you to "sign here," your printed name beneath it like a speech prefix, interpellating you into your role as a legal person whose speech act–signature entails you to perform your contractual obligations. The signing body is absent in the signature, but also *was* present.[28] Or what of court orders, which initiate a whole set of reactions in other courts, other branches of government, and society generally? The hard, flat, ritual locution "It is so ordered," which punctuates most Supreme Court opinions, may set in motion very specific actions by affected parties. Like a good director, those parties must, as readers of the script, fill in the scenes necessary to enact the drama those words imply.

PARATEXT

Paratexts, a concept developed by Gérard Genette, are perhaps the least fruitful area in which knowledge of dramatic conventions might shed new light on the forms of legal texts.[29] This is true for two contradictory reasons: first, because paratexts – page numbers, introductory essays, footnotes, epigraphs – function so precisely in any given form, and, second, because the analytic possibilities of paratexts are generalizable across all types of texts. Legal citations exemplify the former, a legal practice so idiosyncratic that it may learn nothing from drama. Byzantium would blush at the modern prescriptive Uniform System of Citation propagated by *The Bluebook*, a system the intricacies of which

27 On law's deep commitment to "liveness" see Phil Auslander, *Liveness: Performance in a Mediatized Culture* (Routledge, 1999), chapter 4.

28 Derrida, "Signature/Event/Context," 20.

29 Gérard Genette, *Paratexts: Thresholds of Interpretation*, trans. Jane E. Lewin (Cambridge University Press, 1997).

have become, in the words of one critic, "an unhelpfully over-prescriptive approach to citation that has resulted in needless complexity."[30] Drama has no comparable standards for citations, and no internal models that might rescue law from its current citational morass. Headnotes exemplify the second type of paratext, familiar across genres, merely the law's version of introductions. The headnotes produced by Westlaw and Lexis, which summarize legal opinions, are simply a branded form of summary, subject to the same critique as the summarizing introduction for a dramatic (or any other) text.[31]

Might we still have something to learn from drama's paratextual elements? Act and scene divisions, for instance, are essential paratextual forms in drama, with a history that traces changes in dramatic production practices and the logic of dramatic plots. So-called French scenes, as one example, begin and end with the entrance or exit of a character; each configuration of people on stage creates a new scene.[32] Trial transcripts follow a slightly different logic, mandated to indicate such moments as "DIRECT EXAMINATION," "CROSS EXAMINATION," "PLAINTIFF RESTS," etcetera.[33] On the one hand, the transcript records the trial's formal process, its phases and movements, merely indicating the orderliness of the proceedings. Yet the trial, as lived by its participants, may not be quite so orderly. The transcript's headings reassert the proper dramatic script of the trial.[34] Its paratexts insist that the trial was a set of

[30] Christopher Sprigman et al., *The Indigo Book: A Manual of Legal Citation* (Public Resource, 2016), introduction. Compare the periodic, quixotic campaign against the overuse of footnotes in legal writing, exemplified by Abner Mikva, "Goodbye to Footnotes," *University of Colorado Law Review* 56, no. 4 (Summer 1985), 647–54 and Jack M. Balkin, "The Footnote," *Northwestern University Law Review* 83, nos. 1 & 2 (1988–9), 275–320.

[31] For an exemplary study of legal paratexts in literary works, see Robert Spoo, "Legal Paratexts," in Simon Stern, Maksymilian Del Mar, and Bernadette Meyler (eds.), *The Oxford Handbook of Law and Humanities* (Oxford University Press, 2019), 738–56.

[32] B. Rudolph Delson has noted how "outline-style formatting" of Supreme Court opinions, adopted originally to make long opinions "more approachable," encouraged partial voting on case outcomes. "Typography in the *US Reports* and Supreme Court Voting Protocols," *NYU Law Review* 76, no. 4 (October 2001), 1204.

[33] *Guide*, vol. 6., ch. 5, §520.40.20(b)(2).

[34] Marett Leiboff, *Towards a Theatrical Jurisprudence* (Routledge, 2019), chapter 2, calls law's insistence on dramatic structure Aristotelian.

discrete, sequenced events, from opening statements to presentations of evidence and examination of witnesses, to closing statements, and, eventually, to judgment.

DIDASCALIA

Nowhere does the booking of the law's performance matter more than in the realm of didascalia. Didascalia are the dramatist's expressive tool for encoding and directing emotion – from which we interpret meaning, motive, character, and so much else that we must understand to reach just outcomes. Without didascalia, with only dialogue, we risk misunderstanding legal performances entirely.

Two examples from comedy's interaction with law demonstrate the point. One is the famous story from one of Lenny Bruce's obscenity trials.[35] As Nat Hentoff reported during the trial,

> Lenny had to endure hearing his act performed before a three-judge panel by a nonperformer who had more or less memorized it. Nobody, certainly not the judges – who had refused to let Lenny do his own act – thought any of [the witness]'s surrogate act was funny. How could they? It not only wasn't funny. It was awful. . . .
>
> "This guy is bumbling," Lenny kept saying, "and I'm going to jail. He's not only got it all wrong, but now he thinks *he's* a comic. I'm going to be judged on *his* bad timing, *his* ego, *his* garbled language."[36]

As any comic will tell you, and as the officers of Bruce's court refused to acknowledge: it's all in the delivery.

The second example comes from one of the greatest courtroom films ever made, *My Cousin Vinny*.[37] (Once again, the written form of the chapter somewhat stymies the effect of my argument; I recommend a screening.) Early in the film, Ralph Macchio, playing the role of Bill, is interrogated for a crime the audience knows he did not commit. In a

[35] I am indebted to Christopher Grobe for this example.

[36] Nat Hentoff, *Free Speech for Me – But Not For Thee: How the American Left and Right Relentlessly Censor Each Other* (Harper Collins, 1992), 329.

[37] *My Cousin Vinny*, dir. Jonathan Lynn (Palo Vista Productions, 1992).

classic moment of dramatic misunderstanding, Bill believes he has been arrested for shoplifting a can of tuna. Having confessed his crime, Sheriff Farley (Bruce McGill) – seeking a confession to homicide – asks Bill, "At what point did you shoot the clerk?" Bill replies with what an audience member might describe as incredulity: "I shot the clerk," he says, looking stunned, and then repeats the statement with increased confusion and alarm.

Later in the film, the sheriff testifies in court about his interrogation of Bill, reading directly from a transcript. In his reperformance of this legal script, the sheriff uses an entirely different intonation, as though Bill had stated twice, plainly and factually, "I shot the clerk." The sheriff's testimony turns a suspect's statement of disbelief into a declaration of guilt, not by transforming any words, but by altering his delivery of those words. Intonation, like coughing, does not get recorded in a transcript. Sheriff Farley reasonably read Bill's testimony neutrally because, after all, the transcript itself is neutral, recording words, but not tone.

And yet there exists a clear tradition of indicating emotion in a dramatic text. Indeed, this very scene offers an example of that tradition. The screenplay for *My Cousin Vinny* notes, through its didascalia, Bill's attitude during the interrogation. The first "I shot the clerk" is to be delivered, "completely confused, rolling the words over." During the second statement, Bill "gives [a] questioning look to [Sheriff] Farley."[38] The screenplay does precisely what the interrogation's transcript would not: indicates attitude, emotion, tone, delivery.

Why does the law not attempt to put pathos into writing? How many Bills have had their fates sealed by such refusal?[39] It is a commonplace of modern dramatic texts to make clear – in parenthetical description, by using different fonts, or by other means – how a text ought to be acted. Yet legal transcripts do not take up these conventions from drama, reverting instead to an (illusory) pure textuality.

38 Dale Launer, *My Cousin Vinny*, revised February 27, 1991, 12.

39 Bill, fortunately, is acquitted due to exceptional lawyering by the titular Vinny and to expert testimony by Vinny's fiancée. The film, a fish-out-of-water tale of a New York lawyer in the South, derives much of its comedy through the characters' inability to understand each others' accents and intonations.

Though I have reached the end of my discourse, this chapter, I hope, can serve as a beginning. It offers some methods for thinking about legal texts as scripts that either precede or follow legal performances, and suggests how we might employ traditions from dramatic texts for that analysis. My brief examples indicate the deep, unresolved questions about how law textualizes its performances and performs its texts.

In some sense, this study arrives too early. Law does not yet have a proper book history (for instance, of trial transcripts), nor a proper performance history, though both have emerged in recent scholarship.[40] Perhaps, though, to explore either of those areas properly, law must first recognize that each involves the other. Any book history of law must take seriously the legacy and meaning of performance's textual conventions. And understanding law as performance remains challenging in no small part because legal writing seems designed to leave performance out.

Yet performance persists in the conventions of legal writing, printing, and publishing; we just have to look for it. If law is performance, legal texts are performance texts, and we should – at least sometimes – read them that way.

[40] On performance and law, see Julie Stone Peters, *Law as Performance: Theatricality, Spectatorship, and the Making of Law in Ancient, Medieval, and Early Modern Europe* (Oxford University Press, 2022), for "a history of law as a performance practice" and "a history of legal performance as a constitutive idea in western jurisprudence" (9). For some recent essays offering a book-historical approach to law, see Henrike Manuwald, "Book History," Andrew Benjamin Bricker, "The Functions of Legal Literature and Case Reporting before and after *Stare Decisis*," and Steven Wilf, "Legal Treatise," in Stern et al., *Oxford Handbook of Law and Humanities*; Thom Gobbit, ed., *Law | Book | Culture in the Middle Ages* (Brill, 2021); and older work by M. H. Hoeflich, including "Legal History and the History of the Book: Variations on a Theme," *University of Kansas Law Review* 46, no. 3 (April 1998), 415–32.

PART II

AFFECTATIONS

II.0 Carey Young, *Theatre of Punishment* (2017) Photograph from *Before the Law.*

CHAPTER 6

On Dialogue: Or Legal Performance in the Affective Space

Jesús R. Velasco

INTRODUCTION

For most contemporary bookish people, the fabric of theater is dialogue. But we strive to reconstruct in our minds this dialogue as it first appeared in the theater. We have not been to Epidaurus or Athens to attend the theatrical contests played by the *technitai*, the societies of Dionysian actors who brought both Sophocles and Aristophanes to the people. We have not seen Plautus's and Terence's comedies represented in Mérida's Roman theater (where Seneca's gruesome plays may also have been represented). We have not been in the city of Arras in the twelfth century to enjoy, with the rest of the populace, the theatrical contests frequently won by Adam de la Halle. We have not been part of the crowd at the Spanish *corral de comedias* to see with our own eyes Lope de Vega's *Fuenteovejuna*, Ana Caro de Mallén's *Valor, agravio y mujer*, or Calderón's *Alcalde de Zalamea.* When we travel to France or to Italy, it is not to attend court theater with the king or see a play performed for the marriage of a member of the house of Medici. But we strive to imagine them in the theater in three-dimensional space and time, in all their color and movement, to feel the passions the actors conveyed, to experience them in affective spaces. Why don't we do this with legal dialogues?

Julie Stone Peters's *Law as Performance* shows us that performance and theatricality are always at work in law, helping us reconstruct historical legal experience as three-dimensional experience: kinetic, sensory, affective.[1] Peters shows us that what Andreas Philippopoulos-Mihalopoulos has called the *lawscape* is in fact a *theaterscape*.[2] There is no lawscape – Peters demonstrates – without performance. No matter how many times theatricality has been criticized and censored as alien to the production of justice, it always finds its way into law. Focusing on gesture, movement, bodily position, actions that take place both on the thresholds of justice and in the thick of the judicial process, Peters shows us that performance is paramount for justice-making or law-making, or are these synonyms?

And yet, in striving to highlight the importance of the nonverbal elements of legal performance, *Law as Performance* sets aside (as a physicist would set aside air resistance to produce an experiment) one of the most central elements of performance generally and of legal performance in particular: dialogue. Dialogue is a constitutive element of legal performance: as central to it as both sound and silence are to music. In this chapter, in conversation with Peters's work, I take up the question of legal dialogue. Dialogue, as I will suggest, is in fact not only about exchange of words and ideas or the discovery of truth. It always involves the creation of affective space. This affective space establishes mood and emotion and gives meaning to the vocabulary of dialogue: It configures the stage of dialogue and the things that will happen on that stage.

Placing dialogue front and center may immediately bring to mind Bakhtin's *The Dialogic Imagination*, so central to discussions of discourse, literary form, and much more. But Bakhtin treats dialogue as if it were independent of its institutional formalization. Looking to dialogue only as a vehicle for the free play of ideas, the carnivalesque, he fails to register the structures and strictures of dialogue: its regulatory power. Nowhere is the regulatory power of dialogue more evident than in law, where

[1] Julie Stone Peters, *Law as Performance: Theatricality, Spectatorship, and the Making of Law in Ancient, Medieval, and Early Modern Europe*. Oxford: Oxford University Press, 2022.

[2] Andreas Philippopoulos-Mihalopoulos, *Spatial Justice: Body, Lawscape, Atmosphere*. Abingdon: Routledge, 2015. See also the lecture performance about spatial justice Philippopoulos-Mihalopoulos delivered at the University of Turku: https://sites.utu.fi/lawspacejustice/andreas-philippopoulos-mihalopoulos-performing-spatial-justice-full-video.

legislation, handbooks, and manuals strive to script legal dialogue: forcing the translation of the vernacular into orthodox legal language; excluding unorthodox affect.

However, if legal scripts govern dialogues, shaping affect, affect – which can never be fully controlled – also modifies legal scripts. In fact, legal dialogue always takes place in spaces charged with ungovernable affect – spaces where improvisation may undo the script, spaces where perplexity, danger, and the fight for survival are at play. Peters shows us that fight for survival in the ferocious struggles against scripted orthodoxy she describes – struggles that Foucault referred to as "illegalisms" and that he viewed as both inside and outside of the law, with the capacity to turn around the lawscape itself.[3] It is in that fight for survival, on that precarious threshold between law's scripts and improvisation, at once inside and outside of the law, that we can find a poetics of the affective space.[4] At the moment of silence or between silence and speech, on the threshold, performance, improvisation, and danger meet.

6.1 THE LAWS OF DIALOGUE

6.1.A DIALOGUE AS LAW. Dialogue has always been a regulatory form. It is necessary to foundational divisions: to distinguishing lawyer from philosopher, common law from canon law, jurist from prince, and so on. Dialogue makes such distinctions visible: It instantiates them. In the biblical text, the economy of the dialogue works so that alternating voices arrive to regulate life on earth. The first five books of the Bible, the Torah or the Pentateuch, are a long, developing dialogue between God and men, and between God-sent men and other men whose purpose is to announce and formalize a universal law not bound by time.

We might say here that dialogue is at the heart of the foundation of law: To put it in its starkest terms, dialogue founds law, and thus founds

3 Michel Foucault, *Surveiller et punir: Naissance de la prison.* Paris: Gallimard, 1975. See also Pierre Lascoumes. "L'illégalisme, outil d'analyse." *Sociétés et Représentations* (1996): 78–84.

4 See Irina Dumitrescu, "Improv," *Iberian Connections: Glossary*, https://iberian-connections.yale.edu/glossary/improv.

all norms (law in the broadest sense). But dialogue is also subject to particular laws. If dialogue is a regulatory form, engaging in it has always been a highly regulated process. It does not happen by itself, but according to rules, both soft and hard – the distinction is Lorraine Daston's.[5] These rules – or laws – allow one to recognize that what is taking place is a dialogue and not – for instance – a harangue, a monologue, or a cacophony. Dialogue in written form always respects the law of linearity of the linguistic sign (Saussure). It assigns each of the individuals in the dialogue their own *moment of enunciation*. The laws of dialogue regulate its time, its enunciation, its authority. Dialogue thus belongs to a world of the predictable. Literary dialogues, philosophical dialogues, instances of interrogation, theatrical dialogues create the sensation that one is in a culture of conversations whose interactions must be repeated in a particular way. A given theatrical dialogue may appear very different when the actors change, or when the stage changes, or even when the edition changes, but – even if performance is by definition not predictable – the words are composed to be predictable.

Regulating dialogue is no easy matter. This is because humans in general are very bad at listening to a full set of arguments before jumping to conclusions and interrupting the interlocutor – as a Spaniard, I can aver with no shame that an unregulated dialogue generally leads to a deafening polyphony and dissonance next to which Schönberg's *Harmonielehre* would pale. But once it is regulated, it becomes an extraordinary political and legal artifact for the definition of knowledge and for power generally.

6.1.B DIALOGUE IN PERFORMANCE: THE REGULATORY FORCE OF THE AFFECTIVE SPACE. This does not mean that dialogues function in a sterile void. The elements that shape theatrical dialogues appear in all dialogues: All dialogues require alternation; they require different voices, they require conclusions and choral understanding, they require dialectics.[6] Dialogue requires performance, and

[5] Lorraine Daston, *Rules: A Short History of What We Live By*. Princeton: Princeton University Press, 2022.

[6] Ana Vian Herrero, "Los paratextos dialógicos y su contribución a la poética del diálogo en los siglos XV a XVII," in *Paratextos en la literatura española (siglos XV–XVIII)*. Collection

performance elements themselves contribute to dialogue's regulatory function. In the Homeric agora, for instance, Telemachus needs to hold the staff to speak (Od. 2), so that *actual* dialogue may take place and then political and legal decisions can be made. This simple regulation – an object points to the right to speak and engage in discussion – creates the very dynamics in the circulation of power; power is invested in the staff itself. The staff is also a divine attribute – the staff-bearing God, Hermes, or Mercury, who is not only the messenger of the gods, but also Philology's husband – the ruling of the gods and their interpretation are married till death do them part.[7]

Dialogues require a place where all this can happen. They unfold not only through performance but also through performance in specific spaces. It would be wrong to envision performative space only through the Aristotelian concept of *ópsis* (ὄψις) which has to do with vision, or, in Latin *spectaculus*, what there is to be seen: Riccoboni translates it as *apparatus*; William of Moerbeke calls it *uisus*.[8] For performative spaces – the spaces in which dialogue takes place – are *affective spaces*. Aristotle seems to recognize that *ópsis* is affective, but his ideas about *ópsis* produce a certain frustration because he is so confused about the relationship between *ópsis* and affect. In some cases, the philosopher understands in an eye-opening way how the objects visible on stage, those *things* that are there to limit the action to a production of space, are charged with emotional and affective power (1453b1–3). But then he seems to contradict himself, for he says that it is much better when those emotions and affects derive directly from the fable or plot (the *mythos*, Latin translators

de la Casa de Velázquez 111, ed. Maria S. Arredondo, Pierre Civil, and Michael Moner. Madrid: Casa de Velázquez, 2009, 395–446.

7 The marriage and its juicy details were recounted and commented on by Martianus Capella. The Latin text has been edited and translated in France in several volumes by Les Belles Lettres, coll. Budé. An English version is available in William Harris Stahl, Richard Johnson, and Evan L. Burge, *Martianus Capella and the Seven Liberal Arts: Volume II, The Marriage of Mercury and Philology*. New York: Columbia University Press, 1992.

8 I am using the following editions. For the Greek text and the Riccoboni translation of 1585: *Poética de Aristóteles*, ed. Valentín García Yebra. Madrid: Gredos, 1974. For Moerbeke's translation: *Aristoteles Latinus. XXXIII: De Arte Poetica Guillelmo de Moerbeke Interprete*, ed. Erse Valgimigli, Enzo Franceschini, and Lorenzo Minio-Paluello. Bruges: Desclée De Brouwer, 1953. I cite the Bekker reference for obvious reasons.

always call it *fabula*). Just a few lines later (1453b7–8) Aristotle says that it is splendid that feelings like fear or compassion derive from *ópsis*. But then he writes that *ópsis* is less artistic, and also very expensive! He recognizes the power of the affective space, but does not want it roaming freely; he wants it well scripted and inscribed in the plot, with action governing passion.

What is an *affective space*?[9] Affects, Deleuze declared, are "*tout mode de pensée qui ne représente rien*" (all modes of thought that represent nothing).[10] When we say *affective space*, there seems to be a contradiction, because we are talking about something called *space* in which nonrepresentational thinking (*affects*) happen. And yet one feels that affects occur in space.

[9] A note on the definite article: When I say *the* affective space, I always mean this *the* to be of a collective and fluid character, thus avoiding giving the impression that there is only *one* affective space. In one form or another, the notion of *affective space* has been around for a while, and, in my view, it keeps its notional, intuitive character. Architects and sociologists have more recently been preoccupied with this idea, to better understand the emotional universe of subjects – because subjects are at the center of both architectural and sociological ideas of the affective space. See Federico Matteis, *Affective Spaces: Architecture and the Living Body* (1st ed.) Abingdon: Routledge, 2020. Matteis does beautiful work in defining the affective space, and the emotional states of people, based on architectural practices and urban design. In other words, Matteis's affective space is an analysis of the production of physical spaces. I think this is enormously productive for other kinds of work, including the one I suggest here. See also Silvia Gherardi, "The fluid affective space of organizational practices," *Qualitative Research in Organizations and Management*, 18.5 (2023), 1–19. Gherardi defines the affective space as a concept (which I do not think it is):

> The concept of "affective space" focuses on affect as spatialized and space as affective and draws attention to those ephemeral elements which have the power of holding all the practice elements together and give a qualitative tone to what is accomplished in practising. This approach entails a rethinking of space as processual, performative, multiple, affective and fluid. Consonant with the turn to practice, the turn to space and the turn to affect, I focus on the everyday spatial becoming of different organizing practices in order to rise the methodological question of how to conduct empirical research on affective spacing as an ephemeral and fluid phenomenon, that I name "fluid affective spacing."

[10] Gilles Deleuze, *Seminar on Spinoza*, class of January 24, 1978, at Vincennes. www.webdeleuze.com/docs/spinoza/fr/1978_00_02.pdf.

One cannot really quantify affect. But one might say that some spaces are more affective than others. From a merely intuitive perspective, affective space is the physical space where the volume of affects seems so extraordinary and hypertrophic that affects – as passions and emotions – seem to take hold of all the actions. In the affective spaces of institutional performance, affects steer the movement of those cohabiting in this space, even while this movement responds to or triggers a technical or scripted modality of communication. Certain kinds of affect are central to the regulatory power of dialogue.

Performance may be connatural to the production of affective space, but this does not mean that to produce affective space dialogue must literally be performed, as in a theater. Nontheatrical dialogue – while purely verbal – also relies on the production of affective space.

Indeed, affective space is crucial not only to the meaning of the dialogue but also to dialectical elements: It participates in generating the mood of reasoning and argumentation. Mood is sometimes dismissed as peripheral, but it is not at all peripheral. A couple of examples: In Cardinal Nicholas de Cusa's *Trialogus de Possest*, the three interlocutors are not together at first. Only Bernardus and Johannes seem to be together and willing to engage in a conversation with Cardinalis, who is none other than Nicholas himself. It is February 1460 (Nick is only fifty-nine), in the thick of the disputes between the cardinal and the Duke of Austria, Sigismund, who would fight him and imprison him for a few days in April of that year. Bernard of Krayburg (Bernardus) and Giovanni Andrea Bussi de Vigevano (Johannes) find the cardinal sitting by the fireplace. Nicholas looks at them *placido vultu* (with a calm face), telling them that it is too cold, in fact colder than other days, and that they should approach the fire and tell him why they have such serious expressions.[11] Here, the dialogue itself configures the affective space: the fireplace, the distance between Bernardus and Johannes on one side and Nicholas sitting placidly on the other, the doubt about whether they should approach him.

[11] I am reading the following edition: Nicolas de Cues, *Dialogue à trois sur le pouvoir-est: Trialogus de posest.* Paris: Vrin, 2013, 22.

This stream of affects, produced by the space, is entangled with questions of power. Here, the one in danger – Nicholas – is precisely the one who seems so calm and peaceful sitting by the fireplace, concerned only with the question of whether this February is colder than previous Februaries. In the dialogue, the three of them will delve into the question of the Can-Be (*possest*, which recent French translators and editors render as *povoir-est*, not less confusing than the Latin), and therefore the question of the power of God. A purely technical philosophical interpretation that ignored space would obscure the fact that the affective-spatial circulation of political and legal power is at odds with the forms of power circulation predicated by imperial actors and scripted in dialogue.

Let's look at another example: the river in which Phaedrus and Socrates cool their feet in the dialogue that has Phaedrus's name. They are going to discuss important questions about the immortality of the soul, but what they really need to do is to walk and cool their feet. It's hot out there, and – can one philosophize in this heat? This reference to the heat, their feet, and the river is so crucial to the meaning of the philosophical dialogue that it would probably cease to exist if the feet of those philosophers were not bare and wet.

All those elements exist deictically: The dialogue points to them but does not quite show them. The dialogue does not tell you, here is the fireplace, and the mantel is like that, and the fire is crackling, and there are pictures on top of it, nor (even better) does it show them as a simulacrum there, on stage before your eyes. The dialogue does not tell you anything other than the name of the river. But it is essential to the dialogue to imagine it: shallow enough to just cover the feet up to the ankles and no more (one cannot philosophize with the water up to the neck, except metaphorically). These elements of place are ghosts, *phantasmata* in Greek, that must be imagined by being matched to one's experiences with a fireplace or a shallow river (with a few small fish, hardly a school, trying to avoid your feet). In other words, they are neither an object nor an idea, but rather the affective ectoplasm of one's experiences or imaginations.

That experience invites you to identify with characters in the dialogue. Theoretically, you might identify with any of the characters. But this apparent freedom also serves a regulatory function. For dialogues are framed to allow readers initially to identify with the doctrinally incorrect position precisely so that they can be brought to reject that position – so that they can feel that they have arrived at the doctrinally correct position on their own (while the dialogue was of course always leading them there). I will offer an example. John Wycliff, the famous fourteenth-century priest and church reformer, as well as author of political-legal treatises, was also the author of another *Trialogus* or dialogue of three. He imagined a trialogical scene with a "*solidus philosophus*," a "*captiosus infidelis*," and a "*subtilis theologus*." The first one, Alithia the solid philosopher, speaks; the second one, Pseustis the clever unbeliever, objects; and Phronesis the subtle theologian decides.[12] Pseustis may momentarily persuade readers, but Phronesis helps them see that they were mistaken. The endgame is a series of doctrinal sentences laying out the conceptual, social, political, and economic meaning of Christian doctrine.

Alithia (truth) and Pseustis (liar) are character names that derive from the tradition of debate or dispute poetry in the Middle Ages, while the name Phronesis is of Aristotelian descent and indicates not just practical wisdom, but also prudence, which is a dianoetic virtue that has an extraordinary value in medieval political theory.[13] But this is almost *Hegelian* dialectics, in which theses and antitheses need to be addressed by somebody who has the power of synthesis – who can put in practice a multifaceted prudence that includes political, ethical, and philosophical analysis. Phronesis will be in charge of conveying a synthetic truth and making it portable: Readers can ultimately become Phronesis and think and express themselves *as* him.

Thinking *as* him also means partaking of the affective space, getting involved in this creation of a phantasmic place where feelings, emotions, and affects of a certain kind necessarily happen. Nicholas's placid face when he looks at the others from the fireplace is exactly the kind of expression that can transmit tranquility and draw the reader's focus to

[12] John Wycliff, *Trialogus cum supplemento Trialogi: Joannis Wiclif ; illum recensuit, hoc primum edidit, utrumque commentario critico instruxit Gotthardus Lechler.* Oxford: Clarendon Press, 1879, 38.

[13] Pierre Aubenque, *La prudence chez Aristote.* Paris: Presses universitaires de France, 1963.

the complicated matter for discussion. In the midst of political turmoil involving the very person who seems to be so calm, the readers are drawn by that calm to attend in calm themselves. The cooling of the philosopher's feet transmits to the reader the daily experience of philosophy: Philosophizing is not an activity that takes place in a given, hieratic space, but in a placid, cool everywhere. Wycliff may give readers the sensation that they have been thrust into the middle of polarized polemics, torn between truth and lie. But the text also helps readers feel affectively that prudence is central and available to anyone – as Aristotle suggested in his *Ethics* to his son – and therefore that his sentences are portable: capable of being transferred, owned, and used by others.

6.1.C THE AFFECTIVE SPACE BEYOND THE SCRIPT: TURNING OFF THE LIGHTS OF LITERARY HISTORY. The dialogues I have referred to, one could say, are *literary* dialogues. They belong in a generic storage room well described and ordered by the institution we call literary history. It is a boring institution that plays nevertheless a very important role in the organization of knowledge, and it is at the center of the narratives that produce literature itself. Furthermore, literary history is an apparatus that delimits the range within which literary artifacts operate: By designating genres and establishing their rules, literary history also permits and extols intergeneric relations; literary history defines the modes of exchange, relationship, and transformation within a certain space, not unlike a topological theory. Literary history also allows us to say, "well, this is literature," and to be certain that by doing it we are also understanding the *cordon sanitaire* that exists between this act of intellectual creativity and other acts of intellectual creativity – law, for instance. Establishing the limits and generic characteristics of some literary objects activates them only within their own network, where they do whatever work they need to do, while we can sing from the top of the cliff: *Suave, mari magno turbantibus aequora ventis, e terra magnum alterius spectare laborem.*[14]

14 "It is pleasant, when the winds are buffeting the waves on the great sea, to watch from the land the great struggle of another." Lucretius, *De Rerum Natura* II.1–2.

What happens when we turn off the lights of literary history? Literary dialogues turn out to be not only literary; they cannot be constrained within the literary canon. Philosophical dialogues turn out to be not just philosophical. It is like the museum at night. Objects become alive and start doing all sorts of things and keeping all sorts of conversations while we sleep in the peace of our thresholds – Homeric heroes used to have their beds made in a threshold of the palace, probably to be protected by the lintel. What happens when literary history is not watching, is that all things are mixed up, and that in our dreams the literary and the non-literary start conversations (dialogues, as it were) that shape some of the ways we will think at sunrise.

What we learn from turning off the lights of literary history is that affect is not always so tame. Wycliff may use the affective space to draw readers toward prudence. But the history of dialogue is – I would argue – the history not only of affective space as a regulator but of the permeability of the affective space: On one side enter the formalization and regulation of dialogue, and, on the other side enter improvisation, unscripted action, unpredictable affect. The affective space of the dialogue cannot be entirely controlled by implicit directives. It is in fact so vast that it cannot be contained by any kind of organizational principle or institution. Affects are unpredictable: They happen without specific forms of representation, without even being named, qualified, or described.

Dialogues are thus central producers not only of regulatory affect but also of the kind of affective space where unpredictable things can happen. The prevalence of the affect is what makes a dialogue so powerful in its performance: Affect opens up the dynamics of thinking, rather than enclosing it within action and teleological plot. Dialogues are also, as a form, especially good at illuminating the unpredictability of affective space. They show us the fabrication of affective space in action, as it is happening in the theater of the dialogue, as it arises. Appearing to belong to a world that is fully scripted, dialogues highlight the affective space by revealing the tension between scriptedness and affect. The scripted, predictable words are shaped by and issue in a world of unpredictable affects. Telemachus's staff may be a tool of power, signifying the rules of dialogue. It may effectively found law. But it may also foster trepidation, doubt, love, and a thousand and one other unpredictable effects.

6.2 DIALOGUE IN THE LAWSCAPE

6.2.A DIALOGUE AND THE PRODUCTION OF LEGAL TRUTH. I will now turn from dialogue as law and the laws of dialogue generally to look specifically at dialogue in the lawscape. Rituals, linguistic formulae, forms of power circulation, and reasoning are some of the scripted modalities of legal communication, all carefully set up to organize the judicial process in its entirety. The court of law operates according to fictions and rituals. I say fiction with the utmost respect. Fiction, here, does not mean that something is not true, or that it is a lie, or even that it is a kind of literary genre. There is nothing truer than a court of law. My notion of fiction is in conversation with Yan Thomas's work on the artifices of truth.[15] Because the court of law is not a spontaneous element of nature, but rather an institution, it is by necessity artificial, fabricated, fictionalized, just as all artifices of truth are fictionalized. Legal ritual, for its part, does two things. First, it reassures those meeting in specific legal spaces that everything is going to happen according to plan, time, procedure, and proper movement. Second, it establishes its own myth, its own narrative: self-contained and with a clear, auto-poetic etiology. Fictions and rituals guarantee that the dialogue taking place inside the court of law is going to produce something we call *truth*.

Dialogue is central to the ritual production of legal truth. Here we can see with particular clarity the limits of Bakhtin's conception of the dialogic. For legal dialogue is one of the most powerful scripted modalities for organizing law: for controlling the lawscape and all those subject to it. How do we talk about *dialogue* in the court of law? Interrogation – one could easily object – is hardly dialogue. But here is where things get perhaps more interesting. In his *Diálogo en la muerte del marqués de Santillana* (ca. 1458), Pero Díaz de Toledo describes dialogue as a conversation between someone who asks and someone who

[15] Yan Thomas, *Les operations du droit.* Paris: Seuil/Gallimard, 2011.

responds.[16] Interrogations certainly take the form of a dialogue. At the same time, the questioner and the respondent are entirely distinct from each other, with power on one side and subjection on the other. The questioner creates the script for the respondent. And often the interrogation is, quite literally, scripted in advance: The interrogator follows the formula laid down in the interrogation manual.

Like dialogue generally, legal dialogue does its work in part through performance and the affective space. In law (as Peters suggests), space and performance operate together: through (for instance) the architecture of the courtroom, the atmosphere of viewing and being viewed, of hearing and being heard. Affective space in law is crucial for the constitution of the *lawscape* or the *legal atmosphere* (as Philippopoulos-Mihalopoulos also calls it): the affective universe of the law, outside which there is nothing. Law, in other words, takes place through affective microperformances. These are governed by a concentrate of dialogue, with extraordinary consequences for the judicial process. These operations can be seen in action with particular clarity in the microperformances that pervade the inquisitorial system and its many articulated arms, not least in the sacrament of confession.

6.2.B THE CONFESSIONARY. The Fourth Lateran Council of 1215 mandated that all Christians confess at least once a year in front of a confessor and speaking the same language.[17] During the thirteenth

[16] There is an annotation from one sixteenth-century reader in one of the margins, "dialogo quid," joined to the main, central text with a fine line, meaning that this part of the text contains the "quid," the "what is" a dialogue. And Pero Díaz de Toledo wrote: "(dialogo es palabra conpuesta de dos palabras griegas (dia en griego quiere en latin dezir dos (& logos fabla asi que dialogo querra dezir fabla de dos uno que pregunta a otro que responde. /(& los sabios antiguos como socrates (& plato (& tulio en diuersos libros suyos proçedieron en esta manera por explicar mejor (& mas conplidamente su entençion." Pero Díaz de Toledo, *Diálogo e razonamiento en la muerte del marqués de Santillana.* BNM Mss 10226: fol. 2r.

[17] *Constitutiones Concilii quarti Lateranensis una cum Commentariis glossatorum,* ed. Antonio García y García. Vatican City: Biblioteca Apostolica Vaticana, 1988. See in particular *constitutio* 21, but also *constitutio* 9, p. 57:

> Quoniam in plerisque partibus intra eandem ciuitatem atque diocesim permixti sunt populi diuersarum linguarum, habentes sub una fide uarios ritus et mores, districte precipimus ut pontifices huiusmodi ciuitatum siue

century and (still more) in the fourteenth, inquisitors – who had acquired an extensive knowledge of diverse spiritualities active in many different places – began to regulate these legally mandated dialogues between the Christian subject and the confessor.[18] In this legislative moment in particular, we can begin to understand the importance of the techniques of law-writing: how these techniques in fact – without necessarily changing any technical vocabularies – open the door to a juridification of the world – the complex construction of a system meant to manage a wild lawscape. They do this in part through the scripting of dialogue.

Confession involves the celebration of the sacrament of reconciliation in a private setting through oral utterance. Though the place of confession has changed over time – there have been many different formulae for making sure that the direct contact between confessor (in lieu of God) and penitent are undisturbed – confession always happens in a specific location that deploys its own universe of affects, emotions, and feelings. Let us call this setting a *confessionary*. The confessionary became over time an artifact, a small private stage where the actors arrive from different places to engage in dialogue. There, the confessor and the penitent can be isolated from other people, to protect the privacy of the penitent – but also the privacy of the dialogue and the administration of both penance and absolution.

After the Council of Trent, which devoted many canons to the question of confession, Cardinal Carlo Borromeo ordered some modifications of the process of confession (the ritual). At the same time, he ordered the creation of a beautiful piece of furniture, reasonably portable, that is heavily protected and enclosed.[19] Later on, it would come endowed with a latticework window to separate the confessor from the penitent and avoid sexual contact. (In Spanish, those priestly sexual

diocesum prouideant uiros idoneos qui, secundum diuersitates rituum et linguarum, diuina officia illis celebrent et ecclesiastica sacramenta ministrent, instruendo eos uerbo pariter et exemplo.

18 Jacques Berlioz, *Le Pays cathare: Les religions médiévales et leurs expressions méridionales.* Paris: Seuil, 2000.

19 Trento's fourteenth session, celebrated under the papacy of Julius III on November 25, 1551, is entirely devoted to the sacrament of reconciliation. It fosters private confession and makes it preferable to public penance.

predators were called *frailes solicitantes*).[20] The canons of the Second Vatican Council removed the latticework and most of the private elements, with the aim of establishing a true dialogue between the confessor and the penitent. They meet under the lintel, in the threshold, to *facilitate* the dialogue, as the French Catholic authorities explain in their definition of the *confessional*: "*On tend aujourd'hui, en beaucoup d'endroits, à choisir un lieu plus propice au dialogue entre le prêtre et le pénitent pour la célébration de ce sacrement.*"[21] One genealogy of confession could be told from the perspective of this portable stage in which the penitent has been conducted from the spectacle of public penance or their private, unidirectional conversation with God to a private dialogue within a space and stage that contains it, offering different degrees of intimacy between the penitent and the confessor.

Those are elements that envelop the dialogic experience of confession through the configuration of space and place. But texts also importantly shape the experience of confession. Confession handbooks began to appear after the Fourth Lateran Council, and (still more) after the (heavily glossed) codification of Raymond of Penyafort's *Summa de Penitentia et Matrimonio*. Just as inquisitorial handbooks insist on the specific questions the inquisitor must ask and the answers the interrogated may give, so confession handbooks insist on the specific questions the confessor must ask and specific answers penitent may give. Alfonso X's vernacular code of legislation from the second half of the thirteenth century – the *Siete Partidas* (of which more later), and in particular the *First Partida* – contains forty-five laws specifying the rules of confession (from 1.4.17 to 1.4.46). This includes the kind of questions the confessor must ask (*Partidas* 1.4.26), and the ways the confessor must *pescudar*: that is, engage in an inquest into the sins of the penitent (*Partidas* 1.4.25).[22] In

20 Adelina Sarrión Mora, *Sexualidad y confesión: La solicitación ante el Tribunal del Santo Oficio (siglos XVI–XIX)*. Madrid: Alianza Editorial, 1994. Juan Antonio Alejandre, *El veneno de dios: La Inquisición de Sevilla ante el delito de solicitación en confesión*. Madrid: Siglo XXI de España, 1994.

21 "Today in many places we tend to choose a place for the celebration of this sacrament that is more propitious for the dialogue between the priest and the penitent." https://eglise.catholique.fr/glossaire/confessionnal.

22 The verb "pescudar" is the same verb as "pesquirir," and lexically dependent of the noun "pesquisa," which is the Castilian translation of the Latin "inquisitio."

this same section in the *Partidas*, we learn that confessing is a performance in time (in the moment) and, specifically, a performance of the body. Therefore, confessions must take place in person and orally, not by letter or through a messenger. This is because body language does not lie (*Partidas* 1.4.30).

The *Siete Partidas* are particularly important to the history of legal dialogue and its dominion over the body for two reasons. First, they combine canon and civil legislation in a single royal codification. As a result, royal and civil jurisdiction expands to many different branches of the law, thus covering the whole universe of law. Second, the *Siete Partidas* are written in the Castilian vernacular (Spanish, if you wish). In this, they are unlike canon law in general.[23]

Elsewhere, I have studied the importance of the decision to legislate in the vernacular.[24] Briefly, canon law in the Spanish vernacular – as inaugurated in the *Siete Partidas* – created a novel sensation of communication between laypeople and confessors. The *Partidas* do not seem to have been available between the death of Alfonso in 1284 and the moment in which they were first promulgated (with amendments) in 1348. However, around 1316, perhaps in Salamanca, a certain Martín Pérez published a *Libro de las confesiones.* This handbook tailors the questions to be asked to the specific penitent, mandating that the confessor consider the social, economic, and professional circumstances of the penitent. The book was widely read and copied, as well as summarized in numerous manuscripts.

It would take too long to explain how this handbook and others depend on canon law, on glosses, and on the professorial tradition of

[23] For instance, about fifty years after the Lateran canons on doctrine and penitence (around 1224–1226), Raymon of Penyafort – a Dominican close to inquisitorial movements and even closer to Pope Gregory IX, for whom he compiled the *Liber Extra* – produced the *Summa de Pœnitentia.* The latter, obviously written in Latin, was central to Dominican confessors, who were the most observant among all inquisitors for centuries, deployed all over the French Hexagon. Christine Ames Caldwell, *Righteous Persecution: Inquisition, Dominicans, and Christianity in the Middle Ages.* Philadelphia: University of Pennsylvania Press, 2009 and *Medieval Heresies: Christianity, Judaism, and Islam.* Cambridge: Cambridge University Press, 2015.

[24] Jesús R. Velasco, *Dead Voice.* Philadelphia: University of Pennsylvania Press, 2020: chap. 3.

certain schools.[25] The point I want to make here is that we can see in them how the microperformance of confession micromanaged legal subjects precisely through differentiation and specificity. These dialogues, which governed the microperformance of confession through specific questions and potential answers, served two functions. First, while allegedly serving the spiritual health of the penitent, they in fact served the spiritual strength of the universal church. Second, they helped confessors gain exact knowledge of their communities' customs, habits, social relations, forms of spirituality, and so on. In short, they served knowledge as power.

Antonio García y García, the first editor of the *Libro de las confesiones*, used to say that Martín Pérez's book constituted a *radiography* of medieval society because of the interconnection between the questions to be asked and the social, economic, or political position of the penitents. But it is not a radiography. The handbook *purports* to identify the *actor* and the social and professional roles those actors play, so that the confessor can immediately identify their lifestyles, their sins, and so on. But all of the questions are framed to identify a set of predetermined identities. The confessor must ask these specific questions because he must fit every legal subject into the handbook's prescribed taxonomy of legal subjecthood.

As Peter Linehan wrote in his review of García y García's edition, whatever there is in the *Libro de las confesiones*, it certainly does not describe the intricacies of 1316 Salamanca (or any other place, for that matter): It is, in fact, no more correct for Salamanca than for Southend-on-Sea (which, surprisingly, is a coastal city in Essex). For its entire apparatus of ideas about social, economic, political, and professional identities derives not from the people of Salamanca but from canon lawyers of the 1250s. It is not a description but a recipe. In other words, this fake radiography represents a mandate for a well-structured society in which *actors* are connected to *actants* – that is, to the narrative

[25] Scholars have done that already in Antonio García y García's edition: Martín Pérez, *Libro de las Confesiones*. Madrid: Biblioteca de Autores Cristianos, 2002; and in Hélène Thieulin-Pardo, ed., *Confesionario. Compendio del Libro de las confesiones de Martín Pérez: Edición y presentación*. Paris: e-Spania Books, 2012.

roles available through the canon lawyers' dry, unnuanced understanding of narrative actions.[26]

Among the handbooks, the *Libro de las confesiones* is especially illuminating for numerous reasons. First, it is a vernacular handbook whose audience – Martín Pérez proudly explains – is composed of clerics who cannot read Latin (*illiterati*), and who are therefore particularly in need of correct practical and theoretical knowledge to guide their work in the confessional. (He in fact explicitly excludes those who *do* know Latin or may be well versed in the intricacies of canon law, rather comically dismissing them as readers.) Second, the *Libro* is – like confession itself – extraordinarily oral in its style: it addresses the perplexed confessor in the singular second person (*tú*, the singular "you"). Third, it works, in a sense, algorithmically. All dialogic procedures take the conditional form: If the penitent says X, then you say Y. This means that the confessor must not only engage in a careful analysis of the penitent before asking questions, but also that he must choose the question appropriate to the penitent's answers. In other words, not only do the answers depend on the questions: The questions depend on the answers. Fourth, these algorithmic dialogues depend on the highly granular social distinctions the text identifies. These granular distinctions create the sensation that the *Libro* contains a comprehensive account of the social order generally (an account that many of the "illiterate" confessors must have realized was ill-matched to reality, but is often incredibly funny and entertaining: Who wouldn't want a jongleur in their confessional if he looked like the jongleur in the handbook?)

Two other reasons that the *Libro* is especially illuminating – and especially pertinent here – have to do with its specifically legal character. First, Martín Pérez recognizes that this dialogue, which takes place in the confessionary, is essentially of a legal character. The confessionary is the threshold between earth, where the penitent lives, and heaven, from which descends the law that governs confession. Therefore, this piece of furniture – the confessional – is a sort of vessel connecting two spaces

[26] Mikhaïl Xifaras, "Théorie des personnages juridiques," *Revue française de droit administratif* 2 (2017), 275–287. In this work, Xifaras applies Greimas's semiological theory of actants to juridical roles and types.

that otherwise have no physical connection. In this sense, all confession is nothing other than a rehearsal of the last judgment, in which all sins are weighed and a final sentence issued. Second, the confessor appears there not just as someone who has the capacity to give penance and absolve sins but also as a sort of preliminary judge who determines the specific legal status of the sin and – where a court must make a further determination – decides which court is the appropriate one. In the dozens of situations involving excommunication where the confessor does not have jurisdiction to make a decision and impose a penance, he must know which court has jurisdiction over the case.

6.2.C INQUISITIONS. Confessionary interrogations and questionnaires were in fact inseparable from the legal machinery of thirteenth- and fourteenth-century inquisitions: For instance, the inquisitions in southern France starting around 1230, when Gregory IX asked the Dominicans to do "*quaedam inquisitiones*" to better repress the emergence of heresies against the canons of the Fourth Lateran Council of 1215; or the *grandes inquisitions* of 1245 and 1246; or the inquisitions recorded by Jacques Fournier, the bishop of Pamiers, in the first quarter of the fourteenth century.[27] The archives contain a detailed register of the interrogations: snippets of dialogue taking place between inquisitors and the inhabitants of places from Foix to Béziers, from Albi to Toulouse. The inquisitors register these interrogations not only as a service to the widening control of the church but because they

[27] Jean Duvernoy can be considered the pioneer of the studies of the French inquisitions, and his work is both fascinating and meticulous: *Le Registre d'inquisition de Jacques Fournier, évêque de Pamiers, 1318–1325: Manuscrit Vat. latin n 4030 de la Bibliothèque vaticane, publié avec introduction et notes par Jean Duvernoy* (3 volumes). Paris: Tchou, 2004 [1965]. *Le Dossier de Montségur, interrogatoires d'inquisition, 1242–1247*, 1998. *Le procès de Bernard Délicieux, 1319*, ed. Jean Duvernoy, 2001. *L'Inquisition en Quercy: Le registre des pénitences de Pierre Cellan, 1241–1242*, 2001. Emmanuel Leroy Ladurie did focus on the inquisition of Jacques Fournier in Montaillou, in his classical *Montaillou, village occitan de 1294 à 1324*. Paris: Gallimard, 1975. See also the groundbreaking work of Mark Pegg, *The Corruption of Angels: The Great Inquisition of 1245–1246*. Princeton: Princeton University Press, 2001. Mark Pegg, *A Most Holy War: The Albigensian Crusade and the Battle for Christendom*. Oxford: Oxford University Press, 2008. Michael Barbezat. *Burning Bodies: Communities, Eschatology, and the Punishment of Heresy in the Middle Ages*. Ithaca: Cornell University Press, 2018.

themselves have become actors in a drama that represents the multidirectional desire of inquisitorial curiosity.[28]

Inquisitorial curiosity is always filled with a strange violence. It forces the inhabitants of villages (sometimes full villages) to explain what they believe, how they believe what they believe, and their lives and habits. At the same time, it attempts to reduce singular or communitarian forms of spirituality to a doctrine of beliefs. The interrogations result in few trials, but the manuscripts constitute a body of knowledge that allows the church to establish what orthodoxy means and reconfigure the Christian subject.[29] In the records of the Inquisition, interrogation appears as dialogue, but also as a product of the voracious drive of the interrogator.

The dynamic of the desire of dialogue – the desire to perform dialogue – can be seen clearly in the *Siete Partidas.* The *Third Partida* is devoted to procedural law, and chapter 16 of that *Partida* is about interrogation. Law 26 in chapter 16 of the *Third Partida* regulates the interactions that produce witness deposition. After taking the oath according to the Spanish custom (*Partidas* 3.16.25), the judge must take the witnesses, one by one, to a separate space, away from the rest of the parties involved, with only the company of a learned notary ("*algunt escribano entendido*"). The *Partida* underscores the importance of the affective environment. The judge, it explains, must listen to the witness very calmly or *mansamente* (which is an adverb that can also translate as "meekly"). The judge's countenance must inspire peace of mind and reflect absolute absence of antagonism. Likewise, the judge must remain fully engaged with the witnesses, listening to them without interrupting them and looking straight at their faces. It is in these precise and favorable conditions of controlled emotion that the witness can now speak,

28 Duvernoy's last three chapters of *Inquisition à Pamiers, interrogatoires de Jacques Fournier: 1318–1325,* 1966, contain the story of the last Cathar, Simon Bélibaste, who was executed in Villerouge-Termenès in the fourteenth century. This and many other inquisitorial documents were at the origins of some of the most beautiful works of microhistory, including those of Natalie Zemon Davies and Carlo Ginzburg.

29 The whole purpose of the Fourth Lateran Council is, by fighting against "heretical pravity," to establish a clear doctrine which those who have a deviant (according to the Catholic Church) experience of spirituality and religion must repeat and internalize.

with the sensation that interrogation has been replaced with conversation or dialogue.

And yet a fundamental barrier separates the witness from the judge: Even though they seem to speak the same language, this language is filled with polysemic potentiality. The dialogue is profoundly diglossic. A thirteenth-century glossator of the Justinian Code puts it in a very clear way – and Alfonso also explains something similar in the *Seventh Partida* : "*verba legis debent intelligi secundum propriam significationem, non secundum usum communem loquendi*" ("the language of the law must be understood according to its technical characteristics, not according to the common usage of the words").[30] In other words, recognizing that the interrogator and interrogated do not speak the same language, the *Partida* insists that the judge translate the words of the witness into technical legal language to arrive at a correct understanding: one that conforms with orthodoxy.

Of course, the spoken word is not reproducible in writing. No notary could replicate it in written discourse. The spoken word is usually agrammatical: The witness testifies in solecisms, imprecisions, syntactic and semantic fragments, and so on. No matter how peaceful and emotionally stable the conditions in which the deposition takes place may be, living voice, because it is alive, is always raw. Therefore, judges, lawyers, and notaries feel the need to process it, to edit it. The initial editing takes place orally, with the judge translating immediately during the interrogation itself and then transferring this oral translation to writing. The *Partida* explains this rather theatrically, offering a script for the judge or notary: "Now listen to me, for I wish you to hear if I understand you well," the judge must say,

> and he should then repeat what the witness stated. If he remembers what he said, the judge should immediately cause it to be written down, or should himself do so, well and faithfully, so that nothing may be either omitted or added, and after all this has been done, he should cause it to be

30 Gero R. Dolezalek, "Lexiques de droit et autres outils pour le ius commune (XIIe–XIXe siècle)," in *Les manuscrits des lexiques et glossaires de l'antiquit é tardive à la fin du Moyen Âge*, ed. Jacqueline Hamesse. Louvain: Université de Louvain-la-Neuve, 1996, 353–376.

> read to the witness, and if the latter thinks that it is correct, he should admit it. Where he sees that there is anything to correct, this should immediately be done, and after everything has been corrected, the judge should cause the testimony to be read to the witness, and if the witness thinks that it is correct he should say so. (*Partidas* 3.16.26)

A complex process of grammaticalization is going on – a negotiation between the judge, the notary, and the witness – in which the judge and notary transform the witness's speech into orthodox terms, first orally, and then in writing. A process of refinement and purification results in the dead voice (*vox mortua*) of the text. But recognizing the role of dialogue reminds us that the dead voice is always in dialogue with the *viva vox iuris*: the living voice of the sovereign, the *lex animata*. The text is the result of not a single living voice but of the interaction of several living voices, collaborating and negotiating to produce an archivable object that can be used as proof. The process guarantees its survival and future utility for law.

6.2.D OÑA V. FRÍAS: RECONSTRUCTING THE AFFECTIVE SPACE. Few things are more boring than surveying. And yet owning land, or enjoying land by any means – rental, usufruct, colonization, and so on – is primarily a question of surveying.

Surveying is what sets in motion the *pesquisa* or *inquisitio* (hereafter, inquest) that put the Monastery of San Salvador de Oña before the city of Frías in 1280–1281.[31] The jurisdictions of the monastery and city are different: The monastery is an *abadengo* jurisdiction whose head is the abbot; Frías is a *realengo* jurisdiction belonging to the king. However,

[31] Both the monastery and Frías are located in what is today the province of Burgos. The monastery is a great colonial artifact, and its expansion coincides with the expansion of the Order of Cluny, of which it was part since 1033. The city of Frías, in its turn, was – and still is – an important geostrategic node connecting the Spanish *meseta* with the northern ports. It overlooks the valley of the river Ebro from the top of its castle, which belonged to the king from the time that Alfonso VIII gave the city the *Fuero de Logroño* in 1202 to the fifteenth century, when it became part of the *jurisdicción señorial* of the Velasco family. Between San Salvador de Oña and Frías, one can take a walk of three to four hours, which is, by all accounts, not too much (around eleven miles or just over seventeen kilometers).

looking at the map of the dispute – prepared by Isabel Alfonso and Cristina Jular – we can see the extent to which the two territories overlap.[32] Many of the more than 100 witnesses summoned by the two parties to give testimony about links of dependence, customs, taxes, and infractions come from the same places. These are two powerful domains very close together, sometimes sharing the very same territory.

Looking only at the final manuscript representing the *pesquisa*, one might miss two important things. First, there must have been other versions of the documents that transmit this *pesquisa*, given the crossed references contained in the extant manuscript that do not find resolution in this manuscript.[33] Second, there were almost certainly conversations among the witnesses that do not appear in the recorded dialogues: conversations in which the attorneys, arbiters, and witnesses discussed the possible questions in advance and decided on the kinds of answers they would provide.

Pesquisas, inquests, are slow, they take time, sometimes generations. The *Oña* v. *Frías* inquest is, visibly, a very long undertaking.[34] The manuscript condenses time in a way that obscures the oceans of nonrepresentable thoughts and affects that are part of this investigation. For how long have the inhabitants of this region been talking about the inquest, and

[32] Isabel Alfonso and Cristina Jular, "Oña contra Frías o el pleito de los cien testigos: Una pesquisa en la Castilla del siglo XIII," *Estudios Medievales* (2000), 62–88. The case was reproduced in Isabel Oceja Gonzalo, *Documentación del monasterio de San Salvador de Oña*. Burgos: J. M. Garrido Garrido, 1983.

[33] Archivo Historico Nacional, Clero, Códices, L.76.

[34] The first inquest is in 1271, initiated on behalf of King Alfonso X by his son, Fernando, who died in 1275. Sancho IV takes over in 1280. But the whole problem – of the monastery illegally using the Frías lands for hunting, damaging the crops, and so on – seems to originate during the reign of Alfonso VIII, who died in 1214. And the private litigation must date to the foundational year of 1202. Alfonso X does not manage the inquest personally because, as the documents frequently point out, too many things are going on in the kingdom, and he cannot take the time. Likewise, many of the characters who appear in the inquest say that they are busy with *priesas* or urgent occupations: Taking time for the inquest is complicated and often interferes with their daily lives. At the beginning of the case, when the *alcaldes* or judges have already been appointed and are ready to launch the inquest, one of the city officers, Don Belmonte, explains that he cannot comply with the established deadlines as he needs to have his "pan de faze coger" (his wheat harvested): There will be delays and new deadlines must be established. Oceja, doc. 231, p. 242. Ms AHN Códices.L76 fol. 8r.

how? What did they feel about it? Did the inquest make them feel less connected to people from the same villages and populations on the other side of the dispute – people they certainly knew well, since they were neighbors and frequented the same parishes? What did they think and feel about the jurisdictional powers deployed to question them? What did they think and feel about their own answers? The manuscript is silent on such things. We might treat this as a limit to interpretation: We should say nothing of this because our only evidence is textual and documentary and we cannot speculate based on what is not in the texts or documents (*argumentum ex silentio*). Or we might see in these palpable silences an opportunity for interpretation: But how?

We would need to stretch the surface of the manuscript, enlarge it to register the time of the inquest: not, however, the time of the official events (these are recorded in the manuscript) but the time of the nonevents, all the time lost in translation, all the time that has fallen between the folds of the manuscript. There are various ways we might begin to imaginatively reconstruct that nonrecorded time. For instance, the various materialities of the many documents that compose the manuscript – produced in different times and places before they were bound together – can tell us much about the lives that participated in the construction of the manuscript: Binding has made them appear to be of the same age, but not to the paleographical eye, the eye of the material historian. Another way to imaginatively reconstruct that nonrecorded time – that long period during which the inquest was proceeding in the background like white noise – is dialogue itself.

We know from the *Partidas* that the judge both produces a particular affective space for the interrogation and translates the dialogue into orthodox legal terms. We know from handbooks like Martín Pérez's *Libro de las confesiones* that confession is subject to a set of rules: that these rules are a central means of juridifying the populace, interpellating subjects into the orthodox machinery of the law, allowing law to penetrate the daily social economy of their lives. We know that a manuscript like the one recording the inquest strips the event of all of its dialogic and affective texture. But we also know that – even while the *Partidas* or handbooks like Pérez's or records like that of the inquest attempt to contain affect through the control of dialogue – dialogue in the confessional or the courtroom in fact takes place in a true vernacular very different from that processed by judges and notaries. We know that, in the confessional or the courtroom, affect in fact roams freely.

Whatever their official purpose, texts like these allow us to investigate the affective space of legal dialogue. Reconstructing dialogue and affect is not easy. But to understand the legal event, we must reestablish – by stretching out the surface of the manuscript and activating our historical imagination – the order and affective spaces of the dialogue: its actual time, the play of questions and answers, the possible requests for clarification or equivocations, the questions about circumstances later redacted. (Did you see this happen? Have you heard it? When did you say you learned this? And so on.) We must reestablish the moment in which the witnessing process, by interrupting the lives of those to be questioned, also annoys them (they should be doing their shop work, or laboring, or surveying their own lands, or harvesting the wheat). In other words, we should read the documents and let them speak but – thanks to Hayden White – we know documents do not speak by themselves: They need our help.[35] We need to insert ourselves into the affective space, share the threshold with the people whose names, jobs, links of dependence, and other civic details we may know but whom we do not really know because legal process has *fulanized* them (laundered them), turning them into a John or Jane Doe of sorts.[36]

In the *Oña* v. *Frías* inquest, we have a few glimpses of all this, perhaps pale ones, but nevertheless glimpses. The witness testimony presented by Frías is quick and efficient. The notaries who have recorded those depositions have limited themselves entirely to the *substantia*, the direct information essential to the case. The testimony presented by Oña gives us more: We see not only the witnesses' answers – the substance of the events – but also the questions that they have been asked, and how these change from one witness to the other. Oña's attorneys and the notaries who recorded this testimony are much more detail-oriented: They strive to make visible

[35] Hayden White, *Metahistory: The Historical Imagination in 19th-Century Europe*. Baltimore: Johns Hopkins University Press, 1973.

[36] On *fulanization* see Jesús R. Velasco "The Law," in E. Michael Gerly and Ryan Giles (eds), "The Law," in *The Routledge Hispanic Studies Companion to Medieval Iberia: Unity in Diversity*. London: Routledge, 2021, 101–118.

the law's affective spaces doing the political and legal work they do. But even among the Frías witnesses – so sober and so soberly reported – we can see something that may show us the wider affective space of the dialogue. I will give only one example:

> Domingo de Vascuñuelos, our fourth witness, said that he heard his father and his grandfather say that when King Alfonso VIII created the town of Frías, there was a woman who gave Quintana María's tax money [*enfurçiones,* Latin *offertiones*] to Oña for the anniversary, and also the vassals were moved to the vicinity of Frías because they were its natural subjects and it was believed that they would be better protected there; and he also spoke of four plots of land in Çiellaporrata, and he named them in his testimony, saying that he heard his father and other elderly men say that when King Alfonso established the town of Frías, he asked the monasteries for help in the creation of this town [probably by giving land], and that the monastery of Oña provided these four plots of land to support the establishment of the town.[37]

Domingo de Vascuñuelos mobilizes his memory, looking a few generations back – to his grandfather and to other elders in the village. The information he provides is both imprecise and precise: people talking, memories being activated, living voices becoming *dead voice* becoming living voices again by dint of remembrance. The inquest unveils previous dialogues, networks of information passed through family ties and beyond, *communities* of informants who are in permanent and ongoing dialogue outside the courtroom. In this ongoing dialogue lies a truth, sometimes

[37] Domingo de Vascunnuelos, que es el IIII° de los nuestros testigos, que dixo que oyo dezir a su padre e a su auuelo que, quando el rey don Alfonso [VIII] fizo la puebla de Frias, que vna duenna que dio las enfurçiones de Quintana Maria a Onna por su aniuersario e los uasallos que los metio en uezindat de Frias porque eran sus naturales e tenia que serian meior aforados; e dixo, otrosi, de quatro solares que son en Çiellaporrata, e nombrolos en su testimonio, que oyo dezir a so padre e a otros ommes ançianos que, quando el rey don Alfonso fiziera la puebla de Frias, que pidio ayuda a los monesterios para esta puebla e el monesterio de Onna que dieron estos IIII solares en ayuda de la puebla para uezindat. Oceja, 254; ms. 19v°

The *aniuersario* may be her birthday, or it may instead be the birthday or anniversary of either the king or the monastery.

represented as *fama* (fame, rumor): the crucial foundation of any inquisitorial investigation.[38] Through those snippets of reported memory, we can begin to see the true duration of the legal proceeding and have access to elements that do not appear as actions in the document itself, but that lie in the background, appear on the threshold. We can begin to see the world of affects in which legal things happen not just as actions but as passions.

CONCLUSION

When Sinibaldo de' Fieschi (later Pope Innocent IV) argued that only living voices had juridical value, he was thinking precisely of how the law was performed: The body cannot lie, he felt, whereas written texts, scripted documents and transcriptions were unreliable. If anyone wanted to give credit to a dead animal skin (a parchment, or vellum), it could not serve by itself but would have to be supported with the presence of an authoritative person, someone who had actually been present during the agreement, the trial, or any other judicial event.[39] In looking at dialogue, I am not focusing only on the dead voice: the antinatural body of textual documentation. I am focusing on the living voices that can still be found in the margins and between the lines of the text. Dead voice may hide the affective elements that were once part of the original, oral, bodily dialogue, but this does not mean that we cannot try to imbricate ourselves into this affective space and try to understand how it works. We can restore the living voices of the legal dialogue by attempting to find them in the parchment. We can seek those whom the law attempted to erase, those who expressed their resistance to the lawscape from within the lawscape. In this, we can locate that moment of danger that – as Benjamin once put it – flashes like lightning and constitutes history. In a certain way, fragmentarily, this is what I have tried to do in looking at dialogue – not as a corrective, but as a supplement to what Peters has given us in *Law as Performance.*

[38] Julien Théry, "'Fama': L'opinion publique comme preuve judiciaire. Aperçu sur la révolution médiévale de l'inquisitoire (XIIe–XIVe siècles)." In *La preuve en justice de l'Antiquité à nos jours,* ed. Bruno Lemesle. Rennes: Presses Universitaires de Rennes, 2003, 119–147.

[39] Sinibaldo dei Fieschi, Pope Innocent IV, *Super libros quinque Decretalium.* Frankfurt: Sigismundus Feiereabend, 1570: 22.15, fols. 279v–280r.

CHAPTER 7

Performing for the Audience

Simon Stern

AMONG THE COMPLAINTS THAT HAVE BEEN LEVELED AT lawyers for their stilted, insincere, affected, disingenuous, and overly emotional carryings-on in the courtroom, the bill of particulars itemized by commentators in the early modern period offers an especially helpful catalogue. The denunciations from this era cover most of the concerns that typically figure in diatribes against lawyers, while offering an intriguing qualification that anticipates more contemporary concerns. In addition to the usual accusations of lying, obfuscating, and stirring up their audiences, a number of commentators also argued that lawyers degraded public discourse and damaged civil society more broadly by leading people to trust their emotions and to abandon rational grounds of argumentation. These critics were writing at a time long before cross-examination became a regular feature of the trial in common-law jurisdictions, and their objections would take on a new and potentially even more dangerous form when a lawyer's manipulative efforts could be used to badger a witness. Since at least the mid nineteenth century, the theatrics of cross-examination has played a central role in courtroom fiction and drama. Less attention, however, has been directed at judges who avail themselves of similar methods when seeking to amuse or sway the audience, in some instances by impersonating one of the figures in the dispute. Judges from the seventeenth and eighteenth centuries are sometimes cited for their inappropriate efforts at humour or their inability to control their temper, generally with the implication that these are problems of the past. Using a recent US Supreme Court case as an example, I suggest that judges have not abandoned these practices, even if their tactics are somewhat different.

In *Law as Performance*, Julie Stone Peters helpfully synthesizes a number of attacks on lawyers from the early modern period.[1] In what follows, I will first take up some of the questions she raises about commentators from that era, in order to understand what was distinctive about these complaints concerning lawyers' histrionics, as against the many other complaints about the corrupt and deceptive practices of lawyers and judges. Next I turn to the use of cross-examination as it began to develop near the end of the eighteenth century and grew in the course of the nineteenth century. This change in trial procedure allowed lawyers to think of themselves as actors in a way that differs from Peters's main examples, but that persists in contemporary forensic practice. Finally, I ask how Peters's analysis might help make sense of the less obviously dramatic, but nevertheless theatrical behavior, of judges, particularly when they encourage the audience to laugh in response to their questions, posed in the guise of someone who might be confused or surprised by the provisions at stake. This last section brings out an aspect of judicial behavior that is not commonly associated with lawyers' theatrics. Judicial humor takes many forms, which do not necessarily involve something like a dramatic persona. I hope to show, however, that in some instances, judges merge roles – the role of an impartial interlocutor attending to policy questions, and that of an individual to whom the law might apply – in a way that seems highly theatrical.

If we may take it for granted that every courtroom argument depends on numerous decisions, some more conscious than others, about how to use language and gesture to support an argument, the dynamic and interactive aspect of the process nevertheless bears emphasis. I take "forensic performance" to include the array of dramaturgical techniques that inform Erving Goffman's account of "the presentation of self in everyday life,"[2] extending not only to ways of affirming one's own position but also to ways of portraying the various figures or propositions that

1 Julie Stone Peters, *Law as Performance: Theatricality, Spectatorship, and the Making of Law in Ancient, Medieval, and Early Modern Europe* (Oxford: Oxford University Press, 2022).

2 Erving Goffman, *The Presentation of Self in Everyday Life* (New York: Doubleday, 1956).

might be in contention, in a legal dispute. As exhibited in the courtroom, these practices include the use of speech, gesture, and ritual to convey arguments, embody or criticize legal authority, and impersonate a party, witness, or any other participant in an actual or imagined scenario that animates some aspect of the dispute. The audience for these performances may be directed at all or part of the courtroom audience, and also at imagined observers in the larger public. Finally, these performances may be associated with anyone speaking in the courtroom, but are likeliest to be staged by a repeat player familiar with the norms and dynamics that characterize the forensic sphere.

A frequently repeated complaint about legal performances in any register branded as indecorous is that they appeal to the emotions rather than the intellect. The point is made most concisely by the example of the histrions – Greek actors banned in Rome for more than a century not only as foreign thespians, but more importantly also as erotic and physical threats to propriety. The histrions were famous for walking though the audience half-naked and provoking inappropriate excitement. The provision in the *Digest* that records the ban (*infamia*) on the histrions is immediately followed by a ban on citizens maintaining brothels.[3] Complaints about unacceptable courtroom histrionics may not reflect any awareness of the term's origins, but this compacted set of associations nevertheless shows how objections to improper performances may capture a range of anxieties about their dangerous effects.

7.1 THEATRE OF INJUSTICE

In chapter 5 of *Law as Performance*, Peters discusses a litany of complaints dating from the late fifteenth century through the seventeenth century, amounting to what she calls an "anti-rhetorical tradition."[4] Some of these diatribes simply add a theatrical coating while repeating well-worn themes that we encounter in other denunciations of the legal profession, asserting that lawyers gravitate naturally toward the weaker cause, which they strive to dignify as the superior one; that they bribe witnesses and

[3] *Digest*, 3.2.1. Thanks to Peter Goodrich for noting this association.

[4] Peters, *Law as Performance*, 216–25.

judges; that their flowery rhetoric and energetic imagination help them lie and deceive for their clients.[5] However, some of these attacks address the dynamics of forensic performance in ways that pick out more specifically why it is that role-acting in the courtroom can produce distinctive effects that reach beyond the courtroom, and these examples deserve further attention.

Johannes Ferrarius, writing around the middle of the sixteenth century, says that lawyers can seduce "the iye and eare" and "move any manne [to] evill," or "stirr naughtye persones to unquietnesse."[6] He adds that "where the number of Lawyers dooe swarme and flocke together, ... every courte, every private mannes house [is] in a great sturre and tumult by [the] dissensious sutes whiche those craftye marchantes" provoke.[7] Peters observes that Ferrarius's criticisms "reflec[t] the broader associations between lawyers and theatre that became recurrent figures in humanist texts."[8] Giovanni Pico della Mirandola worries that lawyers have an extraordinary ability to "deceive, circumvent, [and] practice sleight-of-hand tricks," amounting to a talent for "transform[ing] things ... as if by ... magical force, ... so that they assume whatever face and dress you wish." The result is "sheer lying, sheer imposture, sheer magic tricks, [which], like so many masks and simulacra, ... dupes the minds of [the] auditors."[9] Juan Luis Vives associates lawyers' "refined and polished style of speaking" with a feminized tradition of oratory,

5 For some compilations of these attacks, see, e.g., Wilfred R. Prest, "Law, Lawyers, and Litigants," in *The Rise of the Barristers: A Social History of the English Bar 1590–1640* (Oxford: Oxford University Press, 1986), 283–326; Paul Raffield, "A Discredited Priesthood: The Failings of Common Lawyers and Their Representation in Seventeenth Century Satirical Drama," *Law & Literature* 17 (2005), 365–95; Jessica Winston, "Legal Satire and the Legal Profession in the 1590s," in Lorna Hutson, ed., *The Oxford Handbook of English Law and Literature, 1500–1700* (Oxford: Oxford University Press, 2017), 121–41.

6 Johannes Ferrarius, *Woorke of Joannes Ferrarius Montanus*, title page, fol. 100v–102v (a translation of Ferrarius's *De republica bene instituenda* [1556], originally published in German as *Von dem Gemeinen nutze* [1533]); quoted in Peters, *Law as Performance*, 216.

7 Ferrarius, quoted in Peters, *Law as Performance*, 217.

8 Peters, *Law as Performance*, 217.

9 "A Ermolao Barbaro (3 June 1485)," in Pico della Mirandola, *Lettere*, ed. Francesco Borghesi (Florence: Olschki, 2018), 93–95; Wayne A. Rebhorn, ed., *Renaissance Debates on Rhetoric* (Ithaca, NY: Cornell University Press, 2000), 57–67. Quoted in Peters, *Law as Performance*, 218.

which has "laid aside its manly garb and put on a woman's attire." This style, "better suited to swaying the minds of the judge and all the bystanders," is "better suited to the stage" than to the courtroom, and it encourages the audience to behave "as if they were being entertained in the theatre."[10]

Erasmus, in his *Ciceronianus* (1528), says that juries "expec[t] and even deman[d] of the advocates an embellished style" that is "designed to misrepresent the truth, . . . to infiltrate the hearer's mind by deception, and finally to carry his intelligence by storm through rousing his emotions."[11] Heinrich Cornelius Agrippa, in *On the Vanity of Arts and Sciences* (1531), writes that the lawyer's art of pleading is "an ancient, but most deceitful Calling, onely set out with the gaudy Trimming of Perswasion, which is nothing else, but to know how [to] over-rule the Judge, and to turn him and winde him at pleasure."[12] Agrippa envisions a lawyer twisting and wriggling in a performance that invites the audience to imagine themselves in the same role: These "Mimmick[s]," he writes, may be seen "looking with their Eyes like men distracted, throwing their Arms about, dancing with their Feet, lasciviously shaking their Loyns, with a thousand sundry sorts of wreathings, wrestings, turnings this way and that way of the whole Body."[13] This description almost makes the advocate sound like the faith healers of a later era, calling on the audience to experience the same sensations he is modeling.

John Jewel pursues the same theme in an "Oration against Rhetoric" (ca. 1548), which will be particularly salient for my later comments on cross-examination. Jewel imagines a wildly histrionic lawyer whose

[10] Juan Luis Vives, *"On the Causes of the Corruption of the Arts (De causis corruptarum atrium),"* in Juan Luis Vives, *Twenty Books on Education (De disciplinis libri XX)* (1531), translated as an appendix in Juan Luis Vives, *De ratione dicendi*, trans. David Walter (Leiden: Brill, 2018), 424–85. Quoted in Peters, *Law as Performance*, 218.

[11] Erasmus, *Ciceronianus*, in *Literary and Educational Writings*, ed. Craig R. Thompson (Toronto: University of Toronto Press, 1978–89), 6:382; quoted in Peters, *Law as Performance*, 219.

[12] Heinrich Cornelius Agrippa, *De incertitudine et uanitate scientiarum declamatio inuectiua* (1531), anon. trans., *On the Vanity of Arts and Sciences* (London: Speed, 1676), 324; quoted in Peters, *Law as Performance*, 220.

[13] Agrippa, *De incertitudine et uanitate scientiarum declamatio inuectiua*, 65; quoted in Peters, *Law as Performance*, 220.

gesticulations are meant to prompt the observers to respond in kind, imaginatively if not physically: "Why that thrashing about of the body? Why that sudden contraction? that waving of arms? that slapping of the thigh? that stamp of the foot? Why is it they speak not with the mouth, not with the tongue, not with the jaws, but with the hand, fingers, joints, arms, face, and the whole body?" The appeal to emotion, Jewel writes, makes a mockery of the usual forms of legal authority, rooted in evidence and expertise: "What good are courts, laws, oaths, rules, ... judges, and magistrates? Why would we appeal to the authority of witnesses, of records, of speakers, of writers, of examinations, of experts in law?"[14] There are trustworthy sources of information, and reliable figures who can explain and interpret them, but these sources are sidelined in favor of the advocate's deceitful rhetorical stratagems. Francesco Patrizi's *On Rhetoric* (1562) also imagines a crowd of auditors reacting passionately to the advocate's oratory. He likens the observers to "a wild beast with many heads that are always barking and that ... deafen its spirit, dazing it so that it cannot see the light or discern the truth ... And the master orator always has the power to awaken that beast and to make it bark from whichever ... of its heads he pleases."[15] There are a number of other diatribes to similar effect, confirming the general sense that lawyers stir up the audience's emotions, play on the jurors' prejudices, and do their best to hoodwink the judge. These denunciations, attacking malevolent actors for provoking wild and impassioned reactions from uncontrollable audiences, imagine affect as a negative response, as if it arises only in a dangerous form, to be contrasted against an implicitly calm and emotionless state that would appear to be the proper register for legal argument. Yet as Jesús Velasco argues in his contribution to this volume, all dialogue and all performance are gauged to generating affect, creating atmospheres of feeling that bring the written word alive. It is *others'* use of rhetoric that deserves to be castigated.

[14] John Jewel, "Oration against Rhetoric," in Hoyt H. Hudson, "Jewel's Oration against Rhetoric: A Translation," *Quarterly Journal of Speech* 14 (1928), 374–75; quoted in Peters, *Law as Performance*, 221.

[15] Francesco Patrizi, *Della retorica* (1562) (Lecce: Conte, 1994), fol. 57r–61v; trans. in Rebhorn, ed., *Renaissance Debates on Rhetoric*, 184–202. Quoted in Peters, *Law as Performance*, 222.

How do these complaints differ from familiar indictments contending that lawyers lie, twist the law to their clients' purposes, create ambiguity where none exists, and generally act out of self-interest? It is, after all, common to see lawyers charged with suborning witnesses, raising spurious allegations, and exaggerating their client's plight while diminishing the adversary's. In some ways the differences are not very great. It seems outrageous that lawyers take facts and evidence and justice, which should be clear, and produce results that are manipulated and contrived, and treat that process as a matter of course. By the same token, that which everyone else considers natural is made through legal processes to appear contrived, and the lawyers take what should be self-evident and claim that it depends on particular circumstances and conditions that make the answer obscure and controversial.

However, most complaints along these lines are limited to the sphere of the courtroom. They apply only to the facts of the case, or to interpretive disputes that arise within the litigation. Lawyers exaggerate their clients' injuries while minimizing those of the other party, or they try to make simple and straightforward questions appear murky and complicated. A lawyer in William Wycherley's *The Plain Dealer* (1676) typifies these criticisms when he boasts of his ability to "extenuate or amplifie Matter of Fact; baffle Truth with Impudence; [and] answer Exceptions with Questions, though never so impertinent."[16] English Restoration satire is full of similar instances, in which lawyers aid clients in bringing spurious claims and putting on false evidence.[17] According to these accusations, the harmful effects of lawyers' behavior are felt within the frame of a particular case, and so, by implication, they are contained to that extent.

Just as the harm is limited in this way, the kind of deception that lawyers practice also has a limited reach in these accounts. The judge may be deceived, and perhaps even the jury, but the ridiculous and offensive circumlocutions of legal language and the contrivances of the conniving

[16] William Wycherley, *The Plain-Dealer*, 3rd ed. (London: Bently, 1677), 35.

[17] For more examples, see J. Douglas Canfield, *Tricksters and Estates: On the Ideology of Restoration Comedy* (Lexington: University Press of Kentucky Press, 1997); Edward F. J. Tucker, *Intruder into Eden: Representations of the Common Lawyer in English Literature 1350–1750* (Columbia: Camden House, 1984).

counsel are seemingly apparent for everyone else to see. The deception is easily detected. The person who exposes these practices does not claim that any deep or acute insight is required to perceive the problem; a simple description of the lawyers' antics makes the lie patently evident to all. The lawyers are not simply indifferent to the truth – they *want* to be believed, and they rely on feigned evidence and false witnesses rather than behaving as if the source were irrelevant.

However, as Peters points out, a crucial part of the complaint about lawyers who act out roles and imitate actions and passions involves their efforts to appeal not only to the jury, but also to the other spectators in the courtroom. When this larger group can be provoked and incited by the lawyers' efforts, the resulting dynamic introduces a problem of a different order. The result is to enlist the audience, in real time, as active spectators to a performance in which they are also contributors to some extent. This immersive and interactive engagement transforms the conditions of the courtroom, yielding what Velasco characterizes as a mood or atmosphere, an affective space governed by the dialogue between the lawyers and the audience.[18] The lawyer seeks to raise the spectators' passions so that they participate, emotionally and bodily, in the drama being staged. They become involved in a way that goes far beyond temporary approval of the legal result. They are not simply laughing or hissing at some statement; the performance shapes their beliefs and produces a shared, communal sense of involvement, in real time, as the audience members affirm and encourage each other's reactions. Their passionate involvement creates risks for the community more broadly, in a way that a lawyer's factual falsehoods or clever interpretive arguments would not.

This participatory role explains why people can be "stirr[ed] . . . to unquietnesse," as Ferrarius put it, and why they have ever-increasing expectations of rhetorical hyperbole. Their demand for melodrama, or whatever theatrical mode appeals to their degraded appetites, does not merely indicate a taste that the lawyers are catering to, but a taste that the lawyers are cultivating and degrading even further.

[18] See Chapter 6 of this volume.

Lawyers may help people get away with murder through specious arguments, and that can do terrible harm, but lawyers who actively engage members of the community, and sway their views by eliciting their emotional responses in court, can degrade public discourse and destroy communal life in an even more thoroughgoing way. Theatrical performances are communal, participatory, and dynamic, and this is what separates them from the other harms that lawyers inflict.

This point about the dynamic and participatory nature of the enterprise may seem obvious but it bears emphasizing. When scholars talk about law in relation to performance, or theatre, or magic, they usually dwell on questions about the efficacy of the performance (à la J. L. Austin), or the contrived nature of the theatrical stage effects, or the advocates' ability to distract and surprise when they draw on their bag of tricks.[19] Accordingly, the analysis tends to focus on the performers and perhaps their control over the audience, as if the observers could be treated as a by-product of the lawyers' efforts. To be sure, there has been a considerable amount of research on juries, and even the wider audience, by scholars of a sociological or anthropological bent, and some work in media studies has sought to explore these issues. But it remains comparatively unusual for research in this vein to see the audience as a significant factor in the analysis.

This gap in contemporary scholarship on the social and cultural production of legal doctrines and norms suggests an observation about the use of systems analysis as a means of understanding legal change. A systems analysis approach would look to statutes, rulings, norms, governments, trials, courthouses, practices of storage and retrieval, lawyers, juries, economies, the media, and other elements to see how iterative

[19] All these facets of performance have been carefully examined in recent work, for instance in Marianne Constable, *Our Word Is Our Bond: How Legal Speech Acts* (Stanford, CA: Stanford University Press, 2014); Marett Leiboff, *Towards a Theatrical Jurisprudence* (London: Routledge, 2019); Alan Read, *Theatre & Law* (Hampshire: Palgrave Macmillan, 2016); Sean Mulcahy, "Methodologies of Law as Performance," *Law and Humanities* 16 (2022), 165–82; Jessie Allen, "A Theory of Adjudication: Law as Magic," *Suffolk University Law Review* 41 (2007), 773–832; Nicholas Blomley, "Performing Property: Making the World," *Canadian Journal of Law & Jurisprudence* 26 (2013), 23–48; Dan L. Burk, "Patent Performativity," *Journal of Intellectual Property Law* 29 (2021), 280–317.

dynamic changes resonate through the system.[20] A significant amount has been written on the decline of the trial and the rise of settlement and plea bargaining as means of dispute resolution in Britain and America,[21] but scholars have not drawn out an implication that follows from the point that Peters makes – namely that as opportunities decline for theatrical performance in the courtroom, and as the nature of that performance changes, that is bound to have systemic effects on other parts of the system and the results that the system produces. The point is not only that settlement and plea bargaining yield results that would not necessarily obtain at trial, nor that evidence may come out at trial that no one sees, when the parties settle – although those are also important considerations.[22] Rather, the point is that the participatory nature of the trial also has significant effects on the outcome and the community in which the trial occurs, and therefore on the system as a whole – effects that are altered in ways that tend to go overlooked as trials become the exception. In sum, Peters's attention to the lawyers' audience brings out important dimensions that conventional treatments of legal performance have tended to overlook.

[20] Systems analysis enjoyed a fair degree of currency in legal scholarship in the 1970s, but it has not been especially prominent in recent legal scholarship. For some recent examples, see Henry E. Smith, "Systems Theory," in Andrew S. Gold, John C. P. Goldberg, Daniel B. Kelly, Emily Sherwin, and Henry E. Smith, eds., *The Oxford Handbook of the New Private Law* (Oxford: Oxford University Press, 2020), 143–58; Richard Nobles and David Schiff, *Observing Law through Systems Theory* (Oxford: Hart, 2013).

[21] George Fisher, "Plea Bargaining's Triumph," *Yale Law Journal* 109 (1999), 857; Conor Hanly, "The Decline of Civil Jury Trial in Nineteenth-Century England," *Journal of Legal History* 26 (2005), 253–78; Shari Seidman Diamond and Jessica M. Salerno, "Reasons for the Disappearing Jury Trial: Perspectives from Attorneys and Judges," *Louisiana Law Review* 81 (2020), 119–64; Kent D. Syverud, "ADR and the Decline of the American Civil Jury," *UCLA Law Review* 44 (1996), 1935–46; Robert J. Conrad Jr. and Katy L. Clements, "The Vanishing Criminal Jury Trial: From Trial Judges to Sentencing Judges," *George Washington Law Review* 86 (2018), 99–167; Sue Lloyd-Bostok and Cheryl Thomas, "Juries and Reform in England and Wales," in Neil Vidmar, ed., *World Jury Systems* (Oxford: Oxford University Press, 2000), 53–91.

[22] These figure prominently among the concerns usually raised about high rate of settlement in place of litigation. See, e.g., Owen M. Fiss, "Against Settlement," *Yale Law Journal* 93 (1983), 1073–92.

7.2 CROSS-EXAMINING MR. COX

I turn now to a later historical context, outside the boundaries of Peters's discussion, involving the rise of cross-examination in trials in Britain near the end of the eighteenth century. For reasons that need not concern us here, cross-examination did not play a significant role in trials at common law before this period. The later eighteenth century marks the first period in which criminal defense lawyers engaged in cross-examination to any significant extent, and the first period in which lawyers started to write manuals about how to conduct a cross-examination.[23] This practice certainly enhanced the drama and overall entertainment value of a trial, and some lawyers became famous for their talent in this area.[24] What seems notable about many of the examples from this era is that sarcasm and ridicule appear to have been very effective methods, even when used in ways that did nothing to help reveal the truth. A notorious and frequently cited example involves Thomas Erskine, one of the first lawyers to make a name for himself by doing this kind of work. Baron Campbell claimed, in his autobiography, to have been present at a trial for payment of a tailor's bill, where Erskine questioned a witness who testified that a coat had been poorly made, with one sleeve longer than the other. Erskine went over the point carefully, asking the witness, "You will swear that one of the sleeves was longer than the other?" When the witness affirmed this, Erskine asked, "Now, sir, will you swear that one of them was not *shorter* than the other?" The confused witness denied the point, and, according to Campbell, Erskine won the case for his client.[25]

[23] On these developments, see Andrew Watson, *Speaking in Court: Developments in Court Advocacy* (Cham: Palgrave Macmillan, 2019); John H. Langbein, *The Origins of Adversary Criminal Trial* (Oxford: Oxford University Press, 2003); Amalia D. Kessler, *Inventing American Exceptionalism: The Origins of American Adversarial Legal Culture, 1800–1877* (New Haven, CT: Yale University Press, 2017); Philip Gaines, *From Truth to Technique at Trial: A Discursive History of Advocacy Advice Texts* (Oxford: Oxford University Press, 2016).

[24] That cross-examination had such dramatic potential was not lost on contemporaries, but perhaps these resonances become most apparent in the almost metatheatrical cases featuring an actor as a plaintiff or defendant in Edmund Kean's 1824 case for "criminal conversation." See "Action for Crim. Con.," *Drama, or, Theatrical Pocket Magazine* 7 (1824), 203–14.

[25] John Lord Campbell, *The Lives of the Lord Chancellors and Keepers of the Great Seal of England* (London, John Murray, 1847), 6:685. On this episode see also Wendie

This story would seem to confirm all the fears of the antirhetorical and the antitheatrical critics. The implication is that people attend trials for entertainment, and are delighted to see a quick-witted lawyer tie the witness up in knots and trick him into producing an answer the lawyer wants to hear, so that he becomes a kind of puppet in the lawyer's ministrations. The result is not a statement that anyone could seriously regard as helping to clarify the issues or expose the truth. It doesn't show the witness to be a liar, but the pleasure of seeing him become a tool in the lawyer's hands is so satisfying that it is treated as a successful performance and the lawyer is rewarded with a victory. If juries are actually making decisions on this basis, then it seems right to worry that cross-examination has simply become one more device that lawyers are using to entertain, amuse, and animate the audience, and that this device belongs to the same dynamic structure that critics were worrying about centuries earlier. One can easily imagine the critics of the early modern period now adding that cross-examination has become another feature of the lawyers' scripted performances, which affects not only the verdict but also the community's expectations. To be sure, there is good reason to think that exposing laypersons to scenes of cross-examination changed their ideas about truth in almost the opposite direction, leading people to demand a kind of consistency and legal-rational "common sense" that few people display in their ordinary affairs. However, if one were of a mind to see this practice as an element in the legal theatre of the era, it would not be hard to find examples to justify that concern.

Although guides on cross-examination started to appear around the turn of the nineteenth century, it would take many decades before a comprehensive and systematic discussion appeared. Guides to legal rhetoric had long recommended that lawyers should avoid affectation, strive for dignity, and modulate their tone and language harmoniously.[26] Gilbert Austin's *Chironomia; or, A Treatise on Rhetorical Delivery* (1806), published around the time that cross-examination was becoming

Ellen Schneider, *Engines of Truth: Producing Veracity in the Victorian Courtroom* (New Haven, CT: Yale University Press, 2016), 56.

26 See Watson, *Speaking in Court*; Gaines, *From Truth to Technique.*

a more prominent part of the trial, was not focused solely on forensic rhetoric, but if offers advice along the lines of its precursors, warning that extravagance, vehemence, and exaggerated gesticulations all serve to degrade the speaker and the audience.[27] Austin's treatment is unusually explicit about the theatrical model that applies to all public speakers and their need to engage with the audience, and to that extent his discussion anticipates some of the suggestions that later commentators would offer.

The first extensive treatment with specific recommendations for cross-examining witnesses was Edward William Cox's *The Advocate: His Training, Practice, Rights and Duties.* This work first appeared serially in the *Law Times* in the early 1830s and was published as a two-volume book in 1852.[28] In discussing the right approach to cross-examination, Cox writes,

> To be a good Advocate you must be a good actor, and it is one of the faculties of an actor to command his countenance. Open gently, mildly; do not *appear* to doubt [the witness]; go at once to the marrow of the story he has told, as if you were not afraid of it; make him repeat it; then, carry him away to some distant and collateral topic, and try his memory upon *that,* so as to divert his thoughts from the main object of your inquiry, and prevent his seeing the connection between the tale he has told and the questions you are about to put to him. Then, by slow approaches, bring him back to

[27] Gilbert Austin, *Chironomia; or, A Treatise on Rhetorical Delivery* (London: Cadell, 1806), 138. On this work see also Peter Goodrich, *Legal Emblems and the Art of Law:* Obiter Depicta *as the Vision of Governance* (Cambridge: Cambridge University Press, 2016), 168.

[28] Edward William Cox, *The Advocate: His Training, Practice, Rights and Duties* (London: Law Times, 1852). For discussions of Cox's work more generally, see Peter Spiller, *Cox and Crime: An Examination of Edward William Cox, 1809–1879, His Career and His Approach to the Criminal Law of His Time* (Cambridge: Institute of Criminology, 1985); Charlotte C. Watkins, "Edward William Cox and the Rise of 'Class Journalism,'" *Victorian Periodicals Review* 15 (1982), 87–93; Raymond Cocks, *The Foundations of the Modern Bar* (London: Sweet and Maxwell, 1983), 64–77; Martin Hewitt, "The Press and the Law," in Joanne Shattock, ed., *Journalism and the Periodical Press in Nineteenth-Century Britain,* (Cambridge: Cambridge University Press, 2017), 147–64; and Gaines's discussion in *From Truth to Technique,* 82–151, based on his article "Writing the Discursive Proto-Culture of Modern Anglo-American Trial Advocacy: Edward William Cox's *The Advocate,*" *American Journal of Legal History* 51 (2011), 333–58.

> the main circumstances, by the investigation of which it is that you purpose to show the falsity of the story.
>
> The design of this maneuvre is, of course, to prevent him from seeing the connection between his own story and your examination, so that he may not draw upon his imagination for explanations consistent with his original evidence; your purpose being to elicit inconsistency and contradictions between the story itself and other circumstances, from which it may be concluded that all or a great part of it is a fabrication.[29]

It will be evident that Cox's ideas about how to handle a witness are very different from the illustration provided by the Erskine anecdote, and they involve a very different understanding of the lawyer's role as an actor. Here there is no question of putting on an act in order to get a rise out of the witness, or to stir the audience; rather, Cox offers a lesson about controlling one's reactions to keep others from anticipating the goal. His treatment points to different implications for the dynamic mode of audience interaction – it would be a mistake to conclude that he is simply trying to remove that element altogether, but his suggestion that lawyers should proceed in a gentle and mild way points to a diminished role for the kind of interaction that concerned the early modern critics of theatrical lawyering.

But there is nevertheless at least one other theatrical angle to the dynamic that Cox envisions, which turns on the result of this kind and gentle procedure: "By slow approaches, bring him back to the main circumstances, by the investigation of which it is that you purpose to show the falsity of the story." The great evidence scholar John Henry Wigmore wrote that cross-examination is efficacious because when "the cross-examined witness supplies his own refutation" in testimony that "immediately succeeds in time the direct examination," the result produces what he calls a "dramatic contrast."[30] Wigmore explains that the difference between refutation in this fashion, as compared to refutation by means of another witness, "is the difference between slow-burning sulphurous gunpowder and quick-flashing dynamite." Wigmore has at this point switched metaphors and abandoned

[29] Cox, *The Advocate*, 402.

[30] John Henry Wigmore, *A Treatise on the System of Evidence in Trials at Common Law* (Boston, MA: Little, Brown, 1904), 2:1702.

the theatrical language, but the language of dynamite hints at a plotter hoist with his own petard, itself a theatrical image that speaks to the pleasure the audience experiences when narrative causation turns on itself to bring off a satisfying conclusion. Cox's treatment and Wigmore's observations show how cross-examination can facilitate qualitatively different interactions with the audience in the courtroom, which do not closely match the ones that worried the critics in the early modern period, but which nevertheless depend on some of the ideas about theatricality that Peters explores.

7.3 SPECIAL GUEST STAR, JOHN ROBERTS

Peters's treatment of histrionic lawyers hints at yet another line of research, involving judges as actors. Judges cannot engage in the same theatrics as lawyers, but that does not foreclose any chance of donning a role during a hearing. There has been a considerable amount of research on the effects of laughter during hearings before the US Supreme Court, but although this work has looked into matters such as what kinds of parties tend to bear the brunt of judicial humor, and whether male or female judges are likelier to attempt this approach and are likelier to be seen as crowd-pleasers, scholars have largely overlooked a prior question – namely how judges go about eliciting laughter from the audience in the first place.[31] By this I do not mean to ask whether certain areas (e.g., administrative law or criminal law) offer more opportunities for guffaws, or whether judicial humor necessarily takes a form that treats a particular person as its target, although both

[31] This line of work has developed over the past fifteen years or so. See, e.g., Ryan A. Malphurs, "'People Did Sometimes Stick Things in my Underwear': The Function of Laughter at the US Supreme Court," *Communication Law Review* 10 (2010): 48–75; Sharyn Roach Anleu and Kathy Mack, "Judicial Humour and Interprofessional Relations in the Courtroom," in Jessica Milner Davie and Sharyn Roach Anleu, eds., *Judges, Judging and Humour* (New York: Palgrave Macmillan, 2018), 141–78; Tonja Jacobi and Matthew Sag, "Taking Laughter Seriously at the Supreme Court," *Vanderbilt Law Review* 72 (2019), 1423–96; Siyu Li and Tom Pryor, "Humor and Persuasion: The Effects of Laughter during US Supreme Court Oral Arguments," *Law & Policy* 42 (2020), 162–85; Robert Urbatsch, "Humor in Supreme Court Oral Arguments," *Humor* 35 (2022), 169–87. For a broader discussion, see Brigitte Adriaensen, Andrew Bricker, Albergo Godioli, and Ted Laros, "The Difficulty of Judging Jests: Introduction," *Humor* 35 (2022), 295–304.

questions are relevant. Rather, I mean to ask how judges signal that they have turned momentarily to stand-up comedy, and more specifically what kinds of personae they assume to show the audience that it has permission to laugh.

A recently argued case, *Colorado* v. *Counterman*,[32] offers a useful illustration of the dynamics of judicial humor and the laughter it strives to elicit. The case posed the question of whether it is constitutionally permissible to use an objective standard for imposing criminal liability on someone for stalking and uttering threats, or whether some degree of subjective *mens rea* is required under the First Amendment because the speech is sufficiently expressive as to require constitutional protection. Billy Ray Counterman had been sentenced to four and a half years in prison for stalking Coles Whalen, a singer-songwriter, and for using Facebook to send hundreds of messages to her. The messages ranged from the mundane (as when he offered to bring tomatoes from his garden) to the aggressive (as when he wrote "Die. Don't need you," and "I'm currently unsupervised. I know, it freaks me out too.").[33] His conviction was based on a Colorado statute that used an objective standard to determine whether his messages were threatening, but he contended that he could not be convicted unless he had some degree of subjective awareness – at least to the point of recklessness – that his messages might be perceived as threats.

In the course of two years Counterman had sent Whalen more than a thousand messages. At oral argument, Chief Justice John Roberts picked out a few that, in his view, did not appear threatening. To make this point, he read these examples aloud and asked Philip Weiser, the attorney general for the state of Colorado, to explain why someone who sent them must be perceived as uttering a threat. In reading these messages, Roberts courted the laughter of his audience, presenting himself as a confused and befuddled "regular guy" who could not understand why his words could be construed as anything

32 Docket No. 22–138, argued April 19, 2023.

33 *Counterman* v. *Colorado*, No. 22–138, brief of plaintiff-appellee, Appx. A, at 6a (available at www.supremecourt.gov/DocketPDF/22/22-138/233120/20220809160009407_Appendix%20–%20ready%20to%20file%20-%20TO%20PRINT.pdf).

but innocuous.[34] He dwelt, for instance, on a message that said, “Staying in cyber life is going to kill you. Come out for coffee. You have my number.” After quoting this example a second time, Roberts added, “I can’t promise I haven’t said that,” and when this remark brought the laughter he was seeking, he read the message a third time. Roberts claimed to find it incomprehensible that anyone could attach a threatening implication to the message, even if it had come amidst hundreds of others that appeared more menacing: “I think that might sound solicitous of the person’s development. I mean, if we’re talking just about what the statements are, how is that – what tone would you use in saying that that would make it threatening?” When Weiser attempted to explain how, in the context of Counterman’s other messages, this one also amounted to a threat, Roberts could not resist another attempt: “Okay. Say this in a threatening way. One of the things he was convicted of, it was an image of liquor bottles, and there was a caption, ‘A guy’s version of edible arrangements.’” Once again, this clever riposte brought down the house. One may speculate that Roberts’ pose, informed by an awareness of those who would later hear the recording, was also designed to convey a certain self-image to the like-minded people in that audience.

It would be idle to imagine any of these messages being spoken “in a threatening way,” since they were sent by text. The invitation to adopt a threatening tone might almost seem like a disavowal of Roberts’s own highly theatrical conduct at this point in the hearing. It is more than a little paradoxical for him to adopt the stance of an average dude, doing his best to comprehend a woman’s point of view but forced to throw up his hands in exasperation because he simply cannot understand what she is going on about. First and most obviously, if Roberts were right to interpret the message as “solicitous of the person’s development,” there would be nothing wrong with using the objective standard he claims to find so worrisome, since it would yield the innocuous meaning he has just

[34] The effect that Roberts sought is best appreciated by listing to the oral arguments, which may be accessed at this site: www.supremecourt.gov/oral_arguments/audio/2022/22-138; the material quoted here begins at 48:40 of the audio transcript; see also pages 53 and following of the transcript available at the same site.

produced. Second, and conversely, the figure he has been purporting to impersonate would be most unlikely to explain himself in Roberts's words. That average dude does not use words like "solicitous," and if he were concerned about someone's "development" he would just say so. By attributing to Counterman a "solicitous" attitude toward Whalen's "development," Roberts inadvertently highlights the contrived nature of the role he is enacting. He is attempting to speak in Supreme Court legalese while also treating the sentiments of the plain Joe as perfectly congruent with the Court's jurisprudence on objectivity. What makes Roberts's act even more notably theatrical, however, is his effort to play the role of a befuddled guy who is honestly trying to do his best, a role that Roberts dons in the hope of getting a rise out of the audience. He seeks that affirmation because it will show that he is not alone in his perplexity, that the other well-meaning, like-minded guys out there share his view. If it were not obvious enough that Roberts's first try was meant to produce this reaction and the reaffirmation it brings, it quickly becomes evident that he finds the response so reassuring that he must try again and again. His act speaks louder than the words he intones.

This example shows how judicial behavior, despite all the constraints imposed on it, may have its own theatrical potential. In the process of attempting to understand a party's arguments, or contemplating their implications, judges often imagine themselves into the role of someone governed by the provisions in question. That is, in effect, what Roberts seeks to do here. When remarking, "I can't promise I haven't said that," he aligns himself with the hapless defendant now astonished to find that an innocuous statement provides the basis for a criminal prosecution. When inviting the attorney general of Colorado to read a test message "in a threatening way," Roberts strives for another encore from the audience, while placing himself in the role of someone who cannot fathom how anyone could perceive the message as a threat. Criticisms of judicial humor generally focus on inappropriate levity in written decisions rather than statements uttered in court, and even when commentators have discussed judges' behavior on the bench, it is usually taken for granted that questions about interpretation and policy are beyond the reach of any such criticism. Yet Roberts's questions illustrate a practice that, if not commonplace, is hardly unusual.

As Peters shows, concerns about legal performance have attended primarily to lawyers' behavior, but her analysis shows how judicial behavior might raise similar questions. At the *Counterman* hearing, Roberts very deliberately seeks to get a rise out of the audience in a way that is meant to affirm the doctrinal point he seeks to establish. More generally, Peters's attention to the audience for legal performances, and her extensive historical analyses of these questions, open up many new avenues for research.

CHAPTER 8

Desiring Children

Vulnerability and the Sex Offender

Jisha Menon

In June 2019, the Almeida Theatre in London premiered an adaptation of *The Hunt* directed by Rupert Goold and adapted by David Farr from Thomas Vinterberg and Tobias Lindholm's Danish film, *Jagten* or *The Hunt*.[1] The stage version recreates the film's plot and focuses on the repercussions that befall kindergarten schoolteacher Lucas Bruun, falsely accused of sexual abuse by six-year-old Clara, the daughter of his best friend. Clara has a crush on Lucas and is upset when he rebuffs her affection. She subsequently suggests to her principal that Lucas had exposed himself to her. Her classmates corroborate her story by adding imaginative and salacious details of their own. The play examines how the accusation galvanizes the close-knit community in a small Danish town and targets the accused. Reversing our associations with predation and hunting, the play depicts how the force of sex panic stirs up primal hunting impulses and incites the townsfolk to mobilize against the threat of pedophilia.

The Hunt focuses on the hunting down of a man falsely accused of pedophilia, and highlights public reactivity to sex panics, especially in relation to children. In the wake of the accusation, Lucas's professional and personal life unravels: He loses his job, his friendship with the girl's father crumbles, and his burgeoning romance with a coworker comes to

[1] For his astute comments on this chapter, in addition to his formidable brilliance and critical generosity, I am indebted to Robert Weisberg. For generative conversations and insightful feedback, I thank Sarah Brophy, Estelle Freedman, Michael Rau, David Sklansky, and the editors of this volume. I am grateful to Westley Montgomery and Zoe Ryu for research assistance. The Violet Andrews Whittier Faculty Fellowship at the Stanford Humanities Center provided much appreciated research support.

a standstill. The effects of this accusation radiate beyond Lucas; they upset his son who lives with his ex-wife. The community's punitive shaming goads vigilantes who assault him, vandalize his house, and even kill his dog. Eventually, Lucas is proven innocent and acquitted, and reintegrated within the community.

Es Devlin's scenic design amplifies the sense of confinement, ostracism, and fragility that ripples through the plot. An exquisitely minimalist and elegant glass house is mounted stage center, its base rotating and exposing the actors, trapped inside, from all sides. The glass carapace heightens an intense sense of exposure, even vulnerability. This glass house is the setting for the school, a church, a courtyard, and a lodge in the woods. Various rituals of masculinity play out within its precincts: Men drink and sing, hunt, and fight in ways that symbolically reinforce masculinist discourses of security regimes and protectionism. The lighting and sound design further enhance the sense of precariousness captured in the scenic design. The close bonds of community may well be imagined like the glass house – at once the work of beauty but also a stultifying enclosure. Carefully choreographed scenes display the increasingly belligerent community hunting down Lucas. An enigmatic antlered stag appears fleetingly within the glass box and reinforces a sense of hunted prey, while also conveying the machismo that undergirds vigilante justice. In *Hunt*, the prey is Lucas, and the hunter is the community.

The play provoked strong responses in the audience, coming on the heels of the #MeToo movement; some audience members were chafed that the play explores in great empathic complexity the horror experienced by someone falsely accused of sexual abuse, even as similarly compelling accounts of sexual survivors seemed scant.[2] For others, its

[2] See, for example, Ava Wong Davies, "Review: HUNTED at Almeida Theatre," *Exeunt Magazine*, March 16, 2022, https://exeuntmagazine.com/reviews/review-hunt-almeida-theatre. Thomas Vinterberg's 1998 film, *Festen* (*Celebration*) inspired by the Dogme 95 movement, enjoyed a highly successful stage adaptation and portrays the lingering trauma experienced by survivors of parental sexual assault. The film exposes powerfully the social denial and collective refusal to take accusations of sexual assault seriously. Turning now to the falsely accused in *The Hunt*, Vinterberg describes how they too are victimized, as are the children who begin to believe the truth of their accusations.

taut storytelling and elegant visual design combined to make for a powerful evening of theatre. Critic Mark Shenton applauded the play for its "churning unease," and described it as a "gripping, unsettling evening – not easy to watch, but impossible to look away from."[3]

To an audience that never doubts the protagonist's innocence, *The Hunt* offers the moral certitudes of comfort, closure, and even catharsis. The townspeople recognize their folly. Innocence, it suggests, is not the exclusive property of children.[4] Lucas is vindicated and enfolded again in the warm, if stifling, embrace of community.[5] Indeed, the dramatic narrative of *The Hunt* unfolds along the lines of what anthropologist Victor Turner describes as "social drama": The false accusation of sexual abuse instigates a breach in the fabric of a tight-knit Danish community. The breach widens into a crisis, fueled by sex panic, which sets off vigilante justice. Ultimately, the police investigation concludes that the allegation is false, and the story

> Of course abuse happens – I made a film about that already. But I think that there's this other danger and it demands new sacrifices, new victims. These victims are not only the men – and sometimes women – who are accused of something they haven't done. But they are also the children who grow up believing they are victims. Those children operate under the grand illusion that something bad has happened to them; they grow up with similar experiences to the children who really did experience it . . . It's rotten, rotten territory.

See Xan Brooks, "Thomas Vinterberg: Back in The Hunt," *The Guardian*, November 22, 2012, www.theguardian.com/film/2012/nov/22/thomas-vinterberg-the-hunt-festen.

3 Mark Shenton, "Review: *The Hunt* at Almeida Theatre," *London Theatre*, May 25, 2022, www.londontheatre.co.uk/reviews/review-the-hunt-at-the-almeida-theatre; Michael Billington, "*The Hunt* Review: False Accusation Unleashes Small-Town Savagery," *The Guardian*, June 27, 2019, www.theguardian.com/stage/2019/jun/27/the-hunt-review-almeida-thomas-vinterberg-rupert-goold.

4 See Robin Bernstein's excellent account of the making of childhood innocence in nineteenth-century America in *Racial Innocence: Performing American Childhood from Slavery to Civil Rights* (New York: New York University Press, 2011).

5 While violent sex offenders were surgically castrated in Denmark until the 1970s, today, they can be detained indefinitely, in addition to undergoing medical castration. Denmark views criminal offending as a social problem rather than a problem of individual pathology. As a result, the country boasts of robust social programs that enable formerly incarcerated people to reintegrate into society. See Nick Pearce, "Danish Prisons: Dinner for Wife and Kids," *New Statesman* 135, no. 4808 (April 9, 2006): 16.

closes on the image of a reintegrated community, which appears, like the glass house, at once solid and fragile.[6] The breach is redressed but leaves its trace: In the final scene, a shooter takes aim at Lucas; the bullet misses him and grazes past his head. Still hunted, still prey, Lucas remains vulnerable to vigilantes unconvinced of his innocence.

In her authoritative study *Law as Performance*, Julie Stone Peters reminds us, "No one living in the age of late modern mass media – when moving images have taken over the public sphere and brought the courtroom into the palms of our hands – would now say that law takes '[n]ihil ex scenâ': "nothing from the theatre."[7] This is especially borne out in the cultural politics of criminal law. Political theatre saturates criminal law, and mainstream media play an integral role in relaying and consolidating pernicious narratives of heightened crime. The politicization of crime is mediated through culture, exaggerating fears over criminality and normalizing ever more draconian penalties. The media-fueled specter of sexual threats to children has resulted in the formation of some of the most severe laws against sex offenders. The repetition of this cultural imagery normalized state and public violence toward "sexual predators," repeatedly cast as nonhuman outlaws.

Evoking animal imagery, medieval English law casts the outlaw as "caput lupinum," a concept that signifies "the head of the wolf." In the famous thirteenth-century text of jurisprudence, *De Legibus et Consuetudinibus Anglioe*, Henry of Bracton writes, "An outlaw also forfeits everything connected with the peace, for from the time he is outlawed he bears the wolf 's head, so that he may be slain by anyone with impunity, especially if he resists or takes to fight so that his arrest is difficult."[8]

[6] While the police are portrayed as measured and reasonable investigators of crime in this film, new Danish sex offender laws have cast the police as punitive agents, required to surveil and strip sex offenders of their civil rights, inhibiting their reintegration into society. See Kasper Jorgensen, "The Police Monitoring of Sex Offenders in Denmark," Masters in Criminology Thesis, Aalborg University, 2021.

[7] Julie Stone Peters, *Law as Performance: Theatricality, Spectatorship, and the Making of Law in Ancient, Medieval, and Early Modern Europe* (Oxford: Oxford University Press, 2022), 301.

[8] Quoted in Desmond Manderson, "From Hunger to Love: Myths of the Source, Interpretation, and Constitution of Law in Children's Literature," *Law & Literature* 15, no. 1 (2003): 87–141.

Decreed via legal fiat, the performative speech act singles out the felon as one who may be legally killed as if they were a predatory wolf. Developing this trope of the wolf-man or werewolf as the outlaw, Giorgio Agamben points out:

> What had to remain in the collective unconscious as a monstrous hybrid of human and animal, divided between the forest and the city – the werewolf – is, therefore, in its origin the figure of the man who has been banned from the city. That such a man is defined as a wolf-man and not simply as a wolf (the expression caput lupinum has the form of a juridical statute) is decisive here. The life of the bandit ... is the life of the loup garou, the werewolf, who is precisely neither man nor beast, and who dwells paradoxically within both while belonging to neither ... Only in this light does the Hobbesian mythologeme of the state of nature acquire its true sense ... at issue is not simply fera bestia and natural life but rather a zone of indistinction between the human and the animal, a werewolf, a man who is transformed into a wolf and a wolf who is transformed into a man – in other words, a bandit, a homo sacer.[9]

Shuttling between animal and person, the sex offender is an exemplary outlaw figure, banned from the precincts of civility, consigned to the outskirts of the city and lurking in the shadows. Situating the felon outside the zone and protection of the law, such a decree sanctions community vengeance. As *homo sacer*, connoting bare life, the law exposes the felon to the wrath of the community. The sex offender stokes an imaginal reservoir and emerges as a hybrid beast, a felon bearing the head of a wolf, and a creature that may be killed with impunity. Jonathan Simon reminds us that "sex offenders are our modern-day monsters, producing tidal waves of public demand."[10] As if presaging a sense of unease and menace, the sex offender hovers between animality and monstrosity, itself a word that draws from "monstrum" for portents, and derives from the verb "monere," which suggests to warn or foretell.

[9] Giorgio Agamben, Homo Sacer*: Sovereign Power and Bare Life* (Stanford, CA: Stanford University Press, 1998), pp. 63–64.

[10] See Jonathan Simon, "Managing the Monstrous: Sex Offenders and the New Penology," *Psychology, Public Policy, and Law* 4, no. 1–2 (1998): 452–467, at 456.

Viewed simultaneously as beast, monster, and specter, connoting an animal appetite and shadowy pervasiveness, the sex offender is imagined outside the bounds of personhood.[11]

On the other side of the spectrum, the performative force of "the victimized child" legitimates severe punitive sanctions. The white child is the exemplary figure of vulnerability and summons our protective impulses. As community members aver in *The Hunt*, "The happiness of our children is everything. Our hopes and dreams rest in these tiny souls."[12] If, for Lauren Berlant, the "infantile citizen" indexes the increasing privatization of civic life, then for Lee Edelman the child remains "the perpetual horizon of every acknowledged politics, the fantasmatic beneficiary of every political intervention."[13] Any notion of utopian political projects is securely fastened on the child, the paradigmatic figure of futurity. The vulnerability of the child marshals the guardian trope within national culture, while simultaneously legitimating harsh penalties for pedophiles and sex offenders.

While the discursive construction of vulnerable subjects enables paternalistic discourses and legitimizes brutal state reprisals, it is also critical to consider how the law itself exacerbates the vulnerability of those accused. How might thinking with vulnerability as a heuristic allow us to consider both the survivor's exposure to interpersonal and systemic violence as well as the sex offender's exposure to carceral state violence and their social abjection from society? The vulnerability of our social relations makes us susceptible to interpersonal, community, and state violence. Can avowing vulnerability as the shared social terrain that risks wounding

11 Robert Werth argues that the anxiety about the pervasive and elusive danger of sex offenders has turned them from monsters to specters. He points out, "while monsters can be brandished (through sex offender registries), located (via GPS monitoring), and monitored (by parole personnel and concerned neighbors), ghosts tend to confound placement (both spatially and temporally) and resist containment efforts. As a result, they trouble confirmation and certainty – which means that they are equally adept at resisting refutation, even if and when they do not exist." See Robert Werth, "More Than Monsters: Penal Imaginaries and the Specter of the Dangerous Sex Offender," *Punishment and Society* 25, no. 4 (2022): 1–21.

12 David Farr, *The Hunt* (London: Faber and Faber, 2019), 9.

13 See Lauren Berlant, *The Queen of America Goes to Washington City: Essays on Sex and Citizenship* (Durham, NC: Duke University Press, 1997); Lee Edelman, *No Future: Queer Theory and the Death Drive* (Durham, NC: Duke University Press, 2004).

unsettle the criminal law binarism that pits vulnerable victims against monstrous offenders? This chapter considers how shaming practices inflicted by the community and the state, in particular, expose and exacerbate the vulnerability of the offender. In the face of such harsh shaming practices, I examine the offender's strategies of psychic management, that range from self-loathing to internalized vigilantism. I consider how vulnerability is politicized but can also offer resources to reimagine the social contract and move us toward more just and humane models of accountability and redress.

The figure of the innocent child, the paradigmatic victim par excellence, evokes powerful protectionist impulses and summons all the resources of the masculinist state. Absorbing and refracting the contradictory discursive and symbolic functions of male social dominance, masculinist state power works through diffuse and multiple channels, drawing on and disseminating the ideologies of the heteronormative family unit. The emergent protectionist discourses acquired a new intensity in the 1980s and legitimated harsher penalties. In the wake of the disappearance of Etan Patz in 1979, and the subsequent emergence of moral panics that surrounded discourses around "missing children," the sex offender came under greater scrutiny.[14] The anxiety around the sex offender, of course, emerged much earlier and impacted shifting gender relations in the political and legal imaginary.

John D'Emilio and Estelle Freedman's pathbreaking scholarship has traced the historical shifts from the nineteenth century emphasis on policing female sexuality to concerns surrounding social and sexual hygiene to a modern preoccupation with controlling male violence.[15] Channeling male lust toward procreative sexuality maintained the ideal of female purity, while also upholding heterosexual patriarchy. However,

[14] Paul Renfro traces the conjuncture of bereaved parents, media sensationalism, and state legislation that propelled a narrative around threats to endangered children. See Paul Renfro, *Stranger Danger: Family Values, Childhood, and the American Carceral State* (Oxford: Oxford University Press, 2020). For the differential treatment given to black children missing during the same period, see Judith Levine and Erica Meiners, *The Feminist and the Sex Offender: Confronting Sexual Harm, Ending State Violence* (London: Verso, 2020).

[15] John D'Emilio and Estelle Freedman, *Intimate Matters: A History of Sexuality in America* (Chicago, IL: University of Chicago Press, 2012). See especially chapter 12.

when sexual mores for women loosened, the sex regulators needed a new figure to police, and the sexual psychopath stepped into this vacuum, allowing a new site for the regulation of sexual behavior. The simultaneous emergence of the sexual psychopath in the 1930s in media, legal, and populist discourses offered a new rationale to crack down on sex offenders, a capacious category that included perverts, homosexuals, and minor offenders. In Freedman's words,

> The disruption of traditional family life during the depression, when record numbers of men lost their status as breadwinners, triggered concerns about masculinity ... the male sexual deviant became the subject of special attention, particularly if he was inadequately masculine (the effeminate homosexual) or hypermasculine (the sexual psychopath). Both categories of deviant males were thought to attack children, thus simultaneously threatening sexual innocence, gender roles, and the social order. The psychopath neatly fit these concerns.[16]

The affective and political power of childhood vulnerability legitimated heightened criminal penalties for those accused of sex crimes. Roger Lancaster points out how sex panics are "less about the protection of children than about the preservation of adult fantasies of childhood as a time of sexual innocence[;] sex panics give rise to bloated imaginings of risk, inflated conceptions of harm, and loose definitions of sex."[17] Drawing on Freedman's work, Lancaster locates the emergence and circulation of sex panics in the 1930s just as the Southern lynch law went into decline. While execution or incarceration emerged as the primary solutions to contain rapacious black criminality, white sex offenders were deemed sick and confined to mental institutions under sexual psychopath laws. Lancaster points out that white and vigilante citizens' and parents' associations that came into being during the sex panics of the Depression and McCarthy era demonstrated the increasing ways in which citizen demands were articulated in a register of

[16] Estelle B. Freedman, "'Uncontrolled Desires': The Response to the Sexual Psychopath, 1920–1960," *Journal of American History* 74, no. 1 (June 1987): 83–106 at 89.

[17] Roger Lancaster, *Sex Panics and the Punitive State* (Berkeley: University of California Press, 2011).

victimhood, thus normalizing and cementing the role of the state as the protector of vulnerable citizens.

It is no surprise then that laws too have been formed in the very names of children. The new laws since the 1990s imposed ever more punitive penalties and restrictions on sex offenders in prison and after release. These penalties often flow into the coffers of the police, court, and criminal legal system, thus offering incentives to continue to expand the scope of the carceral state. This victims' rights' movements coincide with what Malcolm Feeley and Jonathan Simon call the "new penology," which focuses on managing aggregates of dangerous groups and high-risk "populations" rather than rehabilitating individuals to community norms.[18] Chrysanthi Leon reinforces this point in her study where she argues that risk assessment and control, psychological and biological surveillance are increasingly the norms rather than treatment or prevention.[19] Meanwhile, numerous studies show that "sex offenders have among the lowest same crime recidivism rates of any category of

[18] Malcolm M. Feeley and Jonathan Simon, "The New Penology: Notes on the Emerging Strategy of Corrections and Its Implications," *Criminology* 449 (1992): 449–474.

[19] Chrysanthi Leon, *Sex Fiends, Perverts, and Pedophiles: Understanding Sex Crime Policy in America* (New York: New York University Press, 2011). Leon notes that Jessica's Law, in its California iteration, increased sentences for existing sex crimes, added lifetime GPS monitoring of sex offenders, dramatically expanded eligibility for the state's civil commitment, and restricted where released sex offenders may live. She also observes,

> Prison admissions for felony sex offenses remained flat until the 1960s despite extensive media attention to sensational sex cases, punitive public attitudes, and frequent passage of new laws aimed at sex crime. These contradict what we might have expected from accounts about "panics" surrounding sex fiends and psychopaths in the postwar period. It also contradicts penal theorists who consider sex offender punishment as exemplary as well: from 1940 to 1971, there was a 48% decrease in sex offender prison admissions, while the big period of expansion occurred from 1971 to 1984, when there was a 486% increase. After 1984, there were some fluctuations, but nothing comparable to the pre-1984 increase.

Also in 2006, coinciding with the twenty-fifth anniversary of the abduction of Adam Walsh, President Bush signed into law the AWA; the statute contained a plethora of new restrictions, sentences, and requirements for sex offenders. See Corey Rayburn Yung, "Sex Offender Exceptionalism and Preventative Detention," *Journal of Criminal Law and Criminology* 101, no. 3 (2011): 969–1003, at 978.

offender."[20] Indeed, as Corey Rayburn Yung has pointed out, "particular myths of extremely high recidivism rates and 'stranger danger' have largely served to support various restrictions on sex offenders as well as substantiate court opinions upholding those restrictions."[21]

The sheer heterogeneity of criminal acts that the term "sex offender" encompasses itself is striking: It includes rape, indecent exposure, public urination, possession of child pornography, voyeurism, production or distribution of obscenity, bestiality, solicitation of a prostitute, statutory rape, distribution of child pornography, "sexting" by teenagers, incest, and lower degrees of sexual assault, including groping. Pointing out the "sex offender exceptionalism," Corey Rayburn Yung notes:

> While murderers, armed assailants, gang leaders, and spousal abusers return to the streets of America after their sentences are complete, sex offenders are treated differently. The distinction between those who commit sex offenses and other criminals is not so much substantive as it is political. America has begun what can only be described as a criminal war on sex offenders akin to the War on Drugs that has continued for nearly forty years. ... A criminal war is marked by three elements: myth creation, exception-making, and a marshaling of resources.[22]

The image of the vulnerable child provides powerful grist for the mill, sutures "family values" onto the state, and perpetuates the trope of the family as the microcosm of the nation. In the process, the electorate itself is feminized, imagined as vulnerable, and requiring the masculinist

[20] Thomas Ward Frampton, "The Dangerous Few: Taking Seriously Prison Abolition and Its Skeptics," *Harvard Law Review* 135, no. 8 (June 2022): 2013–2052, at 2037. See also David Fiege, "The Supreme Court's Sex Offender Jurisprudence Is Based On A Lie," *Slate*, March 7, 2017, https://slate.com/news-and-politics/2017/03/sex-offender-bans-are-based-on-bad-science.html.

[21] Corey Rayburn Yung, "Sex Offender Exceptionalism and Preventative Detention," *Journal of Criminal Law and Criminology* 101, no. 3 (2011): 973.

[22] Yung, "Sex Offender," 997. He further argues that "In the case of sex offender civil commitment, the circumstances are no more dire than for other serious crimes, the danger is speculative based upon pseudo-science, and the net is far too broad. Because of these aspects of SVP laws, America should fundamentally reconsider its approach to fighting sexual violence. Laws like the federal SVP statute, premised on myths that allocate substantial resources in a never ending war, do not create a just or better society." Yung, "Sex Offender," 1003.

protection of the state. The ever more stringent laws around sex offenders trigger a mimetic rivalry of muscular nationalism between liberals and conservatives. The feminized public that emerges as the beneficiary of law and order is not a prediscursive category; rather sex panics retroactively constitute this public. An addressable object is conjured into being in order to enable the very discourse that gives it existence.[23] Hence "the public" that is at the receiving end of information about endangered children is not a pregiven, a priori collective but rather a discursively constituted category that is constructed through cultural narratives around crime. This rhetorically constituted public then legitimates punitive policies and rewards politicians who politicize crime.

Turning the trope on its head, *The Hunt* focuses on the suffering and vulnerability of the accused. The play reveals how an accusation of sexual assault can devastate one's physical and mental well-being, while also exploring its repercussions on loved ones and its corrosive impact on community relations. In allowing the audience to empathize with someone falsely accused, the film solicits our compassion for Lucas. But how might our reaction shift if the accused was not innocent like Lucas, but indeed guilty of sex crimes against children? Would we be able to retain a sense of moral complexity when the certitudes offered in *The Hunt* are muddied? What if instead of the catharsis and closure that *The Hunt* provides we are left with feelings of ambiguity, or even disgust?

The structural antagonism of criminal law offers competing notions about who constitutes the victim in scenes of criminal offending: the individual harmed by a particular crime or the accused who may also be a victim of larger systemic marginalization and structural deprivation. For the prosecution, the accused is an autonomous, agential legal subject, who must take responsibility for their actions; for the defense, the victimization of the accused remains unacknowledged, subjected as they often

[23] See Michael Warner, *Publics and Counterpublics* (New York: Zone Books, 2002). This auto-telic circularity is a key feature of Warner's conception of the public. Moving away from an understanding of discourse as Habermasian communicative rationality, Warner explores the multigeneric, cross-citational heterogeneous social field of discourse, which projects for the public a concrete livable world and attempts to realize that world through its address.

are to larger systemic disadvantages. These accounts provide images of the accused that oscillate between subjecthood and subjection, evoking earlier debates around individual agency versus social determinism. Eschewing these binary formulations allows us to consider how legal actors are constituted in and through relations of power: Social subjection is the ground for the emergence of legal subjecthood.

While studies have pointed out the victim/offender binary often overlaps or exists in a continuum, with those who harm likely to have been harmed themselves, prevailing criminal law continues to perpetuate a binary model.[24] The antagonism that structures criminal law saturates cultural responses, eclipsing other avenues for redress and repair. Addressing sexual violence does not require draconian penalties; conversely, addressing carceral expansion does not necessitate minimizing sexual violence: this is a false choice.[25] A more capacious notion of justice

[24] See Cynthia Godsoe, "The Victim/Offender Overlap and Criminal System Reform," *Brooklyn Law Review* 77, no. 3 (2012): 1053–1101.

[25] See, for instance, this exchange in Bruce Norris' new play, *Downstate*, where a survivor of child sex abuse, Andy, confronts a sex abuser:

> ANDY: I was assaulted, okay? It was an act of violence.
> DEE: Ya mean an old man sucked your dick.
> ANDY: I was raped by a serial predator. It was a criminal act.
> DEE: Oh honey. If suckin' dicks was a crime I'd be Al Capone.

While the play portrays powerfully the extreme social abjection that people released from jail for sexual offenses endure, it minimizes the traumatic repercussions of sexual violence. Bruce Norris, *Downstate* (London: Nick Hern Books, 2019). For an insightful analysis of this play, see Ryan Donovan, "'It Feels Like Being in Jail All Over Again': Staging the Criminalized Liminality of Sex Offenders," *Theatre Journal* 76, no. 3 (September 2024): 341–358. In legal scholarship, see Aya Gruber's "Sex Exceptionalism," which criticizes "sex exceptionalism" in criminal law and in society at large, and advocates that sex crimes be treated as ordinary assault. Gruber objects, "A simple assault that leaves no injuries is a misdemeanor or no crime at all, but a sexual assault without physical injury or intent to injure is often a serious felony" (770). "Sex crimes," however, is a malleable and differentiated category. Dismissing the specific delineation of *sexual* assault may misconstrue what precisely was injurious about the conduct. It may minimize the psychic injury of nonviolent sexual assaults; may exacerbate existing power imbalances, obscure questions of privilege, coercive control, and sexual entitlement; may neglect the constitutive, systemic force of misogyny in sexual assault, gender violence, and even nonsexual harassment; and may overlook the violation of sexual privacy. Such a move ironically exceptionalizes physical violence as paradigmatic of crimes worthy of punishment, invisibilizes

that is committed to decarceration, while allowing a path toward accountability and healing can simultaneously dismantle the adversarial topology of criminal law.

Thinking with vulnerability as a heuristic moves us beyond the antinomies enshrined in criminal law. While tropes of vulnerability are mobilized to justify paternalistic state coercion of individuals and groups, vulnerability is also a powerful reminder of the interdependence and mutuality of humans. Centering vulnerability may allow us to rethink the foundations of our social contract in ways that acknowledge both our precariousness and the sovereign violence that holds us in its thrall. It allows us to highlight the lack of systemic and structural support that produces precarity in the first place. It provides a larger contextual framework where we can examine the socioeconomic environments of precarity that encourage risk-taking behaviors. It allows us to undo pernicious and pervasive social structures of racism and misogyny. Thinking with vulnerability affirms relational personhood.

Political theorists as early as Thomas Hobbes writing in 1651 emphasize that the corporeal vulnerability of the political subject necessitates a powerful state. The vulnerable political subject joins membership in a rationally devised political body, which grants protection through its awesome power. The threat to corporeal vulnerability is mitigated and overcome through recourse to a "common power" of the "body politique." By consenting to the sovereign power of the formidable state, the diffident subjects secure their mortal safety and material well-being. An overpowering Leviathan state restrains citizens in several ways: Diffident subjects would check their own capacity for criminal offending for fear of the consequences of an absolute sovereign power; the citizens would cede to the state their desire for vengeance and have the state act on their behalf.

The foundations of criminal law are inextricably entwined with the mobilization, circulation, and curation of fear of the Leviathan state. By instilling fear, the sovereign deters criminal behavior and fosters peace

variable injuries that may be sustained by sexual assault, and may end up recirculating the structure of disavowal that enables misogynist dismissiveness of rape. Aya Gruber, "Sex Exceptionalism in Criminal Law," *Stanford Law Review* 75 (April 2023): 755–846.

and security. To regulate social relations within society, the sovereign defines what is socially acceptable behavior; such norms do not exist a priori in a state of nature. The state then enforces these artificial norms. Hobbes suggests that criminals who are punished by the state have consented to this punishment, indeed, "authorized" it. In this way, the state reinscribes the vulnerability of citizens.

If for Hobbes human vulnerability is the precondition that legitimates a powerful carceral state, for Emmanuel Levinas, vulnerability heightens our awareness of the intersubjective constitution of our subjectivity. Preceding our entry into language, this intersubjective, embodied encounter with others ensures that the trace of another is constitutive of the self. Levinasian intersubjectivity pervades the dynamic between actors in scenarios of sexual harm. The sensory flesh memory of another remains long past the event, reminding us that the event has not ended, but rather continues to exert its hold upon us in subtle and powerful ways. The malaise that arises from the scene of sexual harm leaves its lingering trace as a precognitive flesh memory, an intense and affective vulnerability. The face-to-face encounter with another opens us up to vulnerability, while also soliciting our sense of responsibility, as a prereflective opening of an embodied intersubjective self.

Contra the Leviathan state's invulnerable image that induces awe and diffidence in its citizens, the avowal of vulnerability amongst the citizens allows us to conceive of personhood itself as porous, susceptible to identification, and composed of the traces of our social relations. In the domain of legal theory, Martha Albertson Fineman reminds us that vulnerability is not "a substitute term for weakness or disadvantage, . . . but rather calls into focus what we share as human beings, what we should expect of the laws and the underlying social structures, and relationships that organize society and affect the lives of everyone within society."[26] Developing this insight into the arena of political assembly, Judith Butler has recuperated vulnerability as political action and explored its possibility to generate ethical obligations. Vulnerability is not only an invariable feature of social relations, but also gestures a broader condition of

[26] Martha Albertson Fineman, "Vulnerability and Social Justice," *Valparaiso University Law Review* 53 (2019): 341–370, at 342.

interdependency, which changes the dominant ontological understanding of the embodied subject.[27] Rather than think of vulnerability and resistance as antonyms, or as a propensity that disables agency, Butler forwards vulnerability as an agentic mode of political action.[28] These scholars highlight that the analytical paradigm of vulnerability foregrounds our interdependency within social institutions and the need for a public response for our shared vulnerability, especially when increasingly neoliberal policies attenuate the role of social supports for individuals in society.

While cultural productions have played a large role in perpetuating and cementing binary models of good victims and evil perpetrators, a closer look at perpetrators reveals that many are themselves victims who have endured suffering. The prevailing binary models of criminal law fail to capture the complex and shifting subjective terrain of those who commit crimes. While much mainstream media reinforces these binaries, we do see some alternative depictions that bring us into proximity with criminalized people we may not otherwise encounter in life, and indeed, we may deliberately avoid. These more nuanced scenes of proximity with sex offenders portray their vulnerability and their subsequent strategies of psychic management as they grapple with the punitive shaming and "civil torture" from law enforcement and community members.[29]

Steven Fechter's play *The Woodsman*, which opened at The Actor's Studio in New York in 2000, provides an example of a more complex portrait of a sex offender. The play urges us to see the frailty of both survivors and perpetrators under sovereign power and centers vulnerability in the scenario of sexual harm. A modern-day allegory of the story of Little Red Riding Hood, *The Woodsman* portrays the protagonist,

27 Judith Butler, *On Assembly* (New York: Oxford University Press, 2015).

28 Bennett Capers has drawn attention to the limits of the analytical category of vulnerability, pointing out especially that its paternalism/maternalism shortchanges agency and entrenches existing inequities. See Bennett Capers, "On Violence against Women," *Ohio State Journal of Criminal Law* 13 (2015–16): 347–363, at 347.

29 I am grateful to Bob Weisberg for suggesting the phrase "civil torture" as a way of capturing the social and state reprisals experienced by registered sex offenders. Thanks also to Peter Goodrich for pointing out that the Roman term *infamia* signified civil death or outlawry (*utlagarie*) and was a common outcome for sex offenders.

Walter, as both the wolf and the huntsman. Activating the tropes of both animal and savior, the play explores Walter's struggle to reform his darkest impulses. The play draws on the symbolic and psychic reverberations of the medieval English legal concept of the "caput lupinum" or the felon with a wolf's head, an outlaw pariah whose exposure makes him vulnerable to attacks by anyone in the community. The play suggests both the permanent relegation of sex offenders to the category of the outlaw, while also illuminating social practices that prolong perpetual punishment and interminable reprisals.

Released on parole, after serving twelve years in prison for sexually molesting young girls, Walter struggles to cope with life after imprisonment. He is a skilled craftsman who makes furniture. Upon his release, he finds employment at a lumberyard, where he meets and befriends Vickie, a woman with her own experience of childhood sexual abuse at the hands of her brothers. The play unfurls the psychic tapestry of Walter's subjectivity and allows us to see the friction between his social identity as sex offender and his personal identification with the savior figure. The dramatic agon between his identity and his identification propels this narrative, and the audience is presented with a sympathetic and complex portrayal of a sex offender.

Nicole Kassell's 2004 film version casts Kevin Bacon in the lead role as Walter, and he portrays with acuity and depth the psychic turmoil of a self-loathing pedophile desperate to escape his own desires. Both play and film versions enable audience proximity to the character of a sex offender. In allowing us to get close, *The Woodsman* widens the aperture through which we typically view sex offenders. The play fosters an attentiveness that invites us to suspend censure, engender curiosity, and affirm the humanity and personhood of sex offenders, typically imagined as monsters, specters, or animals.

The Woodsman probes the deep and enduring impact of sexual violence and how it transfigures the lives of victims as well as perpetrators. It gestures toward the loss of agency and disorientation experienced by survivors, betrayed by those entrusted with their care. The play delineates the subjectivity of Walter in ways that exceed the bounded autonomous and individual subject of criminal law. By accentuating Walter's vulnerability, the play urges audiences to consider his complex, shifting, and processual subjectivity, and his struggle to change.

Walter's sexual subjectivity is shaped by the primal scene of taking afternoon naps with his sister when he was six and she was four years old. The memory of her fragrant hair both soothes and arouses him. He carries that tenderness and desire into his adult relationship with Vickie, but a darker impulse of that memory triggers his predation of young girls. His self-loathing prompts him to remake himself in the figure of the savior. In this endeavor, he switches between the roles of the police, the father figure, and the vigilante.

The Woodsman portrays Walter's subjectivity as composed of numerous traces: He is at once wolf and huntsman, perpetrator and police. When Carlos, his brother-in-law, talks about his fondness for his daughter, Walter discerns a remnant of his own pedophilic desire. Carlos reminisces about bathing his daughter, "I remember when she was a little thing and I'd give her baths. I'd hold her wet little body in my hands and think, can anything be more perfect? She's the light of my life." Walter warns and pleads simultaneously, "Don't love her too much, Carlos."[30] Walter sexualizes this interaction between father and daughter. Perhaps the description triggers some pedophilic desire in him. He shares his concerns regarding Carlos's behavior to the state-mandated psychotherapist, Rosen, "Carlos has a thing for his daughter, and if he isn't careful, he's going to suffer." Likewise, Walter identifies with the brothers of his girlfriend Vickie who confesses that she was "poked around . . . here and there." Frustrating Walter's and the audience's expectation of resentment or hostility, she says simply, "I love all of them. They are strong, gentle men with families of their own. And if you ask them about what they did to me, they'd call you a liar and then beat the shit out of you."[31] While Walter activates the stereotype of "stranger danger," the play suggests that sexual abuse is a far more familiar and familial occurrence, happening both within the home and beyond.[32] Walter also

[30] Steven Fechter, *The Woodsman* (New York: Dramatists Play Service, 2014): 16.

[31] Fechter, *The Woodsman*, 43–44.

[32] See Paul Renfro, *Stranger Danger: Family Values, Childhood, and the American Carceral State* (Oxford: Oxford University Press, 2020). The book examines how bereaved parents of missing and slain children mobilized their grief into a victims' rights

identifies with "Candy," the man who hovers around shiftily outside a boys' school.[33] He recognizes something of his own rituals of seduction in the movements and patterns of Candy, a name he coins that serves as synecdoche for both person and thing, bait and lure. Acting as a vigilante, while exorcising his own demons, Walter suspects Candy of molesting schoolboys and eventually beats him up. Each of these identifications with real and imagined child molesters also gives rise to its obverse – the savior figure who wants to rescue his niece, his girlfriend, and the schoolboys.

If identity works through a logic of exclusion, demarcating boundaries between self and other, us and them, then identification blurs them.[34] In identifying with others, the porous self both projects onto others and assimilates others into the self. The substitutions and proxies that are set in motion through numerous identifications allow Walter to dodge and evade the fixity of the identity category of "sex offender," a fixity reinforced through shaming punishments such as parole and the sex offender registry.[35] Seeing himself in a plethora of other characters allows Walter to project onto others his "deviance" and normalize his

movement, which created new punitive policies that legitimized increasingly draconian carceral measures.

33 In a deliberate contrivance, Walter defiantly chooses to live across a school but ensuring that he abides by legal regulations that prohibit sex offenders from residing within 100 feet of places where children congregate. His apartment is 105 feet away from the school. Walter reinforces to his parole officer the difficulty of finding places to live that are affordable. Jessica's Law is the informal name given to a 2005 Florida law that mandates a minimum twenty-five-year prison sentence and lifetime electronic monitoring for adults convicted of lewd and lascivious acts against a child. In 2006, California passed Proposition 83, which increased punishment for sex offenders and prohibited probation for some sex offenses, and required GPS monitoring. It also prohibits offenders from living within 2,000 feet of any school or park, but that was ruled unconstitutional in March 2015.

34 See Elin Diamond, *Unmaking Mimesis: Essays on Feminism and Theatre* (New York: Routledge, 1997).

35 Sex offense registration and notification laws, (SORN) a product of the "tough on crime" era, epitomize the lingering and persistent damage of collateral consequences. First established in the 1940s as a way to keep police informed about the locations of habitual sex offenders, the laws dwindled until 1990s when the Clinton Crime Bill brought them back with renewed force. The European Union along with some individual countries, including the United Kingdom, Canada, Australia, and New Zealand, makes registry information available to law enforcement, but not to the

own sense of abjection. In doing so, he unsettles the coherence and stability of the punitive category of sex offender. His grasping stabs at vigilantism are attempts to flee himself, but tearing himself away from this identity proves difficult. Yearning for a self-sufficiency that eludes the stigmatized, Walter turns his self-loathing and vengeance toward Candy, his doppelganger.

Shame dramatizes the inescapable vulnerability of the self: Interlining the boundary between the body and society, shame exposes one's vulnerability.[36] *The Woodsman* explores the power and limits of shame as a technology of punishment, and especially of self-punishment.[37] Formal shaming exists as an ubiquitous tool in the arsenal of criminal sanctions, and "exploits, in a particularly dramatic and explicit fashion, the assumed link between people's sense of shame and their tendency to observe legal norms."[38] Moreover, shame sanctions function as a form of officially sponsored lynch justice that legitimate mob violence.[39] Not only do

general public. Poland is an exception. In the words of Judith Levine and Erica Meiners,

> SORN is based on a fear and a fantasy. The fear is that the outside world is perilous, full of morally corrupting strangers. The fantasy is that the family is a sanctuary, where sexuality is limited to the monogamous relationship of husband and wife, and where the asexual innocence of children, including adolescents, is guarded. But child protection cannot be based on irrational anxieties and saccharine dreams. Public registries and community notification are meant to enhance public safety. They do not. Nor do they help survivors reclaim their well-being. The only thing the registries accomplish is the registrant's social death. There is no reasonable defense for them. They should be abolished. (Judith Levine and Erica Meiners, *The Feminist and the Sex Offender: Confronting Sexual Harm, Ending State Violence* [London: Verso, 2020], 52)

36 For a powerful and moving account of shame, sexual assault, and the law, see Maybell Romero, "Shamed," *Virginia Law Review* 111, no. 2 (2025): 325–377.

37 See Dan Markel on the illiberality of shaming punishments that unsettles the presumption that shaming is compatible with retributive punishments. Dan Markel, "Are Shaming Punishments Beautifully Retributive? Retributivism and the Implications for the Alternative Sanctions Debate," *Vanderbilt Law Review* 52, no. 6 (November 2001): 2157–2241.

38 Toni Massaro, "Shame, Culture, and American Criminal Law," *Michigan Law Review* 89, no. 7 (1991): 1880–1944.

39 James Whitman, "What Is Wrong with Inflicting Shame Sanctions?" *Yale Law Journal* 107, no. 5 (1998): 1055–1092.

shaming punishments harm the offender's dignity, they also incite demagogic politics, especially when imposed on sex offenders. The effect of these shaming punishments is to stigmatize incarcerated people, who begin to see themselves as damaged and incomplete persons.[40]

The Woodsman depicts the interpellative role of the police in installing a sense of shame and self-aversion in Walter. Sergeant Lucas thwarts Walter's attempts at reform and reinscribes his abject status as a social pariah. He lashes out at Walter:

> SERGEANT LUCAS: In my eyes, you are a piece of shit. Think anyone would miss you if I threw you out the window right now? I could say you jumped when I came in. Who are they going to believe? Not you because you'd be a dead piece of shit.
>
> WALTER: What's your badge number? I demand to know your badge number!
>
> SERGEANT LUCAS: My badge number is shut the fuck up! . . . I don't know why they keep letting scum like you return to the streets. It just means we got to catch you all over again.[41]

Rather than prohibiting his predation, the shaming revives the predator. Walter begins his hunt again. An unnerving scene in an urban park follows. Walter frequents the park and may be stalking a diligent eleven-year-old birdwatcher, Robin. It is a fragile scene. Robin is an alert, self-possessed, and thoughtful girl. Walter warms up to her, compliments her, and then asks if she would like to sit on his lap. She is startled, declines politely, then hesitates, not wanting to offend him. He touches her shoulder, then her hair. Her body registers her uneasiness: She closes her eyes, she shudders, she keeps up her nervous chatter. When Walter tries to convince her to go with him to a more secluded part of the park, she blurts out, "My daddy lets me sit on his lap." The words have an unsettling effect on Walter, as he hesitates and shuttles between his role as predator and protector.

[40] See Erving Goffman, who reminds us that stigmatized persons approach every encounter with "normals" not knowing whether others will recognize them as the whole person they experience themselves to be. Erving Goffman, *Stigma: Notes on the Management of Spoiled Identity* (New York: Simon & Schuster, 1963).

[41] Fechter, *The Woodsman*, 53–54.

WALTER: Do you like it when he asks you?

ROBIN: No.

Walter intuits immediately that her father "asks" her to sit on her lap rather than "lets" her sit on his lap. There is a pause. According to the stage directions, "her answer has a strange effect on Walter, as if for a moment he lost his balance. Carefully, he sits down and stares at his hands."[42] The pause resounds in the auditorium, and the audience lingers in this suspended moment. Walter is thrown by her response and loses his sense of footing. Will the minor jolt interrupt Walter's seduction ritual, his programmed pattern of abuse? Walter follows up with an onslaught of questions: Are you two alone when he asks you? Does he touch you? Does he say strange things? Does he move his legs in a funny way? In response, Robin simply drops her head down and sobs quietly. Walter is increasingly more agitated, he fumbles, changes tack, and shifts from the role of predator to protector. In a breathless series of questions, he asks:

WALTER: Have you told your mother?

(She shakes her head.)

You don't want to tell your mother?

(She shakes her head.)

Is there anyone at home you can talk to?

(She is silent.)

Is there a teacher you like at school?

(She nods.)

What's her name?

ROBIN: Ms. Kramer.

WALTER: Tell Ms. Kramer what your daddy does.

ROBIN: I can't.

WALTER: Yes, you can, Robin. You said you couldn't make the sound of a solitary vireo. But you did. Beautifully.

...

[42] Fechter, *The Woodsman*, 53–54.

ROBIN: I don't want to hurt my daddy. . . . You still want me to sit on your lap? I will. I don't mind.

WALTER: No.[43]

The narrative rupture begins with Robin's "No" to his sexual advances and ends with Walter's "No" to Robin's attempt to please him. The scene unfolds in this negative space as Robin deflects, skirts, and dodges Walter's advances. The compressed and stultifying mood initiated by the first "No" begins to unwind and soften with the second "No." The tense atmosphere lifts and the audience collectively experiences an affective shift, a surge of relief. This brief, unnerving scene traces Walter's shifting subject positions as he morphs from parolee to predator to protector, while also tracking Robin's tentative turn from a definitive "No" to Walter's advances to a coerced, less certain "Maybe." The scene tracks the displacement and unmooring of both characters. It suggests her acquiescing to please Walter by relenting to his demands.

Rather than pit perpetrator against victim in the stark binaries of criminal law, the tableau urges us to see what Levinas calls "the internal antagonism" within these characters.[44] Both characters struggle with their inner antagonism, and the scene is saturated with foreboding and a sense of shame. The loss of self-possession is acute in moments when the offender violates Robin's sense of safety in her own sexual subjectivity. This scene portrays the malleable and shifting subjectivity of the sex offender and the potential for change and transformation even in pedophiles, while also revealing the shifting contours of consent, revealing its internal contradictions where conciliation coincides with a desire for sexual autonomy.

Levinas suggests that shame is "the representation we form of ourselves as diminished beings with which we are pained to identify. Yet shame's whole intensity, everything it contains that stings us, consists precisely in our inability not to identify with this being who is already foreign to us and whose motives for acting we can no longer

[43] Fechter, *The Woodsman*, 62–63.

[44] Levinas writes, "The experience of pure being is at the same time the experience of its internal antagonism and of the escape that foists itself on us." Emmanuel Levinas, *On Escape* (Stanford, CA: Stanford University Press, 2003), 67.

comprehend."[45] Shame transfixes Walter; its tentacles claw their way into his subjectivity. His stabs at vigilantism offer a way for him to overcome shame's intensity. His restless oscillation from his roles as parolee to predator to protector agitates against the stigmatizing category of the "sex offender." Yet "the necessity of fleeing, in order to hide oneself, is put in check by the impossibility of fleeing oneself," Levinas reminds us. "What appears in shame is thus precisely the fact of being riveted to oneself, the radical impossibility of fleeing oneself to hide from oneself, the unalterably binding presence of the I to itself."[46] It is at this conjuncture of fixity and fleeing, of attachment and escape that we need to locate the friction between identity and identification. The identity of "sex offender" is a permanent scarlet letter that interpellates Walter, and his grasping identifications with the role of the protector attempt to escape this label. Whereas identity is predicated on the logic of exclusion, differentiating the sex offender from the rest of society, and develops its self-concept through a process of negation and contrast, identification lays bare the vulnerability and openness of the self. Walter's shame grounds him, even as he attempts to flee that immobility by projecting and throwing himself on to other characters.

Although Fechter's focus is very much on Walter, the portrayal of Robin makes vivid her fortitude and vulnerability. She is in the woods to watch the birds. She arrives with her binoculars and notebook in hand, in which she has recorded the names of sixty-seven birds that she has identified. When she sees Walter there, her approach is direct and uninhibited. She rebuffs his cliché line about her being pretty but is drawn in when he analogizes that "Most people only notice birds with the brightest colors."[47] Robin's visceral uneasiness is palpable as Walter begins with verbal then physical overtures. Something is familiar in this scenario; the traumatic repetition returns her to the primal and sordid scene of filial disillusionment. Walter figures as a mimetic proxy, a site of potential attachment, but also a menacing trigger of traumatic memory. While Walter sees in Robin a beautiful solitary vireo, a singular and hardy bird that sings sweet, slow songs, she sees her father in Walter, both the promise of that figure and its betrayal.

[45] Levinas, *On Escape*, 63. See also Goffman, *Stigma*. [46] Levinas, *On Escape*, 63.
[47] Fechter, *The Woodsman*, 59.

Stimulated by that memory and its lingering hold on her present, Robin's self-possession and composure come undone. When pressed with Walter's insistent questions, she is wordless. How to shape into words, give form and coherence to an assault that left her unmoored, shaken, and dispossessed? How to escape this temporally layered scene of assault, its sedimented history, and its repeated incursions into memory? How to overcome this simultaneous impossibility of wanting to flee while remaining riveted to oneself? Robin begins to sob. The unsettling scene of malaise encloses and smothers in an ever-tightening circle that Robin both returns to and attempts to flee.

Robin's vulnerability in turn solicits something from Walter. He responds to her inaudible petition, switches from his sexual advances to more protective gestures. Her inarticulate address summons in him a guardian figure, and he instructs her on how to secure her own safety. Oscillating between uncertainty and suspicion, only partially in possession of their own motives and desires, infiltrated by the presence of real and spectral others, these characters elude the binary categories of criminal law. *The Woodsman* is replete with specters, doubles, and doppelgangers in scenes where characters waver, shuttle, and oscillate between subject positions. It offers images of shifting and shifty persons, *in media res*, still in various stages of arrested formation. The flat polarities of criminal law that divides into victims and perpetrators and elicits pity or vengeance cannot accommodate the internal antagonism of these characters. These scenes of desultory agency and displaced vigilantism layer disappointment over love, betrayal over affection and exceed the binary language of criminal law.

While in David Farr's *The Hunt* catharsis ensues from the vindication of an innocent man falsely accused of child molestation, *The Woodsman* does not offer any such sense of closure. The ending is not redemptive, but rather points to how shaming operates in scenarios of punitive sanction. Walter manages his psychic disquiet by internalizing the vigilante and receives social approval for it. He channels and redirects his sexual energies from predation to vigilantism and develops new techniques of self-governance. If *The Hunt* unfurls a Turneresque paradigm of social drama that culminates in reintegration, such cathartic closure eludes *The Woodsman.* Rather *The Woodsman* suggests that sex offenders inhabit a zone of indistinction between the human and the animal, between the city and its shadowy outskirts, making it impossible for them to reintegrate into society. The play urges us to look beyond the theatre and toward the larger social and legal contexts that continue to hunt down registered sex offenders as predatory wolves in society. Scorned as outlaws, and designated as unreformable, sex offenders bear a wolf-head that licenses carceral, legal, and social violence against them. They are *homo sacer*, decreed by law to exist outside the protections of law. The spatial and social abjection prevents them from reintegrating into society and ironically makes communities less safe.

While criminal law attempts to redress the vulnerability and harm experienced by survivors, it also inflicts penalties and exacerbates the vulnerability of those who cause harm. Thinking with vulnerability as an analytic category attunes our moral and political obligations to each other, and foregrounds the sense of exposure, injuriousness, and mutuality. These plays allow us to see the vulnerability of those who cause harm, while also highlighting the extreme reprisals from community and institutional retribution that dehumanizes sex offenders.

As restorative justice practitioner and assault survivor Danielle Sered reminds us, "We will not work our way out of violence if we continue to believe that solving violence is about managing monsters. Displacing our old stories will require allowing new ones – full stories, messy ones, ones that include wounds and rage and loss and sorrow and ambivalence and – sometimes, though not always – hope."[48] *The Hunt* and *The Woodsman* underline the relational dynamics of encounters that move us beyond the autonomous, boundaried liberal subject of rights that is enshrined in criminal law. Shining a light on real and imagined pedophiles, these plays allow us to see the vulnerability of offenders and their exposure to state and community harm. Moving away from the strident polarities of criminal law, these portrayals depict those harmed and those who harm not as fixed and immutable, but charting a shared social terrain of vulnerability. The arena of criminal law encompasses complex subjects, both acting and acted upon, oscillating between subjecthood and subjection, susceptible to interpersonal, community, and institutional violence.

[48] Danielle Sered, *Until We Reckon: Violence, Mass Incarceration and a Road to Repair* (New York: The New Press, 2019), Kindle edition, 14–15.

PART III

TRANSGRESSIONS

III.0 Carey Young, *Intake Room, Police Station, Bruges, Belgium* (2023). Colour photograph from *Surfaces of Law.*

CHAPTER 9

The Comediography of Law

Peter Goodrich

Hic bibitur

(Francois Rabelais, *Gargantua and Pantagruel*, 1653, 1.1.)

A doubling, both retrospective and prospective, can act comedically as an opening. In the mid 1550s, forced into isolation by the severity of the plague in Toulouse, the constitutional theorist and doctor of laws Jean de Coras embarked upon the translation of an anonymous Latin text, a *Dialogue between the Emperor Hadrian and the Philosopher Epictetus* with the addition of an expansive commentary.[1] Like many in isolation he wished to revert to beginnings and so adopted the foundational theatrical mode of juristic treatise, the dialogue, 'a form very ancient and significant' of pedagogic explication, and here a play between the emperor and his *nomikos*, an adviser on law, in its full sense of speech of the sovereign.[2] The intercourse, of course, could equally have been between prince and chancellor, doctor of civil law and apprentice at the Inns of Court, a philosopher and a student of common law, or even Cardinal Pole and Sir Thomas Lupset in dense interlocution on whether to replace Anglican common law with the Roman *corpus iuris*.[3] What was necessary was

1 Jean de Coras, *Altercacion en forme de dialogue, entre l'Empereur Adrian et philosophe Epictète* (Toulouse: Porterie, 1558). The *Dialogue* had been in manuscript form for more than a century. It was printed in Latin a few years before Coras' *Altercacion* at the end of Alciatus, *Notitia utraque . . . Disputatio Adriani aug. et Epicteti philosophi* [Basle, 1552] and Coras provides both the vernacular Occitan version and commentary.

2 Edward Waterhous, *Fortescutus illustratus* (London: Roycroft, 1663), introduction.

3 Fortescue, *De laudibus legum Angliæ* [1462] (Selden ed., London: Gosling, 1737); St. German, *Doctor and Student* [1525] (London: Selden Society, 1974); Thomas

a dramatisation, a doubling of the beginning through a series of enigmas posed as questions of origin stranded in the dangerous comedy of definitions. Retrospective resolutions to classical conundrums, the literal legitimacy of social and legal forms needs hindsight, the angel of history, to take a contemporary form and performance.

In prospective mode, in review of Peters' magnum opus, *summum*, and pandect of performative law up until 1678, the plague years had thrown Coras to contemplation of the future. Another doubling. The initial question in the dialogue, opening for content, is a genuine enigma: What do we see in the body of a pedagogue? The answer is *epistola*, a letter missive. The question opens the body to knowledge and simultaneously constitutes the subject as a carapace, an envelope and vehicle of epistolisation. The interrogation moves immediately to questions of communication, the encryption of relay and the heavy signifiers of transmission. The next question is thus *quid est epistola?* and the answer is *tacitus nuntius* or silent messenger. Mute eloquence, gesture and writing, body and text in this early sense, imitate the naked corporeal carapace, another skin containing a hidden message. In the argot of the era, a hieroglyph and in addition, in the Latin text, an image of the dialogists, emperor and philosopher, which provides a visual portal and access to the exchange.[4]

The image, from Alciatus' *Notitia dignitatum*, of Hadrian and Epictetus, the former on his throne, sceptre in the right hand, an open palm welcoming and receiving discourse in his left (see Figure 9.1).[5] The image shows rather than says what the protagonists in turn indicate through gesture, the chironomia and indigitation, the dactylograms that perform through visual manifestation, staging, and enactment in the colour print of the early text. Epictetus grasps his robe in his left hand and points upward with the index finger of his right, demanding attention and, according to canon XX of the *Chironomia*, threatening to

Hobbes, *A Dialogue between a Philosopher and a Student of the Common Laws of England* [1681] (Chicago: Chicago University Press, 2010); Thomas Starkey, *Dialogue between Reginald Pole and Thomas Lupset* [1533], ed. Tillyard (Chatto and Windus: London, 1948).

4 Coras, *Altercacion*, 23: 'messager qui ne dit mot'. The reference is to John of Salisbury.

5 Alciatus, *Notitia dignitatum*; the image precedes the 'Dialogue', and can be found in similar though not identical form in the 1436 manuscript of *Notitia dignitatum* in the Bodleian Library (MS Canon. Misc. 378).

9.1 Emperor Hadrian and the Philosopher Epictetus, from Alciatus, *Notitia dignitatum utraque iuris* (1552). Wikicommons.

denounce if attention wanders.[6] It is a pedagogic image of near equivalence, the standing philosopher is at the same height in this exchange as the sedentary emperor; the teacher is master of the sovereign and vice versa, although the dais, throne, and awning indicate nonetheless

[6] John Bulwer, Chironomia *or the Art of Manuall Rhetorique: With the Lawes, Rites, Ordinances and Institutes of Rhetoricians, both Ancient and Moderne, Touching the artificial management of the HAND in speaking* (London: Harper, 1644), 78. Andrea de Jorio, *Gesture in Naples and Gesture in Classical Antiquity* [1832] (Bloomington: Indiana University Press, 2000) at 473, plate XIX, lists this indigitation as indicating.

a hierarchy, and order of transmission. The imperial *scena*, the gold *cathedra*, is a last instance or dignity whereby the image both signifies and conceals that of which it is the representation and doubling. The throne is visually a stage and staging, replete with curtains, fronds, and rod of office. The emperor is after all seated and, it can be added, in the pose of the judge: *sedementariam vitam & recte sedendo.*[7] Hadrian is not just sovereign and messenger, *vicarius Dei*, but also seated and judging. Here then is the crux, a double message, sovereign and didactic, legislative and philosophical, juridical and pedagogical, an amphibological signification which arrives most explicitly in the answer to the third potentially self-reflective question, *quid est pictura? Veritas falsa* – what is a painting? A false truth. Following the order of enigmas, the naked body, the missive epistle, and the painting are all subject to suspicion, both objects of belief, acts of faith, and modes of fantasy, poetic license, and deception. For performative purposes, all three are surfaces, costumes – hirsute skin, chirograph, and epistle – and then paintings that all figure hidden causes. The body hidden by clothes, the epistolary inscription, and the image share the enigmatic status of enacting in variable forms an absent source. Although diversely so, they are not what they represent, no matter how true their figuration. Body, missive, image – the corporeal bears a message that the letter transmits and the picture depicts so as to manifest a trajectory of transmission through the diverse media of its passage.

The false truth of the image is in effect the culmination of the biblical *haec imago* or 'this face', the human similitude of the ineffable and invisible divinity, the unseen cause of causes and message in the envelope that both conceals and relays. Staying with this key topos, the conjunction *veritas falsa*, it is evident that in the terms argued extensively in *Law as Performance*, the theatrical characteristics of the legal process fall directly

[7] Josse Damhouder, *Praxis rerum criminalium*, Venice, Ioannis Antonium Bertanum, 1572, chapter CLIV, 1666, column n° 2: 'Justitia itaque in solio residens indicat omnem justitiæ administrationem debere sedere. . . . Hoc est, debere inferri censuram animo quieto, libero, et ab humanis affectibus desecato. . . . Et recte sedendo, debet judex sententiam pronunciare. In quiescendo enim et sedendo anima sit sciens et prudens, Aristotele teste.' The Aristotelian desideratum was *debere sedere ad judicandum mentis tranquilitatem.*

within the trajectory of the dyad of body and missive that combine to form the performative image of law as enigmatically true and simultaneously false.[8] This thesis gains incremental expression in Peters' advancing argument as to the affective force of oratorical action and the value created by the impression of reality that legal advocates at their best wield. In her formulation 'legal performance is at once a technology of representation and a crucial ethical practice' (86). The jurist's illusions become reality, or are made, which is to say fabricated into actions and juridical determinations: 'The advocate's artful reality effect, heightened through *actio*, did not offer a mere illusion of reality (as the actor's did): it made reality appear as real as it really was' (86). By the end of the book, it is not only the Horatian *jus* or sauce but the sorcery of law that has become the acting of real life. Illusion, play, and revel resemble legal enactment, and juridical *hypokrisis*, as the etymon suggests, is itself a form of illusion; it is a performance, a play, a fantasm that ironically shows law *in actu* and as *legis actio*. This is how law is 'actually performed'. This is 'as real as law gets' (295). And in twenty-first-century terms of nibbles and bytes, this means the rule of theatre in the modality of theatrocracy unwired, reality on speed (302), true and false in an accelerated imaginal form.

COMEDY OF LAW. There are many exempla in the book, but entry for content, and so we begin with a comedy staged in Tothill Fields, the last trial by combat or duelling decision in the English common law tradition. The fields, which were later to become, appropriately enough, a cricket ground and then or also a prison, themselves provide a trajectory from theatre to law to play, as evinced in Peters' flamboyant narrative of the melodrama of the contestants mock fighting after they knew that the case had been earlier resolved. The forum for this particular, now faux, property dispute was an open air, public stage, mimetically reproducing, which is to say doubling, re-enacting and so exposing the scenography of ordinary trial. As this is not the theatre of the law court itself, with its

8 Julie Stone Peters, *Law as Performance: Theatricality, Spectatorship, and the Making of Law in Ancient, Medieval, and Early Modern Europe* (Oxford: Oxford University Press, 2022). All further numerical references in the text are to this work.

architectural confinement and limitations of time and procedure, we are thrown directly into the foolosophy of justice, the *serio-ludere* of the agon of trial and the definitive trajectory of the triunity of *ordo*, then *lex*, then *comœdium*. What we see, where we start, is with the visibility and audibility of the lawsuit, the audience as it used to be called. *Hypokrisis, actio*, delivery, and the last term can be punned deconstructively as de-livery, removal of livery, law putting on its costume so as to get undressed by the gaze of the spectator. This is primarily because comedy is the oldest theatrical form, laughter being, according to Addison, an original sin.[9] The first point to be made is thus that comedy, the ludic enactment, and here re-enactment of law, the *legis actio* or climactic outcome of legal conflict, is the form that legality necessarily takes. Persons, things, actions are replicated in Coras' body, letter, and image and these in turn can be conceived and triggered as *ordo, lex, comœdium.*

In the imaginal context of contemporary transmission, the logical order of juridical progression has to be ludically reversed: *Comedy* is our introduction to the legal, to the epistolarity of transmission, to the bodies of the players. This is serious. A matter as Selden puts it, *instar omnium*, the form and formulary of all, by means of *ius imaginum* or entry of law's dramatis personae.[10] The jocastic de-livery, the undressed performance, exposure of the tersichorean art of law in the variable modes of its social presence are inevitably comic. Lenton makes the point best in the epigraphs to his *Characterismi*: *dum vivo video, et dum video rideo* (*errorem in humanis et terrorem in libris*).[11] To see is to laugh at the pretensions of the costumed animal, the monkey in a toga, and the cachinnating coifed codpiece, the clothed codex conspiring judge. Vision precedes decision. Conflict generates the case, and it is in these all too human escapades, out of the corporeography of adversity, the verbal and gestural articulations of advocacy, that law and the happy hum of order, the capriole and merry dance, are later redacted to the monochrome regimentations of

9 Joseph Addison, Richard Steele, and Others, *The Spectator*, ed. Gregory Smith (London: Dent, 1958), 2:237.

10 John Selden, *Titles of Honor* (London: W. Stansby, 1614) fol. c.4.b.

11 Francis Lenton, Characterismi *or Lentons Leasures: Expressed in Essayes and Characters. Never before written* (London: IE for Roger Michell, 1631) title page. This is truncated in the 1633 edition as *dum vivio video, dum video rideo.*

the page. The initial document, transcribed in memory, transmitted orally, recalled visually, is the comedy, the stage play itself, in which the litigants, spectators, assessors and judges come together to perform in a field. It is in this sense that Rosenstock-Huessy suggests that progress in law may well 'depend on the regulating power of humour'.[12] Peters too notes the legitimating force, the entry into the family line that such legal *ludi* on Tothill Fields will relay.

Returning to the complex conjunction *veritas falsa* as applied to the picture portrayed and to the costumed lawsuit enacted, it is precisely figures of things to which Coras refers in his classically orientated discussion of the Philosopher's response. Illustrating the answer that Epictetus has given to the question *quid est pictura*, Zeuxis and Parrhasius are invoked, the painting of grapes that fools the birds, and the curtain that appeared to conceal a work of art but was in fact itself the painting. The figure of truth is both semblance and dissemblance, false and true, comic and serious, and it is this juxtaposition that needs desideration. What is true or at least evident is the manifestation of legality in the agonistic moment that generates the *leges actiones*, in the performative scene of what in the case of Tothill Fields is a prospective 'tryal by battail' and these, according to the legal antiquarian Sir Henry Spelman, referencing Glanvill, are called *leges apparentes* – laws made visible.[13] What is it then that appears or is rendered apparent by this vast theatrical scene? For Peters the event collapses the difference between court and stage, trial and combat, because both enact the agon of conflict and its resolution via the medium – *comœdium* – of the juridical liturgy of a verdict. The mystery or *arcanum* of legal judgment depends upon the staging of a conflict that will act as the image of a judgment that is invented, which is to say organised and ordained behind the veil of the dramatic agon of dispute. Again, conjunction and disjunction, the alternating current and Janus face of *arcanum iuris* decked out with coif and cloak, robes, furs and taffeta. A sartorial presence, a costume of colours, livery and delivery, habits of the robes and performative exposure.

[12] Eugene Rosenstock-Huessy, *Out of Revolution* (New York: Morrow, 1938), 756.

[13] Reliquiae Spelmaniannæ, in *The Posthumous Works of Sir Henry Spelman Kt* (London: Awnsham, 1698), 50.

One might here recall Nietzsche's cautel, that truth is a metaphor, an illusion so grounded in practice that we have forgotten its illusory roots.[14] How then does this scene act *ad apparentiam* and more specifically how is its falsity a reference to its truth? Peters in paromoion style sides with Parrhasius: This painted cloth, this theatrical staging, is the reality of law. It generates the truth through the fictive process of trial and, as Kantorowicz elaborates, the apposite maxim is *fictio figura veritatis*, fiction is the figure of truth, the form it takes being *veritas falsa*, or that law does not die. Hers is a neo-materialist view in which the excessively dramatic character of the mock trial – the 'battail' after all never took place because settlement had been agreed one day before – can only have representational purposes. The elaborate staging provides an image of legal relations that corresponds to the force of law, that decisions are always *in camera*, hidden from view, as with the accord that preceded Tothill Fields, or that otherwise occurs in judicial chambers, or where *ex tempore* in the unlit theatre of the judicial skull. Performance, in other depiction, is manifestation and outcome, the speeding (publication) of judgment through the spectacle and modality of its theatrical relay. This then is an event, an encounter that in a correspondence theory of knowledge, accurately reflects the legal relation. The performance enacts what is not there, the *arcanum iuris*, or *mysterium*, which is, in its very absence, non-existent except in its theatrical apparition. At the same time, reflection distorts, and correspondence to the real, to the event, is an epistolary exchange, body to body, letter to letter, image to image, diffracted through the very means of its conveyance.

At one level the event depicts the triumph of law over trial by combat: Duels are illegal because settlement should be judicial and symbolic rather than exsanguinated and merely theatrical. Ironically an apparent trial by combat was necessary to show that such violence was not to occur.

[14] Friedrich Nietzsche, 'On Truth and Falsity in their Ultramoral Sense', in *Early Greek Philosophy and Other Essays* (London: Allen & Unwin, 1911), 180, in Maximilian Mügge's translation, reading 'What therefore is truth? A mobile army of metaphors, metonymies, anthropomorphisms . . . truths are illusions of which one has forgotten that they are illusions; worn-out metaphors which have become powerless to affect the senses; coins which have their obverse effaced and are now no longer of account as coins but merely as metal.'

Remaining with the reality of the event, it evidences first the itinerancy of the legal, that law does not, to borrow a phrase, inhabit any specific territory. The trial by combat has no fixed place, no locus or to borrow from Glanvill, *duellum non locum habet.*[15] The theatrical presence of law is its presence, its real – the cloth is the picture – and that means historically an atmosphere and aura of juridism that travels with its personnel and their performances. The itinerant court, the assize, is also a verb, a mobile matterphor, meaning a momentary material symbol, a sudden sitting or temporary theatre, that like the trial at Tothill Fields, appears and fades, arrives and then disperses. The significance, the *verum*, is that of manifestation and not that of duration. The sovereign appears in the person of its judges and other officials. The Emperor Hadrian has left his seat and remained on his throne so as to appear in the vicarious form of his delegates, in his other body, as principal and principle directing the persons, bonds, and comedy – *ordo, lex, comœdium* – of this particular, itinerant case. The emotion has set the law in motion, to perform the page, while writing; *ratio scripta* itself is but the stage, the material sign or physical presence of the jural relations to and with which it corresponds.

The second point is thus that performance embodies, and it is that incorporation *in actu* that creates the corporation of lawyers, the itinerant and expanded *personae*, the real representatives of the absent sovereign in the symbolic form of a mobile legality. No law without incorporation, manifestation, visible presence. The comedy of being there is necessary, the costumed monkey, the sartorial simian, must appear to invent and instigate the commons and consensus of common law or within the civilian tradition, the *ius commune* with its regalia and *universalia*, maxims and mottoes, dicta and dogma. In this rhetorical and performative dimension, it is real presence that might be termed the liturgical transubstantiation of what after all is in practice a Roman Catholic law. The esoterica, the various encryptions, argot and inkpot words of the symbolæographs and other instruments cannot be for lawyers alone but rather the parchment has to become public and

15 *The Balliol Glanvill*, Libri 5 quaestio iii – https://clicme.wp.st-andrews.ac.uk/online-texts/the-balliol-glanvill-a-draft-edition. The root of such a notion lies in the *Decretals* and the maxim *ecclesia non habet territorium.*

become law in the sense of decision which Vico terms *certa lex*, meaning both *scriptum* and particularity.[16] In broader formulation, the performance on Tothill Fields is a scene of determination in which, in the language of *Leges Henrici Primi*, love conquers law, accord vanquishes combat, a comedy closes, but in the same instance a judicial status and *certum* is conveyed.[17] For law even more than for theatre, the show must go on. Something happens, nothing happens. *Veritas falsa* in the sense that the formal, open air proceedings, preceded by 'oyez oyez', re-enact a scene of judgment by way of settlement that had occurred the day before. The theatre of law – but this is always the case – is a repetition, a restaging that makes the juridical *arcana* present *in personam*, just as much in the rite of settlement as in prosecution and execution. It is always, in other words, an indexical form of manifestation, a reference to a chain such that being there is also *veritas falsa*, in the necessary semiotic sense that visual signs are always references, vanishing concatenations that reference absent precedential and experiential forms, and lead from the image to the thing signified, or in the ecclesiastical maxim, *ab imagine ad rem significatam*.

What the lawyers of the period dubbed *anima lex* or *lex loquens* is precisely the scripted performance of the dead letters of the parchment rules. The *leges apparentes* are the public mobilisation of legality in the bodies of participants and the commonality of the crowd, the common audience of common law. The *falsum* of the performative image of the proceedings, the fact of its being mere appearance is, ironically perhaps in modern eyes, the invention of a humanist *certum* in the sense that Quintilian uses and that Vico adapts. While the performance may appear to be a toroid spectacle, a non-event, this misses the point that the encounter itself, in full theatrical couture and custom is gauged to the

[16] The key text is William West, *Symbolæography which may be termed the art, description or image of Instruments. Or the paterne of præsidents. Or the notarie or scrivener. The first part of instruments extra judiciall* [1590] (London: Society of Stationers, 1603), and for commentary, Bradin Cormack, 'Shakespeare, Hamlet, and the Life of Legal Documents', in Donald Beecher et alia (eds.), *Taking Exception to the Law* (Toronto: University of Toronto Press, 2015), 44.

[17] Downer (ed.), *Leges Henrici Primi* (Oxford: Oxford University Press, 1972), § 49, 5a 'pactum enim legem vincit et amor iudicium'.

sensus communis and the old sense of *certum*, which is that of consensus.[18] This may not be *festa fullorum* nor entirely *ad jocunditatem*, but it is theatrical entertainment, the allure of the spectacle and show that also draws the crowd and makes the instant a synonym of the case. One can borrow from Quintilian and his exhortation to learn Latin from the comic poets – *a comicis* – because that is the language, the vernacular that the people speak.[19] Turn it around, speak law, and the *falsum* of appearance and display, manifests the *certum* of the case, the particularity of an event, a decision that is made in exemplary style in the public sphere as an apparition of law and as the sensibility of the commons. In customary form, the lawyers have to learn *a comicis*, just as much as the crowd needs to see and recognise legality. This is, to put a point on it, a two-way street, a dialectic and dialogue in which jurisdictions meet in mutual interdependence: the comedic sensibility as expressed in *auctoritates poetarum*, as the jurisdiction of poets and philosophers.[20] Charles Lamb, in his essay on 'Stage Illusion', surprises by making the comic point well: 'It is . . . a proof of the highest skill in the comedian when, without absolutely appealing to an audience, he keeps up a tacit understanding with them; and makes them, unconsciously to themselves, a party in the scene.'[21] The necessity of such spectacle and histrionic symbiosis, the pluralisation of the commonality of common law, gains direct expression precisely in the *serio-ludere* of the Tothill theatrics and the multiple meanings of the comedy that it stages.

18 For a detailed examination of the *certum*, see Charles J. McNamara, 'Quintilian's Theory of Certainty and *its* Afterlife in Early Modern *Italy*' (Columbia PhD, 2016). *Verum*, in contrast, is *aequitas*: the *in camera* rustle of parchment rules, the archival realm of inscriptions, extant and elaborated in forms and processes unseen by the commons. The *certum*, by contrast, is the decision and application in public, so that law is enacted and emerges as both governed by and informing the *verum* for future cases.

19 Quintilian, *Institutio oratoria* (Cambridge, MA: Harvard University Press, 2001), §36.431–436: *Si quis autem vestrum quaerat unde addiscenda haec vulgaris Latine loquendi ratio, quando lingua intermortua est et ad nos nonnisi auctores Latini pervenerunt, ego dicam: a comicis. Ii namque a solo argumento poetae sunt; caeterum dictionis genere omnino populari utuntur* . . .

20 As recognised by Coke and other common lawyers, but reverting ultimately to Book 50 of the *Digest* and *antiquæ fabulæ* listed there.

21 Charles Lamb, *The Essays of Elia* [1823] (New York: Wiley and Putnam, 1845), 2:21.

Various digressions upon the incertitude of the enthymeme, on the legal rhetoric of the probable, and the *falsum* of verisimilitude are possible at this point, but it is the integral element of the comedic in both order and law, sensibility and judgment that forms the most important focus of the triune conjunction. Just as the comic is necessary, the apparent is real, and the false is always in relation to the true. This can be elaborated in the juristic maxim *fictio figura veritatis,* but it is in its rhetorical form that it is encountered in our study as a feature of the ancient rules of law, *antiquæ fabulæ,* of which Jouvancy provides the following: *quid est fabula – est sermo falsus veritatem effigens, hoc est, falsa quidem et fictio narratio est: at sub fabuloso verborum cortice veritas semper latet aliqua, et utilis sensus* and translates for current purposes as 'drama is a discourse that figures the truth, that is to say that it is false and fictive but, under the cover and artifice of words, traces a truth and a useful sense'.[22] The effigy or portrayal of verdict and veracity, here the staging of peace, through the rites of images, signs, symbols and words, is legally the record of both *veritas* and judgment, *verum et certum,* and it is the curiosity of law, its pragmatic edict, to endeavour in performing to deny its social and imagistic lineage, its other likeness and shadow similitude. The picture provides the equity of decision that performs and legitimates in familial and familiar form, relating decision precisely to *antiquæ fabulæ,* the narrative justification of the juristic tradition. The monotheism of legality, the emphasis on *serio* and not *ludere,* leads to the dissimulated fashioning of the juridical in the mode of denial, via the claim of an abyssal distance of the *leges actiones* from theatre, rite and revel. The imagery of legal ritual and its recording, the bodies that make up comedy, and play a role in their variable linguistic forms are in doctrine supposed to be lost in the monochrome regimentations of the linear page. Repression, however, rules the inscription of instruments and laws whose language is necessarily the bearer of the images of the causes and conflicts that collide symptomatically in the text.

In the classical Roman law of accession, Gaius in his *Institutes* treats the image, *tabula picta,* as an exception to the principle of alluvion: 'If someone has painted upon my panel (*tabula*), namely an image (*veluti*

[22] Joseph de Jouvancy, *Candidatus rhetoricae* [1711] (Paris: Frères Barbou, 1725), 152.

imaginem) ... the opinion preferred [is] that the panel accedes to the image.' The *Digest* is (at one point) in accord.[23] In an age of *pietas*, the image, being closer to the spirit or unseen cause, took precedence over the substance and led more directly, and so too in the view of the warring theologians of the Tothill Fields epoch, *ab imagine ad rem significatam* – from the image to the thing signified.[24] Taking the comic seriously, exploiting the ludic etymon of the illusive and illusion (*in-ludere*, in play), a degree of profanation is necessary to recognise the democratising character of thinking law *a comicis* or in, on, and of the commons. The Tothill *duello* didn't happen, save in symbolic legal form, and so is especially comic, with the gladiatorial costumed champion, the thespian Nayler, refusing to return the glove, stating no, demanding the ritual of combat and occasion of play. In this instance *otium* is *negotium*, the latter containing the former linguistically and legally. Such equality between comedy and regulation, theatre and law serves as a powerful reminder of the *plus ultra* of the rule, of the image that subtends and triggers, that precedes and determines what is said and inscribed. As Peters has it, the illusion is real and the real is illusion, but always understood through the ludic and illusive root of the illusory, in apprehension in common and *a comicis*. Life, one might say, precedes the still life of the legal tableau. The dead letter of the juristic text becomes law only in its performances, both scribal and theatrical, aesthetic and ludic, *ordo et comœdium, verum et certum*.

The point is that law needs its comedy so as to be embodied, to become real and part of what is common. The body of the populace, which is also to say the mood and the sensibility of the commons, its humour and comicality interact with and invent, open up and open up to the juridical in its more public manifestation. The spectacle, for Peters, has to be both *veritas et falsa*, and this entails, within a triune tradition, a third and more expansive point. That law still engages in the agonistic

[23] Francis de Zuluetta (ed.) *Institutes of Gaius* (Oxford: Oxford University Press, 1946) 1:85 (78). *Digest* 41.9.2 (Gaius) ... *sed ex diverso placuit tabulas picturae cedere*. At other points, different fragments provide the opposite conclusion.

[24] From the Oxford Anglican reformer Robert Parker, *A Scholasticall Discourse against Symbolizing with Antichrist in Ceremonies: Especially in the Sign of the Cross* (London: n.p., 1607) 47–48.

procedures, the *leges apparentes* as conducted symbolically in the palaestra of the courthouse or in the extra-foraneous *serio-ludere* of Tothill Fields, and this leads to another conflict, as ancient as the Old Testament, the generative antinomy of wit and judgment. Addison, who is not always the best comic guide, in essay 249 published on Saturday, December 15, 1711, as adverted earlier, recounts reading a sermon in which the Roman priest 'laid it down as a Point of Doctrine, that Laughter was the Effect of Original Sin and that Adam could not laugh before the Fall'.[25] The dogmatic thesis is that laughter is mad but if we recall the context of the exodus from Eden, it was the necessary jocastic act of sartorial awareness, of putting on raiment, costuming up for social presence and performance. The wittier implication, however, is that laughter confronts the sacred with the profane, rule with invention, *verum* with *certum*. Where the Garden was closed and static, an atemporal order of a nebulous law, the exit from such inactuality and stasis is the emblem and exemplum of beginning, just as laughter is the respiratory, facial and pectoral mark of the inauguration, or the inventive beginning of thought.

The purpose of the biblical detour, the reference to the original ban on laughter and the comic, is simply to pose the role of wit as the motor of judgment. Eden is utter boredom, eternal stasis, the absence of events. Comedy is mobility, affect, and the instance of *exeunt*. Laughter moves, it unsettles, innovates, creates, changes by embracing the breaking of the rule so as to escape the confinement of the precedent. Like dreams for Freud, law is 'insufferably witty', because the rule is constantly broken. 'Joke work' is the art of expanding the rule beyond its breaking point. The law of performance, that Peters so brilliantly tracks is the record of comic interventions into judgment, of the mobilising contestation of the rule, rebellion at judgment. From Calefurnia mooning the bench, the heretic Jan Hus laughing and mimicking the ecclesiastics who had sentenced him to death, to the *filius terrae*, clowns, revels and the lord of misrule, to the delightful puns of the fog bound Cambridge wit, Ignoramus, the thrust of legal theatrics is the exception, the mobilising moment of thought that alters or

[25] Joseph Addison, *Spectator*, vol. 2, 237.

alpers the rule.[26] The joke, if one can formulate it so, as evident in Tothill Fields as elsewhere in practice, is that the law is everywhere except in law. That sense of the absurd that is the comedic concomitant of any act of law application, the performance of decision in its ritual, liturgical, effectual sense is always also a susurration or smirking breach of the generality, the guffaw that accompanies the unexpected overturning of a word, role, meaning or posture that preceded it.

The jurist as agelast is far from the mark because order and law depend upon comedy and the trinity of *ordo, lex, comœdium* is an active, inventive and propulsive combination. Borrowing from Sir John Doderidge Knight (spelled here with the elegance of an 'e' as fourth letter, although this is sadly not always the case), the language of law is drawn *a comicis*, from the conversation of the commons, from the dialogic imagination generated by the social use, the history and conflict from which cases emerged and customary norms were drawn.[27] Law then, though I intend no particular order, is the interactive reformulation of the social symbolic, the symbolæographic inscription of the heavy signifiers of status, role, and relationship into a sociolinguistic system that comedy both propels and parodies, and in breaching, innovates in better and worse forms. *Comœdium* finds its place in Blount's *Glossography* as traveling plays that visit up and down the country, using fables 'representing, as in a Mirror, the similitude of a civil and private life, beginning for the most part with some troubles, but ending with Agreement or joy'.[28] The comedy is the imaginative performance of the casuistical, the vaticinate invention of future decisions, while the comediographer, the writer of comedies, is as close to a definition of a lawmaker or poet as legislator as one could devise. What better disarticulation of the case method, of the reporting of judgments, detailing as they do both with the conflict of the parties and its resolution in judicial fiat, than the comediography of law? And both itinerant, the players and the Assize judges, thespians and lawyers traversing their circuits in parallel.[29]

26 Alper Ral, 'Sit, Stand-up, Jump', unpublished paper on file with the author.

27 Sir John Doderidge, *The English Lawyer* (London: More, 1631).

28 Thomas Blount, *Glossographia* (London: Newcomb, 1656) s.v. comedy and comediographer.

29 Haldar, 'The Outdoor Stages of Common Law', in this volume, pages 81–89.

How, finally, does the comedy of the juridical work? It is perceived as a minor genre, a marginal exornation and peripheral drama of gesture and diction appropriate at best to collections of *facetiæ*, merriments or uncommon laws.[30] According to Bossuet in his 'Maxims and Reflections on Comedy', which is printed just after his much lengthier 'Funeral Orations', picking up on Addison's theme, 'peals of laughter (*les éclats de rire*) make one forget the presence of God . . . and the seriousness of the Christian life'.[31] The pleasure given via the eyes and ears promote the body while they 'soften the soul'. Laughter is in effect sacrilegious, a futile, histrionic endeavour, *stultiloquium* that explicitly profanes the Scriptures. It is in that theological condemnation that the power of the theatrical manifests its critical force. The profane quality of the performance of law is a direct challenge to the legislative hierarchy and to the privileged place of lawyers. As Peters shows in multiple vignettes, in the immaculately detailed substance of her history, performativity necessarily brings the populace into law in inventive acts both of transmission and of revolt. When Jan Hus laughs all the way through his ritual defrocking at the end of his heresy trial, the ambiguous character of the performance of law, of comedic challenge, and of the indexicality of the relay of tradition in visual, which is to say imaginal forms is fully on display.

Far from excluding laughter or always compelling gravitas, ingravescence, the tragic modality of legal actions, the decorum of law has to encompass both the Apollonian and the Dionysian, the sedentary and the terpsichorean, formalism and the comedy of carnival or

[30] Restricting myself to the early modern and modern, in the spirit of revels, the Basoche and *Ignoramus*, Martial d'Auvergne and Benoît de Court, I would cite, because they should not be missed, David Murray, *Lawyers Merriments* (Glasgow: Glasgow University Press, 1912); John Willock, *Legal Facetiæ: Satirical and Humorous* (London: London Literary Society, 1887); A. P. Herbert, *Uncommon Law* (London: Methuen, 1935) and its sequels. In broader terms the titles tell the story of the insignificance, which is to say the failure to comprehend law's comedy, as Croake James, *Curiosities of Law and Lawyers* (London: Sampson Low, 1882); Francis Watt, *Law's Lumber Room; Curious Cases and Amusing Actions at Law* (London: Bodley Head, 1895) or even the more recent Laura Little, *Guilty Pleasures: Comedy and Law in America* (Oxford: Oxford University Press, 2019).

[31] Bossuet, 'Maximes et Réflexions sur la Comédie' [1694], in Bossuet, *Oraisons Funèbres. Sermons et maximes* (Paris: Mignot, n.d.), 197, 201.

inversion as in the Hus trial. The theatrical character of law, of trials, but also of architectural, archival, artistic, and now also filmic representations, is essential to the transmission of law as tradition, meaning *sensus communis* as the commonality of law. It is crucially a manner of passing on not the substance of law but its form, its visible exterior, its gestural and aesthetic or decorous modalities. It is the phantasm of normative citizenship, the fantasy of a shared social reality that is relayed in the repetitive formulae and recognisable manual expressions of legal presence, of delivery as enactment. Performance, one can argue, performs the symptoms of law, meaning that the figures or fictions act out hidden causes, prior decisions, previously archived rules and regimentations. In Tothill Fields, to pursue again the exemplum, the legal settlement and decision on title to the property had been made the day before the performative spectacle of an aborted trial by combat. The enactment was in one sense '*make believe*' (3) precisely in the sense of fostering credulity, engaging citizenry and in moving things on.

CONCLUSION

The last point can form the basis of a conclusion, let us say a *con-ludere* of comediography, in terms of what *Law as Performance*, ending as it does in 1678, might convey to the contemporary. What is offered is in one sense a critical symptomatology of performance, gauged to the visible movement of legality, and the mobilisation of its presence. What could be termed the *aura hysterica* of the social is manifested in the style of juridical events that are apprehended most directly in the expressions of pathology that come to public enactment in the mode of trials. These are the optical motors that symptomatically express structural change. In Tothill Fields the end of the trial by battle was enacted for the populace and the dance of the combatants gives ocular expression to the riddle of the death of a particular social form of dispute resolution. That, however, is only a start. The *widdershin* or dancing backward in front of an audience, the gestural mode and its chironomic forms, the nomograms, dactylograms, and further symbolic gestures, such as the Neapolitan Andrea de Jorio so famously collected, are the perduring dynamic of law's transmission.[32] Performance is the mode of setting precedent, the mobile act of scoring decision into public record and social memory. The incidence of the incidental, the supposedly marginal enactment, the histrionics of trial, are in fact the key to the transmission of forms that would otherwise suffer the desuetude of the archive. The law in books, *ratio scripta,* is the memory of the guild, the argot of lawyers, itself drawn from the spectacle of agonistic trials. It is hard law in the view of the judicial author of three comedic volumes of *Miscellany-at- Law,* symptomatically subtitled 'A Diversion for Lawyers and Others'.[33] While Judge Megarry means that the miscellaneous is incidental and occasional, the comedy of events reminds the attentive of the sense of diversion as change, of direction, of attention, and of humour. The narratives and shows, the performances at trial, the records of comedy – *comœdium legalis* – are the transport of precedent and the social relay of law. The diversionary belongs to the miscellaneous style, as Shaftesbury so eloquently expatiated, but it is more than that, it is the symptom of the real, the peripheral facet that encrypts author and cause, and at its best is the essence of wit and vehicle of insight.[34]

Performance, to use the old argot, expresses the soul through the body, but lawyers cannot visibly be too histrionic and must not reveal the extent of the affect that invents decision and so propels precedents that otherwise appear to lie dead on the page. They cover up and go sedentary at the moment that law's art of performance intensifies and threatens to demonstrate the sensible form and imaginal life of legality. Performance historicises and politicises. It breaks out of the closure of the system and pillories the anachronic mode of reason as immaterial and incorporeal. Time, which is of course the medium of change, is operative here comedically. The performance-symptom, the power of law's *comédie humaine* is what Aby Warburg named the *dynamogram,* namely the force of occurrences of

[32] Andrea de Jorio, *Gesture in Naples and Gesture in Classical Antiquity* [1832] (Bloomington: Indiana University Press, 2000).

[33] Robert Megarry, *A Miscellany-at-Law: A Diversion for Lawyers and Others* (London: Stevens, 1955). A second volume appeared with the same publisher in 1973; and a final volume, or so one must surmise, edited by Bryan Garner, appeared as *A New Miscellany-at-Law* (Oxford: Hart, 2005).

[34] Anthony Earl of Shaftesbury, *Characteristicks Volume III* (n.p. 1723), 6–7.

survival in the transmission of forms.[35] It is in seeing the law performed that it becomes both common and alive, reanimated in alternating and changing enactments as law by, with and for us. The dynamogram traces the life of a form, the morphology of figures, the aesthetic of forces and the intensity of affects as they are transmitted through performance. An audience that laughs remembers just as much as the body that is branded or the witness that weeps. The power of the histrionic performance lies in its corporeal and comedic expression, as a litmus of affective force, which the dynamographic history of performance here traces to excellent effect. The decorum of legality has one of its roots in dream and a closer etymon in *dignitas*, meaning office and perdurance as in that which does not die but rather passes on. The dream of law is its decor, its performativity and the oscillating twitch of its wax nose.

The power of legal action lies in its bringing law to light, to public manifestation, both as spectacle and as inscription in memory. The dynamographic function of the theatrical form is thus to instil both the drama and the sensibility of the legal norm, as *sensus communis*, legislative act, and comedy of the social form. The life of law, the offices and dignities of the extant tradition are juridical fictions, antique circumbilifabulations, images inherited as licit forms that collide comedically with the present and action. What Peters achieves in *Law as Performance* is the massive and erudite historical narrative of the mobilisation of Code and precedent, and specifically the moments when theatre challenges the limits of law by making its staging visible. The comediographer depicts the performative passage of laws made visible, alive, comedic in the multiple senses of active, common, comic, becoming imaginal and anachronic survivals, facets of a continuing sensibility that attaches necessarily to the limits of law. For comediography, for the forms that transmit and appear again in these records, in this argument, it is what Warburg terms the seismograph that reaches the level of form and force, the visible movement of invisible agitations, such as those

[35] For discussion of the dynamogram, see Georges Didi-Huberman, *The Surviving Image: Phantoms of Time and Time of Phantoms: Aby Warburg's History of Art* (University Park: Pennsylvania State University Press, 2017), 108–111.

that appear in their paradoxical mode in the drama of Tothill Fields. It is the antinomy of the visible and its unseen cause that instigates the comic punctum, the performative dimension of legality. This is the *ludus,* the joke, the realisation of the limits of the system and the lawlessness of law which is embedded precisely in laughter, in what is impossible to write or say but that can exist only as the motivating affect and mobile poetics of moving from text to action, from *iuris vinculum* to *legis actio,* from *lex* to *comœdium,* and in sum and jape from the regimentation of the page to the anarchy of decision.

CHAPTER 10

The Force of Laughter and a Minor Jurisprudence of Refusal

A Question of Silence *(Marleen Gorris, 1982)*

Başak Ertür*

MARLEEN GORRIS' FEMINIST CLASSIC *A Question of Silence* (1982) features what may well be one of the most powerful fictional court scenes ever filmed: an extended scene of wild laughter that grows and grows to eventually engulf all the women in a courtroom during the trial of three women prosecuted for the murder of a man. The women break the law by committing murder, then by breaking out in laughter, but this is no ordinary breach. Creating a laughterhood among the women in the courtroom,[1] it is a transgression that cannot be re-contained by law, and it re-signifies the murder itself as uncontainable by law's own terms. Placed towards the end of the film, the scene is cathartic, and yet it works only if one has been tuned into that potential of uncontainability all along. The force of the scene is that it taps into a certain embodied knowledge of the here and now, as well as its potential elsewhere. If the knowledge of the here and now is derived from accumulations of lived experience, the knowledge of its potential elsewhere is also embodied, a heterotopia that is conjectured and conjured from within the laughterhood. We know it is (t)here.

There is of course an economy to the chosen setting for this powerful depiction of the force and potential of feminist refusal. Bodily acts

* I am thankful to Alisa Lebow for showing me this film some two decades ago knowing that one day I would write about it, and for still being by my side when I did. I gratefully acknowledge the Leverhulme Trust for the award of a Leverhulme Research Fellowship (2023–24) during which I drafted this chapter.

1 Anca Parvulescu, *Laughter: Notes on a Passion* (Cambridge, MA: MIT Press, 2010), 1. Parvulescu borrows this wonderful figuration, 'laughterhood', from Russian futurist poet Velimir Khlebnikov, and does it justice.

(including acts of speech, but also gestures and indeed laughter) matter in unusually accentuated ways in public trials, where performative operations of law are at their most exposed. As I parse elsewhere by distinguishing between legal performativity and legal performance to think their linkages more carefully, what allows law to operate as if it were fate (the masquerade whereby legal performatives pass as constatives) is more prone to unravelling in this particular setting.[2] This is why trial scenes, fictional or actual, always have strong dramatic potential. But the trial scene in *A Question of Silence* is potent even if read merely literally, as a scene of forensic refusal: the refusal in and of the forum. In critical legal literature, acts of refusal in trials have been figured primarily in terms of resistance and rupture. In this chapter, I draw on another critical legal theme, 'minor jurisprudence', to explore refusal in the alluring terms proposed by Bonnie Honig in *A Feminist Theory of Refusal* (2021): not only as rejecting the here and now, but also as practising the elsewhere in the here and now. Something of a counter-forum emerges in the collective laughter of *A Question of Silence*, but where and what is it? I attempt an answer through a close reading of the film and by juxtaposing its trial scene with a number of other scenes of feminist refusal, to ask after the role and workings of the uncontainable, the untameable, the inassimilable in the forum.

A caveat as I revise this chapter for publication in the immediate aftermath of the bizarre judgment of the Supreme Court of the United Kingdom (UKSC) in *For Women Scotland Ltd.*, and as we witness the even more bizarre ways in which the judgment is interpreted in transphobic campaigns in the UK and beyond. The film this chapter focuses on is now more than four decades old, and its immediate references in feminist literature are also of a period whose radical feminism is nominally claimed today in grotesquely essentialist ways. There has been much feminist thinking over the past few decades, including trans-feminist work, on how to read the seeming biological essentialism of some key feminist texts of the past century. It is beyond the scope of this chapter to delve into that rich discussion, but suffice it to say that when I write of 'women', I do not claim the category as an exclusive territory that must be

[2] Başak Ertür, *Spectacles and Specters: A Performative Theory of Political Trials* (New York: Fordham University Press, 2022).

guarded against incursions. In effect, the appeal to law in *For Women Scotland* for its paternalistic aegis, the call to reinscribe women's 'sex' as a 'characteristic' whose 'protection' requires a practice of exclusion could not be further from the orientation vis-à-vis law that I describe here in terms of feminist refusal.[3]

SHE CAN COMMUNICATE BUT SEES NO POINT IN IT

Our protagonist is Janine van den Bos, a well-respected forensic psychiatrist at the height of her career. She's upper-middle class, attractive, married to a successful lawyer. They make something of a power couple, with an even distribution of power within the couple: he (too) cooks and cleans, she (too) initiates sex, her professional career (too) is all-important, and so on. That's the set-up. The plot? Janine needs to write a report. She is to provide her expert opinion to the court on the mental state of three women involved in the gruesome killing of a man, the proprietor of a boutique for women's clothes. But it is not an easy case to make sense of. None of the women knew the victim or each other before the killing. They all readily and in good humour admit their responsibility for the crime at the police station where they are brought the following day. This is also where they first learn each other's names. None have any prior criminal records or histories of violence. The killing was seemingly unprovoked but very violent, as the forensic pathologist reports to Janine drily:

> injuries to the whole body inflicted by blows and kicks, with hands, shoes and several blunt and sharp instruments like coat hangers and a shopping cart . . . The blows were mainly aimed at the head, the abdomen and the genitals . . . The torso has a deep cut from the Adam's apple, which was also heavily damaged, to the lower abdomen, probably caused by a broken plastic coat-hanger wielded with great violence. The genitals are barely recognizable as such.

[3] In beginning to think about what form feminist refusal might take vis-à-vis the UKSC judgment at this moment, I would invite readers to tap into the force of laughter with the exquisite Emily Grabham, 'Parody Alternative Judgment: For Women Scotland [2025]', *Critical Legal Thinking*, 1 May 2025, https://criticallegalthinking.com/2025/05/01/parody-alternative-judgment-for-women-scotland-2025.

This excess of blood and gore has all the male characters – the inspector, the prosecutor, the judges, even Janine's lawyer husband who has nothing to do with the case – convinced that the three women are insane, or at least were temporarily so at the time of the crime: 'There's no doubt about it, they're completely crazy. But I don't have to explain what you know professionally,' says one official to Janine before she has even met the women. At a later stage in her investigation, 'it's obvious', says Janine's husband, oblivious to what Janine has just been telling him about them. 'These women are completely deranged.' But it is not so open-and-shut for Janine, whose opinion is technically meant to be the one that counts. And the more she engages with the women, the more she sees that something is wrong not with them, but rather with the world that surrounds them.

Janine recognizes them as three 'really very ordinary women' (Figure 10.1): the oldest, Annie, is a waitress at a greasy spoon, a divorcee who is also estranged from her daughter and lives alone. We get a glimpse of her daily banter with the male clientele of the cafeteria, where she bats off the sexist missiles coming her way with raw wit and wild laughter. The other two are younger. Andrea is beautiful, brilliant, single. She works as an executive secretary at an international corporation. Her work there is well above her pay grade, indispensable, and invisibilized.

10.1 Three 'really very ordinary women': Annie, Christine, Andrea. Still from *A Question of Silence.*

There is a scene at a board meeting where she makes a well-reasoned proposal concerning the company's trade activities – her speech is barely tolerated and does not register. She is the only woman at the meeting. Minutes later, the same proposal is offered by another attendee, as if spoken for the first time – 'Good thinking, Bob', says the chair. The third woman is Christine, married to a minor civil servant, mother of three, a housewife. She has stopped speaking altogether. Janine first thinks that it is catatonia induced by the killing, but it turns out that Christine stopped speaking long before the killing, and it is not pathology but a clear choice, a refusal. As Annie has to explain to Janine: 'Do you really wonder why Christine stopped talking? Nobody is listening.'

It is Christine's silence that gives Marleen Gorris' film its original title, *De stilte rond Christine M.*, which translates as *The Silence around* (or surrounding) *Christine M.* Her silence is indeed quite central to the film's plot line, as that which Janine keeps trying to crack. Reading Christine's silence first as pathology, Janine tries to crack it open into speech – any speech. Then understanding it as a choice and the refusal that it is, she tries to pry it open for potential mitigation of punishment. Finally, Janine tries to break through Christine's silence for her own need of connection, once the three women make it clear that they have come to the end of their tolerance for her and her interviews. 'You don't understand people at all, do you?' says Andrea. 'And certainly not women'. The film's English title is *A Question of Silence*, offering a more capacious sense of what it depicts, namely silence in its two related guises:[4] as a condition imposed on women, and as a form that women's refusal takes. As an imposed condition, silence also has to do with that which cannot be mediated through speech: the difficulty of bringing to language the minor but relentless manifestations, operations and effects of patriarchy and sexism. As a form of refusal, silence is about that which is better left unmediated in language: women's solidarity against patriarchy is depicted in the film as a silent agreement that not only needs no words, but is also wary of them.

[4] For more on the various senses of silence in the film, see Lucy Fischer, *Shot/Countershot: Film Tradition and Women's Cinema*. British Film Institute Cinema Series (Basingstoke: Macmillan, 1989), 296–97.

Silence is crucial to the narrative arc of the film, which is character-led and can be read as the story of Janine, an accomplished professional, seemingly a master of her speech, with recognized jurisdiction as an acclaimed and effective forensic psychiatrist, eventually arriving at this silent complicity with the women. She finally fully recognizes the silence of Christine M., and also understands the other silences that initially perplex her, such as that of a number of unidentified women at the boutique who must have witnessed the crime but never came forward to testify. We, the viewers, know what the men of law never figure out but Janine eventually will: that a diverse cohort of four women eye-witnesses silently agree to a pact of silence after watching the maiming, mutilation and killing of the shopkeeper from the beginning to the end of the attack. Yet Janine's own route to this silent complicity is not so straightforward. 'I can't reach them,' she admits, exasperated, at a late stage in her investigation. It is further a personal affront to Janine that the women mock her conviction that her report will actually speak: that it will communicate to the court, register and effect some form of justice, possibly leading to a finding of diminished responsibility and a mitigation in the sentences, particularly if Janine is to pathologize them by declaring them insane for the crime that the women sanely avow and readily take responsibility for. By eventually becoming convinced that these women are all too sane, and finally refusing to pathologize them before the law, despite the prosecutor aggressively pressing her and the chief judge practically begging her to do so, Janine too comes to arrive at silence as a form of refusal, adopting what she says about Christine's silence: 'She can communicate but sees no point in it.'

Janine's eventual arrival at this point of there-really-is-no-point is depicted in the most dramatic scene of the film towards the end, during her testimony as an expert witness in the trial of the three women. It is a wild and astonishingly brilliant scene of women's collective and contagious laughter that erupts in the courtroom and disrupts the proceedings (Figure 10.2). The onslaught of laughter cathartically resolves an extended build-up of tension around Janine's speech in previous scenes. As an expert witness, her speech is supposed to chime into the exercise of juris-diction, the speaking of the law that is taking place in

10.2 The laughterhood. Stills from *A Question of Silence.*

that space, but instead it proves inassimilable. Her statement of expert opinion that 'the three women are completely sound of mind', sends shockwaves through the audience and outrages the prosecutor, who begins to push Janine with a liberal dose of casual sexism, implying that she is speaking as a woman and not an expert, and that she is obviously failing in her duty to be objective. The faceoff continues after a lunch break, during which Janine's husband, who has been watching the proceedings, asks her to hold off on her 'peculiar ideas', express herself 'less vehemently', and be 'more realistic' – that is, to consider the damage she could inflict on her (read: his own) reputation and career if she were to insist on her opinion. Angered but resolved to stay on course, Janine returns to the courtroom and is questioned further on her report by the judge and the prosecutor, who now ask her to provide her opinion as to the motive behind the killing. Janine hesitates to speak what is a matter of silence, but begins to try to put into words what has in the course of the movie become crystal clear: 'It surely didn't escape your attention that these women killed a *man* who also happened to be the owner of a boutique.' The prosecutor dismissively retorts that the case would be no different if one hypothetically swapped genders, say, if the women had killed a female shop owner, or if the killers were three men. This is when Annie's rambunctious laughter first fills the courtroom, then spreads to the four witnesses in the audience, to the other two defendants, and finally to Janine, who makes one last-ditch attempt to explain the situation to a bewildered chief judge before fully surrendering to laughter: 'It's really quite funny,' she says. 'What did you say?' the judge asks, Janine gestures never-mind with a flick of her hand. The wild, contagious laughter continues in waves for nearly three minutes on screen until the end of the scene.

Silence and laughter are thus presented as key manifestations of women's refusal in *A Question of Silence*. Commentators have heard the echoes of Hélène Cixous' influential essay 'Laugh of the Medusa' in the coupling of silence and laughter, and have fittingly situated the film in relation to feminist work on phallogocentrism and within a milieu of thinking about *écriture féminine*. While 'neither self-conscious nor particularly intellectual',[5] nor anywhere as formally daring as the avant-garde feminist filmmaking of its time,[6] the film does take up in a kindred spirit some of the key themes in Cixous' ebullient call for women to 'confirm women in a place other than that which is reserved in and by the symbolic, that is in a place other than silence', for us to 'break out of the snare of silence', 'in order to smash everything, to shatter the framework of institutions, to blow up the law, to break up the "truth" with laughter'.[7] The scene of laughter in the courtroom in *A Question of Silence* is so powerful because after depicting the ceaselessly minor, relentlessly mundane, mercilessly banal operations of patriarchy in every nook and cranny of women's life, the film finally offers the trial scene as a bold literalization of patriarchy and its symbolic authority as 'law', performed with the requisite gravitas on the stage of a trial by men in judicial costumes. And then it just shatters it with something so simple and so readily available as laughter.

5 B. Ruby Rich, *Chick Flicks: Theories and Memories of the Feminist Film Movement* (Durham, NC: Duke University Press, 1998), 320.

6 Laura Mulvey, 'IAS Laughter: Past and Present of *A Question of Silence*', *UCL Institute of Advanced Studies* (blog), 1 January 2021, www.ucl.ac.uk/institute-of-advanced-studies/publications/2021/jan/ias-laughter-past-and-present-question-silence.

7 Hélène Cixous, 'The Laugh of the Medusa' [trans. Keith Cohen and Paula Cohen], *Signs* 1, no. 4 (Summer 1976), 875–93, 881, 888.

OBSCENE PROTEST

What brings me back to this scene is something that jumped out at me in the work that instigated this collection: Julie Stone Peters' *Law as Performance.* This is a book rich in historical detail on the ways in which performance has been central to Western jurisprudence as its constitutive element. In one regard, the dazzling array of resources that Peters has gathered can be read as the long Western history of saning, taming and engineering legal performance; an account of just how much ink and sweat has been spent in trying to subdue this unavowably essential element in law. Then again, what had drawn me to Peters' previous work on law and performance was her incisive formulation of the ever-present risk of the untameability of legal performance, and her formulation of the deep ambivalence that law has to its constitutive dependency on its performance as that which will make it, but might just also break it.[8]

I must already have been looking for the untameable as I was reading Peters' book. I read it as a PDF on my computer, and so I fantasize that what jumped out at me is presented in the form of a pop-up in the actual tangible book, because it is right around the middle, in chapter 4: an image depicting Calefurnia in the court, baring her ass to the judge. Peters gleaned this image from a mid fifteenth-century tract, but she also includes an earlier image of Calefurnia in the book, one that apparently 'circulated widely in late medieval Europe',[9] having first appeared in thirteenth-century illustrated editions of an influential compilation of Saxon law. Calefurnia here is depicted as scolding the judge, cursing him with one hand and holding her crotch with the other. The illustration was included in the compilation to explain the exclusion of women from the forum, accompanied by the caption, 'no woman may be a pleader, nor

8 Julie Stone Peters, 'Legal Performance Good and Bad', *Law, Culture and the Humanities* 4, no. 2 (2008): 179–200. See also Peters' ' Mapping Law and Performance: Reflections on the Dilemmas of an Interdisciplinary Conjunction', in *The Oxford Handbook of Law and Humanities*, ed. Simon Stern, Maksymilian Del Mar and Bernadette Meyler (Oxford: Oxford University Press, 2020), 198–215.

9 Julie Stone Peters, *Law as Performance: Theatricality, Spectatorship, and the Making of Law in Ancient, Medieval, and Early Modern Europe* (Oxford: Oxford University Press, 2022), 143.

may she bring a suit without a guardian'.[10] Then again, Calefurnia defied the judge in this way because she was furious at not being allowed to plead for herself. So what we have here is a fabulous causality, that strange self-fulfilling temporality of patriarchy, whereby the exclusion that is presented as a reasonable response to the obscene protest is in fact the very thing that the protest was a response to. Peters suggests that Calefurnia may have inspired another woman whose obscene protest is featured prominently in the book: Catharina Arndes, a well-respected late fifteenth-century townswoman, who during a confrontation with a delegation seeking to impose the archbishop's new rules on the local women's monastery, effectively chases the clergymen away by lifting up her skirts at them.[11] 'Let the priests tremble', writes Cixous half a millennium later, 'we're going to show them our sexts!'[12]

In her *Laughter: Notes on a Passion*, Anca Parvulescu suggests that there is a 'special relation' between exposed female genitals and laughter.[13] Parvulescu reads Cixous' 'Laugh of the Medusa' as crystallizing this special link, as it introduces a key twist on Sigmund Freud's reading of the myth of Medusa in a brief research note from 1922. Here Freud famously suggests that 'to decapitate = to castrate'[14] and that Medusa's severed and petrified head 'takes the place of a representation of the female genitals', the paradigmatic sight that arouses terror of castration, which Freud describes as what happens 'when a boy . . . catches sight of the female genitals, probably those of an adult . . . and essentially those of his mother'.[15] Cixous' twist is simple and precise: 'You only have to look at the Medusa straight on to see her. And she's not deadly. She's beautiful and she's laughing.'[16] It turns out that the link between women's laughter and public exposure of genitals has a bountiful archive: Parvulescu

[10] Ibid. [11] Ibid., 142. [12] Cixous, 'The Laugh of the Medusa', 885.

[13] Parvulescu, *Laughter*, 110.

[14] See Cixous elsewhere for yet another key twist directly on Freud's equation: 'If masculinity is culturally ordered by the castration complex, it might be said that the backlash, the return, on women of this castration anxiety is its displacement as decapitation, execution, of woman, as loss of her head' (Hélène Cixous, 'Castration or Decapitation?' [trans. Annette Kuhn], *Signs* 7, no. 1 [1981]: 41–55).

[15] Sigmund Freud, 'Medusa's Head', in *The Standard Edition of the Complete Psychological Works of Sigmund Freud*, vol. 18, ed. James Strachey (London: Hogarth Press, 1955), 273–74.

[16] Cixous, 'The Laugh of the Medusa', 885.

draws on Cixous' other works on laughter, on other figurations of Medusa, and also on other ancient figures of 'gaping mouths', such as the old woman, Baubo, who helps bring Spring back to earth, jolting Demeter out of her depression by getting her to laugh at the sight of her aged vulva. There is also the 'exuberantly vaginal'[17] and 'cunt-threatening'[18] Celtic 'old hag' figure of Sheela na gig, powerfully refigured in artist Nancy Spero's work to emphasize that the threat laughingly posed by exposed female genitals is not merely one of castration but also of engulfment ('and essentially those of his mother').[19]

A further term that Parvulescu brings into this discussion of laughter and exposure is the 'revolution', and although I consider 'refusal' a more generative term to think with here, it is worth a brief detour, if only to get us to the question of violence, which I will eventually return to. Parvulescu's route to revolution is via another text on the politics of the figure of the Medusa: Neil Hertz's discussion of a scene of two women on the barricades in Paris during the June 1848 uprising, lifting their skirts at armed soldiers while shouting obscenities at them. This a scene purportedly reported by Victor Hugo (with the preface 'the June uprising … displayed suddenly, to a horrified society, monstrous and unknown forms'),[20] but might well have been fantasized by him, as Hertz is careful to note in his discussion of male hysteria finding expression in the representation of political threats as sexual threats: 'What the revolution is said to be doing figuratively is precisely what – in a moment – each of the women will be represented as doing literally, suddenly displaying monstrous and unknown forms to a horrified society.'[21]

[17] Josephine Withers, 'Nancy Spero's American-Born "Sheela-Na-Gig"', *Feminist Studies* 17, no. 1 (1991): 51–56.

[18] Cherry Smyth, 'Nancy Spero', *Art Monthly* 345 (2011): 34–35.

[19] Here too it may be (though really shouldn't be) necessary to add a caveat: I do not read this invocation of 'female genitals' as pertaining to an ontological truth that inheres in and magically exudes from certain body parts (as, for example, the submission made on behalf of Scottish Lesbians, Lesbian Project and LGB Alliance in *For Women Scotland Ltd.* bewilderingly implies; see 'Submission to the Supreme Court', https://scottishlesbians.org.uk/resources) but in terms of their figurations, say, in psychoanalysis and myth.

[20] Quoted in Neil Hertz, 'Medusa's Head: Male Hysteria under Political Pressure', *Representations* 4 (1983): 27–54, 29.

[21] Ibid.

Women's self-exposure in defiance, medieval European scenes of which we find in Peters' book, is indeed a long-standing repertoire of contention that continues to have currency around the world. Naminata Diabate, who conceptualizes the act in terms of 'naked agency', notes that 'the aggressive disrobing of mature women is a practice documented since medieval times in Africa' as well, and writes of having documented hundreds of acts of naked protest around the world over the past couple of decades.[22] One key suggestion of Diabate's study is that it may be misguided to consider this form of protest always and everywhere non-violent as such, as some instances clearly draw on traditions of genital cursing and thus aim to bring about the social or literal death of their targets.[23] Notably, the Catharina Arndes scene that Peters relates, which apparently may have involved other townswomen joining Arndes in the action but reportedly did not involve any physical contact or scuffle, was described by the chroniclers of the time as 'violent'.[24]

A MINOR JURISPRUDENCE OF REFUSAL?

Forensic refusal breaches orderly legal proceedings, the rituals and paraphernalia of dignity, authority and majesty. The breach causes but a temporary suspension, and it justifies (both retroactively and preventively in that strange self-fulfilling temporality of patriarchy) the permanent exclusion – or at least, the perpetual alienation – of the outragers from the forum, rather than transforming the forum itself. This breach is not quite the 'strategy of rupture' that is based on identifying and exploiting the contradictions in sovereign recourses to law. Forensic rupture, as Emilios Christodoulidis succinctly defines it via Jacques Vergès, is brought about by 'an act of resistance' that 'registers without being absorbed, integrated or co-opted into the system against which it

22 Naminata Diabate, *Naked Agency: Genital Cursing and Biopolitics in Africa* (Durham, NC: Duke University Press, 2020), 11, 8.

23 Ibid., 194.

24 Cordelia Heß, 'Skirts and Politics: The Cistercian Monastery of Harvestehude and the Hamburg City Council', *Medieval Feminist Forum* 47, no. 2 (2011): 57–92, 67.

stands'.[25] Representations of Calefurnia's breach are absorbed into the forum as the commonsensical justification for women's exclusion from the forum. 'The hearing will continue in the absence of the defendants,' announces the chief judge following the breach of collective laughter in *A Question of Silence*, as the laughing women are escorted out of the courtroom.

It is in fact difficult to discern a 'strategy' in this type of breach, particularly when we know how laughter in the courtroom can work strategically: in classic rhetoric, laughter is considered a forensic weapon, and rhetoricians have sought to engineer its tamed and disciplined versions for timely deployment against an opponent whose ridicule may well tip the scales in one's favour. But the laughers of *A Question of Silence* laugh themselves out of the courtroom, just as Calefurnia's exposure results in (the retroactive justification of) her expulsion. How to understand these performances of refusal, particularly in their ancient, mythical and persistent dimensions, as more than just amusing one-liners – that is, as more than acts that merely cancel themselves out once the laughter settles?

The opening scene of Peters' *Law as Performance* is the trial by battle at Tothill Fields in 1571, a time when such proceedings were no longer common. It is a strange and fascinating event that allows Peters to lay out a number of the key questions that drive her inquiry about the centrality of performance to law. But perhaps most importantly, it crystallizes Peters' important point that 'the public spectacle ensures the validity of the legal decision'.[26] The spectacle that can validate can, of course, also invalidate. Yet one thing we come to understand in the course of Peters' discussion is that there are no magically total operations of validation or invalidation, but rather a vast range in between, and this range in between is precisely what makes the inquiry into performance in law and law as performance actually interesting. Valuable in this regard is Peters' literary studies approach of 'dwelling on small but significant moments'.[27] In turn, this reading practice and methodological orientation undergirds a key claim of the book, namely that 'it is not only

[25] Emilios Christodoulidis, 'Strategies of Rupture', *Law and Critique* 20, no. 1 (2009): 3–26, 5.

[26] Peters, *Law as Performance*, 4. [27] Ibid., 22.

sovereigns, legislatures, and judges who create law through grand edicts; so do its subjects, not only through words but through actions large and small'.[28] Peters thus suggests that performance can be understood as a form of 'minor jurisprudence', and then (perhaps too swiftly) adds that sometimes it is 'not minor at all'.[29]

We do not get a more extensive discussion of minor jurisprudence than this one gesture in the book, but Peters evokes the concept with reference to Peter Goodrich's 1996 book *Law in the Courts of Love: Literature and Other Minor Jurisprudences*. This is where Goodrich discussed the fifteenth-century High Court of Love in Paris as 'but one instance of an alternative jurisdiction or forum of judgment drawn from the diversities of the legal and literary past',[30] and suggested that there is 'a much larger and as yet unwritten history of repressed, forgotten and failed jurisdictions'.[31] While Goodrich's key example was indeed that of a specific court and a specific minor tradition of jurisdiction, he proposed the notion in the more capacious sense of jurisprudence, counting, for example, 'lost critical and satirical traditions of jurisprudence', and contemporary critical legal studies as minor jurisprudences.[32] Panu Minkkinen had also used the formulation in a similar sense in his 1994 paper on Kafka's 'minor jurisprudence' – reworking Gilles Deleuze and Félix Guattari's notion of 'minor literature' into 'minor legal literature'.[33] In this regard, Peters' suggestion concerning performance as a minor jurisprudence is borne out by her extensive review of the legal canon on performance, but the suggestion is further that unstudied and perhaps unrehearsed

[28] Ibid., 23.

[29] Ibid. The proposal to see performance *as* a minor jurisprudence in a book on law *as* performance has a strange circularity which becomes somewhat dizzying when we keep in mind the suggestion that the 'law as approaches to legal studies (as opposed to the proliferations of, say, 'law and') and to legal history, such as Peters' book, should be seen as minor jurisprudences (Christopher Tomlins, ed., 'Law as ... Minor Jurisprudence in Historical Key', special issue, *Law Text Culture* 21 [2017]). But this too may be a sign of the inextricable, and perhaps in the final instance inexplicable, centrality of performance to law.

[30] Peter Goodrich, *Law in the Courts of Love: Literature and Other Minor Jurisprudences* (London: Routledge, 1996), 1.

[31] Ibid., 2. [32] Ibid., 2, 5.

[33] Panu Minkkinen, 'The Radiance of Justice: On the Minor Jurisprudence of Franz Kafka', *Social & Legal Studies* 3 (1994): 349–69.

performance practices by law's subjects in the forum may too have the capacity to constitute what may be understood as a minor jurisprudence. I hold on to this for thinking about my juxtaposed scenes of refusal.

A more recent collective re-visitation[34] of Goodrich and Minkkinen's earlier formulations attests that the concept of minor jurisprudence(s) may owe its evocativeness and attractiveness in part to its fuzziness. Commentators tend to problematize both component terms of the phrase, but 'minor' more so. One key question has been around how the minor relates to the major, with some general agreement that it must always be defined as such in relation to the major. Genevieve Painter, for example, writes that 'the idea of the minor needs the major',[35] while Christopher Tomlins puts it in more theatrical terms, proposing that the thinking of minor jurisprudences 'embrace a "major" as their stage or backdrop'.[36] Mark Antaki tries something different in article that explores the boundaries of the concept, tackling it from numerous directions at once and asking it a somewhat discordant set of questions. He asks, for instance, whether minor jurisprudence can be understood as 'not a minor to a major but something beyond (existing?) minor-major dualities'.[37] But he also questions the 'jurisprudence' component of the notion as well. What if, Antaki suggests, '"Minor Jurisprudence" does away with law as we know it and invites us to a life "beside" – but not "in" or "of" or "with" law?'[38] Can minor jurisprudence, he further asks, be understood as 'an anti-, or better yet, a non-, jurisprudence?'[39] In the end, Antaki too opts to preserve the relationship to the major and to jurisprudence as such in the concept. He does this through a more elaborate and sustained engagement with the vicissitudes of Deleuze and Guattari's definition of 'minor literature', which allows him to point out that 'the minor is a "practice" of

34 Tomlins, ed., 'Law as . . . '.

35 Genevieve Renard Painter, 'Law as Minor Jurisprudence: Is It a Mistake?', *Law Text Culture* 21 (2017), 276–98, 293.

36 Christopher Tomlins, 'Law As . . . IV: Minor Jurisprudence in Historical Key. An Introduction', *Law Text Culture* 21 (2017), 1–29, 23.

37 Mark Antaki, 'Making Sense of Minor Jurisprudence', *Law Text Culture* 21 (2017), 54–75, 55.

38 Ibid. See also Goodrich on minor jurisprudences being 'to the side of' law (*Law in the Courts of Love*, 69).

39 Antaki, 'Making Sense', 57.

the major', that they are 'different modalities of the same'[40] and that there is thus 'an inter-belonging of minor and major'.[41]

In thinking about a minor jurisprudence of refusal, there may be some value in holding on to those questions that Antaki raises about the jurisprudentiality of minor jurisprudences and their prepositionality to 'law as we know it', even if these questions may at first seem to push the concept even beyond its own fuzzy boundaries. Here one notable aspect of Goodrich's early definition of minor jurisprudences is that it implies a definition of major jurisprudence as that which is not quite what it makes itself out to be. Minor jurisprudences are 'a challenge to the science of law and a threat to its monopoly of legal knowledge'.[42] They are 'forms of legal knowledge that escape the *phantom* of a sovereign and unitary law' and 'interrupt the *idolatry* of one law'.[43] So the minor is also what exposes, challenges and perhaps thereby undermines the phantasmatic and the imaginary elements that allow the major to constitute itself as such. It is perhaps primarily in this sense that minor jurisprudences are interruptive, that they 'cut holes in the in the fabric of the law', but while actually 'inhabiting institutional space'.[44] Hence the tried and tested utility of 'minor jurisprudence' for theorizing the place of critique vis-à-vis law. But what about refusal? In bringing the concept to bear on my juxtaposed scenes, I wish to repurpose for refusal the questions that have been asked of it regarding critique: How does refusal work within law while also remaining without it? How to think about the elsewhere of refusal that also occupies institutional space? Is it possible to seek minor jurisprudences in bursts and pockets of extra-legality that may spill over the frames that attempt to contain them – frames of, say, madness, crime, contempt? It is suggested that minor jurisprudences are a 'taking away from, abrogating, suspending, unfinishing',[45] but can minor jurisprudences be discerned in a turning away from, withdrawing, refusing?

To return to *A Question of Silence* in attempting to tackle these questions, one key figuration of the women's refusal in the film is their refusal of

[40] Ibid., 68. [41] Ibid., 72. [42] Goodrich, *Law in the Courts of Love*, 2.

[43] Ibid., 2, 4, my emphases.

[44] Peter Goodrich, 'How Strange the Change from Major to Minor', *Law Text Culture* 21 (2017): 30–53.

[45] Ibid., 32.

mediation, particularly the mediation of law. Peter Goodrich writes of 'the foundational character of law as a medium, a symbolic and discursive enterprise'[46] and Cornelia Vismann draws upon the work of Antoine Garapon to propose the 'mediality of the justice system', which, in a criminal case, is meant 'to translate the criminal act into a symbolic form' by providing a frame within which a speechless and unrepresentable act is captured in words'.[47] If Vismann is right in suggesting that the justice system 'seems to have forgotten its own mediality',[48] it is one of the surprising gifts of the film that it represents this mediality so captivatingly, particularly in its subtler moments. The film is bracketed by two obvious guises of law: the police arresting each of the three women at the beginning of the film, and the trial scene at the end. But between these bookends, law is represented mainly through its recording, copying, filing and surveillance practices and technologies (Figure 10.3).

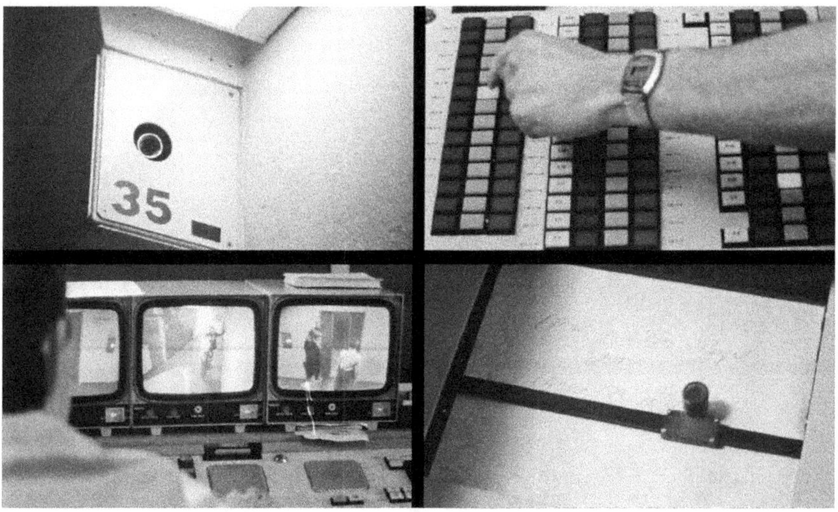

10.3 Law is represented mainly through its recording, copying, filing, and surveillance practices in *A Question of Silence*. Stills from the film.

[46] Peter Goodrich, 'Law', in *Critical Terms for Media Studies*, ed. W. J. T. Mitchell and Mark B. N. Hansen (Chicago, IL: University of Chicago Press, 2010), 249–65, 250.

[47] Cornelia Vismann, 'Tele-tribunals: Anatomy of a Medium' [trans. Sara Ogger], *Grey Room*, no. 10 (January 1, 2003): 7–21, 15.

[48] Ibid., 16.

Indeed, if it weren't for the camera's studious attention to these mechanic workings of legal media technologies, we could mistake the prison that the women are kept in for some kind of residential care unit, a colourful and benign space of confinement with bookshelves, indoor plants and kindly women guards who look more like social workers.

Janine herself is clearly part of this legal apparatus of mediation as a court-appointed psychiatrist, and she is keen to successfully fulfil her duty to mediate between the women and the law. She is never without her tape recorder while interviewing the women, and she spends sleepless nights with this device, playing and replaying extracts from the interviews (Figure 10.4). Her coming around to join in the women's refusal – their silence and their laughter – is often read as the result of a process of identification. Ruby Rich suggests that 'she comes to doubt the women's insanity and to understand their motive as potentially, hypothetically, her own'.[49] Likewise, for Jane Arthurs, in this film '"identification" depends to an extent on an intellectual

10.4 Janine with her tape recorder. Stills from *A Question of Silence.*

[49] Rich, *Chick Flicks*, 320.

alignment with a middle-class professional's growing realization of her own oppression, through a rational process of investigation that reveals the institutionalized forms of patriarchal power'.[50] So the suggestion is not only that Janine comes to identify with the three women through her forensic methods, but also that the viewer is drawn into the film's world of meaning cerebrally by means of the same methods, through a rational identification with her. While the film does indeed work through identification with Janine for viewers who would be inclined to identify with her, in the narrative world of the film, it is not the rationalized bureaucratic process of forensic mediation that brings Janine around, but rather her decisive break with it. At a critical turning point, as the women begin to lose patience with her and push back, we see her lose mastery of her speech in the interviews: her sentences are left incomplete, her tape recorder on pause. Her participation in the laughter in the courtroom is her final break with law's mediality. Is that break therefore to be interpreted as an embrace of immediacy and unmediation? Or is it rather that we arrive at another (a minor?) type of mediation, another modality of 'hearing'?

VIOLENCE

I have emphasized silence and laughter as two key manifestations of women's refusal in *A Question of Silence*. But there is also, of course, the violence. Perhaps because of how the killing is framed in the film, or rather because the entire film is about reworking its framing, commentators on the film tend to shy away from reckoning with the act of killing itself. This avoidance may be seen to be facilitated by its decisively limited visual depiction. We understand what happened to the victim through the dry forensic pathology report, tidily packaged and self-contained. There is eventually a scene of the attack in a flashback: The shopkeeper catches Christine as she steals an item of clothing.

[50] Jane Arthurs, 'Thelma and Louise', in *Feminist Subjects, Multi-media: Cultural Methodologies*, ed. Penny Florence and Dee Reynolds (Manchester: Manchester University Press, 1995), 89–105, 92.

He approaches her, takes it out of her bag and smugly points to the price tag. Christine takes it back and calmly stuffs it and then a few other items into her bag. Amused by this scene of defiance, the other two women join in, taking their time to methodically stuff garments in their bags in full view of the shopkeeper. The women then slowly circle around and close in on him. A push, a push, a slap – he is down. A kick, a shopping trolley, a broken plastic hanger – he stops groaning. Another kick, a broken glass shelf, a heavy glass ashtray, and on it goes: taking their time and acting with calm deliberation, the three women improvise weapons to torture, mutilate and kill the boutique owner. Except for two momentary glimpses of it on the ground before any blood is spilled, the body of the victim remains out of frame: no gore, no graphic visual depiction, only some campily exaggerated sound effects overlaid on a 1980s experimental electronic musical score. 'Stylized through a deliberate, almost ritual execution, and a camera calmly intent on the slayers, not the slain',[51] the scene's pace and choreography indeed unfold as if it were a sacrificial rite, as if the women are 'performing or reenacting an already rehearsed scene'.[52] Perhaps we are watching a modern retake on a mythical scene: Pentheus being torn apart by the bacchants (Figure 10.5).[53]

Gorris' decision to not show the victim's body seems to have served as a kind of license to look away from the violence, with commentators treating the act of killing merely as a metaphor, or an unpleasant yet indispensable plot device. Whereas the legal system, as depicted rather

[51] Sheila Johnston, '*De Stilte Rond Christine M.* (*A Question of Silence*)', *Monthly Film Bulletin* 50, no. 589 (February 1983): 48.

[52] Geetha Ramanathan, 'Murder as Speech: Narrative Subjectivity in Marleen Gorris' *A Question of Silence*', *Genders*, no. 15 (Winter 1992), 61.

[53] With most commentators' mythical associations going towards Medusa and/or the Furies (who get an explicit mention in the film when the prosecutor describes the body as being so mutilated that it was as if it had been attacked by 'a high-heeled army of Furies'), I thought I was alone in this association to the *Bacchae* until encountering Geetha Ramanathan's brilliant reading of the film, where she writes: 'The camera now notes the spatial arrangement of the boutique and pauses at the shaken man in the middle of women who surround him stilly, in mythic remembrance of Pentheus amidst the Bacchae' (Ibid., 66).

10.5 Pentheus amid the bacchants. Stills from *A Question of Silence.*

realistically in the film, can only register the act as crime and madness,[54] most sympathetic readings of the film, in not paying close attention to the formal aesthetics of the killing, tend to frame it as a 'feminist snap'[55] in response to an accumulation of 'the small indignities of women's lives',[56] thus excusing and, worse, explaining it away. But in thinking refusal through, we may need to read the scene of the attack more boldly on its own terms. Geetha Ramanathan does precisely this, and proposes that the killing is in effect a 'speech act' that is an articulation of women's political desire: 'their desire for female solidarity and their desire to undo patriarchy'.[57] Pointing out the significance of the boutique as a male owned female 'public' space in the discursive arrangement of the text,[58]

[54] Perhaps an important counter-point here is provided by Alice Diop's *Saint Omer* (2022), a fiction film closely based on the real-life trial of a woman who killed her fifteen-month-old daughter. The film depicts a female chief judge who manages to orchestrate the procedure in a way that allows a very sensitive form of hearing.

[55] Sara Ahmed, *Living a Feminist Life* (Durham, NC: Duke University Press, 2017), 200–206.

[56] Linda Williams, 'A Jury of Their Peers: Questions of Silence, Speech, and Judgment in Marleen Gorris's *A Question of Silence*', in *Multiple Voices in Feminist Film Criticism*, ed. Diane Carson, Linda Dittmar and Janice R. Welsch (Minneapolis: University of Minnesota Press, 1994), 58–71.

[57] Ramanathan, 'Murder as Speech', 61.

[58] Ibid., 60.

Ramanathan interprets the act of killing as the women reclaiming that space for themselves by acting in concert, and thus 'rewriting their identities as women in a public space'.[59] She reads the silent complicity of the witnesses as their approval, validation and legitimation of the killing as 'an act of battle by the women rather than a sudden spontaneous "feminine" outburst of rage'.[60]

CINEMA AS COUNTER-FORUM

Ramanathan's reading partially problematizes Linda Williams' influential reading of the film as skilfully tapping into what Elaine Showalter has defined as the 'wild zone' of women's culture: a mysterious zone of women's experience that is 'conceived outside the limits of all existing language, all "known" reality'.[61] This is risky territory for feminist artists according to Williams, but necessary to engage with to validate women's 'muted' experiences. She praises Gorris' film for doing so while avoiding 'the pitfalls of a facile or utopian feminist revision'.[62] Williams too reads 'the violence of the crime' as 'a form of speech',[63] but then does not fully follow through with the implications of this. Taking shelter in the film's motif of silence, Williams suggests that the film demonstrates the heroic moment of feminist consciousness as the moment of solidarity 'with an identity that has not yet been spoken and that cannot yet speak itself'.[64] But for Ramanathan, 'The greater act of courage, as the film presents it, is that the women speak to what has been named in such an extraordinary way: female desire as violence.'[65] What is interesting here is that Williams, finding the power of the film in 'its refusal to narrate the positive, utopian identity of women',[66] holds on to an ideal of a feminist utopia that nevertheless must be protected from articulation because it will be just too crass to speak of it.[67] The wild zone is to thrill, it is to excite feminist desires, and to inform feminist aesthetics, but it must do all this while remaining a no-place. But what if that zone is not so much a utopia which

[59] Ibid., 61. [60] Ibid., 63. [61] Williams, 'A Jury of Their Peers', 432. [62] Ibid., 433.
[63] Ibid., 437. [64] Ibid. [65] Ramanathan, 'Murder as Speech', 60.
[66] Williams, 'A Jury of Their Peers,' 439.
[67] Williams dismisses, for example, Cixous' 'pat reversal' of the Medusa figure (433, 439).

shall remain unspoken of and uninhabited, but a heterotopia that is a space and time of rehearsal, a space for prefigurative practices towards another way of living? A heterotopia that thus may well be both very here/now and elsewhere at once, much in the way desire desires?

I borrow the heterotopia formulation from Bonnie Honig's *A Feminist Theory of Refusal*, where she offers an alluring reading of Euripides's play the *Bacchae* as yielding an understanding of refusal as not merely an act, but as having an arc, which has 'the city as its destination'.[68] The arc of refusal means that the heterotopian escape from the city to the Cithaeron, where the women render inoperative their productive and reproductive capacities, has to be followed up by a return to the city to claim it:

> Heterotopias valuably serve as spaces or times of rehearsal where alternative forms of life can be tried out and explored. . . . The bacchants teach the importance of that experience as rehearsal and example when they complete the arc of their refusal by returning to the city to claim it. At that point, it is up to the city: is it ready to receive them?[69]

While the play is commonly read in centuries of reception as the tragedy of Agave (who with her sister and other bacchants 'maddened' by Dionysus, kills her son the king Pentheus on Cithaeron, mistaking him for a lion cub while in bacchic delirium) or that of King Pentheus (who is punished by Dionysus with death by his mother's hand because he refuses to recognize the god as one), for Honig the tragedy is that of the city, because it is not ready to receive the women as they complete their arc of refusal. This argument necessitates a re-signification of the killing of Pentheus, an act that is so 'nauseatingly horrifying' that it 'leads most readers or viewers to condemn the women who committed the violence and to see them as mad'.[70] Then again, we would do well to remember how, Honig suggests, 'the conventional center holds on to power in the face of such challenges . . . : by turning such heterotopias into sites of madness or exception'.[71] Approaching the killing of Pentheus for its

[68] Bonnie Honig, *A Feminist Theory of Refusal* (Cambridge, MA: Harvard University Press, 2021), 2, 103.

[69] Ibid., 71. [70] Ibid., 12–13. [71] Ibid., 96.

political meaning much as Ramanathan approaches the killing in the film, Honig pursues the question of 'what it would mean to see the women's violence as, in some way, deliberate and free: a refusal'.[72] In Honig's reading, the killing of Pentheus is not merely a tragically unknowing filicide, but also and primarily a regicide[73] that is part of the larger and deliberate regicidal project (a 'slow regicide') of the bacchants, a project apparent in their every act. For Honig, 'when the bacchants kill the king, they release everyone and him, too, from the false idolatry of patriarchal sovereignty'.[74] Their return to the city to demand to be celebrated for the 'hunt' is a return that therefore 'has the power to inaugurate a politics',[75] but only if the city is indeed ready to receive the women and their regicidal politics.

While many film critics and feminist film scholars, particularly at the time, read *A Question of Silence* as promoting separatism (on Cithaeron, perhaps), it is possible to read this film with Honig as bearing an arc that involves a return to the city. For this, we must return to the scene of laughter. One rather challenging and compelling proposal that Anca Parvulescu makes is that in thinking about laughter we must 'focus on the burst of laughter itself', rather than doing what most 'theories of laughter' do, which is to focus on the something else that laughter is a response to: 'the comic, jokes, humor, the grotesque, the ridiculous, the ludicrous etc.'.[76] What would it mean to consider laughter in the courtroom scene as untethered from its object, the law? In Parvulescu's reading of the film at the end of her book, the scene already depicts this very untethering:

> Soon all the protagonists, spectators to the spectacle of law, are roaring with laughter. ... Slowly, laughter dislocates itself from its object, the gender-blind court of law, and, by extension, the law itself. It is a laughter that has its own *raison d'être*, apart from any specific laughable

[72] Ibid., 12.

[73] According to Honig, Agave is here faced with patriarchy's double-bind: 'It is simply not possible to kill the king without losing the son, not just because of the circumstantial fact that her son Pentheus is also the king, but more fundamentally because killing the king means killing patriarchy, the structure of kinship to which the position of "son" belongs' (ibid., 82).

[74] Ibid., 66. [75] Ibid., 95. [76] Parvulescu, *Laughter*, 3.

> object. And laughter reproduces itself, laughter asks for more laughter. It not only interrupts, but repeats itself and spreads.[77]

What gets created in this contagion of laughter is a 'laughterhood'[78] of laughers. But this laughterhood is importantly both on screen and off: the contagion of laughter in the courtroom spreads beyond the screen to the film theatre, thus constituting the latter as a counter-forum, a site of minor jurisprudence that emerges precisely due to the avowed medial force of the space.

'Interestingly, at each screening of the film that I attended, this infectious rupture spread to the theater audience, producing a moment of stunning solidarity,'[79] testifies Barbara Kruger. The film 'works on its viewers as forcefully as water on dehydrated food, reconstituting its proper audience even as it unreels upon the screen. … It is a gendered audience to which Gorris appeals, a subversive audience of women scattered throughout the movie theater, rising up in instinctive laughter', writes Ruby Rich.[80] Linda Williams attests to 'the genuine sense of danger and excitement' generated by two screenings of the film she attended,[81] and Sheila Johnston writes of how the 'implied sense of solidarity is – irrationally, perversely – exhilarating'.[82] This, perhaps, is the episode of the 'return to the city' in refusal's arc: the film's own mediality reconstitutes the space of the film theatre as a counter-forum, as the site of a minor jurisprudence of laughter. But what jurisdiction could this refusal have? I will leave two anecdotes here to begin to imagine answers. The first is by Jane Root who worked at Cinema of Women, the film's British distributor at the time of its release in London. It was, she says, 'a film which dramatically divided audiences. Some women stood up and cheered, while other (often male) viewers left enraged. … I was told that the Pizza Hut restaurant next door to one of the cinemas was full, night after night, with couples engaged in deep and sometimes angry

[77] Ibid., 154. [78] Ibid., 1.

[79] Barbara Kruger, *Remote Control: Power, Cultures, and the World of Appearances* (Cambridge, MA: MIT Press, 1993), 201.

[80] Rich, *Chick Flicks*, 319. [81] Williams, 'A Jury of Their Peers', 437.

[82] Johnston, '*De Stilte Rond Christine M.*', 48.

arguments about the film'.[83] And one from Ruby Rich: 'At the New Directors preview in New York, the audience recapitulated the film's own ending: man after man rose to confront Gorris with hostile or garbled questions, only to encounter raucous laughter from most of the women in the audience. Gorris wasn't surprised; she had observed this pattern everywhere the film had shown.'[84] It is in and through this laughter that the city prepares to receive the bacchants upon their return from Cithaeron.

[83] Jane Root, 'Distributing "A Question of Silence": A Cautionary Tale', in *Films for Women*, ed. Charlotte Brunsdon (London: British Film Institute, 1986), 213–23, 213.
[84] Rich, *Chick Flicks*, 324.

CHAPTER 11

Oath Taking and Legal Performance

Marco Wan

IT WAS SUPPOSED TO BE A STRAIGHTFORWARD PROCESS, AND a familiar scene. Following the 2016 elections for the Legislative Council, or Hong Kong's legislature, the incoming lawmakers took their oath of office one by one inside the Council's chamber. However, there was drama that year. When it was his turn, Leung Kwok-hung, a veteran legislator returning for a new term after a landslide victory, approached the stand holding a giant yellow umbrella and other props, and shouted pro-democracy slogans along the way. He read out the oath loudly and aggressively, and also inserted dramatic pauses at unexpected moments. Dissatisfied with the manner in which he took the oath, the Hong Kong government initiated proceedings against him. It argued that Leung's antics rendered his oath invalid and that he should be disqualified from office.

The Court of First Instance (CFI) agreed with the government. It opined that Leung's behaviour at the stand amounted to no more than a 'theatrical performance', and that he had therefore failed to exhibit the sincerity and solemnity required for the oath.[1] The Court of Appeal (CA) affirmed the lower court's decision.[2]

In this chapter, I take the *Leung* case as a point of entry for exploring the relationship between law, theatre, and performance. My question is: what does the courts' characterization of Leung's oath as theatrical performance

* The author would like to thank Albert Chen, Andrew Counter, the editors, and the anonymous readers for their insightful comments on the chapter.

1 *HKSAR* v. *President of the Legislative Council* [2017] 4 HKLRD 115 (CFI, 14 July, 2017), 247.

2 *Secretary for Justice* v. *Leung Kwok-hung* [2019] HKCA 173 (CA, 15 February, 2019).

tell us about the nature and operation of law? In *Law as Performance*, Julie Stone Peters boldly contends that, far from being a set of 'jurisprudential footnotes', legal performance is 'a constitutive idea in Western jurisprudence'.[3] In other words, theatre and performance are crucial to understanding what law is. Moving from the ancient world to early modern Europe, she demonstrates how notions of theatricality ('law needs theatre') and anti-theatricality ('law must avoid theatre at all costs') lie at the heart of how we talk and think about law. By examining the case in light of Peters' insights, I posit that the proceedings can be understood as an encounter between law on the one hand, and performance on the other, that reconfigures the boundary between them in order to expose the nature of law as performance. I then analyse law's strategies at keeping that boundary in place.

I will begin by providing the legal and political context for the *Leung* case in Section 11.1. In Section 11.2, I interpret the case as a clash between Leung's theatricality and law's anti-theatricality. I then home in on law's anti-theatrical language in Section 11.3, and draw on J. L. Austin's lectures on the performative and the constative, as well as Jacques Derrida's reinterpretation of those two concepts, to explore the nature of legal performance. Theatricality and anti-theatricality appear to be on opposite sides in this case – Leung embraces theatre, the government (and the courts) reject it – but as Peters points out, the two are not necessarily polar opposites: while they are often marked out as 'antinomies', they can also be 'proximate' to one another, sometimes 'perilously' so. [4] In the final section, I examine how theatricality and anti-theatricality both stand apart and come together in the courts' reasoning, and contend that the judicial insistence that theatre has no place in the oath-taking process can be understood as an attempt on the part of law to disavow its own performative nature.

[3] Julie Peters, *Law as Performance: Theatricality, Spectatorship, and the Making of Law in Ancient, Medieval, and Early Modern Europe* (Oxford: Oxford University Press, 2022), p. 9. For further discussions of law and performance, see Sean Mulcahy, 'Methodologies of Law as Performance' (2022) 16(2) *Law and Humanities* 165–182 and *Law and Performance*, ed., Austin Sarat, Lawrence Douglas, and Martha Merrill Umphrey (Amherst: Massachusetts University Press, 2018). See also Marrett Leiboff, *Towards a Theatrical Jurisprudence* (Abingdon: Routledge, 2019).

[4] Peters, *Law as Performance*, p. 9.

11.1 THE LEGAL AND POLITICAL CONTEXT

The legal proceedings in *Leung* took place amidst a long-standing debate about the pace of democratization in Hong Kong. China resumed sovereignty over Hong Kong in 1997, after 156 years of British colonial governance in the territory. The Basic Law, Hong Kong's post-handover constitutional document, guarantees fundamental rights and freedom,[5] an independent judiciary[6] and the continuation of the common law system inherited from the British regime.[7] It also guarantees that the capitalist economic system and way of life before 1997 will 'remain unchanged for fifty years' after the retrocession.[8] The idea of 'One Country, Two Systems' is at the core of the post-colonial constitutional order: Hong Kong is part of China, a one-party socialist state, but it is meant to exist as a liberal enclave with 'a high degree of autonomy'.[9] Most importantly for understanding the oath-taking controversy, the Basic Law was understood by many people in Hong Kong at the time to guarantee a gradual transition to democracy: it states that the 'ultimate aim' is for both Hong Kong's leader (the Chief Executive) and its legislators to be selected by 'universal suffrage', and that the pace of democratization is to be determined according to the principle of 'gradual and orderly progress' and 'in light of the actual situation' in the city.[10] In the case of the Chief Executive, candidates for election would be nominated by a committee that is 'broadly representative' of Hong Kong society.[11]

In part because of these constitutional guarantees, questions of when and how Hong Kong would become democratized became a focus of political and constitutional debate in local society. As years passed, however, frustration grew at the slow pace of democratization. This frustration spilled over in Occupy Central, a civil disobedience movement in 2014 that lasted more than two and a half months, during which people occupied the main roads, flyovers and public squares to demand democratic elections. There also arose increasing localist and anti-China sentiments, and localist parties calling for Hong Kong's independence from China formed in the aftermath of Occupy. Alarmed by these

5 Basic Law Article 4.
6 Basic Law Article 2.
7 Basic Law Article 8.
8 Basic Law Article 5.
9 Basic Law Article 2.
10 Basic Law Articles 45 and 68.
11 Basic Law Article 45.

developments, the Central Government in Beijing began to tighten political control over the city, and sought to curb the influence of these pro-democracy and localist parties.[12] Leung belonged to the radical wing of these parties, and was also a prominent figure in Occupy Central. In this context, it becomes obvious that his election victory, and the victories secured by candidates at the same end of the political spectrum, were a major cause of consternation for the authorities in both Hong Kong and Beijing.

Leung was amongst a group of legislators whose oaths were held to be invalid by the courts. The text of the Legislative Council Oath is set out in the Oaths and Declaration Ordinance (ODO): an incoming legislator has to swear that they will 'uphold the Basic Law of' and 'bear allegiance to' the Hong Kong Special Administrative Region of the People's Republic of China, and that they will serve Hong Kong 'conscientiously, dutifully, in full accordance with the law, honestly and with integrity'.[13] The oath can be taken in English or Chinese. The fact that an incoming legislator who does not take a valid an oath is barred from office is closely tied to the history of this ordinance.[14] The ODO was first enacted in 1972; it was revised after the 1997 retrocession but the wording and structure remained essentially the same.[15] The 1972 ordinance was itself largely modelled on the United Kingdom's Promissory Oaths Act (1868). As Han Zhu and Albert Chen point out, there are two differences between the Hong Kong ordinances and the UK legislation that would turn out to be critical to the events of 2016.[16] First, the 1868 act applies to judges and holders of high-level public office in the UK, but it does not apply to

12 For a more detailed discussion of Hong Kong's democratization up to the time of the *Leung* case, see Albert H. Y. Chen, 'The Hong Kong Basic Law and the Limits of Democratization Under "One Country, Two Systems"', 50 *The International Lawyer* (2017), 69–86.

13 Oaths and Declarations Ordinance, Part IV, Schedule 2.

14 Han Zhu and Albert H. Y. Chen, 'The Oath-Taking Cases and the NPCSC Interpretation of 2016: Interface of Common Law and Chinese Law', 49 *Hong Kong Law Journal* (2019), 381–415. For a discussion of the history of the legislation on oath-taking in the UK context, see Enid Campbell, 'Oaths and Affirmations of Public Office under English Law: An Historical Retrospect', 21(3) *Journal of Legal History* (2000), 1–32.

15 Zhu and Chen, 'The Oath-Taking Cases', 391–392.

16 Zhu and Chen, 'The Oath-Taking Cases', 392–393.

legislators, whose oaths are governed by a separate statute known as the Parliamentary Oaths Act (1866). In contrast, the ODO applies to, amongst others, principal officials, judges and legislators. Second, while judges and other holders of high-level public office in the UK are disqualified if they do not take a valid oath under the 1868 Act, legislators who fail to take a valid oath are not automatically disqualified under the 1866 Act: they do not have to vacate their seat, even though they cannot sit in any debate or vote in parliamentary proceedings.[17] In contrast, ODO does not stipulate different consequences for different officials. Zhu and Chen demonstrate that the differences between UK and Hong Kong law can be traced to the structure of colonial governance: they note that the ODO was enacted in Hong Kong 'at a time when all major organs of the colonial government, including both the Legislative Council and the Executive Council, consisted of members appointed by the Governor, and there were no elected representatives of Hong Kong people in the legislature'.[18] Under those circumstances, there was no need to treat legislators more leniently on the grounds that they were chosen by the people, and hence no need for the ordinance to 'distinguish between the legal consequences of failing to take the required oath by Executive Council members and judges on the one hand and Legislative Council members on the other hand'. As a result of this historical legacy, an incoming legislator in twenty-first-century Hong Kong such as Leung whose oath is deemed invalid cannot take office.

There were two separate legal cases in the oath-taking saga of 2016. The first concerned Sixtus Leung (no blood relation to Leung Kwok-hung) and Yau Wai-ching. When the candidates took their oaths, they both carried a flag bearing the words 'Hong Kong is not China'. They referred to Hong Kong as an independent nation, and substituted 'China' with a derogatory word for the country which the Japanese used during the Second World War.[19] The president of the Legislative

[17] Section 5, Parliamentary Oaths Act (1866).

[18] Zhu and Chen, 'The Oath-Taking Cases', 394.

[19] *Chief Executive of the HKSAR* v. *President of the Legislative Council* [2016] 4 HKC 417 (CFI, 15 November 2016).

Council determined that their oaths were invalid, but made the decision to allow them to retake them. This was the point at which the Hong Kong government initiated disqualification proceedings. Moreover, under Article 158 of the Basic Law the Standing Committee of the National People's Congress in Beijing has the power of final interpretation over the constitutional document. Its interpretations are binding on the Hong Kong courts.[20] Before Hong Kong's CFI decided on the case, the Standing Committee issued an interpretation of Article 104, which is the article governing oath-taking. The interpretation states that, according to the true meaning of Article 104 as decided by the Committee, the incoming lawmaker must (i) adhere to the form and content of the oath, without altering, adding to, or omitting any of the words, (ii) take the oath in a solemn and sincere manner, and (iii) sincerely believe in and strictly abide by the pledges in the oath. Furthermore, (iv) if the oath is invalid then the oath-taker will be disqualified from office without the opportunity to retake the oath.[21] Yau and Sixtus lost their case at both the lower courts and on appeal.[22]

The second case involved Leung and three other candidates. In addition to Leung, there was Nathan Law, who adopted what the courts called a 'distinct rising tone' of mockery whenever he pronounced the Chinese character for 'country'. He also prefaced the oath with an opening statement that included the English words 'You can chain me, you can torture me, you can even destroy this body, but you will never imprison my mind,' and concluded his oath with a renewed call for resistance. There was Yiu Chung-yim, who inserted extra words into the oath. And there was Lau Siu-lai, who separated the ninety words constituting the oath by placing six-second pauses between them as she read. Lau subsequently announced on her Facebook page that she intended her performance of the text not to be interpreted as the rendition of a coherent oath of office, but as the vocalization of ninety distinct words

20 Article 158, Basic Law.

21 Interpretation of Article 104 of the Basic Law of the Hong Kong Special Administrative Region of the People's Republic of China by the Standing Committee of the National People's Congress (adopted 7 November 2016).

22 *Chief Executive of the HKSAR* v. *President of the Legislative Council* [2017] HKLRD 460 (CA, 30 November 2016).

that had no connection between them. They, like Leung, lost their case and were barred from taking office.[23] Out of the four legislators in the second case, Leung was the only one who appealed, and he also lost in the CA.[24]

The oath-taking cases generated strong reactions across the political spectrum in Hong Kong. While the behaviour of these legislators was widely condemned as disrespectful and even insolent, the high-handed disqualification of the candidates who were chosen by the electors as their representatives in the legislature gave rise to grave concerns that Beijing was undermining the city's autonomy and interfering with the independence of its judiciary, both of which are constitutionally guaranteed. Particularly troubling was the timing of the interpretation – the fact that it was rendered before the Hong Kong courts had had a chance to decide on the issue seemed to suggest that Beijing was pre-empting a ruling in favour of the candidates.[25]

Given that Leung's oath was the only one explicitly characterized by the courts as theatrical, I will focus on him in the remainder of this chapter. However, the legal and political context indicates that his case constitutes a focal point around which anxieties about the entanglements between politics, law, theatre and performance crystallized, and testifies to the efforts on the part of the authorities to separate them.

11.2 THE GREATEST SHOWMAN?

Leung's rendition of the oath was a political spectacle, and it is worth describing it in some detail. When the clerk called his name, Leung walked to the stand wearing a black T-shirt with the words 'Civil Disobedience' written in Chinese. In his right hand was a big yellow umbrella, the symbol of Occupy Central. Slogans were written on the umbrella, such as 'End One-Party Rule!' and 'Release the Prisoners!'. In his left hand, he held a piece of cardboard on which was written the title

[23] The *Leung* case (CFI). [24] The *Leung* case (CA).

[25] For further discussions of the oath-taking controversy, see Johannes Chan, 'A Storm of Unprecedented Ferocity: The Shrinking Space of the Right to Political Participation, Peaceful Demonstration, and Judicial Independence in Hong Kong', 16 *I.CON* (2018), 373–388 (377–379) and Zhu and Chen, 'The Oath-Taking Cases'.

of a legal decision on Hong Kong's democratization handed down by Beijing; a giant black cross was scrawled over the title. Beijing's decision, commonly known as the 831 Decision to mark the day it was handed down (31 August 2014), was regarded by many as China's way of ensuring that only candidates acceptable to the Communist Party would be eligible to run for the office of the Chief Executive, and it was the immediate trigger for Occupy.

As Leung approached the stand, he shouted slogans such as 'Self-determination for the people!', 'Civil disobedience without fear!', 'We will not be cowed!' and 'I demand double universal suffrage [for choosing both the Chief Executive and the legislators]!' When he read out the oath, he deliberately paused at random points and varied his rhythm in the text to disrupt its flow. The sloganeering began again as soon as he completed the reading. He then took out another replica of Beijing's Decision, tore it up in front of the clerk administering the oath, and, in a flamboyant final gesture, threw the paper fragments into the air.[26]

This was the performance which the CFI condemned, and its description of Leung's oath as theatre was not questioned by the CA. The CFI said that the sloganeering and the destruction of the Decision's replica were simply 'theatrical acts', and as such were 'totally unrelated' to the oath.[27] Moreover, it held that when interpreted against his 'theatrical conducts', Leung's characterization of his own attitude towards the ceremony as solemn seemed sarcastic at best. The import of this 'theatrical performance' in the Council Chamber, according to the CFI, was that the defendant had failed to respect the seriousness and importance of the oath-taking exercise.[28] The Court further observed that he had not demonstrated the sincere attitude the process required. His oath was therefore held to be invalid.

The proceedings can be thought of as a clash between two different conceptions of the place of theatre within the legal domain. The courts' stance can be described as anti-theatrical: in the eyes of law, Leung's theatrical performance signifies pretence, frivolity and impudence. As such, it is antithetical to the qualities that it regards as both prerequisites

[26] The *Leung* case (CFI) 115–119.
[27] The *Leung* case (CFI) 125.
[28] The *Leung* case (CFI) 247.

for, and definitive of, oath taking, including 'sincerity', 'solemnness', 'respect' and 'seriousness' – these are words that appear repeatedly in the judgment.[29] The courts' approach here can be understood as a part of a long-standing cultural suspicion of theatricality. As Jonas Barish has argued, opposition to theatricality has persisted for centuries across multiple cultural domains: from Plato's distrust of mimetic experience to the modernist dramatists' interrogations of their own medium, theatricality has been associated with superficiality, falsity, immorality and danger. The judicial imagination, like the anti-theatrical mind which Barish explores, confers on theatricality the 'savor of forbidden fruit', and casts it as something that tantalizes, provokes, seduces and ultimately corrupts.[30]

Law's anti-theatrical stance lies at the core of a contrast it establishes between Leung's behaviour and the oath taking by pro-Beijing legislators who were allowed to take office. It could be argued that what the courts regarded as problematic here is not the fact that Leung performs, but that he gave the wrong kind of performance: if he had given the correct kind of performance, if he had taken his oath 'properly', he would have been able to take office. As such, what law objects to in reality is not performance per se, but a performance that goes against or beyond the theatrical norms that are legally acceptable. Yet if law does indeed accept some version of performance, it does not recognize itself as doing so. In other words, a crucial dimension of the courts' anti-theatricality is its refusal to associate oath-taking with performance. This non-recognition is reflected in the insistence on 'sincerity' as a defining element of the oath. Sincerity can be thought of as a form of transparency: to be sincere is to allow others to see directly into your heart, to observe your true feelings. By this logic, to do something sincerely is precisely to *not* engage in theatre or performance of any kind. The sincerity requirement, then, is tantamount to a legal requirement that Leung's oath be completely natural, that it give access to his true feelings, that it contain no form of acting. The Standing Committee's interpretation is clear on this

29 The *Leung* case (CFI) 124.

30 Jonas Barish, *The Anti-theatrical Prejudice* (Berkeley: University of California Press, 1981), p. 477.

point: the oath taker must not only strictly abide by their oath, but 'must sincerely believe' in it, otherwise they would have taken 'a false oath'.[31] The demand for sincerity is therefore less a demand for a particular kind of performance, proper or otherwise, than a demand for artlessness and transparency. In the eyes of the law, Leung was playacting, while the successful candidates offered true, unmediated allegiance.

Ironically, though, what is striking about the process of oath taking in this context is that it has an inherently theatrical quality to it: unlike merely signing one's name on a piece of paper and putting it in the post, the legislative oath is publicly enacted and delivered *a viva voce*; as such, it requires an audience to see and hear it. There can be no effective or meaningful oath without sound, body and spectacle.[32] Leung clearly embraced theatricality, and deployed it as a way of advocating for Hong Kong's democratization. Through his performance, he makes bare the essence of oath taking as a kind of political performance and renders visible its inherently theatrical quality.

His oath taking constitutes a performance in two overlapping senses: performance as that which can '*describe* a *particular* form of expression' for a real or imagined audience, as in something theatregoers see in a playhouse, and performance as that which can '*diagnose* a *universal* ontological condition' about an entity such as law.[33] Leung's verbal expression and bodily presentation constitute, firstly, a performance in the more particular or conventional sense of the word: they are designed to draw attention, to put oneself on display for dramatic effect, to entertain and elicit a reaction from the audience. Given the Council's standard practice of filming its meetings and ceremonies, Leung may have had in mind an audience that extended beyond the incoming and existing lawmakers who were in the room with him, but that also included people likely to see the footage from the day on their television or computer screens.

Leung's words and actions can be further construed as a performance in the second, more ontological sense: law and politics come about

[31] Interpretation of Basic Law Article 104, p. 3. [32] I thank Scott Veitch for this point.
[33] Peters, *Law as Performance*, p. 18.

through a series of repeated gestures, and his deeds and utterances are arguably part of an ongoing attempt to bring about a change in the law, to enact a transformation in the political system, to hasten the coming-into-being of a different, more democratic, constitutional order. In *How to Do Things with Words*, J. L. Austin introduces a distinction between constative and performative utterances. He posits that constative utterances are those that describe an existing state of affairs: 'The grass is green' or 'I am hungry' are constative, in that they report on a reality that is already there. Performative utterances, by contrast, do not merely describe reality, but impact upon or enact a change in reality. An example Austin gives is 'I give and bequeath my watch to my brother' in the context of a will: [34] the statement is performative because the act of uttering it is, or at least partly constitutes, the performance of an action. As Başak Ertür succinctly glosses it, 'in Austin's scheme, performative utterances *do* rather than describe; they produce or transform a situation, or at least attempt to do so'.[35]

In this instance, Leung's sartorial choices, his sloganeering, his use of props such as the yellow umbrella, his dramatic tearing up of the mock Decision in public, and the ostentatiousness of his overall delivery and self-presentation can be collectively read as a performance that seeks to be politically and legally *performative*, in the sense of actively adding to, amplifying and furthering the efforts at creating concrete political and legal changes that were gaining momentum in Hong Kong society at the time. As Austin points out, oath making is already a performative act exemplar, and Leung's tactic of using it as a means to push for universal suffrage, political participation and more expansive rights and freedoms takes the performativity in a different direction from what was expected in the Legislative Council. Jacques Derrida has criticized Austin for placing intention at the core of his conceptualization of speech acts, and argues for foregrounding the role of iteration. While it could be questioned whether intention is indeed as central to Austin's framework as Derrida contends, the foregrounding of iteration helpfully brings the

[34] J. L. Austin, *How to Do Things with Words* (Oxford: Oxford University Press, 1962), p. 6.

[35] Başak Ertür, *Spectacles and Specters: A Performative Theory of Political Trials* (New York: Fordham University Press, 2022), p. 54.

force of Leung's performance into view.[36] As footage of his performance was relayed across televisual news channels and various social media outlets, as it proliferated on the front page of the broadsheets, they intensified discontent with Hong Kong's slow pace of democratization and galvanized the public's demand for reform, thereby compounding the impact of Leung's theatre. When seen through an anti-theatrical lens, however, these acts take the form of parodies or bastardized versions of the requisite oath, and as empty gestures with no legal effect. Theatre becomes indistinguishable from theatrics, political performance appears as farce and in a dynamic spanning hundreds of years that Barish has traced, theatricality slides once again into anti-theatricality.

11.3 LAW'S TEMPORAL PERFORMANCES

Leung's faith in the power of theatre was countered by an institutional distrust of theatre as sham in the proceedings, and the courts construed his actions as an empty performance and therefore as the antithesis of law. Yet in what sense might law itself be thought of as performance, as Peters contends? And if it is a kind of performance, is it *merely* performance, or does performance here signify differently such that it is not simply the opposite of the real? One of the doctrinal questions raised in the CA regarding the Standing Committee's interpretation serves as a point of entry: given that the interpretation was rendered after Leung attempted to take the oath, does it have retroactive effect so as to render his oath invalid?[37] In other words, does the interpretation take effect only from the moment it was rendered by the Standing Committee (in which case it does not apply to Leung), or does it take effect before that moment (in which case it does)?

The CA held that the interpretation applies retroactively: like the Standing Committee's other interpretations of the Basic Law, it 'has

36 Jacques Derrida, 'Signature Event Context', in *Limited Inc.* (Evanston, IL: Northwestern University Press, 1977), pp. 1–25.

37 A related question was raised regarding whether the interpretation constituted a clarification of or a supplementation to the Basic Law. The CFA has held that the Standing Committee had the power to both clarify and supplement laws in *Director of Immigration* v. *Chong Fung Yuen* (2001) HKCFAR 211.

retrospective effect back to 1st July, 1997', or the day of the retrocession.[38] As such, the interpretations must be construed to state 'what the law has always been since the coming into effect of the Basic Law on that date'. This question about retrospectivity, or *temporality,* is crucial to understanding the relationship between law, theatre and performance. To understand why this is so, it is helpful to examine the judicial discussion of retroactivity in light of Derrida's contention that retroactivity can be 'fabulous' (in the sense of fiction, or fashioning, or forming).[39]

In 'Declarations of Independence', which examines the significance of the act of signing in the context of the US Declaration of Independence, Derrida posits that the signing constitutes a troubling of the distinction between the performative and the constative which then gives rise to a temporal disjuncture he calls 'fabulous retroactivity'. Derrida asks: what might it mean for the representatives from the thirteen colonies to sign 'in the name and by the authority of the good people'? Specifically:

> Is it that the good people have already freed themselves in fact and are only stating the fact of this emancipation in the Declaration? Or is it rather that they free themselves at the instant of and by the signature of his declaration?[40]

What, in other words, is the nature of the Declaration, and how does it operate? Is it a constative utterance, in the sense that the people in the thirteen colonies have 'already freed themselves', such that the Declaration is 'only *stating* the fact of this emancipation' in reality?[41] Or is it a performative utterance, in the sense that it is the signing of the Declaration that *produces* the state of freedom?

Derrida contends that the Declaration cannot be thought of as either constative or performative, but hovers undecidedly between the two registers. Crucially, he further posits that this undecidability is not a logical fallacy or error in the document, but is constitutive of the very

38 The *Leung* case (CA), 52.

39 Jacques Derrida, 'Declarations of Independence' [trans. Tom Keenan and Tom Pepper], 15 *New Political Science* (1986), 7–14 (10).

40 Derrida, 'Declarations of Independence', 9.

41 Derrida, 'Declarations of Independence', 9 (my italics).

process of origination that the Declaration is meant to announce and achieve. The positing of a politico-legal regime rests on a fundamental 'equivocation', and in the American context, the Declaration depends on this equivocal undecidability to found the nation.[42]

He makes a similar argument in his analysis of the idea of the people in the Declaration. On the one hand, the representatives sign the Declaration in the name of the 'good people' who are already there to lend their authority to the signers. On the other hand, 'this people does not exist', in the sense that the category or concept of 'the people' that functions as the representatives' source of authority does not come into being before the signing. As such, 'the signature invents the signer'. The signature, then, both presumes the existence of 'the good people' and performatively brings them into being as such.

This dynamic is what Derrida calls 'fabulous retroactivity': the signature shuttles between being underwritten by a pre-existing freedom, and enacting the very freedom from which it draws its authority. In the same vein, the representatives sign in the name of the people, while also bringing the people into being through their signatures. The moment of signing produces, in the present, that which is already there all along. The Declaration therefore oscillates continuously between stating a reality and forging it, between the constative and the performative.

Ertür brilliantly teases out the theatrical implications of this relation of undecidability, and traces it back to Austin. She points out that early on in *How to Do Things with Words,* Austin underscores that some performatives can disguise themselves as constatives, in the sense of taking on the form of an utterance that describes the world when it is actually creates or transforms it. Austin calls these utterances 'masqueraders',[43] and as Ertür notes, his metaphor is noteworthy for its theatrical connotations:

> The metaphor brings the excluded theatrical through the back door into Austin's theory, as part and parcel of his initial definition of the performative. The performative, we are told, is that which often disguises

[42] Derrida, 'Declarations of Independence', 10.

[43] Austin, *How to Do Things with Words,* p. 4.

> or passes itself off as constative. So there is already a staging involved in the performative, whereby it disguises the fact of its enactment.[44]

The 'undecidability between the two modes' of the performative and the constative is a masquerade – in other words, a form of theatre, or the 'staging' of a disguise.[45]

When we return to the question of the interpretation's retroactivity in *Leung* and place it in the interpretative frame that Derrida, Austin and Ertür give us, it becomes evident that, as a speech act, the interpretation is characterized by a similar relation of undecidability between the constative and the performative. The CA's reasoning relies heavily on *Lau Kong Yung* v. *Director of Immigration*, in which Hong Kong's CFA held that the temporal significance of a Standing Committee interpretation should be understood in the following way:

> The Interpretation ... dates from 1 July 1997 when the Basic Law came into effect. It *declared* what the law has always been.[46]
>
> The Interpretation has effect from 1 July 1997.[47]

The statements 'The Interpretation has effect from 1 July 1997' and 'The Interpretation ... dates from 1 July 1997 when the Basic Law came into effect' are constatives: they describe or report a state of affairs in reality, the state of affairs being that the meaning of the Basic Law as stated in the Standing Committee's interpretation has been there from the very beginning of Hong Kong's post-colonial existence. However, at the same time, the court acknowledges that the Interpretation '*declared* what the law has always been'. Verbs can be good indicators of performatives: 'I do' (as in a wedding ceremony) 'I order' (as spoken by a judge in court), 'I promise' and 'I bequeath' are some common examples. The verb here – 'to declare' – is a classic performative, a *doing* verb that creates a state of affairs in reality: by *declaring* what the meaning of the Basic Law from the very beginning, the interpretation *produces* the reality that the meaning it contains is the one that the text of the Basic Law has expressed all along. The interpretation is therefore a speech act that hovers

[44] Ertür, *Spectacles and Specters*, p. 65. [45] Ertür, *Spectacles, and Specters*, p. 67.

[46] *Lau Kong Yung* v. *Director of Immigration* [1999] 4 HKC 731 (CFA) 758G (my italics).

[47] *Lau Kong Yung* 759D.

between the two registers of the constative and the performative, between describing and declaring, between stating and generating. If, as Derrida notes, the relations of undecidability between the performative and the constative are constitutive of the act of origination, and if, as Ertür foregrounds, the metaphor of the masquerade brings in the theatrical, then the situation analysed in *Lau Kong Yung* can be interpreted as a form of theatre, in the sense of a performative utterance which masquerades as a constative one. The temporality operative in this instance is a 'fabulous retroactivity' that destabilizes two linguistic registers.

To trace the ways in which the 'performative-constative masquerade' is at work here is not to offer a critique of Hong Kong law or Chinese law per se, nor to imply any wilful political deception by the authorities in the case.[48] Staging, disguise and masquerade – in short, elements of theatrical performance – are unavoidable in any act of linguistic interpretation undergirding a moment of founding, be it by the signatories and readers of the American Declaration of Independence, the members of the Standing Committee, or the judges of the law courts. In fact, the CFA in *Lau Kong Yung* explicitly makes reference to the common law declaratory theory of judicial decisions, the fiction whereby judges do not create law but merely find it, in its reasoning about the retroactivity of the Standing Committee's interpretations.[49] To underscore that undecidability, or masquerade, is constitutive of the speech acts of law is to make a jurisprudential inquiry into what law is and how law operates as a linguistic product and a process of interpretative reasoning.

This masquerade also takes the form of precedential reasoning in *Leung*. In 'Force of Law: the "Mystical Foundation of Authority"', Derrida famously observes that 'the founding and justifying moment that institutes law implies a performative force, which is always an interpretative force'.[50] To interpret in the institutional context of law, to discern a pre-existing meaning in a legal text by turning to previous cases as common law lawyers are wont to do, is to actively posit and

48 Ertür, *Spectacles and Specters*, p. 67. 49 *Lau Kong Yung* 758 G.

50 Jacques Derrida, 'Force of Law: The Mystical Foundation of Authority' (1990) 11 *Cardozo Law Review* 920–1046, 941.

perpetuate that meaning through acts of interpretation. An interpretative act not only restates meaning, but enforces and amplifies it; that is why the 'interpretative force' is also a 'performative force'. When interpreting the text of the Standing Committee's interpretation of Article 104, the CA cites, and re-cites, the previous cases on the nature of the Standing Committee's interpretation: it refers to its own judgment in the Sixtus Leung and Yau case, which states that the interpretation sets out the true and proper meaning of Article 104 'from day one'.[51] It then gives further force to this reading of the Standing Committee's interpretation by citing the CFA's decision in the same case, in which the Appeal Committee similarly concludes that a Standing Committee interpretation represents 'what the law is and has always been'.[52] By building the foundation of its judgment from these precedent cases, the decisions by the courts in each of these cases restate, constatively, what is already acknowledged as the reality of the Basic Law's meaning since the establishment of Hong Kong as a Special Administrative Region of China, but in doing so, they entrench and amplify that reality performatively, as a legal institution, through a highly visible recourse to a purely legal doctrine, that of *stare decisis*. To think of law as performance is emphatically not to think of it as *merely* performance, but to recognize that a continuous process of quotation, repetition and self-referencing lies at the core of the way it constitutes itself. The drama of common law reasoning here is the process through which the 'foundation' of law, or law's originary moment, becomes indissociable from the 'conservation' of law, or the performance of law as law.[53]

CONCLUSION: PERFORMANCE, THEATRICALITY, ANTI-THEATRICALITY

We are in a position to return to the question at the beginning of this chapter. What does the courts' view of Leung's oath as a theatrical

[51] The *Leung-Yau* case (CA) 53.

[52] *Chief Executive of the HKSAR* v. *President of the Legislative Council* 20 HKCFAR 390 (CFA 1 September 2017) at 35.

[53] Derrida, 'Force of Law', 943.

performance tell us about the nature and operation of law? In other words, what is the jurisprudential significance of their anti-theatrical stance? The proceedings can be approached as an attempt, whether conscious or unconscious, to establish a relationship of absolute opposition between law on the one hand, and performance on the other. By adopting an anti-theatrical stance, law casts the performance of a man who embraces, and indeed relishes, his own theatricality as a kind of reckless playfulness that is ill suited for the occasion. At the same time, the anti-theatrical language, or the representation of an invalid oath not as an oath that is problematically performed but as one that is performed at all, enables law to represent the legally valid oaths as, by contrast, pure artlessness rather than instances of performance. In *Leung*, the qualities which law accepts and identifies with, such as solemnity, seriousness and sincerity, are framed as non-theatrical. The legal presents itself as synonymous with the absence of theatre. In other words, by representing Leung's performance as having no place in the legal domain, by framing it as little more than theatrics, the courts' anti-theatricality situates theatrical performance as the antithesis of law.

However, as I have argued in the previous sections, performance is in fact an integral part of law, even though law does not acknowledge it to be so. Both law and the man whom law condemns perform. There are two sets of inter-connected performances on each side. Leung's actions can be said to be a show that deliberately seeks to entertain, shock and even scandalize his audience. At the same time, they enact a form of advocacy and therefore 'perform' in Austin's sense of the word, as a set of utterances and bodily gestures which aim to bring into being a different political and constitutional order.

Law's performance can be understood firstly as a form of linguistic theatre that throws into question the division between the constitutive and the performative, and that enacts a Derridean fabulous retroactivity troubling the linear timelines on which legal reasoning depends. It can also be understood as a performance of law *as law*, in the form of a public citation and recitation of legal authorities that gives rise to a continuing and necessary spectacle of a hallowed 'artificial reason' that can be traced to Sir Edward Coke, whereby the judgment of law proceeds according to a foundation and logic specific to law itself.[54]

What the clash between (the Leung's) theatricality and (the courts') anti-theatricality in the case ultimately reveals is that the two stances are not only 'proximate' to one another, but 'perilously' so: they point to the fact that performance lies at the core of law as much as it lies at the core of the spectacle which the courts condemn.[55] When law and theatre collide, when they are read across one another, they begin to hum and echo in a way which exposes their common foundation of self-constitution in performance. In this uncanny encounter, the boundary between the two arenas starts to blur, the epistemological distinction between them starts to look less certain and law's performances start to become more visible.

In this light, law's anti-theatricality can be read as the symptom of a disavowal of its own nature as performance: the rejection of theatre constitutes a way for law to displace its gaze from the theatrical dimension of its own reasoning and the fictionality which, as Derrida points out, cannot be dissociated from the undecidability which gives rise to the temporal disjuncture known as fabulous retroactivity.[56] In other words, anti-theatricality can be said to be a way of exteriorizing performance: by aligning performance with a figure held to be lacking in the qualities of sincerity, solemnity and seriousness that define law, the courts suggest that performance cannot logically be part of law. The oath-taking saga in Hong Kong shows how anti-theatricality can be a means through which law expurgates performance from its discursive domain and stages its own formal existence.[57]

54 The Case of Prohibitions [1607] EWHC J23(KB).

55 Peters, *Law as Performance*, p. 9. 56 Derrida, 'Declarations of Independence', 10.

57 The term comes, of course, from Stanley Fish. See *There's No Such Thing as Free Speech … And It's a Good Thing, Too* (Oxford: Oxford University Press, 1994), pp. 141–180.

CHAPTER 12

"Naked Athena" and Classical Lines

Wayward Aesthetics of the Exposed Body

Anna Jayne Kimmel

The erasure of the body in civilized societies has everything to do with fear of the very violence upon otherized bodies on which civilization is built.

– Rocío Pichon-Rivière (*GLQ*, 2021: 446)

We cannot address the history of modern surfaces without also asking after the other history of skin, the violent, dysphoric one – the one about racialized nakedness inherited from the Enlightenment so necessary to Western constructions of humanity and the one that speaks of the objectification, commodification, and fetishization of racialized skin, especially black female skin.

– Anne Cheng (*Second Skin*, 2013: 11)

Literature in the legal humanities has begun to turn toward performance as a new site of analysis: as source, representation, and intervention. From *Law and Performance* (2018) to *Law as Performance* (2022), this belated comparison has garnered increasing traction.[1] But methods from dance and performance studies, those wayward disciplines where corporeality supersedes the literary, still make only passing appearances. The repercussions, however, exceed the methodological

[1] Austin Sarat, Lawrence Douglas, and Martha Merrill Umphrey, eds. 2018. *Law and Performance*. Series in Law, Jurisprudence, and Social Thought. Amherst: University of Massachusetts Press; Julie Stone Peters, 2022. *Law as Performance: Theatricality, Spectatorship, and the Making of Law in Ancient, Medieval, and Early Modern Europe*. First ed. Law and Literature. Oxford: Oxford University Press.

toward the most material. This chapter underscores the consequences for this absence by centering the lone figure, "Naked Athena," as a femme body in protest whose choreographic aesthetic of whiteness allowed particular flexibility under the law. Through her balletic performance of resistance, themes of discipline, elegance, and decorum swirl against the indecent, vulgar, and obscene labels afforded other protesters in the same scene. Motivated by this duality, I survey histories of the publicly exposed body as righteously revealed or promiscuously pornographic, a distinction theorized within aesthetics as the difference between nakedness and nudity yet left ambiguous in legal terms.

NAKED ATHENA: AN AMBIVALENT APPARITION

In response to the federal occupation of Portland, Oregon, in 2020, an uncanny figure emerged from the crowded protest scenes which spawned across the nation a rally cry for Black Lives Matter (BLM): a photograph features a young, femme body sporting only a face mask and stocking cap who approaches heavily armed officers and then poses in postures later captioned as ballet. At least ten law enforcement officers stand *en face*, armed, shielded, and planted in a wide, assertive stance. Uniformed, they aggregate as a living barricade. The glare of a police vehicle's headlights illuminates the pavement between the parties as both stage and interrogation, unsure which side is audience and which is performer; positioned directly across from the figure and photographer alike, the car beams cast a haloed glow around her "apparition."[2] Police lights elsewhere cast the periphery in a pale pink haze, a surrealist dreamscape all too real. From within this spotlight, she moves through a series of poses with her full front on display to the onlooking officers. Keeping her identity anonymous, news media christened this woman "Naked Athena," a heroic icon laid bare in a collision of vulnerability and bravery.

This arresting moment marked a summer of racial outcry against anti-Black violence following the murder of George Floyd, wherein inflamed

[2] Richard Read, "Out of Portland Tear Gas, an Apparition Emerges." *The Los Angeles Times*. July 19, 2020.

participation resulted in the contentious call for Oregon's national guard to enter the arena.[3] Armored in the repertoire of ballet as a costume of whiteness, this Naked Athena sidestepped accusations thrown upon other protestors at the same time; rather than a looter or rioter (supposedly) worthy of social, political, and legal critique, nomenclature elevated her status to the divine.[4] Her open flesh starkly contrasted the camouflage fatigues, gear, and helmets of the state agents. In her exposed form, she approached the officers unequivocally unarmed, offering no excuse for reasonable alarm, retaliation, or subsequent justifications of imagined weaponry so often tabulated. She nevertheless caused a stir.

Juridical logics prompt us to emphasize legal moments in which accusations have been made – arrests, trials, and contract breaches – in order to understand the legitimacy of the claims. Less frequently do we pause to consider moments in which allegations have not been raised, in spite of their greater ubiquity. The scene of Naked Athena prompts such inverted attentions, as her nudity and the subsequent nonpolicing of her exposure – aimed directly at police authorities – becomes the focal point of my attention. I do not intend to exalt this singular figure and consequently overshadow the pressing stakes of the larger protest movement. Such words continue to need to be written and read. But here, I read deeply into what this scene reveals about the entanglement between legal and performance aesthetics and the subsequent corporeal ambiguity which emerges when not understood together. Obscenity doctrine and discernment of indecency coheres at this nexus, wherein perceptions of offense and calculated shock define prevailing orders of modesty. If clothing fashions a particular type of containment for the naked body, ballet styles a different restriction on the otherwise natural

[3] The 2020 BLM protests in Oregon lasted more than 100 consecutive nights; in the month of June, protestors established an "occupied zone" autonomous from police force in an abolitionist utopian vision. By July, federal forces were deployed to Portland under Protecting American Communities Task Force, but strongly criticized for the use of unmarked vehicles and officers.

[4] Others would, however, critique the widespread circulation of her image as representative of the protest. Affiliates of the BLM movement, for example, questioned that her performance may have unwittingly distracted from the rallying cause, which "Jen" herself acknowledged later in a podcast.

body and facilitates the civilizing transition from perverse nakedness to permissible nudity. Unclothed and unnamed, the nude dancing body becomes site of critical concern for those of us attuned to the covert ways in which race, gender, and sexuality continue to animate legal hierarchies. This extends to the discernment of the obscene body in motion.

In the case of Naked Athena, her splayed legs and masked face could have been invoked to depict her as lewd, perverse, kink, or otherwise outside the normative bounds of the law. She herself would clarify an antagonizing intent when reflecting, "This fury arose in me ... I said, I want to be naked. I want to confront them."[5] However, perhaps due to her slim figure and light skin, news media instead scripted her as "urban and civilized," "an apparition." No charges were filed against her wayward actions. Such a reading, while on the one hand progressive for its openness to sexuality and the nude body, foregrounds an ableist and racialized legal aesthetic in which nudity is elevated to rhetoric of deity when ascribed to white femininity: what Robin Bernstein laconically names as a "holy obliviousness" and Rebecca Chaleff extends to the imperial project of the ballet blanc.[6] The variously applied boundaries of obscenity seemingly emerge from a legal history in which whiteness has been constructed as property, secured and otherwise performed within hierarchies of race and desire.[7]

Instead, the deviance on display was read as nonviolent, arousing neither fear nor aggression, instead deflated by the vulnerability of exposed skin susceptible to wounding. In a world in which Blackness itself is already feared as a weapon, however, I caution against the conclusion that nakedness itself was enough to protect. Rather, her aesthetic

[5] Jen, cited in Rose Minutaglio, "Portland Protestor 'Naked Athena' on Why She Stripped Down." *Elle*. July 29, 2020.

[6] Robin Bernstein, 2011. *Racial Innocence: Performing American Childhood from Slavery to Civil Rights*. New York: New York University Press, 8; Rebecca Chaleff, 2020. "Dance of the Undead: The Wilis' Imperial Legacy." Ed. Susan Manning, Janice Ross, and Rebecca Schneider. *Future of Dance Studies*. Madison: University of Wisconsin Press. 413–430.

[7] Cheryl I. Harris, 1993. "Whiteness as Property." *Harvard Law Review* 106 (8): 1707–1791. See also Ian Haney-López, 2006. *White by Law: The Legal Construction of Race*. Rev. and Updated, 10th anniversary ed. Critical America. New York: New York University Press.

legibility as a normative figure featured her perceived whiteness in spite of self-identification as a non-Black person of color, an interpretation further reinforced by her performance of the classical lines of ballet. The particular politics of her framing underscore this aesthetic ambivalence: a *New York Times* article suggests her to be a "light-skinned person of color," though others originally suggested her to be white.[8] From the embedded racial ambiguity we can conclude she passed as white, willfully or not. This motivates my reading of her whiteness in spite of factual claims toward her self-identified race. Additionally, I want to highlight the ways in which Naked Athena was allowed to remain anonymous, at most claiming the name (and potential pseudonym) "Jen" on a radio show after the event; anonymity itself can serve as a marker of racial privilege as people of color are historically over-surveilled. I intentionally draw attention toward the aesthetic logics of her circulation in excess of her politics for, as I will argue, it allows us to understand this nonpolicing within a larger narrative of modernism, not divorced from colonial efforts of *missionne civilisatrice*. From her performance and its mediated attention, I theorize an aesthetics of the legal rooted in racialized interpretations of the lewd, the indecent, and the obscene that can be traced through classical and modern aesthetics when read via dance studies.

The readings of Naked Athena that emphasize the balletic repertoire synthesize an underlying tension of race and privilege in the narrative surrounding the protest. On the one hand, such an interpretation passes as justified: Her straight spine, flexible limbs, and symmetric poses follow the aesthetics of ballet rehearsed for centuries. One photograph in particular mimics the balletic position of a *posé*: Her right leg lifts until her foot is pressed against the inside of her left knee as if in the resting position of a flamingo, her arms lifted overhead in informal *port-de-bras*, chin raised slightly. Yet a closer analysis contradicts such claims of this corporeal genealogy: Her supporting leg remains in parallel rather than the external rotation definitive of ballet training, her palms flex outward in her overhead reach against a balletic carriage, and her foot rests flatly

[8] Mitchell Jackson. "Who Gets to Be a 'Naked Athena'?" *The New York Times*. July 25, 2020.

in its entirety against the inside of her leg rather than articulated through a pointed position. In this sense, the media outlets who instead chose to read her gestures as reminiscent of yoga positions had as much grounds for doing so, not least for the symmetry, flexibility, and static nature of the various positions associated with the non Euro-American practice. Her ascription as goddess further builds upon formulations of the Apollonian frame as the moral fetishization of the upright body as dignified and noble reflective of a normative, idealized body rooted in an ableist and classist aesthetic.[9]

I belabor this point of ambivalence to suggest that the choice not to center yoga, or the choice to center ballet in spite of the inaccuracy of the naming, suggests a decision based upon something other than corporeal analysis. The imposed passing then, assisted by quasi-balletic signals of class and race, begets a legal interpretation of white femininity that presumed nonthreatening intent. Translated to the street, the postures veil a confrontational (if still peaceable) disposition, with entrenched perceptions of decorum overriding legal lines of decency. Allowed to exit the scene without notable physical harm or arrest, her performance as a ballerina rendered her legible as an obedient, docile, and civil body in spite of her overt protest, willful defiance, and illicit gestures.[10] She escaped the bodily scrutiny leveraged elsewhere. Under this viewing her repertoire veils the politics beneath the choice to not police her public nudity as race, law, and aesthetics become entangled in unarticulated ways. Jen acknowledged the interpretative lens of nudity when she summarized intent: "My nakedness is political. It's my expression."[11] Her nakedness was nevertheless converted into a sheath of nudity, attesting to the politics projected onto her surface.

9 Drawing upon Mikhail Bakhtin's reading of *Rabelais*, Owen Smith goes on to challenge the distinction between the noble body and folk body as upheld through corporeal techniques and racial assumptions. Owen Smith, 2005. "Shifting Apollo's Frame: Challenging the Body Aesthetic in Theater Dance," in *Bodies in Commotion: Disability and Performance*, ed. Carrie Sandahl and Philip Auslander. Ann Arbor: University of Michigan Press, 87–101.

10 Once exposed, she was impacted by a rubber bullet to the foot, which drew blood. I do not mean to minimize this harm. She did not, however, report more serious injury or physical threat that others recounted during these escalated nights of protest.

11 Jen, cited in Minutaglio, "Portland Protestor."

EXPOSED FORM: A REVIEW OF PUBLIC INDECENCY

Oregon has unique leniency in its nudity laws, allowing for some exposure of the human figure without invoking indecency, be it public or private. In many ways echoing the Miller test for obscenity, the state tolerates nudity so long as there does not exist "the intent of arousing the sexual desire of the person or another person," or in the case of its private indecency laws, so long as exposure would not "reasonably . . . be expected to alarm or annoy the other person."[12] Portland maintains its own authority on the matter, declaring under City Code 14A.40.030 (Indecent Exposure): "It is unlawful for any person to expose his or her genitalia while in a public place or place visible from a public place, if the public place is open or available to persons of the opposite sex." Despite clear appreciation for the demonstrative force of the body, these legal codes place a greater emphasis on intent than reception – a term decidedly linked to the theatrical and performative and left largely undetermined in the legalese.

Not all exposure, however, is created equal. Given the historic hypersexualization of Black and Brown bodies, the invocation of "reasonable alarm" opens the possibility of racial bias in its interpretation as some figures are deemed inherently sexual a priori to the establishment of intent.[13] In most US states, indecent exposure laws are significantly gendered, as public lewdness extends to the exposure of all genitalia but only female nipples (exceptions occur in Hawaii, Maine, Ohio, New York, and Texas). This binarized legacy extends from *The People & C. Respondent* v. *Ramona Santorelli and Mary Lou Schloss* (1992), whose

[12] The public indecency law prohibits sexual acts in public, including exposing one's genitals for sexual gratification. The private indecency law prohibits exposure of the genitals to a person who does not consent in a manner that would alarm or annoy that person. For more, see Or. Rev. Stat. section 163.465 and Or. Rev. Stat. section 163.467 (Appendix 2).

[13] For more on the racist invocations of obscenity, I turn to Kimberlé Crenshaw, who deftly presents the selective application of obscenity prosecution by comparing the contentious case of the 2 Live Crew – an all-Black, male rap group whose sexually explicit lyrics were charged as obscene – and Madonna – a white female pop star who "acted out masturbation, portrayed the seduction of a priest, and insinuated group sex on stage" but was never prosecuted for obscenity.

topless summer solstice picnic in Central Park intentionally led to their arrest and contestation of Penal Law § 245.01, to the *desnudas* performers of Times Square whose patriotically painted torsos leave little left unseen amongst other critical flashpoints in the legal regulation of the exposed form. It becomes further gendered given the antiwoman logic that female genitalia are less threatening than male genitalia for which public exposure/indecency laws are more stereotypically invoked (even while modesty of the femme form has received greater social scrutiny). Legal anxiety toward the trans body and homophobic attitudes only accentuate the disparate application of obscenity laws on the aesthetics of race, gender, and sexuality.

Legal concerns toward indecent exposure, public lewdness, and the obscene have been challenged under First Amendment protections of expressive material, including contemporary evaluation of immoral and scandalous remarks.[14] Classified as a misdemeanor, penalties for public exposure and indecency occur rather infrequently – as in the case of the Naked Athena whose performance went unrecorded before the law. From interpretations to the First Amendment's expressive freedoms to the Fourteenth Amendment's Equal Protection Clause, discerning nudity under legal provision remains an ambiguous task.[15] Even when toplessness and other partial nudity has been deemed permissible, arrests still frequently occur, as artist-advocate Holly Van Voast intentionally accentuates through performative interventions. Idiosyncratic and incomplete, these collective errancies in this law's application raise the questions: What purpose does obscenity doctrine serve if so subjectively enforced? Who is it meant to protect? Phrased in its inversion, who is it meant to criminalize?

[14] For consideration of a history of First Amendment expressive activity as it relates to scrutiny surrounding the exposed body, symbolic expression, and queer association, I turn to Paul Siegal 's work, "A Right to Boogie Queerly: The First Amendment on the Dance Floor," in *Dancing Desires: Choreographing Sexualities on and off the Dance Floor*, ed. Jane Desmond. Madison: University of Wisconsin Press, 2001. 267–283. For more recent address, see also the Supreme Court case *Iancu* v. *Brunetti* 588 US 388 (decided June 24, 2019).

[15] For example, see Anita L. Allen, 2006. "Disrobed: The Constitution of Modesty." *Villanova Law Review* 51: 841; James H. Taylor, 1992. "Constitutional Law: Nude Dancing's Marginal Status under the First Amendment." *Florida Law Review* 44: 141.

An answer lies submerged in the entangled histories of law, aesthetics, and the nude. These categories, if often kept separate in academic discourse, converge to solidify hierarchies of race. Motivated by the famed nudity of twentieth-century performer Josephine Baker, humanities scholar Anne Cheng writes on the intimacies of modernism and primitivism as a site for understanding implications of racial difference. "The march of progress," submits Cheng, "is thus equated with the suppression and erasure of erotic material excess, deemed to be the exclusive and natural domains of sexual and savage primitives."[16] Modernity, morality, and flesh become overlapping projects. To make this argument, Cheng draws upon Adolf Loos's *Ornament and Crime* (2013), the title itself linking aesthetics and law. If Cheng emphasizes an aesthetic teleology that disappeared nakedness in its march of progress, such momentum reanimates through legal codes which regulate that very aesthetic space.

I return to Cheng's argument, however, as Naked Athena offers a near-perfect inversion of Cheng's primary case study, Josephine Baker: an anonymous twenty-first-century figure versus a twentieth-century celebrity, performed in the context of public protest versus proscenium-cabaret stage, a white-coded body performing ballet versus a Black body performing theatrical dance. Both examples center live events with visual and film circulation of the youthful, able-bodied female "wearing her nakedness like a sheath."[17] Located within these aesthetic developments, "the trope of skin/surface thus occupies a central place in the making of modern aesthetic and philosophical theory," writes Cheng. To this list, I would add legal codes, as concerns of morality sharpen at the same time, if in distinct and unacknowledged ways. Civil codes that restrict the naked body echo the aesthetic values of modernism, at least modern architecture, "defined as specifically the liberation from 'primitive' and 'feminine' inclinations."[18] A comparative reading, then, allows us to extend the aesthetic argument of Cheng toward new contexts, including legal domains with material stakes in the present moment.

[16] Anne Cheng, 2000. *Second Skin: Josephine Baker and the Modern Surface.* New York: Oxford University Press. 24.

[17] Cheng, *Second Skin*, 1. [18] Cheng, *Second Skin*, 25.

CONTESTED MYTHOLOGY: CLASSICAL AND CONTEMPORARY VIEWS

Naked Athena of Portland, however, is far from the first woman to invoke her white femininity in exchange for legal protection. Against interpretations that Naked Athena's acceptance is a contemporary phenomenon indicative of some teleological progress of moral acceptance or anticonservative Christian becoming of society, I want to return to the Greek narrative of Phryne, uncanny in its parallels. One might be quick to recall her fabled biography (and question the adoption of Athena for this anonymous 2020 figure given her association as the goddess of warfare in lieu of the more analogous Phyrne): a Greek *hetaira* known for beauty, Phryne became infamous during her trial for impiety (or *asebeia*), having "removed her robes, let down her hair and walked into the sea in full view of the other celebrants."[19] When the orator Hyperides defended her around 350 BCE, rhetoric alone failed to persuade the jury of her innocence. In an improvised act of sexuality, Phryne disrobed before the court. When the jury saw her bare breasts, she was acquitted: *non Hyperidis actione ... sed conspectus corporis.*[20] The imagery of bare breasts in the courtroom as defense repeats throughout the centuries as a celebrated motif of protest when cast upon the white figure. Such reproductions include Orientalist Eugène Delacroix's *Liberty Leading the People* (1830), amongst other lauded examples. Yet rather than rhetoric of the primitive used at the time to describe the culture of colonized peoples who were similarly disrobed, Delacroix suggested instead that his painting depicted the "modern subject," again calling into question the racialized and heterosexual aesthetic gaze that undergirds sociolegal interpretations of indecency.[21]

[19] John Keefe, 1975. "An Ivory Figure of 'Phyrné': A New Attribution." *Bulletin of the Art Institute of Chicago (1973–1982)* 69 (4): 12–14.

[20] Trans: "Not by Hyperides actions ... but by the sight of her body." Helen Morales, 2011. "Fantasising Phryne: The Psychology and Ethics of *Ekphrasis*." *The Cambridge Classical Journal* 57 (1): 71–104.

[21] Delacroix regularly featured the female nude in his work, including *The Triumph of Religion* (1821). See *Eugène Delacroix (1798–1863): Paintings, Drawings, and Prints from North American Collections* [Held at the Metropolitan Museum of Art, New York, April 10–June 16, 1991]. Metropolitan Museum of Art, 1991.

Although the facticity of these events are disputed, including if Phryne disrobed herself or if this act was executed by the orator Hyperides (390–322 BCE), what remains consistent across the various accounts is that the revelation of Phyrne's breasts induced acquittal – that is, that her nude body was a legal advantage, not an illicit act of indecency (if accounts of the partiality of her nakedness differ). Reflecting on Phryne, classics scholar Ioannis Ziogas summarizes that "Female beauty, like [the] male heroism" of exposing wounds to evidence military courage, "acts as a barrier that checks the punitive hand of law."[22] Ziogas invites us to read Phryne's "irresistible beauty" in context of *The Trojan Woman* and the judgment of Helen, affirmed as nudity given its intertextual references to Greek myths and the divine. The parallel extends theorization of the aesthetics of law toward a larger attention to beauty and desire.[23] These themes slide analogously into the twenty-first century through repeated motifs in the scene of Naked Athena in which body made bare remained protected before the law. The masculinist bent of the intended audience repeats across each of these narratives, although in the most contemporary case, the all-male jury has been replaced by the masculine authority of the police.

I return to this courtroom performance by Phryne, not simply because it reveals a tension between rhetorical authority and embodied expression as evidence in legal scenes of judgment. Rather, I am also invested in the aloof shifting between nudity and nakedness presented in its retelling. For example, Quintilian asserts that "people believe that Phryne was acquitted not by Hyperides' speech, however admirable it was, but at the sight of her stunning body, which she bared by drawing aside her tunic."[24] Others yet "introduced Phryne in pitiable garb, beating her naked breast and tearing her tunic, and the jurors saw and acquitted her out of pity."[25] This shift in language toward the naked

[22] Ioannis Ziogas, 2018. "Law and Literature in the Ancient World: The Case of Phryne," in *Law and Literature*, ed. Kieran Dolin. Cambridge: Cambridge University Press. 79–93.

[23] Ziogas, "Law and Literature," 83.

[24] Quintilian, *Institutio Oratoria* 2.15.9. Cited in Ziogas, "Law and Literature," 79.

[25] Christian Walz, *Rhetores Graeci* (Stuttgart, 1832–1836), 7.335. Cited in Ziogas, "Law and Literature," 80.

simultaneously invokes the wretched, far from the stunning sight of nudity previously framed. The jurors' reactions shift in these retellings too, as their affective response modulates from awe to pity respectively; the semantics, more than translational difference, code for ambivalence of law and the uncertainty of fleshly revelation.

Implicit to the logics of these retellings compiled here lies a juridical value in the aesthetic distinction between the naked and nude lost in contemporary applications of the law that continues to animate legal debate. This affective shift toward the exposed body, then, reflects the continued ambiguity associated with the articulation of emotional and aesthetic reception. Turning back to scholar Anne Cheng, she writes: "In spite of our political sophistication today, we still have few tools and little language for addressing what I call visual pleasure in the contaminated zone: those uneasy places of visual exchange where pleasure, law, and resistance converge."[26] This distinction also accounts for the varied reactions to exposed bodies across legal history, not least the "irreverent performances" of Calefurnia and Catherina Arndes featured by Julie Stone Peters.[27] Such is the renewed sophistication called for in this chapter, wherein knowledge from aesthetics and performance studies can inform corners of legal ambiguity still held within invocations of public exposure.

NUDE VERSUS NAKED: A MORALIZING AESTHETIC CODED BY LAW

Underneath the ambiguous articulations of the exposed body percolates an aesthetic distinction between the naked and the nude form already rehearsed within discourses of art history. Canonical authorities on the matter write:

> To be naked is to be oneself. To be nude is to be seen naked by others and yet not recognized for oneself. A naked body has to be seen as an object in order to become a nude. (The sight of it as an object stimulates the use of it

[26] Cheng, *Second Skin*, 167. [27] Peters, *Law as Performance*, chapter 4.

> as an object.) Nakedness reveals itself. Nudity is placed on display. To be naked is to be without disguises.[28]
>
> To be naked is to be deprived of our clothes, and the word implies some of the embarrassment most of us feel in that condition. The word "nude," on the other hand, carries, in educated usage, no uncomfortable overtone. The vague image it projects into the mind is not of a huddled and defenseless body, but of a balanced, prosperous, and confident body: the body re-formed.[29]

Clark's aesthetic interpretation of the nude permeates public imagination including interpretation of legal codes that police the undressed body, if it has been critiqued as sexist and elitist. Interpreting Clark's *The Nude*, Harry Berger links the aesthetic values of affect, culture, and race when he asks "who the unembarrassed and uncivilized minority" might be, before going on to associate nakedness with the female body in particular.[30] Each, while discrete, acknowledge the sensitive differences between the naked and the nude as an aesthetic marker laden with sociocultural investment.

Across the larger lexicon, nudity becomes associated with the artistic, the refined, and the sublime whereas nakedness becomes proxy for excess, vulnerability, and shame – the contrasting values assigned to the dual forms of Naked Athena and Josephine Baker, respectively. Across both weave concerns for proximity, exposure, intimacy, legibility, and recognition. Nudity signals the transformation of naked toward an ideal of "proportion, symmetry, and harmony" – that is, the forms of ballet most legible to a mainstream public.[31] Read under these aesthetic conditions, nakedness, but not nudity, is disavowed under the American legal tradition, if its language does not always parse it with such clarity.

28 John Berger, 1997. *Ways of Seeing: Based on the BBC Television Series with John Berger. A Book Made.* 37. pr., 1. publ. 1972 by British Broadcasting Corporation and 1977 by Penguin Books. London: British Broadcasting Corporation.

29 Kenneth Clark, 1972. *The Nude: A Study in Ideal Form.* A. W. Mellon Lectures in the Fine Arts 2. Princeton, NJ: Princeton University Press.

30 Harry Berger, 2005. *Situated Utterances: Texts, Bodies, and Cultural Representations.* 1st ed. New York: Fordham University Press, 363.

31 Berger, *Situated Utterances*, 366.

The distinction between the naked and nude body that took place across the fields of visual arts, medical research, and religious morality. Ideals of nudity over nakedness presume a moralizing stance endowed with Christian dogma. For many, nakedness as an illegal act follows the original sin in the fall from paradise, as sexuality became an illicit behavior and virginity cherished.[32] Contemporary Euro-American orientations toward the unclothed body continue to follow from Christian, medieval, and Enlightenment era traditions, replete with moralizing overtones. When Berger writes that "to be naked is to be deprived of our nudity," he implies it to be deprived of dignity, that is, without legible values before social norms – indicators codified by legal codes in the names of public decency.[33] If Berger views the nude as a "fictional ideal of the body," its implications linger in material and ideological ways despite any supposed facticity.[34] For example, reviews of an ivory figure of Phryne suggest that "the sculpture also tells much about mid-nineteenth century taste, which considered nudity acceptable if the subject were of a moralizing or 'improving' nature."[35] Such manifestation includes contemporary interpretations of codes of public decency and reveals larger tensions within the secular and separatist attitudes claimed by the US government.

Language of intention and consent contained within contemporary public exposure law repeat within critical formulations of the nude. "Consent is crucial when it comes to nakedness," writes queer theorist Rocío Pichon-Rivière. She continues: "On both sides of the intentional relation that is perception, consent is necessary to have intimacy rather than mere exposure."[36] This commentary productively challenges the legal language of indecent exposure, in which reception usurped intent. Power dynamics continue to vibrate: "While … the history of colonial

[32] For example, Elizabeth Grosz writes: "While the Greek nude began with the heroic body proudly displaying itself in the palaestra, the Christian nude began with the huddled body cowering in consciousness of sin" (cited in Berger, *Situated Utterances*, 367).

[33] Berger, *Situated Utterances*, 365.

[34] Berger, *Situated Utterances*, 374.

[35] Keefe, "An Ivory Figure," 14.

[36] Rocío Pichon-Rivière, 2021. "Nudes and Naked Souls: Critical Phenomenology of Skin Disclosure and Hemispheric Trans Theory." *GLQ: A Journal of Lesbian and Gay Studies* 27(3), 431–450, 446.

sexual violence explains why skin exposure got to be seen as a loss of dignity, I add that nudity enforcement to this day perpetuates that economy of dignity. I think that the assumption implicit in the equation . . . is that being naked is always-already exposing oneself to domination by an abusive other (perhaps even 'asking for it')."[37] That nudity might be a sheath but nakedness an invitation to violence synthesizes the stakes of transdisciplinary engagement across law, aesthetics, and performance.

Beneath this terminology of the nude or naked amasses a question of the revealed body and its racialized reception. As dance choreographers and critics have probed in the US racialized society, can anything but the white body be seen as universal?[38] Put otherwise, does the racialized body – in dance or drawings or scenes of protest – always signal the particular? Afterall, as Margaret Miles writes in *Carnal Knowing*, "The nude body achieves universality at the expense of particularity."[39] By consequence, in a raced society, can the exposed body ever be viewed as nude and not naked, and thus not in violation and need of police response once exposed? Even as laws shift, aesthetic attitudes of the police state can be slow to keep up.[40]

Interpreted through these aesthetic frames, indecency laws criminalize the naked body but not the nude body. Such an observation forces acknowledgment of the racialized aesthetic practice behind this distinction. Although these binaries are false imaginaries of imperial import, their force still saturates contemporary legal theory. Nudity becomes an artful abstraction while nakedness becomes shorthand for the primitive, contributing to aesthetic categories of the civilized and uncivilized body. This canon invites simile between nakedness and the bare body, on the one hand, and the political body, on the other hand, in which only the latter engenders protection. As Ernesto Lacau distinguishes, "In Art

[37] Pichon-Rivière, "Nudes and Naked Souls."

[38] Choreographer Miguel Gutierrez frames this question most poignantly in the article, "Does Abstraction Belong to White People?" (2018) as he recounts a stream of personal events in which the politics of race tainted reception of contemporary dance. Michael Gutierrez, "Does Abstraction Belong to White People?" *The BOMB*. November 17, 2018.

[39] Cited in Berger, *Situated Utterances*, 364.

[40] Holly van Voast's punk drag performances as Harvey van Toast, specifically incited arrest to call attention to the non-uptake of the legal decision in *The People* v. *Ramona Santorelli and Mary Lou Schloss*, for example. These episodes reveal a delay of at least two decades between the decision of a court and a shift in police attitudes.

History the distinction is often made between *the nude* (a body represented as it is, without reference to dress, as in Ancient sculpture) and the *naked* (where the absence of dress is fully visible, as in Northern painting of the Middle Ages and early Renaissance).[41] When scholars such as Berger locate nudity's "historical provenance in the art of antiquity," they omit any acknowledgment of non-Western tradition in which the unclothed body held its own aesthetic implications.[42] The distinction between nude and naked, then, separated low and high art across geopolitical lines. Put more assertively, "colonialism is a history of racist nudity enforcement," which reverberates throughout contemporary politics of the publicly exposed body.[43]

CIVILIZED OR CIVILIZING: CODES OF EXPOSED FLESH

Beyond the singular instance of Naked Athena's permissible protest, the wider argument of this chapter suggests the conflation of the civil body – as legal, political, and social being – and the civilized body – as aesthetic, ranked, and historical – that is, the Western body. As Julie Stone Peters argues, legal actors were historically trained in an aesthetics of decorum, disavowing the indecency of bodily gestures and dictating that one "should move around gracefully."[44] If she theorizes this performative act of dignity via rhetoric and oration, or what Cicero has termed the "eloquence of the body," it is also a choreographic space in which aesthetics of Western law were solidified. Such disciplined decorum became expected of the civilized body outside of the courtroom and halls of authority (where ballet also began). Whereas the line of each choreographed gesture for the ballerina connotes a sense of composure and premeditation, gestures on the non-balletically codified figure arouse potential anxieties toward the unruly, the wayward, the unrest.[45]

41 Judith Butler, Ernesto Laclau, and Slavoj Žižek, 2000. *Contingency, Hegemony, Universality: Contemporary Dialogues on the Left*. Phronesis. London: Verso, 88–89.

42 Berger, *Situated Utterances*, 365.

43 Pichon-Rivière, "Nudes and Naked Souls," 445.

44 Peters, *Law as Performance*, 105–106.

45 There are, of course, notable examples to the contrary; be it early modernist ballets like *Le Sacre du Printemps* or non-Western styles characterized as ephebic, the illegibility of control was met with frenzy.

By considering these entangled aesthetic legacies via dance studies, we can begin to untangle the racializing force of law that continues to be enforced today in spite of law's supposed neutrality.

In *Law as Performance*, Julie Stone Peters draws our attention to decorum via Cicero's theorization on bodily eloquence. If not explicit, traces of civilizing aesthetics animate this text. Consider the following commentary by Thierry of Chartres on Cicero's *De inventione* (ca. 1130–1140):

> There was a time at the beginning of the world when men were savage and lived in the manner of beasts, [using] only their bodily strength, without any reason. At this time there was a certain man who was wise and eloquent, [and] recognized that . . . man was open to persuasion; and so . . . the wise man began to use eloquence and he drove out the savagery and brought men together to live by law, and he instructed the assembled people in the laws of living according to what is right.[46]

As Peters points out, there is an ethical ambiguity for Cicero on bodily eloquence as it contains both danger and virtue; strength sparred against reason. But there is also an aesthetic ambiguity that maps all too well onto the distinction of nude contra naked within concerns for indecency. For Cicero, decorum is that which has "three elements: beauty, tact, and taste" against the crude, the explicit, the vulgar.[47] Indeed, the legal containment of the naked body over the nude body expresses a civilizing function of law rooted in Euro-American aesthetic concerns for the appropriate body – that is, the civil body.

Beyond religious themes of purity, however, attention toward the nude body has frequently been invoked in state of nature philosophy, which parallels Eurocentric imaginaries of the (un)civilized as a political philosophical state of being. The protective valence of whiteness that shrouds Naked Athena bears traces to American modern and postmodern dance aesthetics in which the natural body was celebrated and

[46] Cited in Peters, *Law as Performance*, 98.

[47] M. Tullius Cicero, 1913. *De Officiis.* With an English translation by Walter Miller. Cambridge, MA: Harvard University Press. 126.

whiteness was assumed as the epitome of (legal) neutrality.[48] Dance historian Ann Daly's scholarship on choreographer Isadora Duncan, an American icon and pioneer of the modern dance tradition, illustrates this lineage of concert dance's attention toward the divine. Reflecting on Duncan's desire for the natural body as embraced by the Greeks, Daly writes:

> Nature was Duncan's metaphorical shorthand for a loose package of aesthetics and social ideals: nudity, childhood, the idyllic past, flowing lines, health, nobility, ease, freedom, simplicity, order, and harmony. Through a series of correspondences, she elided Nature with science, religion, the Greeks, and finally, Culture. The Natural body was thus "civilized" (and white) as opposed to "primitive" (and Black). Functioning as the foundation trope for her artistic practice, the grace and clarity of the Natural body thus served to purify and elevate. . . . Functioning, too, as the foundational trope for her social agenda, it provided not just a blueprint for social order and harmony but also a template of social *control*, at a time of backlash against immigrants.[49]

Influenced by Dionysian values, Duncan sought to be "done into dance" as an act of divine purity – a Naked Athena prior to its pop-cultural circulation in 2020.

Duncan's aesthetic line of inquiry stands not as an exception but an exemplar of a larger dance movement that continues to dominate Euro-American concert dance. Cheng too highlights the importance of Isadora Duncan as an "apt example of the intimacy between neoclassicism and primitive and orientalist tropes."[50] From royal origins of court dance in France to modern figures like Martha Graham and Isadora Duncan, there exists in concert dance a prevalence of Greek and Roman themes that shape the affiliated movement vocabularies of grace, dignity, and decorum. As Clark writes, the nude represents "a far

[48] Dance scholar Thomas DeFrantz reflects on the juxtaposition of Black modernism, asking about the possibility for an American public to ever view the Black body outside of a racialized context.

[49] Ann Daly, 2002. *Done into Dance: Isadora Duncan in America*. Middletown, CT: Wesleyan University Press, 89–90.

[50] Cheng, *Second Skin*, 127.

wider and more civilizing experience" than the naked, which has been deemed closer to the natural state. This aesthetic standard extends to less codified places, including ballroom culture where the American standards of whiteness are performed for categorical likeness or realness. But this invocation of the natural body in dance extends beyond the reach of art aesthetic into the realm of the legal, as concerns for the nude body become policed under law.

WAYWARD AESTHETICS AND BEAUTIFUL FUTURES

Julie Stone Peters establishes the theatrical manipulations and rhetorical theories inherent to the courtroom, as lawyers and litigants attempt to persuade a particular affective response to given evidence, reminiscent of Phryne's courtroom stunt. She writes that, in the courtroom, "the body may express the divinity of the human form; it may signify; it may entertain. Or it may be ... indecorous, accidental, leaky, or sublimely obscene."[51] Yet queued by terms such as *hypokrisis, action*, and *pronuntiatio*, Peters narrows performance and bodily expression toward its animation in oral delivery – an emphasis on orator Hyperides over the gestures of Phryne. And in spite of her chapter's title, "Courtroom Oratory, Forensic Delivery, and the Wayward Body in Medieval Rhetorical Theory," waywardness and race fall from view (appearing only once on the penultimate page of the chapter). From Phryne's narrative to Naked Athena's performance, the exposed figure resurfaces these attentions when read in light of contemporary concerns for the indecent body.

The subtle yet strategic shifts between nude and naked opens space for wayward aesthetics of the exposed. Saidiya Hartman opens *Wayward Lives* (2019) with a cast of characters, nudging the reader into a liminal but illuminating space betwixt the theatrical and the theoretical, the performative and the political, the not-quite-real but more-than-mere-fiction. In other words, the possible. For Hartman, the wayward is the minor and anonymous figure, if not all together erased figure, of Black femme life in the twentieth century who "refuse[s] the terms of visibility imposed on them" – or she who capitalizes on the inability for history's

[51] Peters, *Law as Performance*, 95.

gaze to see them any other way.[52] The wayward, then, assumes her own agency in deciding if she is to be viewed as naked or nude, uncivil or civilized, and ultimately, lawful or not. Perhaps Naked Athena is wayward as she dislocates classical ballet to open fire and pavement. Perhaps she is wayward as she approaches police authority against instinct to retreat. Or perhaps she rehearses a wayward aesthetic for as she bares it all, she refuses the protest to be about anything other than skin.

Hartman dwells on a different nude image as she breathes life into the beautiful experiments of wayward lives, including that of a young Black girl lying naked on an arabesque sofa for a prying, pseudo-scientific gaze, "a forensic picture of an act of sexual violence not deemed a crime at all."[53] In the case of Naked Athena, her verticality subverts characterization as a living odalisque mapped onto the other nude and anonymous figure. Her balletic postures render her legible as beautiful, as beyond the need for legal intervention into civilizing matters. I pause on Hartman's haunting questions when considering the images together: "Was it possible to annotate the image? To make my words into a shield that might protect her, a barricade to deflect the gaze and cloak what has been exposed?"[54] Time, place and historical contrast are markedly different as I shuttle between these two images, but nevertheless I am struck by the profound difference between the perceived flesh of these scenes. For the wayward youth of Hartman's attention, no authority recognized the legal violations inflicted upon her. For Naked Athena, no authority recognized the legal codes of which she herself was in violation. Read in their intimate reliefs, together these two figures contribute to a larger history of racialized femininity – one I have aimed to read here within legal discourse of the indecent.

Naked Athena's actions and subsequent nonpolicing invite an entanglement of race, gender, and aesthetics of the unclothed body read through contemporary legal regulations of public exposure. Articulating the politics of aesthetic categorization, Hartman writes: "Beauty is not a luxury; rather it is a way of creating possibility in the

[52] Saidiya V. Hartman, 2019. *Wayward Lives, Beautiful Experiments: Intimate Histories of Social Upheaval.* First ed. New York: W. W. Norton & Company, 18.

[53] Hartman, *Wayward Lives*, 33. [54] Hartman, *Wayward Lives*, 26.

space of enclosure, a radical art of subsistence, an embrace of our terribleness, a transfiguration of the given. It is a will to adorn, a proclivity for the baroque, and the love of *too much*."[55] Exposure may very well be that *too much* when not predetermined as promiscuous, lewd, or indecent. My aim has not been to offer a normative or moralizing vision of the future of nudity in the United States, but to gesture toward the very real stakes held within the aesthetic values of law. The balletic performance in the heightened public scene of protest allowed for this reading, one scene of many in which wayward aesthetics of the civil body have been coopted toward classical lines.

APPENDIX

APPENDIX 1

The Miller test was developed in the 1973 case *Miller* v. *California*. It has three parts:

- Whether "the average person, applying contemporary community standards," would find that the work, taken as a whole, appeals to the prurient interest,
- Whether the work depicts or describes, in a patently offensive way, sexual conduct or excretory functions specifically defined by applicable state law,
- Whether the work, taken as a whole, lacks serious literary, artistic, political, or scientific value.

The work is considered obscene only if *all three* conditions are satisfied.

APPENDIX 2

Oregon Revised Statutes Crimes and Punishments § 163.465

1. A person commits the crime of public indecency if while in, or in view of, a public place the person performs:

[55] Hartman, *Wayward Lives*, 33.

   a. An act of sexual intercourse;
   b. An act of deviate sexual intercourse; or
   c. An act of exposing the genitals of the person with the intent of arousing the sexual desire of the person or another person.
2. Public indecency is a
   a. Class A misdemeanor.
   b. Notwithstanding paragraph (a) of this subsection, public indecency is a Class C felony if the person has a prior conviction for public indecency or a crime described in ORS 163.355 to 163.445 or for a crime in another jurisdiction that, if committed in this state, would constitute public indecency or a crime described in ORS 163.355 to 163.445.

Oregon Revised Statutes Crimes and Punishments § 163.467

1. A person commits the crime of private indecency if the person exposes the genitals of the person with the intent of arousing the sexual desire of the person or another person and:
   a. The person is in a place where another person has a reasonable expectation of privacy;
   b. The person is in view of the other person;
   c. The exposure reasonably would be expected to alarm or annoy the other person; and
   d. The person knows that the other person did not consent to the exposure.
2. Private indecency is a Class A misdemeanor.
3. Subsection (1) of this section does not apply to a person who commits the act described in subsection (1) of this section if the person cohabits with and is involved in a sexually intimate relationship with the other person.
4. For purposes of this section, "place where another person has a reasonable expectation of privacy" includes, but is not limited to, residences, yards of residences, working areas and offices.

CHAPTER 13

Coda / Cauda / Cado

What I Learned from Performing Law*; or, Thereby Hangs a Tail*

Julie Stone Peters

> ***coda***: *Période musicale, vive et brillante, qui termine un morceau.*
> – *Trésor de la langue française* (ca. 2020)

> ***coda***: see *cauda.*
> ***cauda*** or (low) *coda*: a tail. . . . *caudam trahere,* i.e. to be mocked, *coda illa Verrina.* – The privy member.
> ***cado***: to fall, fall down, descend.
> – T. Lewis Charlton, *An Elementary Latin Dictionary* (1890)

> ***coda***: an implement for driving horses, goad or whip, . . . animating, inspiring . . . exalted by the inspiring.
> – Sir Monier Monier-Williams, *A Sanskrit-English Dictionary* (1872)

Invited to write something as a finale to this extraordinary collection of essays, I was unsure what to call it. "Conclusion" was clearly wrong: the essays did not invite conclusion, but its opposite, opening up a new world of thought. I tried "Envoi" – was I not sending these essays forth? – but Peter Goodrich, as coeditor, gently nixed that idea: "Envoi" was already taken, he noted, and surely secondhand Derrida at this late date was a bad idea. It suddenly struck me: "Coda"! Since my musical education had ended when I was eight (about the same time as my mathematical education), I wasn't too sure what a coda was. So I decided to look it up. When I found it in the *Trésor de la langue française*, I was delighted: "*Période musicale, vive et brillante, qui termine un morceau.*"[1] My termination would be lively! Brilliant! Musical! Of course, all that Italian *sprezzatura* might need a bit of Latin gravitas. So I turned to T. Lewis Charlton's *Elementary Latin Dictionary*. There, under "*coda*," I read: the "low" (vulgar) form of *cauda*: a tail; also "the privy member" (as Charlton delicately puts it); and, in the locution *caudam trahere*, "to be mocked" (literally, to drag one's tail).[2] Oh, what a falling off was here![3] Not just a tail, but a dragging "privy member" subject to mockery! Before my eyes, the vowels were rearranging themselves, anagrammatically, into the word "*cado*": I descend . . . I fall.

Then I remembered Calefurnia's *cauda*. It appears in a pair of images at roughly the center of my book: apparently the most popular part of the book, so I take the liberty of reproducing the images here (in the hope of boosting sales) (Figures 13.1 and 13.2).[4] In the first image, which comes from a c.1295–1304 illustrated manuscript of the thirteenth-century code of laws called the *Sachsenspiegel*, a brush-like tail protrudes from Calefurnia's backside. Here, one might say with Shakespeare's Touchstone, thereby hangs a tale.[5] For the image of her tail in fact comes with a tale explaining a legal rule: Calefurnia was angry "because her demands could not proceed without a spokesman," and so, "in a fit of rage," she "misbehaved before the emperor" (the judge in the case). She thus "forfeited [for] all [women]" the right to bring a suit or plead in court. A later commentary concludes that this "misbehavior" took the form we see in the second image: there, she turns her back to the judge, bends over, lifts her skirts, and – as Başak Ertür puts it – "bar[es] her ass to the judge." (Ertür envisions this as a pop-up.)[6] Mooning

1 Trésor de la Langue Française informatisé, https://www.atilf.fr/ressources/tlfi/ ("coda").

2 T. Lewis Charlton, *An Elementary Latin Dictionary* (Oxford: Clarendon Press, 1891), 115.

3 I steal the exclamation here from a Ghost who complains of his widow's bad taste in men (*Hamlet* I.v l.54).

4 Julie Stone Peters, *Law as Performance: Theatricality, Spectatorship, and the Making of Law in Ancient, Medieval, and Early Modern Europe* (Oxford: Oxford University Press, 2022), 143–5.

5 For the phrase (with the implied pun on tale / tail), see e.g. *Taming of the Shrew* IV.i l. 54; and *As You Like It* II.vii l. 29.

6 See Ertür's essay in this collection, 221. Unless otherwise noted, all in-text references are to essays in this collection.

13.1 Calefurnia (tail exposed) tells her tale to the judge in an illustrated manuscript of the *Sachsenspiegel* (ca.1295–1304). Heidelberg University Library, Cod. Pal. germ. 164.

13.2 Calefurnia moons the judge in an edition of Martin le Franc's profeminist *Champion of Women* [*Champion des dames*] (1488). Sig. s8r. Newberry Library, Chicago, Special Collections.

the judge, embracing her fallen condition, Calefurnia seems to declare (with that prolific author Anonymous), "the law is an ass."

Calefurnia (and her creators) may be innocent of etymological tales. But, turning tail on the law while goading the judge, she nonetheless expresses the origin of the origin of the word *cauda* in the Sanskrit *coda*, which signifies (according to Sir Monier Monier-Williams's *Sanskrit-English Dictionary*) "an implement for driving horses, goad or whip."[7] (Presumably

[7] Sir Monier Monier-Williams, *A Sanskrit–English Dictionary Etymologically and Philologically Arranged with Special Reference to Greek, Latin, Gothic, German, Anglo-Saxon, and Other Cognate Indo-European Languages* (Oxford: Clarendon Press, 1872), 327.

for driving asses too.) The Latin *cauda* ("*coda*" in the vulgar form) clearly emerged from the Sanskrit, in one of those frequent metonymic transfers between subject (whip) and object (tail). The two in fact continued to merge in English penal metaphors, for instance in the cat-o-nine-tails (a tail that whips tails) or "whipping at the cart's tail" (using a tail to whip a tail hitched to a tail). One can see (again thanks to Sir Monier Monier) that the ambiguity of the Sanskrit adjectival forms – "animating," "inspiring," "exalted by the inspiring" – similarly merge subject and object. For the *coda* is both a goad that inspires and the thing inspired.

It may appear that I am simply chasing my tail here, but what precedes has in fact led me, however dizzily, to some of the things I would like to say. First, this thing I am calling a coda is both mine and that of the marvelous contributions here that have inspired it. They are the exalted subject – the consciousness – of which this is the mere object, coming to life only because their ideas have animated my words, as I have tried to think alongside them. Second, the essays in this collection offer radically new ways of thinking about the conjunction of law and performance: that is, they are not the tail (appended to my book); I am the tail appended to theirs. Third, I have treated these essays as an invitation to "attempt a self-criticism" (to paraphrase Nietzsche).[8] In taking up this invitation, I may be fated to *caudam trahere*: to drag my tail or, like Calefurnia, expose myself, in defiance of my own dignity. But if in this I fall (*cado*) from the heights to which I aspire, it is, I think, a Fortunate Fall, and the occasion for it – these essays – a great gift: a *cadeau*.

THE REVENGE OF THE ONTOLOGICAL *ID*, OR THE METHODOLOGICAL *ÜBER-ICH* UNBOUND

Among the central things these essays have helped me see anew are the methodological rules I laid down for myself in writing my book. The aim of these rules – a set of strict prohibitions – was to keep my eye on a sharply defined topic: law *as* performance; "law itself" as a

[8] In 1886, Nietzsche appended his "Attempt at Self-Criticism" to the text of the *Birth of Tragedy* (1870–1), and included it in the section on *The Birth of Tragedy* in *Ecce Homo* (1888).

performance practice. It seemed to me that these prohibitions would allow me to say something very specific: not merely that law is performative, or that performances can influence law, but that "showing doing" is central to law in a very concrete institutional way. I wanted to show the centrality of sensory, kinesthetic, embodied, enacted expression to law as an institution, law's modes of self-expression. These prohibitions were clearly self-imposed, but they seemed to come to me in the stentorian voice of a scholarly *Über-Ich.* No stage plays or other modes of extralegal performance, even if their subject was law! No mere verbal *rulings*, even if their subject was performance! No attention to legal words alone (however "performative" those words)! That would be cheating.

But, a confession: while I tried not to, I did sometimes cheat, rebelling against my scholarly superego. No fiction allowed, and yet I couldn't resist Calefurnia, a creature of wild fantasy with only the faintest resemblance to her origins in the first-century BCE plebeian Caia Afrania. My last chapter ended with the "Trial of the Sorcerer" at the Gray's Inn revels in 1594, featuring the Sorcerer and the Prince of Purpoole.[9] Those moments of rebellion were symptoms, pointing to the tension between my methodological boundaries and the book's central claims. For instance, if I tried to separate fictional texts from "the things real people did in real legal arenas" (to focus solely on the latter), I also insisted that "[l]aw and its aesthetic representation are not always radically distinct kinds of things."[10] If I tried to segregate the extralegal from the legal, I also insisted that "real law" could not be hermetically sealed off from theatrics, or anything else. If I tried to sideline texts to focus on performance, my sources were of course mostly texts: texts whose lively textuality I treated as key to how people viewed and understood legal performance. My central claims – which sought to deconstruct the false ontological boundaries separating fiction from the real, law from not law, text from performance – were in fact deconstructing my methodological boundaries. Ontology was at war with methodology, surging up like a primal drive from the book's depths to flout its prohibitions. Just as, in the image, Calefurnia wags her *cauda* defiantly at the law, so did my ontological *Id* wag itself defiantly at my methodological prohibitions.

[9] Peters, *Law as Performance*, 144, 286–7. [10] Peters, *Law as Performance*, 5.

In his essay, Jesús Velasco generously likens me – methodologically speaking – to a physicist: "as a physicist would set aside air resistance to produce an experiment," so *Law as Performance* set aside texts, fictions, the "extralegal" (he implies) in order to test its central hypothesis (120). True, I tried to be scientific, but (as he also suggests) marvelous things happen when one opens the window, lets the air flow back in over the barriers, and watches ideas free themselves, take flight, and soar. That is what the essays in this collection do: something like what Velasco describes as the museum at night, when at dusk objects come to life and begin to "d[o] all sorts of things and kee[p] all sorts of conversations while we sleep, ... mixed up, and ... in our dreams ... shap[ing] some of the ways we will think at sunrise" (129).

What follows is my attempt to describe all the things that have come to life in this collection, while registering the ways that the essays here shake loose the distinctions that sustained my methodological strictures, unbinding the rigid dichotomies on which they depended. In this animated museum that is also a legal dreamscape, we have the *hetaira* Phryne, her breasts bared for the jury; beer-belching judges; a modern-day Little Red Riding Hood; an oath-taking legislator with a giant yellow umbrella and an X through the laws; "Naked Athena" the ballerina; Lady Rhetorica as a courtesan (meretrix); "the oscillating twitch of [law's] wax nose."[11] We have assize circuits modeled on the cosmos, open-air moothills and courts of piepowder, the scripting of visible affect and courtroom tears, chironomia and indigitation and dactylograms, legal didascalia, silence and laughter, and the "mute eloquence" of the letter.[12]

THE PLAY OF THE TEXT, OR THE WORD UNBOUND

> [P]erformance [is] a distinctive form of expression, palpably different from ... textual expression. [8]
>
> – *Law as Performance*

[11] See Kimmel 276–9, Haldar 92, Menon 179, Wan 245–46, Kimmel 258–70, Hutson 56, Goodrich 211.

[12] See Haldar 83–4, Mukerji 80, Goodrich 194–95, Miller 114–15, Ertür 213–38, Goodrich 194.

If the letter of the law is mutely eloquent, it also actively mutes eloquence. As Derek Miller puts it, "legal writing seems designed to leave performance out" (116). The "all too human escapades" that law strives to master, writes Goodrich, "the corporeography of adversity, the verbal and gestural articulations of advocacy, . . . the happy hum of order, the capriole and merry dance" (and, let it be said, also the toll of the bell and the death march) "are later redacted to the monochrome regimentations of the page" (198). In Lorna Hutson's description, "once codified or assimilated to the body of knowledge called law," legal decisions "are promptly abstracted and insulated from th[e] crowd-pleasing compromises of their origins," that is, from the "[a]uditory and sensory reactions and distractions" that shaped them (36). The legal severing of performance and text is not a natural occurrence but an act of force: looking at the history of legal performance, notes Ertür, one realizes "just how much ink and sweat has been spent in trying to subdue [it]" (221).

Miller offers us a concrete critical program for seeing where text has suppressed performance: seeing between the lines of "the legal performances" that texts "encode or anticipate." "By searching for dialogue, speech prefixes, stage directions, paratext, and didascalia," he writes, "we will find some of law's essential performances – sometimes concealed, sometimes hiding in plain sight," showing us "what legal texts prioritize and exclude, . . . the slippages between legal texts and legal performances" (102). He vividly illustrates such slippage in his evocation of a scene from the film *My Cousin Vinny* (114). A college student named Bill believes the police have arrested him for accidentally stealing a can of tuna from a convenience store, but in fact they have arrested him for the murder of the convenience store clerk. After Bill admits to taking the tuna, the sheriff asks him: "At what point did you shoot the clerk?" Bill repeats with increasing incredulity: "I shot the clerk, . . . I shot the clerk. . . . " In court, the sheriff reads Bill's "statement" as a confession to murder: "He said, 'I shot the clerk. I shot the clerk.'" As Miller points out, it is very hard to render this tonal slippage in a purely textual medium: You would have to hear it (115), or, better, to see it.

So too would you have to hear and see the tonal slippage in the Hong Kong legislator's oath-taking ceremony that Marco Wan discusses. In his account, dissident legislators used the oath-taking ceremony as an opportunity to protest Beijing's political control and the slow disintegration of democratic governance. Their protest took the form not only of visible theatrics but of aural effects meant to estrange the words of the oath: ironic tones, extreme pauses. Nathan Law, for instance, adopted a "'distinct rising tone' of mockery whenever he pronounced the Chinese character for 'country'" (244). Veteran legislator Leung Kwok-hung "read out the oath loudly and aggressively [and] inserted dramatic pauses at unexpected moments" (244). Lau Siu-lai paused for six seconds between each of the words as she read. All of the protestors lost their cases and were barred from taking office.

In both of these cases, law works retroactively: in *My Cousin Vinny*, its transcription takes control of oral meaning; in the Hong Kong cases, it crushes tonal insubordination. But law also proactively scripts performance, as Miller suggests. If "*[a]nima lex*" is "*lex loquens*" (speaking law), *lex loquens* often consists in "the scripted performance of the dead letters of the parchment rules" (Goodrich 202). One can see such scripted performance at work in the confessional and inquisitorial dialogues Velasco describes. Working "algorithmically" (as he writes), they may appear to instantiate a legal "I-thou": the interrogator's follow-up questions depend on the answers of the penitent or the accused. But they are in fact coercive catechisms: "scripted strophe-antistrophe[s]" that "forc[e] the translation of the vernacular into orthodox legal language" in order to "produce an archivable object that can be used as proof": a text that constitutes legal "truth" (121).

Nevertheless, all that "ink and sweat" spent "trying to subdue [performance]" ultimately fails. As in the Hong Kong ceremonies, the extempore thrusts itself into the scripted scene, disrupting the text. "[O]n one side, enter the formalization and regulation of dialogue," writes Velasco, "and, on the other side ente[r] improvisation, unscripted action, unpredictable affect," which "may undo the script" (121). If "legal writing seems designed to leave performance out," it cannot. For law restlessly "move[s] between texts and acts," as Miller writes (97).[13] In *My Cousin Vinny*, the tonal slippage is not merely from performance to text,

[13] Or, as Velasco puts it, "the dead voice (*litera mortua*) of the text . . . is always in dialogue with the viva *vox iuris*, . . . the *anima lex*" (140) (and see Velasco, *Dead Voice: Law,*

but from performance to text to performance: from the police station, where Bill's words are "redacted to the monochrome regimentations of the page"; to the courtroom, where the sheriff's voice invests those "monochrome regimentations" with new meaning, transforming incredulity into confession. What these instances remind us is that the dichotomy between text on the page and embodied performance is a false one: law consists in both the textualization of performance and the performance of the text, and the textualization of the performance of the text (and so on, in a never-to-be-disentangled set of transferences). Is performance "a distinctive form of expression, palpably different from . . . textual expression"? I'm not so sure.

The idea that text and performance can be severed becomes especially doubtful when one looks at the centrality of the performed word in the rhetorical tradition. Both when memorizing their speeches and when preparing to improvise, legal orators drew on a set of established techniques, as Lorna Hutson reminds us: a repertoire of both verbal and performance devices guided by long-standing rhetorical principles. Quintilian may have admired Demosthenes's response when asked to name the three most important elements of oratory ("Delivery, . . . delivery, . . . delivery"). But, as she points out, Quintilian's discussions of delivery look like a sideline, when set beside his elaborate discussions of *inventio, dispositio, elocutio, status,* proofs, narrative, and other verbal skills. Hutson rightly insists that we not elide "the contribution of rhetoric as *inventio* with its contribution as performative technique" (55). She also reminds us that, in the law court, the script – wrought through *inventio, dispositio, elocutio* (and so on) – could not be severed from performance. If the art of the orator lay in verbal and narrative technique, verbal and narrative technique *was* performance technique.

This never ceased to be true, as we can see in the eighteenth- and nineteenth-century guides to cross-examination that Simon Stern discusses. In *The Advocate: His Training, Practice, Rights and Duties* (published serially in the 1830s), Edward William Cox explains that the

Philosophy, and Fiction in the Iberian Middle Ages [Philadelphia: University of Pennsylvania Press, 2020]).

advocate must at once "be a good actor" and a master of narrative manipulation:

> [G]o at once to the marrow of the story he has told, as if you were not afraid of it; make him repeat it; then, carry him away to some distant and collateral topic, and try his memory upon *that*, so as to divert his thoughts from the main object of your inquiry, and prevent his seeing the connection between the tale he has told and the questions you are about to put to him. Then, by slow approaches, bring him back to the main circumstances, by the investigation of which it is that you purpose to show the falsity of the story. (Stern 158)

For Thomas Erskine – lawyer for a tailor-plaintiff who demanded payment of his bill (from a perhaps improvident client) – the key was not only to trap the witness but to get a rise out of the audience. As Stern tells the story, the witness "testified that a coat had been poorly made, with one sleeve longer than the other." The dialogue that followed went something like this:

> ERSKINE: You will swear that one of the sleeves was longer than the other?
>
> WITNESS: Yes. . . .
>
> ERSKINE: Now, sir, will you swear that one of them was not *shorter* than the other?
>
> WITNESS: Yes.[14]

Erskine won the case.

THE MANIFOLDS OF SPACE AND TIME, OR PERFORMANCE AND LAW UNBOUND

> I have tried to keep my eye squarely on performance in legal arenas. . . . [Historical legal records] describe events in the world at large, [but] are frustratingly silent on . . . how events in specifically legal arenas looked, sounded, felt; . . . in short, performance by and before the law. [21]
>
> – Peters, *Law as Performance*

[14] Stern 156. I've altered Stern's account here, transforming it into a dialogue and interpolating the witness's affirmative answers as: "Yes."

Accounts of moments like Erskine's trap have the structure of theatrical *peripeteia*: emotional, narrative, and performative concentration; recognition, reversal, and a moment of awe. We *could* take the trial as the paradigmatic legal performance, envisioning it as akin to theatre (in its normative institutional setting): a roughly two-hour spectacle in a fixed location with a beginning, middle, and end. Certainly, both rhetorical theorists and contemporary commentators often encourage us to think of trials as having that structure: both Cicero and Quintilian have theatre in mind as a model. But trials have their own temporality, far longer and more temporally and spatially diffuse than theatre's. They partake of a more expansive mode of performance: not delimited in space and time or governed by the human visual and auditory sensorium. In this, we might pay heed to Subha Mukherji's warning that we must not "essentialise" performance (71). For performance appears in this collection as a kaleidoscopically mutable thing. For instance, the assize trials Piyel Haldar describes may have been "theatrical and even melodramatic events," as he writes, but "the performance of law took place on a wider stage than those [stages] provided by the assize courts themselves" (Haldar 83). What is it "to keep [one's] eye squarely on performance in [specifically] legal arenas, . . . performance by and before the law"? What counts as performance and where are the boundaries of legal arenas? I am not sure.

Haldar's account of the assize circuits as performance spaces stands as a particularly helpful challenge, given the importance of the circuits to Anglo-American law. "[A]ssize trials and the court buildings in which they were held were no more than nodal points in [an] organized network of communication that extended over the entire social and geographic terrain," writes Haldar. "[I]t was the itinerancy of the regional circuits themselves," the "paths and routes between shires and assize towns," that "provided a larger, more significant, stage for the presentation of law" (83). Certainly, the nineteenth-century lawyer-novelist-archivist John Cordy Jeaffreson envisioned the assize judges' processions from town to town as a magnificent spectacle for the entertainment of the populace:

> When they moved, crimson and gold, burnished steel and floating ancient [pennants] gladdened the eye: [and] the ear was addressed by the blare of trumpets. (Haldar 85, quoting Jeaffreson)

At the same time, as Haldar shows, the circuits called upon a larger, more mystical spatial, visual, and auditory imaginary. Providing choreographic direction, the Crown acted as "an all-seeing mechanism, a *primum mobile* in a Pythagorean/heliocentric system, that set the whole mechanism of the circuits in motion," following the era's "Pythagorean poetics" (Haldar 83). Haldar quotes Sir Francis Bacon:

> You that are Judges of the Circuits are as it were the planets of the Kingdom. ... Do therefore as they do; move always and be carried with the motion of your first mover, which is your sovereign. (Haldar 83)

As Haldar reminds us, material and symbolic space cannot be disaggregated. "In their circuits and revolutions," he writes, "microcosm resembled macrocosm and revealed the greater order of the universe" (83).

While the assize circuits had a spatial and temporal form that was entirely different from that of the piepowder courts Haldar discusses, both had a profound relationship to the land that was at once material and symbolic. The circuits traveled "paths wired into the landscape." The piepowder courts, held in marketplaces during market fairs, located law in the earthiness of the marketplace, a fact registered in their name: the *pye-poudre*, or *curia pedis pulverizati*. According to Blackstone, that name derived from the dusty feet (the "*pied poudré*") of the suitors to the court: the "travelling merchants, itinerant chapmen, shepherds vagabonds and drovers" who "by their motion raise *pulverem vel lutum* (dust and mud)" (Haldar 90).

It is not only in Haldar's essay that we can see legal performance as something far more spatially and temporally fluid than the normative model of theatre would suggest. In Anna Jayne Kimmel's "Naked Athena," for instance, legal performance takes place in the space of the political demonstration: a space of ceaselessly shifting boundaries, as the conflict between protestors and police unfolds. There, we can see the time of the event as similarly mutable, expanding space as time expands. Does the legal performance take place in the moment the photographer captures the protester, arms and legs spread wide, seemingly suspended in air? Or does it take place in the more extended time of the police crackdown, or of the protest itself? Or does it take place in the time of the transmission of the photograph and its manifold interpretations (its "beautiful futures" [276])? Or is its time (as Kimmel seems to argue) that of the long history of representations of the naked and the nude, the primitive and the civilized, – of "racialized interpretations of the lewd, the indecent, and the obscene" (262)? The time of performance moves as it moves in us, expanding and collapsing, crossing planes of experience, its speed ever-changing (a high-speed train one moment, then the slow and steady rhythm of a heart). So does legal time, which is not, of course, only the time of the trial or execution or the endless-seeming time of prison, but the time (as Velasco puts it) of "memories being activated, living voices becoming *dead voice* becoming living voices again by dint of remembrance," those "snippets of memory" that register "the true duration of the legal proceeding" (145).

The central question here is: should we view the photograph Kimmel shows us as outside the frame of law? To place a "*cordon sanitaire*" around law (to use Velasco's phrase [128]) – treating some things as inside law, and others as outside law – is to replicate law's own historic project of erecting a wall around its domain, attempting to preserve a hermetic space in which law can retain its institutional purity. We find an expression of that project in the *Siete Partidas*' insistence that "the language of the law must be understood according to its technical characteristics" (Velasco 139): technical legal language is itself a technique for sealing law off from the vernacular world. But, as Velasco suggests, the "juridification of the world" means that "there is nothing" outside of "the affective universe of the law" (131). Law violates its own boundaries, seeps "under the lintel, [across] the threshold," travels through the latticework of the confessional (Velasco 133). It works not only through action but through inaction, as Kimmel points out: not only when it raises allegations but when "allegations [are] not raised" (Kimmel 260). It is there in its own "palpable silences": in "time lost in translation; all the time that has fallen between the folds" (Velasco 142).

THE *VERITAS FALSA*, OR THE REAL UNBOUND

> [I]n the temptation to interpret the politics and poetics of [fictional] text[s], it is very easy to lose sight of the things real people did in real legal arenas. [22]
>
> – Peters, *Law as Performance*

If law is everywhere – if we cannot separate the legal from the extra-legal – the distinction between "the things real people did in real legal arenas" and fictional texts representing law begins to collapse. The "real" of law is a fiction, as the etymology of "fiction" reminds us (*fictio*, a making or fashioning): law is eternally in the process of being fabricated. The legal subject is an imaginary subject, created simultaneously by law and by the media representations that (as Jisha Menon writes) "rela[y] and consolidat[e] pernicious narratives" (the "repetition [of] cultural imagery") (168). Even courts of law are "artificial, fabricated, fictionalized, just as all artifices of truth are fictionalized" (Velasco 130). Law's scenes and personages are as "fantasmatic" as those of the theatre.

This recognition is central to Hutson's account of the parallel formation of legal and theatrical rhetoric in the early modern period. Discussing Ludovico Ariosto's 1509 play, *I Suppositi* (*The Supposes*), Hutson argues that both law and early modern theatre developed rhetorical supposition as a crucial means of fabricating realities beyond the immediately visible world (44). Both lawyers and playwrights asked listeners to imagine worlds elsewhere, outside of the immediately perceptible scene, "to infer, from characters' uses of probable arguments, all the backstories, motives and hidden truths of [a] play's story" (44). Such inferential logic was key to "the newly illusionistic power of theatre to make audiences think they have seen things they haven't seen, and to infer and imagine the fictional world of the play," creating the kinds of expansive and yet coherent fictional worlds on which our experience of fiction still depends today (48).

Subha Mukherji similarly insists on the parallel between legal and theatrical fictionality in what she describes as a "provocation against [the] assumption of a fundamental difference between the fiction of the theatre and the truth and reality of the law court" (63). Mukherji seeks to replace hierarchy (the treatment of "real" law as superior to theatrical fiction) with "a horizontal placement of legal and theatrical engagements" (64). Paradoxically, the distinction between theatre and law is necessary to her deconstruction of that distinction. To explore the "pain and pleasure of the *scaenius* of law," she writes, we "need the *scaenius* of the theatre" (76). Theatre – in its difference from law – turns out to be ideally suited to revealing the fictionality of law. It is uniquely capable of "tuning into the fiction, construction, and the affective realties underpinning 'real' trials." It "can mine this dimension of the ontology of law the more freely because it does not share institutional law's investment in factual truth or its veridical telos" (64). It is "at home in *hypokrisis*," and can thus make visible "[t]he epistemic yearning" to expose the *hypokrisis* that "structur[es] judicial encounters, the proficiency of legal representation at playing to it, the semiotic remit of subject-positions" (76).

We can see this yearning to expose judicial *hypokrisis* in early modern plays like *King Lear*, in which (writes Mukherji) "the fantastic nature of the trial [on the heath] lays bare the performative insides of the legal machine, its fictive ontology" (64), while "tuning into the fiction, construction, and the affective realties underpinning 'real' trials" (64). And we can see it in contemporary plays like those Menon discusses: David Farr's 2019 adaptation of *The Hunt* and Steven Fechter's 2000 *The Woodsman*. Both plays show how theatre – in providing an alternative legal-affective space – may alert us to the affective realties underpinning trials today, and specifically to the emotional realities of "criminalized people we may not otherwise encounter in life." Both highlight the ways in which relations of power shape the social subjection that is "the ground for the emergence of legal subjecthood" (176): subjecthood that often appears hardened into binaries (criminal / victim, child abuser / savior).

The Woodsman's "specters, doubles, and doppelgangers" offer a challenge to such binaries, revealing what Menon (following Emmanuel Levinas) calls "the internal antagonism of these characters" (186). "[O]nly partially in possession of their own motives and desires," characters are "infiltrated by the presence of real and spectral others": they "waver, shuttle, and oscillate between subject positions," somehow "elud[ing] the binary categories of criminal law" (188). Reading these plays through Levinas and Judith Butler, Menon suggests how attention to "vulnerability" might "move us beyond the antinomies enshrined in criminal law" (177). "Thinking with vulnerability" may allow us "to rethink the foundations of our social contract in ways that acknowledge both our precariousness and the sovereign violence that holds us in its thrall" (177). "If for Hobbes human vulnerability is the precondition that legitimates a powerful carceral state," she writes,

> for Emmanuel Levinas, vulnerability heightens our awareness of the intersubjective constitution of our subjectivity. Preceding our entry into language, this intersubjective, embodied encounter with others ensures that the trace of another is constitutive of the self. (178)

Vulnerability and resistance are not antonyms. For (writes Menon) vulnerability "gestures [toward] a broader condition of interdependency" that reveals interdependency as "an agentic mode of political action" (179).

Pointing to the ways that theatrical fictions reveal the fictionality of law, Menon and Mukherji implicitly invoke the age-old claim about the paradoxical truths of fiction, which we find (via Goodrich) in the third question in Jean de Coras's dialogue between Hadrian and Epictetus: "*[Q]uid est pictura? Veritas falsa* – what is a painting? A false truth" (196). Similarly, "*[Q]uid est fabula*[?]" (asks the pedagogue Joseph de Jouvancy). In Goodrich's translation (which helpfully renders *fabula* as "drama"):

> Drama is a discourse that figures the truth, that is to say that it is false and fictive but, under the cover and artifice of words, traces a truth and a useful sense. (204)

Theatrical fictions figure truth, revealing the fictionality of law, its *vera falsitas* (true falsehood). So the fictionality of law reveals the truth of theatrical fictions, its *veritas falsa* (false truth). It is tempting to reverse these: for after all, theatre is really true even in its supposed falsehood, and law false even in its supposed truth. Both (as Hutson shows us) depend on "supposes," hypotheticals, counterfactuals, falsehoods that may be true or truths that may be false. As Goodrich writes: "The theatrical characteristics of the legal process" produce a "performative image of law as enigmatically true and simultaneously false" (197). In this enigmatic image, law is "a performance, a play, a fantasm which ironically shows law *in actu*, and as *legis actio*" (in the act, as legal action) (197), fabricating the real. As Marco Wan puts it, in law, "the performative masquerades as the constative, bringing a new order into being."[15]

[15] Remark at conference on "Law as Performance," Cardozo Law School, April 2, 2023.

THE LAST LAUGH: THE CODA-CAUDA AS A "MINOR JURISPRUDENCE OF REFUSAL"[16]

Hic bibitur [Here she is drunk]

– Petrus Bonumdives

Will the last person to leave please trash themselves?

– Abbie Berman

In the courtroom in Marleen Gorris's 1982 film, *A Question of Silence*, three women laugh. In Başak Ertür's account, they have committed a horrific and seemingly unmotivated murder, shown in a slow flashback in which the women "improvise weapons to torture, mutilate and kill [a] boutique owner" (232). They "all readily and in good humour admit their responsibility" (215). During the trial, when the prosecutor says that the case would be no different if the killers were men or if the shopkeeper were a woman, one of the defendants begins to laugh. The four witnesses begin to laugh, then the other defendants, and finally the female lawyer for the defense. The laughter is wild, contagious, and lasts for nearly three minutes on screen (time it, and you will see how long three minutes is: a three-minute laugh violates all narrative-cinematic norms). They are laughing at what Goodrich describes as "the costumed animal, the monkey in a toga, and the cacchinnating coifed codpiece clothed, codex conspiring judge" (198). They are laughing at us.

Ertür points out that "[i]n classic rhetoric, laughter is considered a forensic weapon." Rhetoricians "have sought to engineer its tamed and disciplined versions for timely deployment against an opponent whose ridicule may well tip the scales in one's favor" (225). We can see this use of laughter – timely deployment of ridicule against an opponent – in Simon Stern's evocation of slick lawyer Thomas Erskine's humiliation of the witness in the case of the tailor, as well as in an anecdote Stern tells us about Chief Justice John Roberts. An alleged stalker was on trial for sending more than a thousand text

[16] I borrow the phrase from Ertür's title, which of course draws on Peter Goodrich's coinage of the phrase "minor jurisprudences" in his *Law in the Courts of Love: Literature and Other Minor Jurisprudences* (London: Routledge, 1996).

messages to his victim, including some with threats, for instance "Don't need you," "Die." But Roberts, who was determined to cast the victim as a hysterical woman threatening male prerogative, chose to read one message aloud during oral arguments: "Staying in cyber life is going to kill you. Come out for coffee. You have my number." He then remarked, "I can't promise I haven't said that": laughter. (According to Stern, he was so pleased that he read the message three times) (162). In our pleasure in Erskine's one-upmanship, it's easy to forget that this is a nasty legal trick. Harder in Roberts's case if you've ever been stalked. Being funny isn't always funny.

But the laughter that Ertür finds in Gorris's film is of an entirely different kind. It is more like what Anca Parvulescu describes in her account of the film's key scene:

> Slowly, laughter dislocates itself from its object, the gender-blind court of law, and, by extension, the law itself. It is a laughter that has its own *raison d'être,* apart from any specific laughable object. And laughter reproduces itself, laughter asks for more laughter. It not only interrupts, but repeats itself and spreads. (Ertür 237)

Ertür helps us to a better understanding of the views that Goodrich reports: Bishop Bossuet's claim that "peals of laughter (*les éclats de rire*) make one forget the presence of God" (208); or that of the Roman priest who (according to Joseph Addison) "laid it down as a Point of Doctrine, that Laughter was the Effect of Original Sin and that Adam could not laugh before the Fall" (206). *Cado, ergo rideo* (I fall, therefore I laugh). As Goodrich writes, "[l]aughter is in effect sacrilegious" (208).

In *A Question of Silence,* the women forget the presence of God the Father, eat the apple, refuse Adam's dominion. They turn "palpable silences" into resounding refusal: registered not in the language of the so-called civilization that has silenced them (words, or Cicero's elegant "eloquence of the body," or the balletic posture attributed to "Naked Athena") but in hyperbolic, raucous cacophony. Here we have a feminist version of Foucault's "*illégalismes populaires.*"[17] We might be

[17] For "*illégalismes populaires,*" see e.g. Roger-Pol Droit, *Michel Foucault, entretiens* (Paris: Odile Jacob, 2004), 67.

tempted to think of this zone of laughter as utopian, suggests Ertür, but utopia is always in the future, remaining "unspoken of and uninhabited" (235). What if "that zone is not so much a utopia [as] a heterotopia?" she asks (drawing on Bonnie Honig):

> a space and time of rehearsal, a space for prefigurative practices towards another way of living? . . . both very here/now and elsewhere at once, much in the way desire desires? . . . 'spaces or times of rehearsal where alternative forms of life can be tried out and explored.' (Ertür 234, quoting Honig)

Such heterotopias are "wild zone[s]," creating an arena that is at once its own place and "a no-place" (Ertür 235). Citing Barthes's *S/Z*, Mukherji describes how a text may hold back "'one last meaning . . . whose place it keeps free and signifying'": This holding back of meaning is how "'law's subjects'" turn subjection around into irreducible subjecthood, acutest at its vanishing point (69).[18] In the courtroom in *A Question of Silence*, subjection becomes irreducible subjecthood, vanishing into the heterotopia of laughter.

Here, I return to my coda, or rather, to Calefurnia's *cauda*. Citing Hélène Cixous (via Parvulescu), Ertür notes that there is a "'special relation' between exposed female genitals, the revolution and laughter." In Freud's reading of the myth of Medusa, the "Medusa's severed and petrified head 'takes the place of a representation of the female genitals'" (Ertür 222). As Ertür writes, "Cixous's twist is simple and precise: 'You only have to look at the Medusa straight on to see her. And she's not deadly. She's beautiful and she's laughing'" (222). "Let the priests tremble," writes Cixous, "we're going to show them our sexts!" (Ertür 222).

Calefurnia's *cauda* does not change the law prohibiting women from bringing their own cases. And Gorris's laughing murderesses do not escape law's vengeance. And Wan's wildly theatrical oath-takers? They too lost their cases, tempting one to say: not all performatives that masquerade as constatives succeed in their masquerades. Not all bring a new order into being. For Wan the "oath-taking saga" – which showed how law "stages its own formal existence" by "expurgat[ing]

[18] Mukherji borrows the phrase from Wallace Stevens.

performance" (257) – clearly failed. But law changes. Who is to say what "uncanny encounter[s]" (257) – what moments of fantasmatic legal poetics help it to do so? And – as the other "uncanny encounter[s]" of recent years make us wonder – who is to say which ones will bring good, and which will bring evil?

Index

INDEX

For EU product safety concerns, contact us at Calle de José Abascal, 56–1°, 28003 Madrid, Spain or eugpsr@cambridge.org.

www.ingramcontent.com/pod-product-compliance
Ingram Content Group UK Ltd.
Pitfield, Milton Keynes, MK11 3LW, UK
UKHW021540160726
473348UK00004B/462